Developmental Dilemmas

The restructuring of socialist economies in the former Soviet Union, and East and Central Europe following the fall of the Berlin Wall in 1989 belong to the largest projects of social engineering ever undertaken. At once, policy-makers were confronted with fundamental questions such as whether to dismantle the core institutions of the communist state, what new institutions to create, how to articulate anew the relationship between plan and market, and in what time frame. In the view of neo-liberal economics, privatization is a *conditio sine qua non* for a well-functioning market economy. However, if there is one area of reform that demonstrates that society and societal change are less pliable and malleable than social engineering and neo-liberal economics suggest, it is land reform.

China's chosen path of land reform is unique in scale and ambitions among the (ex)socialist states: a government-owned and controlled land market that prohibits private ownership and a free land market; yet, with the ideological compromise of paid lease and transfer of use rights. In conceptualizing development, some scholars deem competitive markets and private, secure property rights protected by "the rule of law" critical preconditions for stable economic growth. *Developmental Dilemmas* demonstrates that the Chinese case seemingly defies the need for privatization of land ownership. Peter Ho argues that the successful creation of new institutions hinges in part on choice and timing in relation to the particular constellation of societal economic, political and cultural parameters. Disregarding these could result in rising inequality, bad land stewardship, and the eruption of land-related grievances.

With contributions from a leading team of specialists, this volume offers an authoritative and in-depth analysis of the main constraints in China's land administration; the potential sources of land disputes; the socio-economic impact of agricultural land, forest, and grassland policies; and the alternatives in land tenure that could lead to a socially acceptable, ecologically sustainable and economically viable land use. This volume will be of interest to students of development studies and contemporary China, and will address a wide readership of professionals interested in the economics of transition, legal anthropology, natural resource management, and gender and rural development.

Peter Ho is Professor of International Development Studies and concurrent Director of the Centre for Development Studies at the University of Groningen, The Netherlands.

Asia's transformations

Edited by Mark Selden

Binghamton University and Cornell University, USA

The books in this series explore the political, social, economic and cultural consequences of Asia's transformations in the twentieth and twenty-first centuries. The series emphasizes the tumultuous interplay of local, national, regional and global forces as Asia bids to become the hub of the world economy. While focusing on the contemporary, it also looks back to analyze the antecedents of Asia's contested rise.

This series comprises several strands:

Asia's Transformations aims to address the needs of students and teachers, and the titles will be published in hardback and paperback. Titles include:

Confronting the Bush Doctrine
Critical views from the Asia-Pacific
Edited by Mel Gurtov and Peter Van Ness

Japan's Quiet Transformation
Social change and civil society in the 21st century
Jeff Kingston

State and Society in 21st Century China
Edited by Peter Hays Gries and Stanley Rosen

The Battle for Asia
From decolonization to globalization
Mark T. Berger

Ethnicity in Asia
Edited by Colin Mackerras

Chinese Society, 2nd edition
Change, conflict and resistance
Edited by Elizabeth J. Perry and Mark Selden

The Resurgence of East Asia
500, 150 and 50 year perspectives
Edited by Giovanni Arrighi, Takeshi Hamashita and Mark Selden

The Making of Modern Korea
Adrian Buzo

Korean Society
Civil society, democracy and the state
Edited by Charles K. Armstrong

Remaking the Chinese State
Strategies, society and security
Edited by Chien-min Chao and Bruce J. Dickson

Mao's Children in the New China
Voices from the Red Guard generation
Yarong Jiang and David Ashley

Opium, Empire and the Global Political Economy
Carl A. Trocki

Japan's Comfort Women
Sexual slavery and prostitution during World War II and the US occupation
Yuki Tanaka

Hong Kong's History
State and society under colonial rule
Edited by Tak-Wing Ngo

Debating Human Rights
Critical essays from the United States and Asia
Edited by Peter Van Ness

Asia's Great Cities

Each volume aims to capture the heartbeat of the contemporary city from multiple perspectives emblematic of the authors' own deep familiarity with the distinctive faces of the city, its history, society, culture, politics and economics, and its evolving position in national, regional and global frameworks. While most volumes emphasize urban developments since the Second World War, some pay close attention to the legacy of the *longue durée* in shaping the contemporary. Thematic and comparative volumes address such themes as urbanization, economic and financial linkages, architecture and space, wealth and power, gendered relationships, planning and anarchy, and ethnographies in national and regional perspective.

Titles include:

Hong Kong
Global city
Stephen Chiu and Tai-Lok Lui

Shanghai
Global city
Jeff Wasserstrom

Singapore
Carl Trocki

Beijing in the Modern World
David Strand and Madeline Yue Dong

Bangkok
Place, practice and representation
Marc Askew

Asia.com is a series which focuses on the ways in which new information and communication technologies are influencing politics, society and culture in Asia. Titles include:

Asia.com
Asia encounters the Internet
Edited by K.C. Ho, Randolph Kluver and Kenneth C.C. Yang

Japanese Cybercultures
Edited by Mark McLelland and Nanette Gottlieb

Literature and Society is a series that seeks to demonstrate the ways in which Asian literature is influenced by the politics, society and culture in which it is produced. Titles include:

Chinese Women Writers and the Feminist Imagination (1905–1945)
Haiping Yan

The Body in Postwar Japanese Fiction
Edited by Douglas N. Slaymaker

Routledge Studies in Asia's Transformations is a forum for innovative new research intended for a high-level specialist readership, and the titles will be available in hardback only. Titles include:

1 **Developmental Dilemmas**
Land reform and institutional change in China
Edited by Peter Ho

2 **Japanese Industrial Governance**
Protectionism and the licensing state
Yul Sohn

3 **Remaking Citizenship in Hong Kong**
Community, nation and the global city
Edited by Agnes S. Ku and Ngai Pun

4 **Chinese Media, Global Contexts**
Edited by Chin-Chuan Lee

5 **Imperialism in South East Asia**
'A fleeting, passing phase'
Nicholas Tarling

6 **Internationalizing the Pacific**
The United States, Japan and the Institute of Pacific Relations in war and peace, 1919–1945
Tomoko Akami

7 **Koreans in Japan**
Critical voices from the margin
Edited by Sonia Ryang

8 **The American Occupation of Japan and Okinawa***
Literature and memory
Michael Molasky

* Now available in paperback

Critical Asian Scholarship is a series intended to showcase the most important individual contributions to scholarship in Asian Studies. Each of the volumes presents a leading Asian scholar addressing themes that are central to his or her most significant and lasting contribution to Asian studies. The series is committed to the rich variety of research and writing on Asia, and is not restricted to any particular discipline, theoretical approach or geographical expertise.

China's Past, China's Future
Energy, food, environment
Vaclav Smil

China Unbound
Evolving perspectives on the Chinese past
Paul A. Cohen

Women and the Family in Chinese History
Patricia Buckley Ebrey

Southeast Asia
A testament
George McT. Kahin

Developmental Dilemmas

Land reform and institutional change in China

Edited by Peter Ho

Routledge
Taylor & Francis Group
LONDON AND NEW YORK

First published 2005
by Routledge
2 Park Square, Milton Park, Abingdon, Oxon OX14 4RN

Simultaneously published in the USA and Canada
by Routledge
270 Madison Ave, New York, NY 10016

Routledge is an imprint of the Taylor & Francis Group

Typeset in Baskerville by Wearset Ltd, Boldon, Tyne and Wear
Printed and bound in Great Britain by MPG Books Ltd, Bodmin

British Library Cataloguing in Publication Data
A catalogue record for this book is available from the British Library

Library of Congress Cataloging in Publication Data
A catalog record for this book has been requested

ISBN 0–415–36239–3

Only those who make a living from the land can understand the value of land.

Fei Xiaotong, *Xiangtu Zhongguo*, 1947

In loving memory of Zhao Jiasong. My 'whitelighter' who taught me why the small hermit lives on a mountain, and the great hermit lives in a town.

Contents

Figures

Tables

Contributors

Tony Banks is the social impact advisor for the New Zealand Agency for International Development (NZAID) since 2004. For a decade prior to that he was a lecturer in the field of development management and international rural development at Massey University, New Zealand. His research focus has been on local-level institutional arrangements for rangeland management in China and he has published in *World Development* (2003), *Mountain Research and Development* (2003), *Development and Change* (2001), and *Development Policy Review* (1999).

Loren Brandt is a Professor in the Economics Department at the University of Toronto, Canada. Most of Professor Brandt's work is focused on the economics of institutional change in China's past and present economy. Among other works, he has published on China's labor and credit markets in the 1930s, the nature of growth during the Nationalist Period, issues of rural reforms and macro-economic economic policy. He also teaches several classes on applied econometrics and the economic development of China.

Cristina Brasili is Professor of Political Economy and Regional Development Policy in the Faculty of Statistics at the University of Bologna (Italy). Her main research areas are regional cohesion and convergence in the European Union and the Italian agrifood system and local and agrifood districts development. Her recent publications include *Perspective of the Agri-Food System in the New Millennium* (CLUEB, 2003); *Convergenza economica delle Regioni Europee ed allargamento ad Est* [Economic Convergence and Eastern Enlargement in EU Regions]; (il Mulino) 3/2003, and *L'evoluzione del sistema agroalimentare in Emilia-Romagna* [Development of the Agrifood System in Emilia-Romagna Region] (CLUEB, 2003).

Daniel W. Bromley is Anderson-Bascom Professor of Applied Economics at the University of Wisconsin-Madison, USA. Professor Bromley has published extensively on: (1) the institutional foundations of the economy; (2) the legal and philosophical dimensions of property rights; (3) the economics of natural resources and the environment; and (4) economic development. He has been editor of the journal *Land Economics* since 1974. He is a Fellow of the American Agricultural Economics Association, and is listed in *Who's Who in Economics.* He is currently serving as Chair of the US Federal Advisory Committee on Marine Protected Areas. Daniel Bromley has written and edited 11 books, the most recent of which are: *Economic Interests and Institutions: Conceptual Foundations of Public Policy* (Blackwell, 1989); *Environment and Economy: Property Rights and Public Policy* (Blackwell, 1991); *The Social Response to Environmental Risk* (Kluwer, 1992) (with Kathleen Segerson); *Making the Commons Work: Theory, Practice, and Policy* (ICS Press, 1992); *The Handbook of Environmental Economics* (Blackwell, 1995); *Sustaining Development: Environmental Resources in Developing Countries* (Elgar, 1999) and *Economics, Ethics, and Environmental Policy* (Blackwell, 2002) (with Jouni Päävola).

John Bruce is a lawyer, and for twenty years worked with the Land Tenure Center at the University of Wisconsin-Madison where he served two terms as director. He has worked on tenure issues in China since 1979, initially as consultant to the Ford Foundation and the World Bank, and continues his involvement there through the current projects of the World Bank. He is currently Senior Counsel (Land) in the Legal Department of the Bank, and serves also as senior land tenure advisor in the Bank's Agriculture and Rural Development Department.

Michael Carter is Professor of Agricultural and Applied Economics at the University of Wisconsin. He is co-editor of *World Development* and director of the BASIS Collaborative Research Support Program that studies rural poverty alleviation strategies in Africa, Asia and Latin America. Professor Carter's research focuses on the nature of growth and transformation in low income economies, paying particular attention to how inequality in the distribution of assets shape, and are shaped by, economic growth. His recent publications include "Asset Smoothing, Consumption Smoothing and the Reproduction of Inequality under Risk and Subsistence Constraints," (with Fred Zimmerman). *Journal of Development Economics*, 71(2) (August 2003): 233–260; "Getting Institutions Right for Whom? Credit Constraints and the Impact of Property Rights on the Quantity and Composition of Investment", *American Journal of Agricultural Economics* 85(1) (February 2003): 173–186 (with Pedro Olinto). "Morals, Markets and Mutual Insurance: Using Economic Experiments to Study Recovery from Hurricane Mitch," in C.B. Barrett (ed.) *Exploring the Moral Dimensions of Economic Behavior* (Routledge, 2004) (with marco Castillo); and "Land Ownership Inequality and the Income Distribution Consequences of Economic Growth," in G. Cornia (ed.) *Inequality, Poverty and Growth in an Era of Liberalization and Globalization* (Oxford University Press, 2004).

Roberto Fanfani is Professor of Political Economy and Agrifood Economics at the University of Bologna (Italy). He has been Dean of the Faculty of Economics (University of Modena), and Dean of the Department of Statistics (University of Bologna). His main research interests refer to the Common Agricultural Policy, agri-food development and perspectives, structural changes and regional development. His key publications include *The Italian Agriculture* (Il Mulino, 2001), *The Territorial Specialization of the Food Industry* (Inea, 2001); and *Perspective of the Agri-Food System in the New Millennium* (Clueb, 2003).

Li Guo is an economist in the East Asia Rural Development Sector Unit of the World Bank and is working on the World Bank's lending projects in China, Indonesia, Cambodia, Mongolia, Philippines, Laos, and Ghana, particularly in the fields of land management and poverty reduction. His research focuses on development issues in rural China, especially on land property rights, social capital, and income inequality and he has published widely in academic journals such as the *American Economic Review*, the *Journal of Comparative Economics*, and *China Quarterly*. Some of his recent publications include "Does Guanxi Matter to Nonfarm Employment?" *Journal of Comparative Economics*, 31 (2003) (with Xiaobo Zhang); "Hazards of Expropriation: Tenure Insecurity and Investment in Rural China," *American Economic Review*, 92(5) (2002) (with Hanan Jacoby and Scott Rozelle); "Land Rights in China: A Comprehensive Review of the Facts, Fictions, and Issues," *China Journal*, 1 (2002) (with Loren Brandt, Jikun Huang and Scott Rozelle).

Nico Heerink has been Beijing Office Co-ordinator and Research Fellow with the International Food Policy Research Institute (IFPRI) since January 2004. Before joining IFPRI he was an Associate Professor at Wageningen University, The Netherlands. His research activities have concentrated on economic policy reform and sustainable agricultural development, income inequality and economic development, international trade and the environment, rural public investment, and the economics of low external input agriculture. He obtained his MSc in econometrics from the University of Groningen, The Netherlands, and his PhD in economics from the European University Institute in Florence, Italy. Since September 2001, he has held an honorary appointment as concurrent Professor at Nanjing Agricultural University. Some of his recent publications are "Income Inequality and the Environment: Aggregation Bias in Environmental Kuznets Curves." *Ecological Economics*, 38 (2001): 359–367 (with A. Mulatu and E. Bulte); "Food Insecurity, Soil Degradation and Agricultural Markets in West Africa: Why Current Policy Approaches Fail." *Oxford Development Studies*, 29 (2001): 189–207 (with N. Koning and S. Kauffman); and *Economic Policy and Sustainable Land Use: Recent Advances in Quantitative Analysis in Developing Countries.* (Physica-Verlag, 2000) (with H. van Keulen and M. Kuiper).

Peter Ho is Professor of International Development Studies and concurrent Director of the Centre for Development Studies at the University of Groningen, The Netherlands. He is member of the Academic Committee of the International Institute for Asian Studies (IIAS) in Leiden and of the Steering Committee of the European Conference on Agriculture and Rural Development in China (ECARDC). From 1997 until 2002, he served as the personal Chinese interpreter for the Dutch Minister of Foreign Affairs. He has published widely on issues of green social movements and civil society, natural resource management, and environmental policy in China. His recent publications include *Institutions in Transition: Land Ownership, Property Rights and Social Conflict in China* (Oxford University Press, 2005) and *Rural Development in Transitional China: The New Agriculture* (Frank Cass, 2003), co-edited with Jacob Eyferth and Eduard B. Vermeer.

Jikun Huang is the Founder and Director of the Center for Chinese Agricultural Policy (CCAP) of the Chinese Academy of Sciences (CAS). His research covers a wide range of issues on China's agricultural and rural development, including work on agricultural R&D policy, water resource economics, price and marketing, food consumption, poverty, and trade liberalization. In the past 15 years he published more than 160 journal papers, more than one-third of them published in international refereed journals. He is co-author of seven books. He has received the Outstanding Scientific Progress award from the Ministry of Agriculture four times, the Award for China's top ten outstanding youth scientists in 2002, and the Outstanding Achievement Award for Oversea Returning Chinese in 2003. He serves as policy adviser to the Chinese government. Some of his recent publications include "China's War on Poverty: Assessing Targeting and the Growth Impact of Poverty Program," *Journal of Chinese Economic and Business Studies*, (3) 2003: 299–315; "Producer Benefits from Input Market and Trade Liberalization: The Case of Fertilizer in China," *American Journal of Agricultural Economics*, 85(5) (2003): 1223–1227 (with Qiao, Fangbin, Bryan Lohmar, Scott Rozelle and Linxin Zhang); "China Aggressively Pursuing Horticulture and Plant Biotechnology," *California Agriculture*, 58(2) (2004): 112–113 (with Scott Roxelle); "Trade Reform, Household Effect, and Poverty in Rural China," *American Journal of Agricultural Economics*, 85(5) (2003): 1292–1298 (with Ninghui Li and Scott Rozelle).

Shashi Kant is an Associate Professor in the Faculty of Forestry, at the University of Toronto, Canada. He is a recipient of Ontario Premier's Research Excellence Award. He has published more than 50 papers in a wide range of journals and books. He specializes in forest resource economics and forest management systems with an emphasis on the economics of sustainable forest management (SFM). His main research interests are consumer choice theory, including theory of preferences revealed in non-market situations; institutional and evolutionary aspects of forest management; and production analysis of co-management production processes Some of his publications are: "Economics of Sustainable Forest Management (Editorial)," Forest Policy and Economics, 6(3–4) (2004): 197–200; "A social choice approach to sustainable forest management: An Analysis of Multiple Forest Value in Northwestern Ontario," *Forest Policy and Economics,* 6(3–4) (2004): 215–227; Ecosystem Choices without Discounting and Prices," *Environmental Monitoring and Assessment,* 86 (2003):105–127; "Extending the Boundaries of Forest Economics," *Forest Policy and Economics,* 5 (2003): 39–56. "A Theoretical Model of Optimal Forest Regimes in Developing Economies," *Journal of Institutional and Theoretical Economics,* 157(2) (2001): 331–355 (with R. Berry); "A Dynamic Approach to Forest Regimes in Developing Economies," *Ecological Economics,* 32 (2000): 287–300.

Zongmin Li is an economist, a former staff member of the former Research Center for Rural Development, a research institute under China's State Council. She gained her Master's degree in economics from the University of Beijing and her PhD in Development from the Land Tenure Center of the University of Wisconsin-Madison. She has worked with the Ford Foundation and a variety of Chinese NGOs on women's land issues in China. She has been a consultant to the World Bank, UNIFEM, and other international donor organizations, and is currently the Chief of Party of the USAID's Central Asia Land Tenure Reform Project, working in Kazakhstan, Uzbekistan and Tajikistan.

Xiaolin Pei worked as a policy researcher in the China State Planning Commission, Beijing, in the 1980s. He earned his PhD in Economic History at Lund University, Sweden, and was Assistant Professor there from 1999 to 2000. From 2000 to 2001 he was a visiting scholar in the East Asia Program at Cornell University. Dr Pei is now a senior researcher at the Van Vollenhoven Institute, Leiden University, The Netherlands. His recent publications include, *The Institutional Root of China's Rural Industry and Gradual Reform* (1998). His current research interests are China's land system and land law.

Frank N. Pieke is Lecturer in modern politics and society in China and a Fellow of St Cross College at the University of Oxford. He is Director of the Institute for Chinese Studies and Deputy Director of the ESRC-funded Centre on Migration, Policy and Society (COMPAS), where he heads the centre's research programme on "Sending Contexts". His most recent book is *Transnational Chinese: Fujianese Migrants in Europe,* (Stanford, CA, 2004) (with Pál Nyíri, Mette Thunø and Antonella Ceccagno).

Futian Qu is Vice-President and Professor at Nanjing Agricultural University. His research activities have concentrated on sustainable agricultural development and resource economics and management, economic policy reforms and sustainable land use, farmland institutional transition and allocative efficiency. He obtained his PhD in agricultural resource economics from Nanjing Agricultural University. Some of his recent publications are "Institutions, Policies and Soil Degradation: Theoretical Examinations and Case Studies in Southeast China," *Chinese Journal of Population Resource and Environment*, 2(1) (2004): 14–21 (with Tan Shuhao, Huang Xianjin and Nico Heerink); "Rural Market Development and Village Economics Approach,' *China Rural Survey*, 54(1) (2004): 44–55 (in Chinese) (with X. Shi, F. Qu, N. Heerink and M. Kuiper); and *Sustainable Resource Use and Sustainable Economic Development*, (Beijing, 2000) (with N. Heerink and Z. Huang).

Scott Rozelle is Professor in the Department of Agricultural and Resource Economics at the University of California, Davis, and is the U.C. Davis 2000 Chancellor Fellow. Dr Rozelle's research focuses almost exclusively on China and is concerned with three general themes: (1) agricultural policy, including the supply, demand, and trade in agricultural projects; (2) the emergence and evolution of markets and other economic institutions in the transition process and their implications for equity and efficiency; and (3) the economics of poverty and inequality. He is fluent in Chinese and is the chair of the International Advisory Board of the Center for Chinese Agricultural Policy. He is also a member of the Giannini Foundation.

Shuhao Tan is a PhD researcher at Wageningen University and a lecturer at Nanjing Agricultural University, mainly teaching resource and environmental economics. Her PhD research topic is "Land fragmentation, farm household production decisions and soil degradation in China." Her research interests are economic policy reform and sustainable agricultural development, resource use and environmental change. Some of her recent publications are Tan Shuhao, Qu Futian, Huang Xianjin and Nico Heerink (2004) "Institutions, Policies and Soil Degradation: Theoretical Examinations and Case Studies in Southeast China," *Chinese Journal of Population Resource and Environment*, 2(1) (2004): 14–21 (with Qu Futiqan, Huang Xianjin and N. Heerink); "Farm Households' Behavior and Soil Conservation: From a View of New Institutional Economics," *Soils*, 36(2) (2004): 141–144 (in Chinese); "On Economic Policy Reform and Regional Soil Degradation: A Case Study of Jiangxi Province," *China Land Science* (in Chinese) (2001) (with Li Li, Xu Ai-hui and Wa Shinxiu).

Weiguo Wang is Professor of Economic and Civil Law, and Dean of the Faculty of Economic and Civil Law at the China University of Politics and Law, Beijing. His recent publications include *Exploring the Verity of Legal Studies in the Age of Reform* (*Gaige Shidai de Faxue Tansuo*), (Falü

Chubanshe, 2003) and *Legal Construction of China's Land Property Rights* (*Zhongguo Tudi Quanli de Fazhi Jianshe*) (Zhongguo Zhengfa Daxue Chubanshe, 2002) (with Guanghua Wang). Weiguo Wang has served as a national advisor to various commissions of the National People's Congress on the Land Administration Law, the drafts of the Bankruptcy Law and the Property Rights Law.

Yang Yao is Professor of Economics at the China Centre for Economic Research, Peking University. He is editor of *China Economic Quarterly*. Professor Yao's research interests are rural land tenure and institutional changes in China. His recent and forthcoming publications include "Local versus Global Separability in Agricultural Household Models: The Factor Price Equalization Effect of Land Transfer Rights in China," *American Journal of Agricultural Economics* 84(3) (August, 2002): 702–715 (with M. Carter); "Land Tenure Choice in Chinese Villages: The Rational versus the Political Model," *Land Economics*, forthcoming; and "Political Process and Efficient Institutional Change," *Journal of Institutional and Theoretical Economics*, forthcoming.

Yaoqi Zhang is an Assistant Professor in the School of Forestry and Wildlife Sciences, at Auburn University, USA. He has authored and co-authored more than 20 papers in a wide range of journals and books. His main research interests are private forests, land tenure evolution, human–nature interaction, land use change, and non-market valuation of environmental and natural resources. Some of his recent key publications are: "The Impacts of Economic Reforms on the Efficiency of Silviculture: A Non-parametric Approach," *Environment and Development Economics*, 7(1) (2002); "Economics of Transaction Costs Saving Forestry" *Ecological Economics*, 36(2) (2000); "Econometric Analysis of the Causes of Forest Land Use Change in Hainan, China, " *Canadian Journal of Forest Research*, 30 (2000); "Deforestaton and Forest Transition: Theory and Evidence from China," in the book *World Forests from Deforestation to Transition?* (2000); "Impacts of Economic Reforms on Rural Forestry in China," *Forest Policy and Economics*, 1(1) (2000); "The Forest Sector in China: Towards a Market Economy," *World Forests, Society and Environment* (1999).

Preface

In the past decade, the People's Republic of China has boasted the world's highest growth rates. By allowing entry to the World Trade Organization (WTO) the international community not only confirmed the importance of China's economy in the world, but also the successes associated with economic reforms. Whether the widely touted optimistic prognosis for the Chinese economy is justified remains to be seen. During the first years of the twenty-first century, the central authorities have grown increasingly concerned about a possible overheating of the Chinese economy. Less visible to the outside observer, however, are certain structural problems that still await a solution. Of the three basic means of production – land, capital and labor – the first has remained effectively beyond the reach of market forces. In the rural areas – where the majority of China's land resources are located – there is no free transfer of land holdings and mortgage on land, while the locus and nature of ownership are still unclear.

In order to assess the current stage of China's land reforms and its effects on Chinese farmers, a seminar entitled "Rural Land in China: Land Rights and Sustainable Use" was held during the International Convention of Asia Scholars in Berlin (ICAS, 9–12 August 2001). Four chapters in this volume originate from the lively discussions and exchanges during this scholarly encounter – in particular, the contributions by Pieke, Fanfani and Brasili, Pei, and Tan, Qu and Heerink. However, as I was convinced that China's land reform is a timely, yet insufficiently highlighted issue in academic terms, I embarked on an arduous process to put together a book on this topic.

Looking for the people who are doing good work in this area is at times daunting and discouraging, but then finding them and learning from their experiences is very rewarding. Working together with them is even more rewarding. During this long process several people have helped me produce the book that you now have in your hands. First, I would like to thank Mark Selden for his unlimited support in shaping the papers into a publishable form. Mark has been my counsel and friend for many other issues. I would also like to thank Robert Ash, Richard

Edmonds, and Vivienne Shue for reviewing the papers in this volume. I hope the reader will enjoy this book as much as I enjoyed putting it together.

Peter Ho
Groningen,
3 March 2005

Introduction

The chicken of institutions or the egg of reforms?

Peter Ho

The fallacy of social engineering

In their comprehensive study on agricultural development, Stevens and Jabara (1988) optimistically noted:

> As agricultural development occurs, new and modified organizations and institutional arrangements are therefore required. If we can identify the new functions that need to be performed as economic and social change occurs, we should be able to identify the organizational and institutional requirements.

Would it not be wonderful if the social sciences indeed disposed so simply of a theory with the powers to explain and predict institutional needs in relation to social change, as Stevens and Jabara envisioned in the quote above? Alas, the existing social theories might come a long way in explaining the "why" of institutions, however, they are still quite removed from accurately *predicting* institutional requirements. One area in which this has become obvious is the study of transition, in particular, the reform process from a centralized economy predicated upon socialist and communist ideas, to a free market economy.

The restructuring of socialist economies in the former Soviet Union, and East and Central Europe following the fall of the Berlin Wall in 1989 belongs to the largest projects of social engineering ever undertaken. At once, policy-makers were confronted with fundamental questions such as whether to dismantle the core institutions of the communist state, what new institutions to create, how to articulate anew the relationship between plan and market, and in what time frame. The dilemma in reforming centrally planned economies to market economies boiled down to "shock therapy" versus guided development. It became the ultimate "politician's dilemma": must politics create new institutions to propel reform, or is reform – once the spirit is released from the bottle – an autonomous process that drives institutional change? What comes first: the chicken of institutions or the egg of reforms?

In the view of neo-liberal economics, privatization is a *conditio sine qua non* for a well-functioning market economy. This premise, enshrined in the "Washington Consensus" became the guiding principle for many social engineering programs of the World Bank and the International Monetary Fund in the former Soviet Union and Eastern bloc countries (Amsden 1997). Armed with this notion, Ministries of Privatization were set up that redistributed state and collective assets to the public, to workers and collective members, and to former owners whose property had been expropriated. In hindsight, one bitter lesson learnt is that society and societal change are less pliable and malleable than social engineering and neo-liberal economics suggest. Not least because of the disastrous results of rapid voucher privatization in Russia, we have been taught modesty and the realization that there is no single blueprint for economic reform (see, for example, FAO 1994). Private property protected by law, the principle of "getting-the-prices-right," and the emergence of effectively functioning markets are the outcome of a given society's historical development and institutional fabric. In other words, the successful creation of new institutions hinges in part on choice and timing in relation to the particular constellation of societal, economic, political and cultural parameters (Spoor 2003; Swinnen 2001; Wyplosz 2000). This critical theme is the backdrop against which the various contributions of this edited volume have been written.

Studying institutional change, regardless of whether it is focused on transitional or developing economies, may prove most fruitful when focused on its structuring of the means of production – land, labour and capital. This book does exactly that: it singles out land as an object of study and places it in the context of one of the world's largest and most populous countries undergoing institutional reform, the People's Republic of China. Land is one of the most important resources of humankind, although in modern, industrial society this is often overlooked. Therefore, Rowton Simpson rightfully reminds us that:

> Land is the source of all material wealth. From it we get everything that we use or value, whether it be food, clothing, fuel, shelter, metal, or precious stones. We live on the land and from the land, and to the land our bodies or our ashes are committed when we die. The availability of land is the key to human existence, and its distribution and use are of vital importance.
>
> (1976: 3)

On occasion, however, newspaper articles on the forced evictions of indigenous people in Brazil or the expropriation of white farmers in Zimbabwe put the land question right in the centre of public attention (van Royen 2001: 4). They also reveal how politicized the land question can become and suggest its profound social and economic consequences.

Before turning to the Chinese experience, it is necessary to review the critical issues and leading scholarly themes in the social engineering of land reform.

Land reform – creating credible institutions

One of the most telling and far-reaching measures to effect institutional change concerns the redistribution of land holdings through land reform. In its most politicized form, land reform equals revolution and is the ultimate means available to revolutionary movements or a nation–state in winning over the populace or destroying vested elites. Examples of this abound in history, ranging from ancient Greece to twentieth-century Mexico, Brazil and, of course, China (Tuma 1965: 20–27, 129–146). In the developmental context, however, land reform is generally equated with economic restructuring and is narrowly conceived as pertaining to surveying and granting title, land consolidation, and settlement programs through which state land is transferred to settlers. Land reform, however, actually comprises many more facets than that, as it is a complex mix of political and economic objectives. Land reform or "land-to-the-tiller" programs commonly feature state actions to transfer use and ownership rights to land; the change of social relations and class structure; and the improvement of the agricultural sector's economic performance (Lippit 1974: 138–146; de Janvry 1981: 383). In short, land reform aims at the transformation of rural society as well as profoundly impacting rural–urban and state–society relations. Or as Raup stated, land reform programs "combine redistribution of rights in land and the supporting measures that are necessary to achieve three objectives: social justice, political health, and agricultural output expansion" (1967: 270).

In the former Second World where communist regimes have become transitional economies, land reform programs are distinct from the Third World where newly established nation–states replaced the pre-war colonial or semi-colonial states. In contrast to developing countries in the South, transitional economies share what may be termed a "socialist property rights structure."[1] According to Marxist theory, class antagonisms and capitalist exploitation are to be avoided by socializing the means of production by putting them under common ownership, where they are at the disposition of the whole people organized as a state or a collective.[2] Despite the differences, land reform programs in both Second and Third World countries inevitably touch on three critical issues: (1) tenure security and economic development; (2) the position of informal and customary institutions vis-à-vis statutory laws and regulations; and (3) the role of state governance in guiding transition and development processes. These common themes might bear lessons for our understanding of development and transition that transcend simplistic Second and Third World classifications.

In thinking about land reform one generally does not escape from such notions as modernization and economic progress. As societies evolve from predominantly traditional, agrarian economies to industrialized, highly capitalist and technology-intensive economies, one might discern clear-cut stages of institutional development that appear or can even be brought about under specific social, economic and political conditions. In the 1960s, Rostow proposed a theory in which he envisioned five sequential growth stages from (1) traditional society; (2) the preconditions for take-off; (3) the take-off; (4) the drive to maturity; to finally (5) the age of high mass consumption. He believed his model useful "to regard the process now going forward in Asia, the Middle East, Africa, and Latin America as analogous to the stages of preconditions and take-off of other societies in the late eighteenth, nineteenth, and twentieth centuries" (Rostow 1960: 139). Although much criticized at the time, Rostow's model has been and continues to be influential in conceptualizing agrarian change as growth-stage theories rise and fall with the shifts of scholarly paradigms.[3] Similar evolutionary and deterministic lines of thinking frequently appear in the discussions on land reform and its institutional requirements.

Many economists of the property rights school have argued that insecure property rights lead to dampened investment behaviour and the mining of natural resources.[4] The principles of the property rights school can be traced back to the writings of Gordon on the over-exploitation of resources held under open-access,[5] and Coase on the relation between property rights assignments and Pareto-optimal outcomes (Coase 1960: 1–44; Gordon 1954: 124–142). In their reasoning, a clear assignment of property rights is a precondition for economically efficient resource allocation and, eventually, environmental sustainability. The writings of the property rights school provided the legitimization for privatized property as the sole most efficient and secure institutional arrangement. Thus, in the restructuring of markets, secure, private property should be among the ultimate objectives of development. The wish of national governments to establish private and secure property rights justified many large-scale land titling projects undertaken by multilateral and bilateral aid agencies all over the world. Although the ascendancy of the principle of private and secure property rights has never been as complete as its critics or proponents might want us to believe, the arguments of the property rights school have remained influential to date. In a recent article, Miceli *et al.* confidently maintain:

> One of the least controversial principles in the economics of land markets is the notion that the more clearly defined the property rights, the greater the land market efficiency. . . . Registration may be the preferred choice for developing countries that are in transition to market economies and private property systems.
>
> (2000: 370, 387)

Contrarily, the empirical evidence is less unequivocal and as we will see below, the Chinese experience is a case in point. For one thing, many studies on African countries have demonstrated that land registration has had a negligible or no impact on investment behavior and farm income.[6] It should be noted that the scholarly and political discussions on secure property rights and socio-economic development are blurred on two accounts. First, if we define tenure insecurity as the likelihood that the land user might risk losing his land rights (and associated income flows) at a certain point in the future, it should simultaneously be understood that eliminating such a threat can be accomplished through formal, as well as informal, institutions. In other words, increased tenure security does not necessarily require the issuance of formal land titles defined and recognized under statutory law.[7] Second, in contrast to the assumptions of Western economic advisors who served on advisory boards to national governments in the former Eastern bloc, secure tenure should not be equated with private property *per se*. Efficient resource allocation and greater incentives for resource conservation do not exclude the possibility of vesting tenure security in a community of users because, as Bromley aptly noted, "common property represents private property for the group of co-owners" (1991: 25). This leads us to the second critical issue in land reform and institutional change: the relative position of customary and informal institutions versus the statutory legal system.

One of the marked changes in Western European development has been the weakening and gradual disappearance of customary and informal land arrangements under the sway of increasing industrialization and rationalization. In the lowlands of Holland, a textbook example of spatial planning taken to its rationalized limits, traditional commons such as the *Marken* and *Meenden* have virtually vanished. In Britain, for centuries a system of land cultivation popularly termed the common or open-field system existed, under which unfenced village land was jointly cultivated under a triennial rotational system (first year wheat, second year spring crops, and third year fallow). During the second half of the eighteenth and the first half of the nineteenth century, landlords in England and Scotland increasingly appropriated these commons and invested capital to practice scientific, mechanized agriculture quite at odds with the open-field system. This movement that forever changed the British rural landscape from flexible fields divided merely by "balks" of grass into fixed, registered landholdings is known as the "enclosure movement." Enclosure in Britain did, however, have its drawbacks. Forced land eviction without proper financial compensation was not uncommon as peasants' customary claims – as elsewhere in the world – were generally non-codified, and thus difficult to prove against the landlords' claims. The renowned historian Sir George Trevelyan writes:

> In the redivision of the open fields and common wastes among individual proprietors and farmers, there was no intention to defraud the

> small man, but no desire to give him more than his apparent legal claim. Often he could not prove a legal claim to the rights he exercised in the common. Oftener his legal rights to keep cows or gees there, ... were compensated with a sum of money which was not enough to enable him to set up as a capitalist farmer ... The compensation might, however, pay for a month's heavy drinking in the ale house. And so he became a landless labourer.
>
> (1942: 457)

And Arthur Young – a forceful proponent of enclosure – noted in 1801 "by nineteen out of twenty Inclosure Bills the poor are injured and most grossly."[8]

At a certain point in time, any national government that has embarked on the path of economic reform is confronted with the question of what position informal institutions should be accorded relative to the formal, statutory institutional framework. In land reform the question is whether to disregard or recognize land claims that predate the statutory legal system. Due to its unwritten and fluid features, customary tenure is generally seen as irreconcilable with a modernized economy that needs registered plots with clearly established ownership for efficient land market transactions. Economists of the property rights school will bring the argument to bear that the flexibility and fluidity of customary land tenure arrangements are tantamount to tenure insecurity and will lead to market inefficiencies.[9] For this reason, governments frequently opt for the nationalization or privatization of commons. Yet, as many scholars have convincingly shown, customary and communal arrangements might under specific conditions actually function with significantly lower transaction costs than state or private arrangements.[10]

On the other hand, in certain cases – such as Zambia and Mozambique – nation–states have attempted to recognize informal and customary tenure with varying degrees of success.[11] The fixation of customary land claims in formal institutions, however, does entail certain dangers. The Dutch land rights jurist Sonius remarked:

> It should be realised that this [customary] law is by no means found always and everywhere in its undiluted form, and moreover that under the influence of the rapid political and economic developments ... it shows clear signs of modification, with all the social complications that this entails.
>
> (1963: 3)

The paradox inherent in Sonius' remark is, of course, his assumption of an "undiluted form" of customary law which simultaneously demonstrates "signs of modification" when subjected to social change. In fact, the fixation of customary law is a *contradictio in terminis* as its basic features are its fluidity and unwritten character. In Indonesia, the national government has unsuccessfully sought to fit customary systems into rigid notions of "traditional" *adat* law that in fact ceased to exist when, during the early 1930s, the influential lawyer van Vollenhoven described, and thus, fixed them in time.[12] The issue of time is crucial in the nation–state's conceptualization of and dealing with customary land claims. In the *Pocket Law Lexicon,* Motion defined customary law as "unwritten law established by long usage"(1951: 419) which immediately raises the question: what is long? In England, this is defined as that which exists for so long that "the memory of man runneth not to the contrary," a limit strangely fixed at the date of the accession of Richard I in 1189 (Simpson 1976). In communist China, memory runs considerably shorter with a limit that stops at 1950.[13]

Regardless of whether customary land claims are formalized through statutory law or not, if not properly handled by the state, these might give rise to violent and protracted land disputes.[14] Where there is a clash between traditional and modern institutions with overlapping competencies, yet with different norms and clienteles, land-related grievances are easy to surface. In land-scarce regions, where an increasingly marketized and commodified agricultural sector expands its influence into traditional rural society still governed by communal, informal arrangements, farmers are under threat of indiscriminate eviction from their land. This situation calls into question the role of state governance in guiding institutional change – the final critical issue in land reform.

How to strike the right balance between state intervention and market forces? On the one hand, the state is responsible for creating the necessary institutions to stimulate the emergence of a land market or guide its development. Land features two characteristics that sets it apart from most other goods – immobility and a virtual indestructibility – which makes it an ideal collateral in market transactions. To realize this potential it is necessary that land is endowed with secure, clearly defined and easily transferable ownership rights. It is at this point, that according to neoliberal economists the role of the state should come in to establish cadastral systems that ensure broad access to information for individuals and entrepreneurs to enable an informed use of their rights. In fact, recent studies in Thailand and Honduras have pointed to the need for titling to improve credit supply.[15] On the other hand, however, the state should also regulate land markets in line with its overall social objectives, which include protection of weaker social groups such as poor farmers, women and ethnic minorities. These two aims of land policy are sometimes difficult to reconcile:

> There may be many circumstances where formal titles will not have an effect on access to credit. ... At low levels of income and in the absence of other mechanisms for social security, land serves as a social safety net. Foreclosing on the land of households who have defaulted

> on credit would deprive them of the basic means of livelihood and may not be socially desirable which is essentially the reason for customary systems restricting the marketability of land. Even where formal law decrees that land should be fully tradable, such legislation may be impossible to implement.
>
> (World Bank 2003: 36)

By proceeding with land titling under conditions of low economic development, the state risks creating what I would term an "empty institution" rather than a "credible institution." The latter touches on the crucial concept of "trusting the system" or in the words of Diermeyer *et al.*, the "fundamental question of property rights: do economic and political actors believe that property rights are credible?"[16] If not socially accepted, a state-driven institution such as a cadastre will remain a mere empty shell; a situation reminiscent of the formal registration of land lease rights in China, where notarized household contracts are often but a "paper agreement" as rural collectives can still appropriate and redistribute leased land whenever deemed necessary.

For this reason, "getting the institutions right" is maybe more critical in the state-guidance of transition and development than "getting the prices right." At times, economic restructuring unleashes forces in society that require strong state intervention in the market place. As land resources become increasingly marketized and commodified, the state should ensure that the emerging land market does not result in a rapid concentration of land in the hands of a powerful few. This inevitably implies the control of market forces through the restriction or even prohibition of land sales or certain types of land rental. China, Uzbekistan and recently, North Korea,[17] are clear examples of transitional economies that have consciously opted to refrain from the privatization of land ownership while reserving the control over land for the state. In May 2002, the Russian Duma passed a law that allowed for the private sale of agricultural land. Yet, in response to parliamentary concerns over land speculation by foreign investors, President Putin secured an amendment to the law shortly afterwards. Through the amendment foreigners are no longer allowed to buy and sell agricultural land but only entitled to lease for a maximum term of 49 years (AP/Reuters 2002: 6; NRC Correspondent 2002: 4).

Although much high-quality research has been conducted on the land tenure reforms in the People's Republic of China, most of these studies are fragmented and isolated. There are few works that bring together the various efforts in one comprehensive study of transition and development.[18] This volume unites contributions from various disciplines – economics, law, anthropology, sociology and statistics – in the attempt to analyze land reform, which has been central to understanding all dimensions of China's multifaceted economic reform. There are three important areas in which the study of the Chinese experience will facilitate an understanding of transition and development processes. First, China has – out of ideological, as well as practical considerations – opted to implement a specific, hybrid land tenure structure for the agricultural sector under reform. Under the principle of complete state and collective ownership of land resources, privatization of rural land use rights has been effected through state-allocated use rights and commercial lease. It is no overstatement to say that this chosen path of land reform is unique in scale and ambitions among the former socialist states.[19] Second, after more than twenty years of reforms, it has become obvious that the Chinese experience is at odds with important premises of neo-liberal economics. Particularly notable is the fact that private land ownership has not proven essential for the effective functioning of the rural economy. And finally, at this writing, China is drafting its first Property Law that will form the foundation for the nation's land ownership and use rights structure for decades to come. This poses fundamental issues with far-reaching social, economic and political implications for the central leadership.

Land in twentieth-century China: from "destroying landlords" to private lease

The history of land policies in the People's Republic is in many ways also a chronicle of twentieth-century China. With the promise of "land to the tiller" Mao Zedong built his rural power base, which brought him victory over the nationalist forces. Land reform encompassed a wide range of issues including ownership, tenancy, rents, hired labor, state revenues and debts. It had a profound impact on Chinese society: with the overthrow of the rural elite and roughly equal land distribution within rural communities, the entire power structure was turned topsy-turvy. The timing and intensity of land reform differed over time and place. In the 1930s and early 1940s land reform in "revolutionary base areas," such as Shaan-Gan-Ning, was carried out with minimal social disruption. Primarily relying on rent and interest reduction and tax reforms, rich peasants and even landlords retained sufficient land to survive. However, in the politically charged atmosphere of the civil war of 1945–1949, land reform took a radical turn, costing the lives of many rich peasants and landlords. During the "speak bitterness" meetings peasants were encouraged to accuse the landlords paraded before them. Those accused of bullying the peasant class – murder, arson, rape and beatings – were not spared. An estimated 800,000 landlords were executed as "counterrevolutionaries" (Madsen 1991: 624).

Land reform in China was one of the largest and most far-reaching examples of land expropriation in world history. In the land reform process, between 200–240 million acres of arable land were redistributed to approximately 75 million peasant families.[20] In addition, the 1950s' land reform also heralded the end to the customary property rights structure as it had existed up to the late imperial and republican era. When the Communists took power in 1949, all forest, grassland and wasteland was declared state property; one year later this was formalized in the 1950 Land Reform Law.[21] With this act, the Communist government proclaimed the principle of *res nullius* or "open to acquisition on the basis of being unowned" over land resources which in fact were inhabited by ethnic minorities and Chinese colonists, and used under unwritten, customary and communal arrangements. The disregard of customary and informal tenure has remained a potential source of fierce land-related grievances in China today.

The second period of cataclysmic changes in ownership and control over land began with the establishment of the Higher Agricultural Producers' Cooperatives in 1956. From that moment, private land ownership was effectively abolished, leaving land in the hands of the state or the collective. Until decollectivization in the mid-1980s, there were basically only two areas in which significant change took place in land tenure rights: the level of collective ownership and the extent of household use rights to cultivate and market products of the small plots of land allocated to households. First, the disaster of the Great Leap Forward (1958–1962) forced the central leadership to decentralize land ownership from the commune to the production team, that is from units of several thousand households and multiple villages to units of 20–30 households within a natural village. This ownership structure was laid down in Party regulations promulgated in 1962 – the Sixty Articles – and remained in place for over two decades until the demise of the collectivist institutions. Second, the freedom to cultivate household plots and to market the produce shifted with the political winds. Before 1958 when rural China was overnight organized into huge administrative units – the people's communes – farmers were allocated use rights (not ownership) to small plots of collective land for their own purposes (the so-called *ziliudi*). Depending on the region, farming was more or less privatized with managerial responsibilities vested in the household in the wake of the failure of the Great Leap and the famine that resulted. In some areas individual farm households negotiated contracts under which they had to deliver grain quota to the state at fixed low prices. The surplus grain produced above the quota could be sold freely on private markets.[22] These rights were rescinded twice (and subsequently reinstalled), as the political pendulum swung sharply during and after the Great Leap Forward and the Great Proletarian Cultural Revolution (1966–1976). (Madsen 1991: 647–648)[23]

The Plenum of the 11th Central Committee of the Communist Party in December 1978 marked the beginning of the economic reforms and the beginning of the end of collectivism. The lease system, termed the Household Responsibility or Household Contract Responsibility System, was the outcome of regional experiments borne out of dire need in the poverty-ridden county of Fengyang in Anhui Province.[24] The experimentation with land leases was carried out under the aegis of Wan Li, the provincial governor of Anhui Province. The contract system proved to be the ultimate solution in reconciling the Chinese state's ideological premises – state and collective ownership of the means of production – with the bare necessity of having to revive the agricultural sector dampened by years of collectivism. In the four years prior to the economic reforms in 1978, grain production had stagnated at a level of around 280 million tons (State Statistical Bureau 1990: 12). By allowing private lease the rural collectives hoped to stimulate farmers' incentives – an undertaking that ran counter to conservative forces within the Communist Party. It was not until governor Wan Li was promoted to the Politburo, and the Fengyang experiments had received support from influential leaders such as Chen Yun and Hu Yaobang, that the Household Responsibility System gained political visibility. The extraordinary results of the land leases – a bumper grain harvest in 1984 that surpassed a total production of 400 million tons (an increase of 30 percent on 1979) – sounded the death-knell over the commune system and silenced many doubters within and abroad China. It also provided sufficient legitimacy for the state to extend the Household Contract Responsibility System to forestry, animal husbandry and fishery.

When the people's communes were dismantled in the early 1980s and household contracts replaced collective agriculture, this was trumpeted as the "second land reform." After more than three decades, the use right to rural land, and control over one's labor were once more returned to the tiller through lease. But the early period of the land lease system was not without setbacks. Its very strength, the decentralization of managerial and use rights to individual farm households, also proved its main weakness. Land reform had led to an extreme fragmentation of land resources and its management. In a few years, collective land was contracted to over 160 million households with an average of around 0.5 ha per family. In addition, as a survey of the early 1980s indicated, the family land was frequently scattered over as many as 11 to 15 small plots of widely varying quality in terms of fertility, topography, and texture (see Croll 1994: 21). The individualistic and fragmented agriculture posed serious difficulties for agricultural modernization. Due to the loss of economies-of-scale, it became difficult to introduce improved seeds and varieties, apply advanced agrochemical inputs, use modern technical equipment, and maintain the former collective irrigation, drainage and road infrastructure.[25]

On the other hand, the Household Responsibility System has definitely established itself as the mainstay of Chinese agriculture. After 1989 the grain harvest never dropped below 400 million tons and has steadily increased to a record of over 500 million tons during two consecutive years in 1998 and 1999 (State Statistical Bureau 2001: 380). One might wonder on the basis of what particular institutional constellation China's agricultural and rural development has been built.

The institutional foundations of China's land reform

After more than two decades of reforms, China's economy appears to many as having decisively turned to the "capitalist" development path. Yet, of the three means of production, only capital and labor have been privatized, while land ownership is still firmly in the hands of the state and the collective. Contrary to other transitional states, the Chinese government refrained from privatizing land ownership, a decision that initially stirred up heated academic and political debates on ownership. Camps were divided into advocates of outright nationalization of land resources, those who felt that privatization was essential for economic development, and moderate reformers who propagated gradual development of the rural land lease system. However, the very successes of the Household Responsibility System took the political wind out of the sails of the proponents of nationalization and privatization, and proved the moderate reformers right on two accounts. First, in contrast to the concerns of neo-liberal economists the privatization of use rights rather than ownership rights has proven economically viable. Second, the central government's decision to maintain the Marxist-Leninist principle of state and collective ownership has to date also avoided the large-scale land-related grievances over pre-revolutionary ownership that ruptured transitional economies such as parts of the former Soviet Union, East Germany and Kyrgyzstan.

As a result of these developments, foreign and Chinese observers shifted their attention from the ownership issue *per se* to the functioning of the land lease system itself. The question became: is the rural lease sufficiently secure to safeguard good land stewardship and long-term investments? At the start of decollectivization the national government allowed farm households a lease period of only five years, which was extended to 15 years in 1984. To safeguard farmers' economic incentives, the lease term was extended with another 30 years on top of the original contract in 1993 (Cheng and Tsang 1996: 44; Reisch 1992: 15–16). The initial results of rural surveys conducted in the early 1990s on the functioning of the lease system were worrying. The Communist Party's Central Policy Research Office found that tenure was everything but secure: in all 274 sample villages, the local authorities had readjusted land distribution rights since the first lease after decollectivization. And in 54 percent of the cases, land had been readjusted more than three times.[26] Chinese politicians, economists and social scientists warned that persisting tenure insecurity would inevitably lead to low investments in, and eventually, the squandering of land resources.

After over a decade of local experimentation with land lease with little intervention from above, the national authorities decided that the time had come for a strong pro-active stance on their part. In August 1997 the Secretariat of the Communist Party and State Council proclaimed a directive that prescribed a stable lease period free from reallocations for 30 years (*san shi nian bu bian*).[27] To show the state's determination to end tenure insecurity once and for all, the principle was subsequently enshrined in the Revised Land Administration Law of 1998. Provincial governments were instructed to give farmers – for the first time since decollectivization – individual, standardized, and notarized contracts. This renewed issue of lease contracts since the late 1990s is known as the "second round of lease" (*di'erlun chengbao*) (Secretariat of the State Council 1997; Land Administration Law 2001: 13) as the initial contract period of 15 years stipulated in 1984 expired. Research conducted a few months after the proclamation of the 1997 directive showed that the degree of tenure security had not significantly changed (Wang 1998: 56–57). Moreover, a high official within the Ministry of Land Resources noted that he did not expect tenure insecurity to end soon as he believed the ban on land reallocations would run counter to the social and demographic reality of rural China (Wang 2002). His remark indicates a possible misconception of the role of institutional change in development. Rather than focusing on the question whether tenure is secure or not, politicians and academics might ask themselves whether the current constellation of the Household Contract Responsibility System is found to be *credible* by social actors.

Surprisingly, neither the alleged *insecurity* of land lease nor the fragmentation of land have exerted serious negative effect on agricultural production and economic growth.[28] As shown earlier, since the late 1980s grain production has been steadily on the rise, hovering around levels of an annual production of 500 million tons. Moreover, ever since the start of the reforms, the Chinese economy has demonstrated impressive growth rates which certainly in the 1990s were to a great extent propelled by the rural economy. From 1991 until 1998 the average annual growth rate in GDP was 10.8 percent, with an overall average of 20.6 percent coming from the primary industry (China Statistical Bureau 1999: 21, 56). There are also no straightforward indications that insecure land tenure leads to bad stewardship of the land. On the basis of a household survey in five villages, Kung and Cai (2000: 276–308) concluded that the "allegation of farmers neglecting to preserve the soil fertility of their contracted plots is wholly unfounded." Furthermore, the political concern that private forest lease would result in clear-cutting by farmers in search of "easy money" proved unnecessary. An exhaustive study by Zhang *et al.* (2000) using data from four provinces over 1978–1995 concluded that "land tenure reform in general has had a positive effect on forest land expansion." While noting inter-provincial differences, the authors found that "the positive impact of the reform on timber harvesting has not taken place at the cost of forest land cover" (Ibid: 27) Again, these were not isolated findings.[29]

Even more astounding are the findings that tenure insecurity is actually supported by a majority of the rural populace and has been from the very start. According to the 1987 survey of the Central Policy Research Office,

80.6 percent of the 10,679 households (40 percent of the total observation households) held the opinion that contract land had to be readjusted if household size increased.[30] In a renewed survey in 1997 the Central Policy Research Office found that 62.8 percent of the sample households still advocated land redistribution.[31] These findings have been confirmed by a multitude of other studies.[32] How can we explain this paradox inherent to China's land tenure?

Farmers might not be certain whether the land they till is still theirs tomorrow. The owner of agricultural land, the rural collective, ultimately has the strongest voice in determining land allocation as opposed to the farmer who holds a contract on it. Yet, the uncertainty over land use has had no apparent negative consequences for the rural economy; it does not result in widespread misuse of land resources; and – most astonishing of all – it rallies widespread social support from the rural populace. The key to the wide social support for the land lease system lies in two words: social security. The 70 percent registered rural residents of the Chinese population,[33] represent widespread hidden unemployment at the countryside. For those millions of peasants active in the agricultural sector, the tiny plot of land they till is a basic security.[34] Under these conditions, the institutionalization of a culture of egalitarianism that ensures equal access to land for all outweighs the need for secure tenure. In this sense, we might liken the frequent land reallocations under the household contract system to an informal, yet, *socially credible* institution not much different from customary, communal tenure arrangements in developing nations elsewhere in the world (World Bank 2003: 36). The crux of the matter is whether such informal rights systems – be they traditional institutions dating back to pre-revolutionary times or tenure arrangements resulting from local experiments since the late 1970s – can persist in the face of a rapidly changing socio-economic environment.

Institutional requirements for transition

Development and transition processes imply change and the question is not *whether* socio-economic parameters and institutions will change but *when*. The winds of change have already manifested themselves in Chinese rural society. In *The Political Economy of Uneven Development*, Wang Shaoguang and Hu Angang (1999: 12) note that "the First World and Third World coexist within China." I would suggest that in China the First and Third worlds do not as much coexist, as that one world emerges within the other, which is the cause for much social and political friction. The Chinese Third World is represented by the rain-fed, subsistence agriculture where smallholders are literally "tied to their land" through egalitarian land distribution. Yet, it is precisely there, where the limits of existing institutions are being increasingly challenged through social conflict and political calls for reform that the First World emerges.

We can witness these processes at work at the rural–urban interface and the wealthier, coastal regions of China. For years, Zhejiang Province has been in the vanguard of local experiments with new tenure arrangements. A textbook example is Xinfeng village in Shaoxing County, which received nation-wide media coverage through an article in the *Nanfang Weekly*. The majority of rural labor of Xinfeng (96.5 percent) has found employment outside agriculture, as a result of which the proportion of non-agricultural income on the total rural income had risen to 76 percent in 2001. For the fields left behind by this large-scale labor migration, the village collective established a shareholding cooperative that sub-leased the land. Whereas, in the past, 478 farmers tilled 23.5 ha of village land, 13.6 ha is now sub-leased to three farm households and the remaining 9.9 ha to the Zhejiang Ridian Company (a former village enterprise). The increase in economies-of-scale opened up the way for more capital-intensive, mechanized agricultural operations, such as market gardens and commercial grain production (see Huang 2001: 2). In research carried out by Liu, Carter and Yao, empirical evidence is furnished on the relation between institutional change and the level of socio-economic development. They demonstrated that the need and the willingness to pay for secure, privatized property rights extended furthest in regions where land is of modest economic importance because of ample off-farm employment and relatively abundant land per capita.[35] What does this imply for the role of state governance in guiding these developments?

To date, the Chinese government has been extremely reluctant to introduce market forces into the rural land market. Whereas some observers would dismiss this reluctance as government failure to create efficient institutions, it actually demonstrates an extreme, and justified, caution in balancing the conflicting interests of China's First and Third Worlds. The national government has prohibited the sale of state and collective land ownership, and restricted the sale of land use rights. Understanding the Chinese land market inevitably means that one first has to familiarize oneself with an opaque, but "politically correct" discourse that avoids certain ideologically tainted terms, such as sale (*mai* or *chushou*) and lease (*dian*).[36]

Carefully avoiding the term "land sale," the Land Administration Law euphemistically stipulates that "the State exercises according to the law, a system of *valued use* for state-owned land" [italics added].[37] In practice, this boils down to the urban, state-owned sector. In the rural collective (cropland) and state-owned (forest, grassland and wasteland) sectors, the Constitution only allows the *non-commercial* transfer of use rights, although Chinese jurists and politicians expect that in the future the free sale (and mortgage) of use rights will be incorporated in law. This issue, which requires a constitutional amendment, is still heatedly debated and nothing about it is stipulated in the latest revision of the Land Administration Law. Through the establishment of a two-tier urban land market, the government keeps strict control over land transactions. On the "first-level market" (*yiji shichang*) the central state[38] "assigns" (*churang*) the use rights of urban state-owned land to buyers for a fixed period varying from 40 to 70 years[39] through auction, tender or negotiation. On the "second-level market" (*erji shichang*) land users can "transfer" (*zhuanrang*) or "contract" (*chengbao*) the use rights obtained on the first-level market to other users in return for payment. However, the period for the "transfer" – nothing more nor less than land lease – cannot exceed the original term stipulated on the first-level market.

Despite the regulatory vacuum, the free transfer, sale and mortgage of rural land use rights have become commonplace in the wealthier and coastal regions of China. There is nothing unusual about this, as a national advisor on land rights to the National People's Congress laconically remarked "if it is not forbidden, it is allowed (*wu jinzhi, ji xuke*). It just provides maneuvring space for local experimentation."[40] More problematic than the emergence of these hidden, informal rural land markets, however, is that the lack of clear regulations has created ample opportunities for abuse and rent-seeking behavior. The steep rise in the value of urban land has enticed corrupt village authorities to sell off land to the ever-expanding cities, and caused officials to approve the construction of factories, office towers and apartment buildings on land originally set aside for agricultural production.[41] Since the late 1990s, the problem of arable land loss due to construction activities has received the highest political priority and was one of the driving arguments to revise the 1986 Land Administration Law.[42] A potential source of social conflict is gradually emerging as land users are increasingly becoming the victims of forced evictions. Under the title "Stealing the Land," an article in the *Far Eastern Economic Review* noted with alarm that

> through a mixture of ambiguous laws, inept monitoring and greed, local officials are grabbing land from the people who farm it. The result is growing fury in the countryside . . . Confiscation is the hottest issue in the countryside and has sparked large-scale riots in southern Guangdong and Fujian provinces (Jiang 2002).

In October 2002, Mu Suixin, the former mayor of Shenyang, was sentenced to death on corruption charges that included the seizure of land from farmers. And in May 2003 Zhou Zhengyi, a Shanghai magnate in real estate, was arrested for illegal land expropriation. After bribing municipal officials, Zhou's real estate development company had succeeded in buying land far below market prices from the Shanghai municipality. The residents, whose old flats were to be torn down to make way for luxurious apartment blocks and shopping malls, were subsequently confronted with forced eviction. Zhou was charged by the public prosecutor with having driven over two thousand people out of their homes without proper financial compensation.[43]

These stories point to the necessity for secure, privatized property rights protected by law as commercialization progresses. One of the preconditions for secure and privatized property rights to surface in a market situation is a system that records changes in the specific rights to the land and the holders of these rights, as well as the qualities of the land in terms of boundaries and surface area. In the absence of such a system, the informed use of rights and free transfer of land become impossible. The need for land registration puts the ownership question right back at the center-stage of attention, a situation that the Chinese government has tried to avoid. If ownership is conceived in the civil law tradition as the absolute right that unites all other rights – such as use, management, inheritance, alienation and disposal – the question "who owns the land?" should be equal to "who controls the land?" But this principle is not self-evident in the Chinese context, which is the reason for the explosiveness of the land question in China.

There are many potential sources of land-related grievances. In a transitional context, one might think of the resentment and rancor among the thousands of forcefully expropriated landlords and rich peasants during Land Reform. Yet, of all problems this issue might be the least difficult to handle. Although hesitant in the beginning, the collapse of the communist world in 1989 increasingly strengthened the central leadership in its conviction that the ideological pillar of state and collective ownership should not be abandoned. China would not go down the road of some of the former socialist states: there would be no privatization of state and collective land ownership. For one thing, this determination has succeeded in smothering secret hopes of former owners or their descendants for a return of expropriated land.

A much thornier question is the recognition of collective ownership. This might sound a little odd for a country whose rural sector a few decades ago was still organized around communes, brigades and teams. A major source of land disputes stems from the fact that in Maoist China, the rural collective – particularly the natural village – was too weak an institution to effectively represent the interests of its members. Although formally vested with land ownership, the village frequently lost out against the local state and higher collective units, the brigade and the commune, that expropriated land without financial compensation. Resolving conflicts of this kind cannot simply be a matter of returning "stolen land." Due to the long-term and substantial investments since expropriation, the design of compensatory mechanisms will have to involve both the expropriated owner and the new, albeit illegal owner. As long as it is unclear who must or has the capacity to pay for such financial redress, poking up old conflicts might be better left aside according to the government.[44] Finally, the structure of Chinese land ownership under which forest and grassland are held under state ownership unless legally proven otherwise implies a concurrent impossibility to recognize any other land rights that existed prior to nationalization. This question typically concerns the land claims by ethnic minorities – nomadic pastoralists and forest tribes – and the colonists who reclaimed "wasteland" for agricultural purposes.

As many national governments and international donors have found out to their dismay, land registration is one of those social engineering projects that are bound to stir up violent conflict, because registration means recognition. The fear of raking up such land disputes, in the absence of adequate mechanisms for conflict resolution and ways to compensate owners or ex-owners, has brought the Chinese leadership to opt for a "hands-off" approach: stop rural land registration and shroud collective ownership in mist. During the revision of the Land Administration Law in the late 1990s, the Deputy Chairman of the National People's Congress Legal Committee acknowledged that the regulations on collective land ownership should be changed because "delegates of the NPC Standing Committee remarked that it is unclear who represents the land ownership . . . of the farmers' collective." He added, however, that revising the law at this point would be impossible under the current conditions (Li 1998: 3). But perhaps the Chinese government must be prepared to force through land registration and face these conflicts in certain regions in order to avoid worse conflicts.

We have come full circle. The sphere of applied science, in which transition and development studies find themselves, sooner or later leads back to the "politician's dilemma": must the political process create new institutions to propel socio-economic change, or is institutional change dictated by the forces of society and economy? In the case of the former, institutions must create the pre-conditions for reform, which was the rationale to apply the "shock therapy" of voucher privatization in the former Soviet Union. But the failure of *glasnost* in Russia led many to believe that guided, gradual reforms under which institutional change follows the changes in society is the answer to the riddle of transition. In case the latter proves true, institutions must follow the forces of change unleashed by reforms. Oi and Walder, however, retort that "while these arguments are appealing on intellectual grounds, the earlier failure of such evolutionary reforms in Hungary justified scepticism about calls for gradual reform" (1999: 2).[45] Rather than conceptualizing economic restructuring in terms of a "chicken or egg" dilemma, we should understand it as an intricate interplay between institutions and socio-economic parameters. At times this might require government restraint and creating ample space for regional economic forces to push the national limits through experiments. At other times this might require forceful state intervention to change the rules of engagement in which transition and development occur to the extent of risking the creation of socially incredible, or even *empty* institutions. The fascinating side of China's land reform to date is that it has led to a dichotomized society in which both approaches are a political inevitability. For this reason, the Chinese case offers important insights into the factors that lead to failure or success in guiding transition and development processes. The pitfall that the state needs to avoid in economic reforms is to impose blueprint institutional concepts with scant regard for the current socio-economic parameters. To provide analysis and evaluation of institutional change for policy-makers to rely on is the ultimate challenge for academic research.

The contributions: institutions and property rights

Before introducing the chapters, it is imperative to clarify the main concepts and theoretical notions used in this volume. By institution, we follow Douglass North's definition "the rules of the game in a society or, more formally, ... the humanly devised constraints that shape human interaction" (1990: 3).[46] The second major concept that runs through the chapters is that of property rights. In the scholarly literature, the words "institutions" and "property rights" are frequently used side by side – even to the point that the distinction between them becomes blurred.[47] In particular, when social scientists define property rights as a "social relation"[48] the two terms blend into one. In effect, the idea of a property right as a "social relation" is unworkable when simultaneously used with the term "institution." For analytical clarity: a property right is an institution, yet an institution is not necessarily a property right. Analysis would be considerably clearer when restricting its use to the statutory and customary legal sphere. This is why the contributions here construe the concept of property rights in the Demsetzian or common law tradition of a "bundle of rights".[49] A property right can include – depending on temporal and geographical variations – such rights as the right of use, alienation, usufruct, access, management and right of way.

The volume is divided into three parts. Part I, "Institutional change, politics and administration" starts with a chapter by Daniel Bromley. This contribution is a theoretical reflection on the predominant premises of contemporary economics that influence our thinking and conceptualization of transition and institutional change. According to Bromley, contemporary economics remains imprisoned by the Manichean tradition bequeathed to us by Adam Smith and Karl Marx. Instead of the neoliberal emphasis on private property rights as the cornerstone of the market economy and "getting prices right," it is argued that the economics of transition should be redirected to three guiding principles: (1) do no serious harm; (2) emphasize the working rules that define economic incentives rather than the ownership structure of assets; and (3) focus on transitional *strategies* rather than transitional *tactics*. By comparing the economic reforms of East and Central Europe with that of China, these principles are examined and validated in more detail.

The following chapter by Weiguo Wang reviews the restructuring of the land property rights in China, with particular reference to land use rights. In line with the current parliamentary discussions in China, Wang starts from the premise that China will never allow private land ownership as Russia has since 1991.[50] On this basis, he attempts to draw inferences concerning what legal reforms of state and collective property rights structures would be required in order to establish a well-functioning system of land use and lease rights. Wang's viewpoint is representative of a growing group of academics and lawyers in China who argue that the key to this issue lies in a reconsideration of the legal position of land use and lease rights as personal rights or *droits de suits*. These rights are opposed to the so-called "real rights," which include the right to buy and sell land. The "real" versus "personal" property rights debate is one of those discussions that even jurists find difficult to follow, as it relates to the specifics of English real property law that, although widely exported, was termed "manifold, intricate, tedious and uncertain" by Francis Bacon, Lord Chancellor in 1618 (cited in Simpson 1976). In China today, the rights to land use and lease are defined as personal rights, which means that if the user is deprived of its land rights only a "personal action" can be brought in court: a payment of their value instead of restoration of the land (or the "real" thing) itself. Wang calls for transformation of contract rights into real rights that would allow legal protection to contracting households, as well as a free transfer of contract rights. His appeal for real rights is in many ways equal to an appeal to establish in China a British system of freehold and lease-in-perpetuity (in Chinese, *yongdianquan*).

Due to the rapid commercialization of the countryside since the economic reforms, the transfer of land holdings has become more frequent. Many infrastructural projects have been undertaken to cope with the growing needs for transportation, living, industrial and agricultural enterprises and environmental protection. In Chapter 3, Frank Pieke examines the new institutional demands placed on the land use planning system. His contribution starts with an analysis of the development of national land use planning since the promulgation of the first Land Administration Law in 1986. This chapter starts by discussing the main contradictions in national rural development policies. After this, rural spatial planning and its role in agricultural development policies are reviewed, followed by an analysis of the current procedures and mechanisms of rural land use planning. The second half of the chapter presents an in-depth case study, drawing on fieldwork data collected in Taicang in southern Jiangsu. While noting the growing need for integrated land use and spatial planning essential to balance and coordinate diverse economic sectors, the Taicang case study demonstrates that spatial planning in China remains riven by conflicting policy objectives: food security, environmental protection, and urban and industrial development.

Part II, "Land tenure and economic relations" consists of five chapters, each of which shed light on the relation between land tenure security and economic behaviour. The first by Rozelle, Brandt, Guo and Huang systematically describes the organization and utilization of China's cultivated land resources. The authors observe substantial differences among villages in the property rights that households enjoy. Most villages in which farmers seem to enjoy relatively long-term security, have established a private property regime, just short of permitting purchase and sale of land. However, in some villages, tenure is insecure and farmers' use of the land appears to be constrained in a variety of ways as a result of demographic pressure, political reasons, or a lack of sufficient off-farm employment. The policy question examined here is this: how effective have these alternative regimes been in providing households the necessary incentives to ensure rational land use and investment, while simultaneously helping local communities meet distributive objectives? This question is further explored through empirical analysis in Chapter 5 by Michael Carter and Yang Yao. Through analysis of panel data from 80 villages, Carter and Yao show that the egalitarian land distribution created by the earlier reforms is becoming less equal over time, and that different regions within China have variously relied upon administrative and market-based responses to this new economic challenge. To examine the functioning and desirability of these alternative mechanisms, the authors present regression models of the determinants of both market and administrative land reallocations, as well as the insecurity-induced investment costs of the latter. Results show that administrative reallocations respond to increasing inequality in endowments, but that these non-market reallocations come at a significant cost in terms of foregone investment. In Chapter 6, Roberto Fanfani and Christina Brasili analyze China's first agricultural census, with particular reference to land use, household types and plot size. They demonstrate the big differences in the structure and characteristics of farm households across the 30 provinces of China. Compared to the collectivist past, when agriculture showed much less diversification, the increasing differences in land use, cultivated and sown area between the main types of agricultural households and non-households (state, collective and village) reflect the widening regional disparity unleashed by the agrarian reforms. The authors compare census data on labor, household size and type, land holdings and land use with previous surveys to redefine the geography of Chinese agriculture at provincial and county level. The changed regional and territorial reality will pose new challenges to policy-makers in terms of the design of agricultural and rural development policies. In Chapter 7, Tan, Qu and Heerink take up an important issue in China's rural development: institutional constraints posed by land fragmentation. The existence of land fragmentation is commonly regarded as a great burden to agricultural production, because it hinders modernization, causes inefficiencies in production and involves large costs to alleviate its effects. The impact of land fragmentation on land use and agricultural development will become more pronounced now that China has entered the WTO. In order to keep up with increased international competition, the rural sector will be forced to develop intensive, mechanized agriculture with greater economies of scale. This inevitably involves land consolidation into larger plots. Tan *et al.* demonstrate that land fragmentation in contemporary China is driven by four factors: (1) the land distribution process of the first and second round of lease under the Household Contract Responsibility System; (2) the (partial) reallocation of land due to demographic factors; (3) government-induced land consolidation programs; and (4) the renting in and renting out of land assigned to households. The chapter concludes that land fragmentation is likely to remain high and will form a serious constraint on the improvement of land productivity needed to meet the challenges of the WTO.

Chapter 8 by Xiaolin Pei delves into a novel and unexplored terrain: the relation between China's structure of land property rights and rural industrial growth. The high growth of township and village enterprises is one of the most remarkable features of China's transition to a market economy. Generally, there are two current explanations for the rapid rural industrialization. First, the statist argument claims that the success of collective township and village enterprise is due to "local state corporatism": local government and business enterprises merge together as one efficient industrial firm. The other school argues that the organizational form of township and village enterprises – a hybrid between state and private ownership – has given them the economic advantage over state-owned enterprises. Pei, however, shows that the rural industrial growth was due to the rapid increase in the number of workers. The primary mechanism that moved this vast rural labor surplus from the farm to the rural industrial sector, argues Pei, was neither the planned system nor markets, but collective land ownership.

Part III, "Rethinking property rights: natural resources and gender," looks at property rights reform in relation to issues that have received less scholarly attention: the management of natural resources such as rangeland and forest, and just as important, the impact of land reform to rural women. To varying degrees, the contributions in this Part call for a rethinking of property rights reform when dealing with these issues. In Chapter 9 by Tony Banks it is argued that property rights of rangeland are distinctly different from agricultural land or cropland. For this reason, it is important to take these differences into account when thinking about the reform of rangeland tenure. Based on a new institutional economics perspective, Banks shows that seemingly inefficient aspects of rangeland tenure, notably communal arrangements and "fuzzy boundaries," may actually facilitate the realization of certain benefits that have been missed in the conventional analysis and could represent "opportunity costs" of further rangeland privatization. Although these characteristics also give rise to efficiency concerns, Banks argues that these lead to improved external exclusion which benefits sustainable management; to larger economies of scale with respect to herd supervision; to an enhanced provision of social insurance; and to the abatement of environmental risk. However, the features of collective and "fuzzy" or insecure tenure of agricultural land are exactly the main concerns of the central state, which is why privatization and land titling are encouraged. Banks argues against this and concludes that it is irrational and undesirable to strive for a convergence between rangeland and cropland tenure.

In Chapter 10, Yaoqi Zhang and Shashi Kant argue that to effectively evaluate the economic performance of collective forestland reforms, one needs to move beyond notions such as ownership, and property rights as a "bundle of rights." These notions overlook other rights related to economic incentives. With this aim in mind, Zhang and Kant propose using a property rights framework that distinguishes between physical asset rights and economic rights. Their chapter does not aim to assess the economic performance of property rights reforms in terms of physical asset rights and economic rights. Instead the chapter attempts to highlight the various critical aspects of physical asset rights and economic rights on collective-owned forestland, and their current status. In addition, it examines the changing role of the government from forest owner to a specialized protector of rights.

The last chapter by Zongmin Li and John Bruce studies a much neglected issue in China's land reform – women's access to land. In fact, this chapter is one of the first scholarly studies that specifically deals with gender and land rights in China. Over the period of reform, men and women have played increasingly different economic roles in their families and their communities. At the same time that gender roles have changed in response to the dramatic changes in the rural economy, China has reinforced property rights to farm households. Over the years, it has become clear that this change has affected men and women in different ways. One development of particular concern to outside observers is the growing landlessness of women. This chapter argues that the landlessness on the part of women is growing as the result of interaction between legal reforms intended to increase tenure security for households, and through the resurgence of traditional patterns of patrilocal residence and patrilineal inheritance of land. While the central government has recognized and sought to deal with this problem in the 2002 Rural Land Contracting Law, the authors demonstrate that the principal remedial provisions face implementation problems and there is a need for further action.

The various contributors to this volume assess the Chinese land reform through the changes in institutional requirements that socio-economic conditions dictate. Whereas the authors agree that private and secure property as the institutional cornerstone for modern society is not a precondition to effect successful transition, both in terms of stable economic development and the protection of weaker social groups, the question is whether it might surface as an essential institution over time. In this sense, it must be understood that private property is not to be equated with private ownership. In fact, some chapters are testimony to the rising importance of secure and privatized, or at least altered, institutions in the course of transition. In different ways the contributions in this volume are a measure of the past, present, and future changes in the Chinese agricultural sector and the nature and significance of transition processes.

Notes

1 This is not to say that there were no wide regional differences in the degree of collectivization between the socialist states. For example, in Hungary and East Germany, collective farms dominated most of the agricultural land, whereas in Poland and Yugoslavia individual peasant farming remained the main form of production.
2 For more information on the features of the socialist legal structure and ownership, see Zweigert and Kötz (1993: 303–304).
3 See the discussion in Stevens and Jabara (1988: 130–131).
4 See, for example, Dorner (1972), World Bank (1974), and Johnson (1973).
5 In fact, quite similar to Garrett Hardin's argument on pastoral resources 14 years later. See Hardin (1968: 1243–1248).
6 See, for example, Atwood (1990: 659–671) and Pinckney and Kimuyu (1994: 1–28). A good review of these studies is provided in World Bank (2003: 30).
7 This is illustrated by the case of peri-urban Ecuador, where informal property rights developed by communities over time had to some extent come to substitute formal property rights. It implies that titling must be done with extreme caution in communities where informal rules exist. See Lanjouw and Levy (1998).
8 Cited in Simpson (1976: 248).
9 Sjaastad and Bromley counter this argument by noting that

> the conventional propositions that indigenous tenure provides insufficient investment incentives, and at the same time leads to rent dissipation, are contradictory. Each may have some merit on its own, but both cannot hold at the same time. The very act of rent-dissipating capture is largely analogous to overinvestment in the extreme case, an investment that yields no direct returns but only more secure rights to land. . . . The key to understanding this is to see that many of the activities related to farming have a dual function – one that is productive and one that is tenurial. If the general investment climate of a rural community is overly cautious, because of market failure, risk aversion, or for other reasons, it is possible that indigenous tenures may provide investment incentives that are superior to freehold, as well as a path towards tenure security more efficient than state intervention in the form of imposed titling programs.
>
> (1997: 549–562)

10 See the large body of literature on common property. Some influential writings are Ostrom (1990), Wade (1987: 95–106), and Bromley (1992).
11 See Wily (2002).
12 See van Vollenhoven (1918) and (1931) and Slaats (2002).
13 The law states "all land deeds that predate Land Reform are invalid" (Sun 1998: 111)

14 The Nicaraguan and Rwandan experiences are a case in point. See Everingham (2001: 61–93); Andre and Plateau (1998: 1–47).
15 See Feder and Nishio (1999: 143), Lopez (1997) and Lopez and Valdez 2000).
16 For a discussion of the credibility of institutions, see Diermeyer *et al.* (1997: 20). In fact, this question also relates to issues of empowerment, democratic representation and decentralization. However, as I here focus on market rather than political reform, these questions are left for the following chapters in this volume to address.
17 See Reuters (2002: 4). In the article it is pointed out that despite intentions for economic reform, North Korea will stay away from privatization of land.
18 See, for example, Walker (1991), Chen and Wills (1999) and Land Tenure Center (1995).
19 This situation very much resembles the Vietnamese system. See also Chan *et al.* (1999).
20 For more information on land reform in China, see also Gray (1990: 266–267, 290) and Lippit (1974: 98–100).
21 Articles 16 and 18 of the 1950 Land Reform Law, in Sun (1998: 109).
22 The grain procurement system of "unified purchase and supply" was established in the fall of 1953.
23 For a local account of the swings in privatization and recentralization of the control over land, see Chan *et al.* (1992: 19–27).
24 In fact, in Anhui Province two different systems co-existed prior to the ascendance of the Household Contract Responsibility System. The first system, known as the *bao chan dao hu*, under which production was contracted to the household, devolved the responsibility for the cultivation of given plots of land to the household. The household was provided with agricultural inputs by the collective, but was not allowed to decide what to cultivate, nor could it sell the agricultural produce on its own. The second system, the *bao gan dao hu* or *dabaogan*, was the direct predecessor to the Household Contract Responsibility System, which allowed the household both managerial rights as well as the right to sell crops under the condition that the state grain-quota had been met. See also Unger (2002: 99–101).
25 See Vermeer (1998) and Selden (1998).
26 Of the sample villages, 20.1 percent readjusted once, 25.9 percent twice, 30.7 percent three times, 12.8 percent four, 2.9 percent five and 7.6 percent six times or higher (Bangongshi 1992: 437).
27 Notice 16/1997 in Sun 1998: 377.
28 Nor is rural house construction significantly affected by it as a recent article demonstrated. See Sergeson (2002: 927–955).
29 As Rozelle *et al.* write: "afforestation effort is greatest on Forest Household Responsibility System and private plots. ... Descriptive statistics show that within the non-state sector ..., increases in forest area happen most frequently when individuals have more control and income rights" (2000: 44).
30 Unfortunately, there are no similar figures at the village level. See Bangongshi (1992: 329) and Kung and Liu 1997: 34.
31 Of the 36.1 percent farmers that opposed land redistributions, 46.7 percent thought their villagers' committee could safeguard a policy of stable land lease, 22.9 percent said that land was abundant and uneven land distribution would not incite social conflict, 17.1 percent said that income from land was no longer important because of alternative employment opportunities, and 13.3 percent stated that land distribution was too cumbersome and they were unwilling to redistribute after the first time. See Wang (1998: 57).
32 See Kung and Liu (1997: 33–64) and Hu (1997: 175–186).

33 Of a total of 1.25 billion people in 1998, 69.6 percent were registered as rural population. See National Bureau of Statistics 1999: 111.
34 A mere 0.14 ha per capita in 1998 (National Bureau of Statistics 1999: 390).
35 The research was based on a survey of 80 village in four provinces, Henan, Jiangxi, Zhejiang and Jilin (Liu *et al.* 1998: 1789–1806).
36 For official definitions and explanations of the terms of the Chinese land market used in this text, see Ma (1991: 93, 183, 891, 989). Although dating from 1991, the regulations on the land market described in this book are still valid today.
37 Article 2, Revised Land Administration Law in Fang (1998: 207).
38 Since the 1998 revision of the Land Administration Law, the central state is the sole owner of state-owned land and can only be represented by the Ministry of Land Resources and its subordinate organs in order to avoid indiscriminate land sales by local governments. See Articles 2 and 5, Revised Land Administration Law, in Fang (1998: 207).
39 According to the official legal interpretation, urban housing land can be assigned for 70 years; industrial land for 50 years; land for educational, scientific, cultural, health care and sports purposes for 50 years; land for commercial, touristic and recreational purposes for 40 years; and other categories not included in the above for 50 years. See National People's Congress Legal Work Committee (1998: 40–41).
40 Wang (2001).
41 Chengri Ding notes

> Huge profits provided economic incentives for illegal land transactions while loopholes in land regulations and laws tempt people to take risks with little fear of consequences. These hidden markets had caused substantial revenue losses to the state and local governments, adversely affecting urban development under the guidelines of urban comprehensive plans, increased social inequality and corruption.
>
> (2003: 109–120)

Similar problems have also been observed by David Zweig (2000).
42 See Xiang (1986: 2). A notice on the protection of arable land (CCP Document 1997/11), jointly promulgated in 1997 by the Communist Party Secretariat and the State Council, demonstrates that land loss is still regarded as an urgent problem.
43 See Jiang (2002: 56–59). Recent cases of forced land evictions were recorded by van Pinxteren (2003: 4).
44 See also Ho (2001: 387–414).
45 See also Walder (2002: 231–253).
46 The sociologist Babbie defined an institution as "a relatively stable and integrated set of symbols, beliefs, values, norms, roles and statuses relating to some aspect of social life" (1980: 114). Commons wrote, "sometimes an institution seems to be analogous to a building, a sort of framework of laws and regulations, within which individuals act like inmates. Sometimes it seems to mean the 'behavior' of the inmates themselves" (1961: 69). There is a wide body of literature available on institutional change and the relationship between institutions and economic behavior. One of the earliest, influential articles on the topic was written by C.J. Wolf (1955: 867–883).
47 The research in which property rights and institutions are brought together in one analysis is the study of so-called "common property" or "common pool resources." See Ostrom (1990), Kiser and Ostrom (1982) and Nicholson (1988).
48 Hoebel cited in Hann (1998: 4).

49 See also Demsetz (1967: 347–359).
50 In fact, the Russian Duma passed a law on 16 May 2002 that allows the free sale of rural land for the first time since 1917. See NRC Correspondent (2002: 4).

References

Amsden, Alice H. (1997) "Bringing Production Back in: Understanding Government's Economic Role in Later Industrialization," *World Development*, 25(4): 469–480.

Andre, C. and Plateau, J.P. (1998) "Land Relations under Unbearable Stress: Rwanda caught in the Malthusian Trap," *Journal of Economic Behavior and Organization*, 34(1): 1–47.

AP/Reuters (2002) "Poetin verbiedt Verkoop Russische Grond aan Buitenlanders (Putin bans the Sale of Russian Soil to Foreigners), *Spits*, 20 June, p. 6.

Atwood, D.A. (1990) "Land Registration in Africa: The Impact on Agricultural Production," *World Development*, 18,(5): 659–671.

Babbie, E.R. (1980) *Sociology: An Introduction*, Belmont, CA: Wadsworth.

Bangongshi, Nongcun Guding Guanchadian (ed.) (1992) *Quanguo Nongcun Jingji Dianxing Diaocha Shuju Huibian, 1986–1990* (A Compilation of Data from the National Rural Survey, 1986–1990), Beijing: Zhonggong Zhongyang Dangxiao Chubanshe.

Bromley, Daniel W. (1991) *Environment and Economy: Property Rights and Public Policy*, Oxford: Blackwell.

Bromley, Daniel W. (ed.) (1992) *Making the Commons Work: Theory, Practice and Policy*. San Francisco: ICS Press.

Chan, Anita, Kerkvliet, Benedict and Unger, Jonathan (1999) *Transforming Asian Socialism: China and Vietnam Compared*, Lanham, MD: Rowman and Littlefield.

Chan, Anita, Madsen, Richard and Unger, Jonathan (1992) *Chen Village under Mao and Deng*, 2nd ed, Berkeley, CA: University of California Press.

Chen, Jean and Wills, David (1999) *The Impact of China's Economic Reforms upon Land Property and Construction*, Aldershot: Ashgate.

Cheng, Yuk-shing and Tsang, Shu-ki (1996) "Agricultural Land Reform in a Mixed System: The Chinese Experience of 1984–1994," *China Information*, 10(3/4) (Winter 1995/Spring 1996): 44.

China Statistical Bureau (ed.) (1999) *China Statistical Yearbook 1999*, Beijing: China Statistics Press.

Coase, R.H. (1960) "The Problem of Social Cost," *Journal of Law and Economics*, 3: 1–44.

Commons, J.R. (1961) *Institutional Economics*, Madison, WI: University of Wisconsin Press.

Croll, Elisabeth (1994) *From Heaven to Earth: Images and Experiences of Development in China*, London: Routledge.

de Janvry, A. (1981) *The Agrarian Question and Reformism in Latin America*, Baltimore, MD: Johns Hopkins University Press.

Demsetz, Harold (1967) "Toward a Theory of Property Rights," *American Economic Review*, 62: 347–359.

Diermeyer, Daniel, Ericson, Joel M., Frye, Timothy and Lewis, Steven (1997) "Credible Commitment and Property Rights: The Role of Strategic Interaction between Political and Economic Actors," in David L. Weimer (ed.) *The Political*

Economy of Property Rights: Institutional Change and Credibility in the Reform of Centrally Planned Economies, Cambridge: Cambridge University Press.

Ding, Chengri (2003) "Land Policy Reform in China: Assessment and Prospects," *Land Use Policy*, 2(20): 109–120.

Dorner, P. (1972) *Land Reform and Economic Development*, London: Penguin.

Everingham, M. (2001) "Agricultural Property Rights and Political Change in Nicaragua," *Latin American Politics and Society*, 43(3): 61–93.

Fang, Weilian (ed.) (1998) *Zhonghua Renmin Gongheguo Tudi Guanlifa Shiyong Jianghua* (A Practical Discussion of the "Land Administration Law of the People's Republic of China"), Beijing: Zhongguo Minzhu Fazhi Chubanshe.

FAO (ed.) (1994) *Reorienting the Cooperative Structure in Selected Eastern European Countries: Summary of Case Studies*, Rome: FAO.

Feder, G. and Nishio, A. (1999) "The Benefits of Land Registration and Titling: Economic and Social Perspectives," *Land Use Policy*, 15(1): 25–43.

Gordon, H.S. (1954) "The Economics of a Common Property Resource: the Fishery," *Journal of Political Economy*, 62: 124–142.

Gray, Jack (1990) *Rebellions and Revolutions: China from the 1800s to the 1980s*, Oxford: Oxford University Press.

Hann, C.M. (1998) "The Embeddedness of Property," in C.M. Hann (ed.) *Property Relations: Renewing the Anthropological Tradition*, Cambridge: Cambridge University Press.

Hardin, Garrett (1968) "The Tragedy of the Commons," *Science*, 162: 1243–1248.

Ho, Peter (2001) "Who Owns China's Land? Policies, Property Rights and Deliberate Institutional Ambiguity," *The China Quarterly*, 166, June: 387–414.

Hu, Wei (1997) "Household Land Tenure Reform in China: Its Impact on Farming Land Use and Agro-Environment," *Land Use Policy*, 14(3): 175–186.

Huang, Guangming (2001) "Xinfeng Cun de Tudi Gufen Hezuoshe" (Land Shareholding Cooperative of Xinfeng Village), *Nanfang Zhoumo*, 14 June, p. 2.

Jiang, Xueqin (2002) "Stealing the Land," *Far Eastern Economic Review*, 7 February: 56–59.

Johnson, D.G. (1973) *World Agriculture in Disarray*, New York: St. Martin's Press.

Kiser, Larry L. and Ostrom, Elinor (1982) "The Three Worlds of Action: A Metatheoretical Synthesis of Institutional Approaches," in Elinor Ostrom (ed.) *Strategies of Political Inquiry*, London: Sage Publications.

Kung, James Kai-sing and Cai, Yong-Shun (2000) "Property Rights and Fertilizing Practices in Rural China: Evidence from Northern Jiangsu," *Modern China*, 26(3), July: 276–308.

Kung, James Kai-sing and Liu, Shouying (1997) "Farmers' Preferences Regarding Ownership and Land Tenure in Post-Mao China: Unexpected Evidence from Eight Counties," *The China Journal*, 38 (July): 33–64.

Land Administration Law of the People's Republic of China (2001) Article 14, English version, Beijing: China Legal Publishing House.

Land Tenure Center (ed.) (1995) *Transition of China's Rural Land System: Proceedings from the International Symposium on Rural Land Issues in China*, Madison, WI: University of Wisconsin.

Lanjouw, J.O. and Levy, P.I. (1998) "Untitled: A Study of Formal and Informal Property Rights in Urban Ecuador," *Yale Economic Growth Center Discussion Paper*, No. 788.

Li, Boyong (1998) *Quanguo Renda Falü Weiyuanhui guanyu "Zhonghua Renmin*

Gongheguo Tudi Guanlifa (Xiuding Cao'an)" Shenyi Jieguo de Baogao (Report on the Results of the Review of the "Land Administration Law of the People's Republic (Revised Draft)" by the Law Committee of the National People's Congress), Speech at the 4th Session of the Standing Committee of the 9th National People's Congress, 24 August, p. 3.

Lippit, V.D. (1974) *Land Reform and Economic Development in China: A Study of Institutional Change and Development Finance*, White Plains, NY: International Arts and Sciences Press.

Liu, Shouying, Carter, Michael R., and Yao, Yang (1998) "Dimensions and Diversity of Property Rights in Rural China: Dilemmas on the Road to Further Reform," *World Development*, 26,(10): 1789–1806.

Lopez, R. (1997) *Land Titles and Farm Productivity in Honduras*, mimeo, Washington, DC: World Bank.

Lopez, R. and Valdez, A. (2000) *Rural Poverty in Latin America*, London: Macmillan Press.

Ma, Kewei (ed.) (1991) *Tudi Da Cidian* (Great Dictionary of Land), Changchun: Changchun Chubanshe.

Madsen, Richard (1991) "The Countryside under Communism," in Roderick MacFarquhar and John K. Fairbank (eds), *Cambridge History of China, The People's Republic*, Part 2: *Revolutions within the Chinese Revolution 1966–1982*, Cambridge: Cambridge University Press.

Miceli, Thomas J., Sirmans, C.F. and Turnbull, Geoffrey K. (2000) "The Dynamic Effects of Land Title Systems," *Journal of Urban Economics*, 47: 370, 387.

Motion, A.W. (1951) *The Pocket Law Lexicon*, London: Stevens and Sons.

National Bureau of Statistics (ed.) (1999) *China Statistical Yearbook 1999*, Beijing: Bhina Statistics Press.

National People's Congress Legal Work Committee (ed.) (1998) *Zhonghua Renmin Gongheguo Tudi Guanlifa Shiyi* (An Interpretation of the Land Administration Law of the People's Republic of China), Beijing: Falü Chubanshe.

Nicholson, Norman (1988) "The State of the Art," in Vincent Ostrom, David Feeny and Hartmut Picht (eds) *Rethinking Institutional Analysis and Development: Issues, Alternatives and Choices*, San Francisco: ICS Press.

North, Douglass (1990) *Institutions, Institutional Change and Economic Performance*, Cambridge: Cambridge University Press.

NRC Correspondent (2002) "Verkoop van Boerengrond in Rusland" (Sale of Farmers' Land in Russia), *NRC Handelsblad*, 17 May, p. 4.

Oi, Jean C. and Walder, Andrew G. (1999) "Property Rights in the Chinese Economy: Contours of the Process of Change," in Jean C. Oi and Andrew G. Walder (eds) *Property Rights and Economic Reform in China*, Stanford, CA: Stanford University Press.

Ostrom, Elinor (1990) *Governing the Commons: The Evolution of Institutions for Collective Action*, Cambridge: Cambridge University Press.

Pinckney, T.C. and Kimuyu, P.K. (1994) "Land Tenure Reform in East Africa: Good, Bad, or Unimportant?" *Journal of African Economies*, 3(1): 1–28.

Raup, P.M. (1967) "Land Reform and Agricultural Development," in H. Southworth and B.F. Johnston (eds) *Agricultural and Economic Development*, Ithaca, NY: Cornell University Press.

Reisch, Erwin M. (1992) "Land Reform Policy in China: Political Guidelines and Tendencies," in Eduard B. Vermeer (ed.) *From Peasant to Entrepreneur: Growth and Change in Rural China*, Wageningen: Pudoc.

Reuters (2002) "Noord Korea knot oude Planeconomie" (North Korea Restricts the old Planning Economy), *NRC Handelsblad*, 20 July, p. 4.

Rostow, W.W. (1960) *The Stages of Economic Growth: A Non-Communist Manifesto*, London: Cambridge University Press.

Rozelle, Scott, Huang, Jikun, Husain, Syed Arif and Zazueta, Aaran (2000) *China: From Aforestation to Poverty Alleviation and Natural Forest Management*, Washington, DC: World Bank Operations Evaluation Department.

Secretariat of the State Council (1997) *Zhonggong Zhongyang Bangongting, Guowuyuan Bangongting guanyu Jinyibu Wending he Wanshan Nongcun Tudi Chengbao Guanxi de Tongzhi* (Notice by the Central Secretariat of the CCP and the Secretariat of the State Council on the Further Stabilization and Perfectioning of the Contract Relations of Rural Land), No. 16.

Selden, Mark (1998) "Household, Cooperative and State in the Remaking of China's Countryside," in Eduard B. Vermeer, Frank Pieke and Woei Lien Chong (eds) *Cooperative and Collective in China's Rural Development: Between State and Private Interests*, New York: M.E. Sharpe.

Sergeson, Sally (2002) "Subduing 'The Rural House-building Craze': Attitudes toward Housing Construction and Land Use Controls in Four Zhejiang Villages," *The China Quarterly*, 172, December: 927–955.

Simpson, R. Rowton (1976) *Land Law and Registration*, Cambridge: Cambridge University Press.

Sjaastad, Espen and Bromley, Daniel W. (1997) "Indigenous Land Rights in Sub-Saharan Africa: Appropriation, Security and Investment Demand," *World Development*, 25(4): 549–562.

Slaats, Herman (2002) "Adat law and land registration in Indonesia," paper presented at the international conference on "Land Registration and Spatial Planning in Transition Countries," 31 October–November, Wageningen.

Sonius, H.W.J. (1963) *Introduction to Aspects of Customary Land Law in Africa as Compared with Some Indonesian Aspects*, Leiden: Universitaire Pers Leiden.

Spoor, Max (ed.) (2003) *Transition, Institutions, and the Rural Sector*, Lanham and Oxford: Lexington Books.

State Statistical Bureau (ed.) (1990) *Quanguo Gesheng, Zizhiqu, Zhixiashi, Lishi Tongji Ziliao Huibian – 1949–1989* (A Compilation of Historical Statistics of all Provinces, Autonomous Regions and Municipalities – 1949–1989), Beijing: Zhongguo Tongji Chubanshe.

State Statistical Bureau (2001) *China Statistical Yearbook 2001*, Beijing: China Statistics Press.

Stevens, Robert D. and Jabara, Cathy L. (1988) *Agricultural Development Principles: Economic Theory and Empirical Evidence*, Baltimore, MD: Johns Hopkins University Press.

Sun, Jianhong (ed.) (1998) *Tudi Quanshu Shiwu Zhinan* (Practical Compass on Land Titles), Beijing: Zhongguo Dadi Chubanshe.

Swinnen, Johan F.M. (2001) "Lessons from Ten Years of Rural Transition", paper presented at the CESTRAD Conference, "Transition, Institutions, and the Rural Sector," The Hague, December 11–12.

Trevelyan, George Macaulay (1942) *A Shortened History of England*, New York: Longman, Green and Co.

Tuma, Elias H. (1965) *Twenty-Six Centuries of Agrarian Reform*, Berkeley, CA: University of California Press.

Unger, Jonathan (2002) *The Transformation of Rural China*, London: M.E. Sharpe,.

van Pinxteren, Garrie (2003) "Protesterende Chinezen verdreven" (Protesting Chinese Driven Away), *NRC Handelsblad*, 17 June, p. 4.

van Royen, Marjon (2001) "Braziliaanse 'Bosbewoners' zonder Rechten" [Brazilian "Forest Dwellers" without Rights], *NRC Handelsblad*, 9 November, p. 5.

van Vollenhoven, C. (1918 and 1931) *Het adatrecht van Nederlandsch-Indië* (Adat Law of the Dutch Indies), Vols I and II, Leiden: KITLV.

Vermeer, Eduard B. (1998) "Decollectivization and Functional Change in Irrigation Management in China," in Eduard B. Vermeer, Frank Pieke and Woei Lien Chong (eds) *Cooperative and Collective in China's Rural Development: Between State and Private Interests*, New York: M.E. Sharpe.

Wade, Robert (1987) "The Management of Common Property Resources: Collective Action as an Alternative to Privatisation or State Regulation," *Cambridge Journal of Economics* 11: 95–106.

Walder, Andrew G. (2002) "Markets and Income Inequality in Rural China: Political Advantage in an Expanding Economy," *American Sociological Review*, 67: 231–253.

Walker, Anthony (1991) *Land, Property and Construction in the PRC*, Hong Kong: Hong Kong University Press.

Wang, Guanghua (2002) Deputy Director General for Land Titling, personal communication.

Wang, Huimin (1998) "Dangqian Nongcun Tudi Chengbao Jingying Guanli de Xianzhuang ji Wenti" (The Present Situation and Problems Facing the Management and Administration of Rural Land Lease), *Zhongguo Nongcun Guancha*, 5: 56–57.

Wang, Shaoguang and Hu, Angang (1999) *The Political Economy of Uneven Development: The Case of China*, New York: ME Sharpe.

Wang, Weiguo (2001) personal communication.

Wily, Alden L. (2002) *The Legal Basis for Land Administration in an African Context*, Washington, DC: World Bank.

Wolf, C.J. (1955) "Institutions and Economic Development," *American Economic Review*, 45: 867–83.

World Bank (1974) *Land Reform: Sector Policy Paper*, Washington, DC: World Bank.

World Bank (2003) *Land Policy for Pro-Poor Development*, Washington, DC: World Bank.

Wyplosz, C. (2000) *Ten Years of Transformation: Macro-economic Lessons*, CEPR Discussion Paper, no. 2254, London: Centre for Economic Policy Research,

Xiang, Zhongyang (1986) *Guanyu "Zhonghua Renmin Gongheguo Tudi Guanlifa (Cao'an)" de Shuoming* (Explanation of the "Land Administration Law of the People's Republic of China"), speech at the 15th Session of the Standing Committee of the 6th National People's Congress, 15 March, p. 2.

Zhang, Yaoqi, Uusivuori, Jussi and Kuuluvainen, Jari (2000) "Impacts of Economic Reforms on Rural Forestry in China," *Forest Policy and Economics*, 1: 27.

Zweig, David (2000) "The 'Externalities of Development': Can New Political Institutions Manage Rural Conflict?" in Elizabeth J. Perry and Mark Selden (eds) *Chinese Society: Change, Conflict and Resistance*, London: Routledge.

Zweigert, K. and Kötz, H. (1993) *An Introduction to Comparative Law*, Oxford: Clarendon Press.

Part I

Institutional change, politics and administration

1 Property rights and land in ex-socialist states

Lessons of transition for China

Daniel W. Bromley

The past decade has seen unprecedented transformations in the political and economic landscape of Central and Eastern Europe and the former Soviet Union. The People's Republic of China is in the midst of its own major institutional changes. The European transitions have paid considerable attention to what is now called "privatization." Indeed, as set out in the Introduction, the general approach in advising governments on economic transition is that private property rights constitute the *sine qua non* of economic transitions. After all, if a nation is moving from a centrally planned economy to a market economy, how is it possible to get there without private ownership of the means of production? In one important respect, this change in property regimes has come to *define* what it means to be a transition economy.

Paradoxically, the economic transition in China is both profound and unique precisely because it has been proceeding – with what most observers consider to be quite impressive success – without the incessant rhetoric of "privatization" that has characterized the transition process in Central and Eastern Europe and the former Soviet Union. Nowhere is this more apparent than in agriculture. Chinese agriculture is still characterized by non-individualized ownership of land – ownership of agricultural land resides either in the hands of the state or other non-individualized arrangements. In the light of these facts, and in view of the quite incredible variation of institutional arrangements embedded within this allegedly "inefficient" structure of ownership, the obvious question to be asked – and some authors here indeed ask that question – is this: how is it possible that China can continue to feed itself, and how can it become a legitimate market economy, without the full-scale imposition of private property as a basic institution? Or, in a variation of this question, is it possible that Chinese agriculture can function "efficiently," and can the economy become vibrant, in the absence of private property in agricultural land?

These questions beg a more fundamental question. That question concerns various ways to provide reasonably parameterized expectations to economic agents. We see that contemporary economics tends to place the entire burden of expectations on some ill-defined notion of "property rights" and the resultant, though equally vague idea of "tenure security." Part of this concern apparently arises from the common perception that only owners of land have tenure security. Another part springs from an apparent failure to see that in many of the varied institutional arrangements in agriculture, Chinese farmers have a range of powerful incentives to bring forth ample production. The picture is not uniformly bright, as it could not be in such a large and institutionally diverse economy.[1] But it is my contention that the common causal link that runs from ownership to security to optimal production has been much overdone. China is a fascinating laboratory for economists precisely because so many received "truths" are challenged by the empirical evidence. Simply put, agricultural production has many "causes" – only a few of which we fully understand. Indeed, the term "property rights" is vague enough to cover a number of institutional aspects of varying importance to the process of modifying incentives of individual economic agents.

The aim of this chapter, therefore, is to provide conceptual clarity on the institutional structure of an economy, and to place discussions of "property rights" in its proper context. In particular, I seek to expose the ideological (normative) base of the conventional wisdom regarding the private ownership of land. I also will assess the transformation processes in Central and Eastern Europe and the former Soviet Union, and will draw inferences as to what these changes imply for the institutional restructuring now underway in China. The bulk of the attention will concern the role of land markets and the process of land privatization. I will suggest that successful transitions must adhere to three essential principles: (1) *do no serious harm*; (2) emphasize the *working rules* that define economic incentives rather than the ownership structure of assets; and (3) focus on transitional *strategies* rather than transitional *tactics*. First, I need to lay the conceptual foundation for the idea of economic transition in general, and the ownership of land in particular.

The dueling dogmas of land

Much of the political and economic ferment of the twentieth century can be understood as the inevitable residue of intellectual agitation of the eighteenth and nineteenth centuries – with Adam Smith and Karl Marx providing the conceptual core of the dominant competing visions. That relatively minor part of Adam Smith's massive work on moral philosophy which is selectively invoked in contemporary economics concerns comprehensive self-interest and thoroughgoing possessive individualism. A world organized along these narrow Smithian lines was precisely the world surveyed by the critical eye of Marx as he contemplated the horrific human toll accompanying Britain's Industrial Revolution. And of course the manifold horrors of brutal Stalinism provide the backdrop against which the triumphalism of market-based capitalism now pervades most thought and conversation. To hear some tell it, we have finally arrived at the end of economic history.

Unfortunately, much of contemporary economics remains imprisoned by the Manichean tradition bequeathed to us by Smith and Marx. This reality is nowhere more apparent than in the tendentious literature concerning land ownership and property rights in transition economies.[2] Indeed, a major theme in contemporary market triumphalism entails the celebration of private property as the *sine qua non* of economic progress. Following World War II, with the creation of the World Bank and other international lending programs, it was imagined that with investment and technical assistance many of the poorer economies would soon "catch up" with the nations of the industrialized world. Since the 1970s the reigning prescription concerning development policies has been consistent in its push to *get prices right*, and to mimic the institutional conditions found in the developed world in general, and the United States in particular.[3] One key aspect of the prescription concerns land privatization and land titling as the necessary precursors to agricultural investment and growth. To quote from a recent study very much in this tradition:

> The evolution of property rights and their effect on investment are central issues in the political economy of development. Moreover, the role of the state in codifying and protecting such rights is regarded ... as important to providing the preconditions for economic growth. Such issues are particularly pressing in Africa, given its relatively poor economic performance and the fact that individualistic notions of ownership are not, as yet, fully accepted. Thus it is often argued that a state structure governing property rights needs to be developed before growth can resume.
>
> (Besley 1995: 903–904)

This view mirrors a long line of similar thinking over the past decade.[4] The work on property rights brings a firm conviction about the benefits of so-called "tenure security" – despite persistent conceptual and empirical ambiguity in respect to the precise meaning of "security" (Sjaastad and Bromley 1997, 2000). Indeed, one sees in this work the naïve presumption that the mere issuance of a title is sufficient to provide security of ownership – even in those nation–states where the general rule of law is the exception rather than the norm. One cannot expect a title to protect owners against arbitrary and capricious actions and outcomes perpetrated by other economic agents – or by government itself – if the general legal foundations of an economy are in disarray. In the face of widespread institutional incoherence and corruption, why a mere title is thought sufficient to bestow tenure security remains one of the abiding mysteries of much of this work. Indeed, it is very often true that the only parties rendered more secure by the issuance of titles are those who lend money to small farmers and demand title as collateral for that pecuniary favor. For non-performing loans, those holding title usually have a secure claim on the assets represented by those titles. We see that titles can actually *decrease rather than increase* tenure security among certain classes of farmers and small entrepreneurs.[5] Ironically, those farmers most in need of protection from predatory economic agents are usually the least likely to gain that security from the mere fact of having received a title. Despite this empirical reality, one continues to see simple models of titling and investment offered up as the necessary development "fix."[6]

There are several other points to be noticed. Specifically, in keeping with the general tradition of this literature, Besley postulates a direct and positive correlation between economic development and the prevalence of private property – and then laments that Africa is a place where "individualistic notions of ownership are not, as yet, fully accepted." That private property might *not* hold decisive causal significance in development trajectories seems, apparently, beyond serious thought. Moreover, we see here the explicit normative content of the Washington Consensus – if other countries wish to achieve "development," they must embrace private property and possessive individualism as we have it in the West. This line of work seems less a research program dedicated to the prospects of revealing plausible reasons for economic development – or lack thereof – than it seems a research program dedicated to the justification of why *all* nations must adopt a very particular property rights structure with which Western economists happen to be familiar. Notice that property regimes in this research program are not seen as *choice variables* for policy. Rather, property regimes are presented as necessary and particularistic *blueprints* to be exported to transition economies where they must be adopted in their entirety.

It warrants notice that the call for secure property rights is accompanied by the companion belief that there is only one form of property rights that will do the necessary work. That property structure is private (or *individual*) property rights pervasive in that part of the world from which most "development" advice and funding now emanates. In fact, there are several different types of property regimes within which individuals can have a variety of rights and duties (Figure 1.1). Despite this, the enduring commitment to individual property regimes persists, perhaps because it happens to mirror how we do economics. That is, the methodological commitments inherent in contemporary economics lead inevitably to but one institutional (property rights) form. This determinism leads the unsuspecting reader to suppose that when it comes to property regimes, there are no choices to be made.

Recall that the core of orthodox economics is possessive individualism – all our models, and all our metaphors, start with the utility maximizing *individual* who can only gain utility by acquiring higher levels of income in order to enjoy higher levels of consumption. Because the individual is the *sufficient unit of analysis* in contemporary economic theory and practice, it

We might usefully think of three general property regimes, and one regime that is not defined in terms of property rights at all.

STATE PROPERTY

The political community is the recognized owner of the asset. Individuals in the political community may benefit from the asset but must observe rules of the government agency responsible to the political community. Examples: national forests and parks, military bases, government office buildings, some agricultural land in China.

PRIVATE PROPERTY

Individual members of the political community have a recognized *right* to benefit from the asset, subject to legislative mediation and judicial review. Non-owners have a *duty* to allow owners to behave as above. Examples: fee-simple land and buildings, automobiles, personal objects.

COMMON PROPERTY

A group of owners holds rights in common, including the *right* to exclude non-owners. Individual owners have specific *rights* and *duties* with respect to their ability to benefit from the asset, subject to legislative mediation and judicial review within the larger political community. Non-owners have a legal *duty* to respect boundaries of the regime. Examples: irrigation districts, condominiums, the Swiss alps (pastures).

RES NULLIUS

There is no legally recognized group of users or owners. The asset is available to anyone – it is an open-access resource. Examples: the high seas fishery (outside of national 200-mile limits), the atmosphere (in the absence of pollution laws).

Figure 1.1 Property regimes.

is logically impossible for any other property regime to fit with standard maximizing models. This doctrine of methodological individualism remains one of the central value judgments of economics.

As a value judgment, methodological individualism is no worse than any number of other possible normative commitments. The problem, however, is that most of contemporary economics proceeds as if methodological individualism were some divinely inspired truth about which there can be no further discussion. This is not the place for that discussion, but it is the place to explore how that normative presupposition biases and distorts conversations about – and analyses of – the role of land and property rights in land as nations undergo institutional evolution toward a more thoroughgoing market orientation. The essential point here is that economic analysis of land and property rights should not be carried on at a level, and in a manner, that will lead the reader to miss the essential circularity in this approach. The very essence of applied economics must always remain the honest quest for the sufficient reasons for particular policy prescriptions, not the eager advocacy of certain prescriptions because they are the inevitable entailments of simple normative models.

When atomized utility-maximizing algorithms are constructed, in which income (or wealth) is the only thing giving of utility, we should not be surprised to discover that tenure security increases income (or the utility of income) when tenure security enters such models as a factor that increases income. It could not possibly be otherwise.[7]

Do such models reveal to us what is best for economic policy in transition economies? Or do such models justify what is best for the fictitious and quite autonomous utility-maximizing agent defined by these models? The fundamental intellectual challenge, therefore, is not to develop simple models demonstrating that Chinese farmers will attain the highest possible levels of utility (or income) if only they had complete atomized control over – and absolute security with respect to – land and related assets. Such models are now commonplace and are distinctive by their comprehensive circularity; they "prove" what their very structure prefigures them to prove. Rather, the only correct approach is to draw upon economic theory in an effort to see if there are ways and means to enhance incomes, and to stimulate agricultural production, without the necessity of abandoning enduring cultural values concerning the place of the individual within a community of many individuals – family, village, local river valley, or hillside. If we can do this, we can thereby show that applied economics is a valuable analytical aid to governments who seek development assistance on their terms, not ours. If we cannot (or will not) do this, we expose orthodox economics as nothing but applied engineering dressed up with monetary weights.

The issue, I insist, has yet to be correctly framed. Indeed, the standard framing of the issue reduces a complex social issue to, as above, a simple engineering problem – do whatever is necessary to increase income (or utility) in a constrained maximization problem with one or two arguments over which maximization shall occur. Nation–states – but especially those in the midst of fundamental transformations – are not in need of simple engineering-type solutions to complex economic and social problems.[8] More precisely, they do not need – and probably do not want – to be told that the answer to their agricultural production problem is to be found in uprooting and destroying existing and plausibly valued social and cultural norms and traditions. Few governments are at liberty to adopt socially impertinent economic advice, even if for some odd reason they should wish to do so. Enhanced agricultural production need not entail social destruction.

Therefore, it seems the better part of wisdom to give serious thought to how the issue should be framed. I offer the following plausible framing:

> What institutional arrangements in their entirety are most likely to lead to the maximum net value of sustained agricultural production (including a growing income for households) from a system in which the nation–state wishes to avoid the individualized ownership of the primary means of production (land)?

Some may denounce this framing on grounds that it preordains inefficiency. In doing so, they merely reveal their own conceptual confusion over the fundamental difference between efficiency and productivity (Bromley 1989, 1990; Saraydar 1989). More seriously, they reveal the normative content of their allegedly value-neutral analytical apparatus. Recall that the Indirect Theorem of Welfare Economics (often called the Second Welfare Theorem) tells us that *for any given arrangement of property rights and endowments*, competitive markets will sustain a Pareto optimal allocation of resources. And since there are no grounds within economics to compare various Pareto optimal states, the economist's advice must stop there. That is, economics cannot reveal to us which of the infinitely many Pareto optimal states is socially preferred (Blackorby and Donaldson 1990; Boadway 1974, 1976; Boadway and Bruce 1984; Bromley 1990; Chipman and Moore 1978; Coate 2000; Gillroy 1992; Gorman 1955; Graaff 1957; Little 1950; Mishan 1969, 1980; Samuels 1974; Samuelson 1950). The choice of which Pareto optimal state is preferred is – to make an obvious point – a political decision. That is, after all, why nation–states have political leaders, legislatures, and courts rather than asking economists to make such fundamental decisions.

It is for precisely this reason that Sen called the Indirect Theorem of Welfare Economics the "revolutionary's handbook" (Sen 1993). All that can be compared is levels (and net values) of total production (and its specific composition) under various property regimes – an empirical task of sweeping impossibility since the intervening variables cannot possibly be overcome. We are, it would seem, back to Smith and Marx. The choice of property regimes – more correctly, the choice among a complex of institutional arrangements pertinent to agriculture, of which property regimes are but one element – is a matter of social commitment to alternative *Pareto-incomparable* futures. History plays a role here for the simple reason that any social commitment is necessarily informed by prevailing ethical norms; it could not be otherwise.[9] But within those prevailing social commitments, each generation brings its own imperatives for continuity and change – driven by the necessity that *the economy is always in the process of becoming*. It is precisely in this spirit that the renowned Chinese politician (Deng Xiaoping) was known to observe, "It doesn't matter whether the cat is black or white, as long as it catches mice." If I might be allowed a slight paraphrase, *it does not matter who owns the land, as long as it produces rice.*[10]

On institutions

To say that institutions – including property regimes – are matters of collective (political) choice is not to say that, given some particular property regime, the other institutional arrangements pertinent to agriculture will have no effect on incentives, and thus on productivity. Indeed, certain institutional arrangements under the same land ownership structure are clearly more conducive to entrepreneurial behavior and agricultural production than others. There is no reason why the nation–state (or indeed the collective) could not insist that it remain the ultimate owner of the means of production. Having retained ownership does not preclude the state from crafting or enabling the creation of incentive-compatible institutional arrangements – we call them efficient contracts – that will induce farmers to undertake considerable initiative, hard work, good management of the enterprise, and therefore the production of bounteous harvests. Indeed, the history of pragmatic institutional innovation in Chinese agriculture over the past three decades is precisely concerned with this issue (Ho 2001; Pei (this volume); Xue-Lascoux and Bromley 1996). Moreover, if we have learned anything from the abundant literature on agricultural contracts and share cropping, principal–agent arrangements can take many forms. In transition economies there is little reason why the government (or the collective) could not remain – with respect to land – the principal, and the farmer remain the agent.[11] The essence in economic policy is to make sure that contracts conduce to the things that the principal and the agent care about – total production, economic returns to both parties, social protection for the weaker party to the contract (the agent), and some concern for the integrity of the local environment.

This latter dimension is of special importance. American and European agriculture models are replete with cost-sharing arrangements – and side-payments – that serve the essential role of bribing farmers to stop destroying nature. These payments are a central component of most environmental legislation so that farmer-led opposition to necessary institutional change might be overcome. Why those bribes are necessary in the first place is rarely discussed, but the primary reason is that most landowners imagine that their ownership gives them the absolute right to do as they please with the land – even when the offsite costs of those actions are serious (Bromley 1997, 2000b; Bromley and Hodge 1990). The idea that private ownership of land is both necessary and sufficient for wise and sustainable use of natural resources is a particularly widespread fiction.[12] Yet the literature on the many benefits of private property rights in agriculture is oddly silent on the many social costs associated with atomization. If the state retains ownership of land it need not engage in the costly American and European-style bribing of farmers to prevent them destroying nature. Nor are costly regulatory schemes necessary. If farmers persist in socially unwanted agricultural practices, it ought to be easy enough to find others who will abide by socially ascertained environmental practices.

I have suggested above that the proper way to approach the transition problem is in terms of institutional design. Specifically, the interesting question becomes: *what institutional structure will provide the proper incentives to encourage production from a land base that remains under a regime of state (or communal) property?* By framing the issue in this fashion, it is clear that the usual preoccupation with property rights is both overwrought and very often misplaced. The key issue in economic policy is not property rights *per se* but rather the expectations and incentives that are parameterized by the full complement of institutional arrangements – *working rules* – of the economic system. This full complement *includes* property regimes, but it does not stop there (Bromley 1989, 2005). Institutions are politically formulated rules that define the boundaries of socially acceptable individual and group behavior.

In democratic states these collective determinations occur in the parliaments and the courts. In societies where democracy is still evolving, other means and structures exist for the promulgation of these working rules. Regardless of their source, institutions are the result of public policy which is correctly understood as collective action in liberation, restraint, and expansion of individual action. Institutions are the product of "collective action" because they emanate not from autonomous behavior by individuals but from conscious collective decision making (Bromley 1989, 2005). Institutions simultaneously liberate and restrain because a restraint for Alpha is liberation for Beta when both are interested in a particular economic outcome. Moreover, institutions can go beyond mere liberation in that they bring the coercive power of the state to bear on the interests of individuals. Indeed, to have a *right* is to have that marvelous knowledge that the state stands ready to protect your interests by imposing duties on all others with designs on your settings and circumstances. By "standing ready" I mean that the right holder has the ability to *compel* the state to come to his/her defense. Notice that the state is not at liberty to decide if it will act on behalf of the individual with a "right." Rather, to have a right is to have the capacity to *command* that the state come to your assistance. We see that collective action that bestows rights serves to "expand" the individual's domain of action by enlisting the state as a compliant ally against other claimants. In strict terms, institutions are the working rules that indicate:

> [what] individuals must or must not do (compulsion or duty), what they may do without interference from other individuals (privilege or liberty), what they can do with the aid of collective power (capacity or right), and what they cannot expect the collective power to do in their behalf (incapacity or liability).
>
> (Commons 1968: 6)

Notice that institutions bestow secure expectations on parties engaged in a variety of economic transactions. And notice that rights and duties exist not just with respect to land (or other assets) but concern all manner of social and economic settings and circumstances. That is, a tenant could have a rather full complement of rights and duties *vis-à-vis* an owner without being the fee-simple owner of the land being tilled. Indeed, urban property markets in many European cities operate quite well on these same principles; central London is a realm of ground leases where dwellings are owned by one party and the underlying land is owned by others. The landowner sells the lease rights to tenants for a specific period of time and tenants obtain mortgage financing to purchase the right of occupancy over that period. There is no literature of which I am aware that laments the inefficiencies of the London property market. Nor are there indications that the tenants in residence fail to take proper care of the dwellings they happen to inhabit. As above, I insist that the current fetish for "ownership" is much overplayed. The relation between rights, property, and property rights is depicted in Figure 1.2.

With this conceptual introduction to the realm of institutions, I now turn to three essential principles that ought to guide the process of institutional change in the service of economic transition: (1) do no serious harm; (2) emphasize economic incentives rather than the ownership structure of assets; and (3) focus on transitional *strategies* rather than transitional *tactics*.

RIGHTS

Rights allow an individual to *compel* the coercive power of the state to come to her assistance. Rights do not entail passive support by the state but rather active assistance for those with rights. That is, the state stands ready to be enlisted in the cause of those to whom it has granted rights. We say that rights *expand the capacities* of the individual by indicating what one *can do with the aid of the collective power* (Bromley, 2005; Commons, 1968; Macpherson, 1973).

PROPERTY

Property is not an object but is instead, a *value*. When one buys a piece of land (in the vernacular, a "piece of property") one acquires not merely some physical object but rather *control over a benefit stream arising from that setting and circumstance that runs into the future*. That is why one spends money (one benefit stream) in order to acquire a different benefit stream ("ownership" of a new benefit stream arising from the fact of ownership). Notice that the magnitude of that new benefit stream is a function of the legal parameters associated with it. The price paid to acquire that new benefit stream is none other than the expected discounted present value of all future net income appropriable from "owning" the thing. This is why property is the *value*, not the object (Bromley, 1991; Macpherson 1973, 1978).

PROPERTY RIGHTS

Property rights bring together legal concepts of *rights* and *duties* with settings and circumstances (including objects) capable of producing income (Bromley, 1991, 2005; Christman, 1994; Hallowell, 1943; Hohfeld, 1913, 1917). Property rights parameterize the nature and extent of income appropriable from control of income-producing settings and circumstances. Trademarks, copyrights, and patents are forms of property rights. All are forms of rights in property (the future value), and duties for non-owners.

Figure 1.2 Relation between rights, property and property rights.

Do no serious harm

When I say that institutional change should "do no serious harm" I have in mind the imperative to avoid the hasty and ill-considered reforms introduced into Central and Eastern Europe and the former Soviet Union in the early 1990s. The ravages of imposed "shock therapy" in these economies were fairly complete – and the damage done to human and physical capital lingers to this day (Murrell 1995, 1996; Stiglitz 2002). Averaging across 22 transition economies in the region, GDP actually *declined* in six of the ten years between 1990 and 1999. In the mid-1990s some of these countries experienced year-on-year declines of 15–30 percent. Ukraine experienced a decline in GDP in *every* year of that decade, Moldova suffered nine years of GDP decline, and for Russia there were eight years in which GDP growth was negative. At the other end of the spectrum Armenia suffered only three years of decline in GDP over the decade, while in Poland, where the transition started somewhat earlier (and where the *status quo ante* situation was much less severe), there were only two years out of ten in which GDP growth was negative. The Washington Consensus – or perhaps, more correctly, the "transition according to the Harvard Institute for International Development" – remains one of the more contentious chapters in the uneven history of foreign assistance. Hindsight is, of course, relatively easy. But careful thought at the time would surely have suggested that sweeping voucher privatization and price liberalization, coupled with the complete absence of the necessary *legal foundations of capitalism*, were almost certain to create social and economic chaos. And that is precisely what happened. We cannot possibly say that no serious harm was done, nor is it plausible to suggest that the long and persistent hardship could not be foreseen.[13]

The flawed transition recipe was not confined to the industrial sector – though perhaps because opposition was more easily mobilized in rural areas, and because widespread privatization in agriculture was more difficult to implement, the damage there is less severe than that inflicted on the industrial sector.[14] Sweeping agricultural privatization was advocated in much of Central and Eastern Europe and the former Soviet Union. Most privatization initiatives were resisted by rural residents – which resistance was then quickly blamed on the "communistic leanings of the backward and romantic" rural population. A more honest assessment would reveal that the cautions and concerns of rural residents were simply used to good effect by those politicians and nomenklatura wishing to return to the former regime. Regardless, full-scale agricultural "privatization" in most of these countries remains unfinished – and for a large share of the rural population that seems to be quite fine indeed.

For the agricultural heartland of the former Soviet Union, it is pertinent to point out that wheat yields are said to have been approximately 85 percent of those attained in the Prairie Provinces of Canada – one of the world's premier wheat regions. The central issue therefore, in the Soviet grain sector, was not a matter of *production* – it was a matter of *harvests and deliveries to mills and to consumers.*[15] Despite this, there was an initial burst of enthusiasm in the early years of post-Soviet agriculture to fragment the large state and collective farms so that family farms might be put in their place. Those in favor of fragmentation cited the need to give land to rural residents who had worked and lived on collective and state farms. Part of this was no doubt fueled by the same romantic vision pervasive in America about the many wonders of the "family farm." Part of it, to be sure, was fueled by the notion that a market economy could not function without small family farms on their own little parcel of land. And part of it was fueled by the nascent rejection of Marxist-Leninist doctrine – and the related Stalinist imperative of an industrialized agriculture. Finally, many rural and urban residents, perhaps descendants of those killed or dispossessed in Stalin's massive collectivization of the 1930s, saw privatization as simple justice (Conquest 1986).[16] For a variety of reasons – including political ideology from within, and economic and political ideology imported by Western advisors – the deconstruction of Soviet agriculture was seen as necessary, inevitable, and desirable.

There was, to be sure, serious opposition to this initiative. Most rural residents had little cash to participate in a land market and there was a concern that full marketability of land would lead to the dispossession of those who had spent their lives on collective or state farms. It was feared that those with ready cash would simply acquire all of the best land and the worst would be left for the economically disadvantaged, or remain in the state sector. In addition, given the limited social and economic infrastructure available in rural areas, there was a legitimate fear that a full-blown land market would lead to widespread absenteeism in which the new urban-based owners would have no desire to live on – or even near – their new possessions (Wegren 1995). Rural Russians certainly need no reminder of the many ravages visited on them by absentee landlords (Blum 1961). Yet another reason concerns the inevitable scale economies of cereal agriculture. Given the enormous size of wheat farms in Argentina, Australia, Canada, and the United States, it seems curious indeed for Western advisors to encourage a policy of fragmentation of such farms in the former Soviet Union.

Given all these factors, and the almost total absence of arrangements to facilitate a viable land market – real estate agents, reliable information about land and its inherent productivity, mortgage finance – the initial impetus for privatization has cooled considerably. For the most part, many of the large farms have been legally restructured into joint stock companies with the workers and some urban residents now enjoying shared ownership.[17] But much agricultural land remains in the public domain (Wegren 1995).

We see that the first principle – *do no serious harm* – suggests that transition policies must be guided not by ideology but by careful analysis. If the agricultural plant is reasonably productive on its own terms, then the rather complete absence of factor and product markets is to blame for problems too often laid at the feet of state (or collective) ownership. An honest assessment of the Soviet state farm reveals that it was, in essence, a "corporate" rural village. Its "outputs" included schooling, local transportation, veterans' pensions and care, health care, general social services, childcare, and a few other functions that Stalin imagined could be better controlled than if left to rural villages dominated by kulaks and traditional landlords. Looked at in this light, the legendary stories of the "inefficiencies" of Soviet state and collective farms are not to be believed.[18] And when we recall the utopian stories about the share of Soviet food output attributable to "private" plots, it would be well to keep in mind the opportunistic theft of seeds, fertilizers, pesticides, machinery, and labor away from the state sector to these precious little parcels. Indeed, these happy stories of private plots might explain much of the ardor for the rush to "privatize" Soviet state and collective farms under the false belief that there is something inevitable about the assured bounty from "private land."[19]

Incentives matter

The vast literature in development economics serves to reinforce an important point about agriculture in transition economies – prices matter. There is a long and excellent history of research in the developing world that focuses on all of the reasons why farmers remain economically disadvantaged. The core idea in this work is that farm-gate prices are generally inadequate to induce the kind of production that would be needed to boost the economic surplus available from rural areas – such surplus then providing an important economic engine for urban and industrial growth (Mellor 1990; Timmer 1990).[20] If low prices are an impediment to increased production, the obvious question remains: why are those prices allowed to remain low? The answer is that governments in developing countries tend to subsidize the price of staples as an indirect means to increase the real income of many wage and salaried workers. If governments can hold down the price that farmers receive for their production, then the necessary budgetary outlay for the subsidies will be less than if prices to farmers were higher.

Prices matter, but the more complete story is that the full complement of institutions (working rules) matter because it is these rules that parameterize the choice domain faced by farmers – and therefore it is from this institutional structure that prices emerge. The issue then is not simply one of getting prices right. The central issue in transition economies is to *get institutions right.*

Specifically, I mentioned above the concepts of rights, duties, privileges, and no rights. In practical terms farmers need secure expectations regarding contracts, the terms and conditions of various credit instruments, input prices, output prices and a host of other variables that influence the net economic payoff of particular actions. This does not mean that the farmer needs perfect certainty. It means, instead, that there must be institutional means whereby some of these uncertainties can be arbitraged away. A highly developed institutional structure would provide avenues for hedging both price risk and yield risk. In addition, well-developed credit markets would provide both short-run and long-run credit at competitive prices. Agricultural extension services – either public or private – would provide essential managerial knowledge when needed. This full complement of institutional arrangements, and facilitative organizations, constitutes the essential correlated activities that can turn an indifferent agricultural sector into a productive and vibrant going concern. Each component of this system serves to narrow the range of surprises for the farmer, and in that sense these components comprise the essential institutional components of a viable agricultural sector.[21] These components serve to parameterize expectations, and thus they reduce the "noise" associated with those variables central to optimal choice. To the extent that signals contain less noise, the information content is enhanced. And informative signals constitute the essence of proper incentives in a market system (Bromley and Chavas 1989). These signals are enhanced by a market economy that is grounded on a well-functioning legal system devoted to that purpose.

We see, therefore, that the process of economic transition is one in which institutional arrangements – the working rules of the economy – are the dominant variables of choice. Choices with respect to rules are driven by a collective determination of the performance indicators deemed appropriate for the economy under study. The institutional setup of an economy is concerned with the nature of incentives that inform – and constrain – individual maximizing behavior.

While markets indeed serve as signaling devices, the larger structure of institutional arrangements must be suited to that purpose. In the economies of Central and Eastern Europe and the former Soviet Union we still find very high information costs, very high contracting costs, and very high enforcement costs. In such circumstances, bad signals result in poor economic performance. The transition to a market economy requires the greatest attention devoted to the nature and extent of signaling. From much of the literature on transition economies, one might easily gain the impression that privatization was both necessary and sufficient for markets to appear. However, privatization is not an end in itself but is rather a means to some other end. That end is better signaling and hence better incentives transmitted to economic agents.

The legal foundations of the market in a well-functioning nation–state provide a *collective consumption good*. That is, the legal foundations of exchange are a collective good in the sense that, once available, these institutional arrangements are available to all participants in the economy, and their use is not subject to rationing by congestion. These institutional arrangements constitute the legal structure that reduces transaction costs and allows markets both to arise, and to emit meaningful signals that reflect marginal values with some social significance. Recall that not all prices are of equal normative significance. Those from distorted or imperfect markets hold no normative significance for the economist or the policy maker. For the most part, conventional economics – and conventional approaches to the economic transformation problem – have failed to address the problem of the sequential nature of institutional innovation. And this brings us to the final component of a coherent process of economic transition.

Transitional strategies

The "shock therapy" that characterizes the transition process in Central and Eastern Europe and the former Soviet Union was flawed on three grounds: (1) it was wrong in its particulars; (2) it was wrong in its hasty and complete imposition; and (3) it was wrong for its preoccupation with tactics rather than with a coherent long-run transition strategy.[22] The central motivation among western advisors seemed to be one of undertaking a very large number of transition tactics immediately and thoroughly.

This motivation reveals the extent to which the process of transition has been badly framed from the very beginning. Specifically, the economic transitions now underway in Central and Eastern Europe and the former Soviet Union are not correctly understood if they are seen as a passage from "plan to market." Rather, these transitions can only be understood if they are seen as the inevitable changes from being part of – or strongly influenced by – the narrow geo-political agenda of the Soviet Union, to this no longer being the case. The concept of transition must recognize the chief implications of this – the end of the Council for Mutual Economic Assistance (CMEA), greater decision-making power for national authorities, and foreign finance and aid coming from the international community rather than exclusively from the USSR. But to equate this with some profound change from "plan to market" (or "state to market") is a serious mistake.

The proper way to view economic transition is to see it as a careful and thoughtful reformation of the economic institutions of society, not as a conscious destruction of those institutions. In agriculture, this would mean focusing early efforts *not* on the ownership structure of land but rather on the institutional arrangements that govern the production and marketing of agricultural output. Here the early emphasis should be on input markets including the usual factors of production, but also concerning production credit and technical assistance. Notice that a preoccupation with the control and ownership of land introduces uncertainty when just the opposite is required. When the larger institutional structure of an economy is being reformed, farmers need greater assurance, not less, that they will be able to reap where they have sown. In this regard, orthodox prescriptions give too much emphasis to property rights in land, and too little emphasis to the full array of institutional arrangements that parameterize a wide range of decisions by entrepreneurs.

With stability in the control of land reassured for the intermediate run, and with production arrangements equally secure, the next focus of attention must be on the marketing channels for agricultural production. As indicated above, this aspect was clearly the weak link in the Soviet agricultural system. It is here that one encounters the central importance of storage and distribution facilities, agricultural processing facilities reasonably close to centers of production and rather extensive networks of marketing advice.

Transition lessons for China

Lessons from the economic transition in Central and Eastern Europe and the former Soviet Union offer important insights that are pertinent to a range of possible modifications in particular institutional arrangements – including property regimes. In each of the transition countries, property rights systems prior to 1990 were to varying degrees characterized by state ownership and control of productive resources, with a limited or sometimes non-existent private sector.[23] The fall of Communism and the dissolution of the Soviet Union in the early 1990s impelled radical alterations of the existing system. From this common starting point, the transition countries have followed highly divergent paths – both in terms of policies and certainly in terms of outcomes in formulating property regimes.

Given the importance of agriculture in terms of contribution to total national output – and in terms of employment in nearly all of the transition countries – the structure of property rights in agriculture has been of particular concern. In the Soviet period, agriculture was characterized by two types of enterprise: state and collective farms, both of which were typically large in scale. Within these two organizational regimes most families relied on small household plots. While the overwhelming majority of agricultural output came from the state and collective farms, household production from these individually controlled (but not privately "owned") plots was significant in a number of commodities including vegetables, and to a lesser extent meat, and dairy products.

Since the early 1990s, the issue of what to do about the organization of agricultural production has been an important one for all of the transition countries. The standard policy prescription from the IMF and World Bank, as we might expect, has been aggressive restructuring predicated on the exaggerated promises of privatization of land. The privatization process has proceeded along two lines: (1) re-organization of state and collective farms into private entities; and (2) expansion of small-scale private household farming and the transfer of portions of large state farms to smaller private concerns – so-called "peasant farms." In general, the focus has been on the second approach, as dismantling socialist farms has proven easier than substantively restructuring them. In terms of land ownership, transition countries were advised to transfer all agricultural land to private ownership as rapidly as possible.

Yet few of them have done so for a variety of reasons. Russia has established joint stock companies for some former state and collective farms, but widespread privatization has not proceeded very far. Indeed, the Russian parliament only recently approved a privatization plan. Poland retained a small-farm agriculture throughout the Soviet period, with private ownership being largely unaffected by other changes in the Polish economy. There were large-scale state farms in part of the country, but Polish agriculture remained largely private in a general sense. Hungary had large-scale state farms and some efforts have been made to return them to private ownership. Interestingly, three Central Asian states offer important lessons in the role of private ownership of agricultural land. We begin with a discussion of Uzbekistan, a country that has fared relatively well in the process of transition, despite a legal prohibition on private ownership of land. I then compare the state of land markets in Kyrgyzstan and Turkmenistan.

Uzbekistan: economic successes under state ownership

One of the most successful of the transition countries in terms of economic growth in the post-socialist period has been Uzbekistan. In 1997, output was 86 percent of the 1990 level, higher than any of the other former Soviet nations, and only slightly behind the average for the Central and Eastern European countries. This strong performance has been something of a mystery to analysts, as the pace of pro-market reforms in Uzbekistan has been slow. For instance, the EBRD ranks Uzbekistan 22nd out of 25 countries in terms of progress towards small-scale privatization and price liberalization. Uzbekistan has pursued policies of import substitution in industry, in contrast to the IMF–World Bank approach of trade liberalization.

One of the key reasons Uzbekistan has been able to defy expectations has been its cotton industry. Cotton is the backbone of the Uzbek economy, and it is second only to the United States as an exporter. Cotton has provided Uzbekistan with a ready source of hard-currency export earnings, partly because cotton was a relatively easy commodity to market in Western Europe and Turkey when the Soviet distribution system collapsed. Zettelmeyer (1999) finds that cotton production is one of three important factors solving the "Uzbek growth puzzle" accounting for Uzbekistan's exceptional growth performance. He offers the view that

Uzbekistan was able to rely on this consistent source of export earnings to finance the state industrial sector, mitigating the disruptions caused by the dissolution of the Soviet Union. Hence, the agricultural sector has played an important role in Uzbekistan's strong growth performance in the post-transition period.

Uzbekistan was one of only four transition countries where gross agricultural output was greater in 2001 than in 1990.[24] Ironically, in terms of "market-oriented" reforms, there has been little progress. Agricultural production is characterized by major state involvement, and many sectors – including cotton – remain subject to the centrally planned system of state orders of inputs and outputs. In the words of one analyst, "farms have been superficially transformed, but without any structural change" (Craumer 1995: 44)."

In terms of land ownership, Uzbekistan is one of a handful of transition countries in which private ownership of land is expressly prohibited by law. State ownership of agricultural land is specified in the Uzbek Constitution, and has been subsequently reinforced with further laws. Private ownership is prohibited out of a desire to avoid land speculation and excessive concentration of ownership, and also because of persistent water resource problems. Uzbekistan is not naturally suited to agriculture, and nearly all farming requires irrigation. Unsurprisingly, water is in short supply – the primary source of irrigation water is the Aral Sea, which is rapidly drying up. Hence, the argument for state control over agriculture is that the delicate management of water resources requires a major role for government.

Uzbekistan has also had some success in increasing food production through the expansion of household and peasant farming. A priority in Uzbek agricultural policy has been to stress the reduction of food imports through the expansion of domestic production and the country has had some success in this regard through private farming. Between 1990 and 1994, the share of these types of farms in total agricultural production increased from 28 percent to 41 percent. Moreover, expansion of household and peasant farms is likely to be particularly difficult in Uzbekistan given the water constraints mentioned above. All agricultural land must be irrigated, hence, there is no reserve of usable but fallow agricultural land for potential private farmers to occupy. Household and peasant farms must negotiate with state farm managers in order to secure use rights. Despite this constraint, Uzbekistan has fared relatively well at increasing private sector production.

The Uzbek agricultural sector is not without its problems, especially with regard to water resources and declining productivity. However, it is clear from the foregoing discussion that Uzbekistan been relatively successful from the standpoint of overall agricultural output, and that this success has played an important role in the relative mild transitional "recession." Hence, it is possible for a transition country to achieve desirable results in its agricultural performance without privatizing land. Moreover, the increase in food production and expansion of household and peasant agriculture suggest that Uzbek farmers are responding to incentives – and that private ownership of land is not a precondition for creating these incentives.

Turkmenistan and Kyrgyzstan: private versus state ownership

The cases of Turkmenistan and Kyrgyzstan illustrate the fact that private ownership of land is not sufficient to stimulate land markets. Turkmenistan is the only Central Asian country in which private ownership of land is guaranteed by the Constitution. The government has engaged in a concerted effort to issue legal title to land owners. Unlike some other transition countries, the process of titling is detailed and complete. The parcel of land for which the title is issued is clearly demarcated and indicated in relation to adjacent territories on a scale map that is part of the title document.

Despite this clear commitment to land titling, use rights and transfer of land are heavily restricted in Turkmenistan. New land allocated to private farmers cannot be sold or given as a gift, and use rights are not clearly delineated. Thus, though private ownership of land is widespread in Turkmenistan, the rights of the owner consist solely of freedom from unlawful expropriation by the state. Consequently, the trading or leasing of land is virtually non-existent. Though reliable data are not available, a recent study found that in Turkmenistan "land markets do not yet exist, due to legal constraints on transactions" (Lerman and Brooks 1998: 162). Turkmenistan thus serves as a rather extreme example of the irrelevance of land titling in the absence of other factors.

By contrast, some semblance of a land market has begun to take hold in Kyrgyzstan – yet, as in Uzbekistan, private ownership of agricultural land is prohibited by law. Though land markets in all of the non-Baltic former Soviet states have proven slow to develop, Bloch and Rasmussen (1998) found that in certain regions of Kyrgyzstan, almost one-third of the farms had managed to acquire use rights to land beyond their initial holdings, mostly through rental contracts. This activity has occurred despite the fact that state-sanctioned certificates to the use rights on parcels of land are difficult to obtain, and have been available only for a short time.

As discussed earlier, the central issue in transition economies is *getting the institutions right* – including fostering an environment that rewards productive behavior. Creating a market for land use rights is consistent with this aim.[25] However, as the cases of Turkmenistan and Kyrgyzstan make clear, private ownership of land is neither necessary nor sufficient for the development of markets for use rights in land. In the service of creating a well-functioning institutional environment – even one in which market mechanisms play a central role – private property and land titling are hardly matters of concern.

It is also worth noting the justifications offered by the Uzbek and Kyrgyz governments for prohibiting private land ownership. The importance of managing water resources, as well as the fears that the irrigation system will deteriorate in the face of massive farm restructuring, figure as major issues in these considerations. Additionally, there is the fear that land will become concentrated in the hands of the wealthy, particularly foreigners. Finally, ethnic tensions persist in Central Asia, and the issue of land has fostered conflict in the past. Particularly, an ethnic conflict in 1990 resulted in hundreds of deaths in the Osh region of Kyrgyzstan over precisely the issue of land access. Given these very real concerns, exhortations from outside experts to privatize agricultural land had better rest on solid empirical foundations. Yet, privatization of land has not yielded output or productivity gains, it does not imply the *creation* of functioning land markets, nor is it necessary for *progress* in the creation of functioning land markets. Perhaps it is time to realize that different circumstances call for different forms of property rights, and resistance to private ownership may be recognition of this fact, rather than a stubborn and irrational resistance to reform.

Conclusion

We see that the first principle – *do no serious harm* – suggests that transition policies must be guided not by ideology but by careful analysis and the pragmatic evaluation of emergent phenomena. If the agricultural plant is reasonably productive on its own terms, then perhaps the rather complete absence of coherent marketing channels is to blame for problems too often laid at the feet of state (or collective) ownership. Many agricultural concerns in China seem to resemble "corporate" rural villages. Their purposes (multiple "outputs") may include schooling, transportation, local manufacturing (TVEs), health care, general social services, and perhaps childcare. Indeed, the chapter by Pei Xiaolin in this volume makes the case that much of the vibrancy of China's economy over the past several decades is plausibly related to two considerations: (1) the pragmatic adaptation of economic policy to emergent phenomena; and (2) the collective/village control of agricultural land that provided an *internal means* whereby labor could readily flow into and out of agriculture in response to signals in the larger economy. Most of that labor flowed out of agriculture, but there have certainly been seasonal and annual fluctuations as economic conditions evolved. While some might consider a vibrant land market as the necessary means to facilitate this sort of labor mobility, it appears that the collective control of agricultural land "internalizes" those necessary adjustments in factor proportions. In this sense, an outmigrant remains "vested" in the village agricultural enterprise until firmly established elsewhere.[26]

Second, the process of economic transition is one of rethinking all the institutional arrangements in an economy – not simply the ownership of land. To focus on just one dimension of this institutional mix is to fetishize land ownership at the expense of a more complete understanding of the institutional foundations of a market economy. It is to grasp at ideological prescriptions necessarily embedded in one particularistic economic vision of the "ideal" world.

Finally, the process of economic transition has been falsely framed. The central issue here is the extent of devolution of agent autonomy down through an articulated system of incentives and sanctions. When extreme autonomy is granted to individual agents, it is inevitable that the collective must then step in to address and to mitigate the perverse and pervasive "externalities" that are the necessary entailment of thoroughgoing atomization of choice. At the other extreme, when individuals have no choices to make, they figure out how to manipulate the system to their individual advantage. Much economic advice seems to advocate complete privatization and marketization with the implicit normative idea that complete autonomy for the individual is the abiding truth of modernity. Lost in these normative allegories is any recognition that a nation–state is, above all else, a collective undertaking.

Economic transitions are precisely concerned with the slow and gradual adjustment of not just the *economic* institutions of daily life. Transitions are also concerned with a re-calibration of individual domains of choice – both perceived and desired – by those individuals embedded in the going concern. Economic transitions entail gradual and mutually consistent evolutionary adjustments in three realms of daily life: (1) the modes of production and reproduction operating at what we might regard as the "domestic economy" (the household); (2) the structural dimensions of an economy (institutions) that define realms of possible and/or desired (and impossible and/or undesired) actions by members of those socioeconomic entities; and (3) the belief systems that legitimize those structures and thus their inevitable manifestations at the household and individual levels. Economic transition is not simply social engineering (or architecture) writ large. Economic transition is the essence of social and cultural transformation. One cannot have a market *economy* unless one first has a market *culture* and a market *society*. Many economic efforts to build models revealing the many wonders of privatization of agricultural land resemble machines without people. Or, the people in such models have no identity, no history, no culture – and the only future they seem to have is, in Veblen's caustic phrase, that of agile globules ricocheting around in instantaneous response to endless signals of monetized gains and losses. Efforts to convince us of the many marvels of privatization are doomed to incoherence precisely because they abstract from the inescapable reality that people – but especially farmers – do not inhabit a world defined only in terms of who owns the land they use.

The essential point here is that most policy advice concerning land and land ownership in the transition economies has been predicated upon a tendentious understanding of economic processes in the agricultural sector, and a narrow analytical approach that pre-ordains the "optimal" institutional arrangements with respect to land. Sadly, this normative agenda has been pushed off on the developing countries of the so-called "Third World" since the 1970s without clear evidence of good effect. And therein lies the real lesson about economies in transition – they have become the victims of the same bogus policy advice that has been dispensed with such confidence, and without clear empirical support, for at least 25 years. Why this dogma persists cannot be adequately explained, except that its origins within received economic theory appear to immunize it from serious intellectual challenge.

The issues facing Chinese agriculture are too complex to be captured with simplistic and pre-ordained analytical approaches. The essential challenge is to seek innovative institutional arrangements that will promote a viable and productive agriculture – and also to seek ways to improve the quality of rural life in China – while remaining intellectually open as to which particular constellation of institutions will produce particular beneficial and undesirable outcomes at particular moments in the never-ending saga of economic evolution. All economies, rather than being on or near some wondrous equilibrium trajectory are, in fact, *always in the process of becoming*. In that sense, *every* economy is a transition economy.

If there is a single lesson for China to take from the European transitions, it is that economists "knew" what was necessary and sufficient by way of institutional reform without the benefit of a clear understanding of the economies under consideration, and in the absence of a coherent theory of the transition process. Unfortunately, these empirical and theoretical lacunae failed to induce caution and prudence on the part of those who imagined that they knew precisely what needed to be done. The decade of social and economic chaos in Central and Eastern Europe and the former Soviet Union reveals just how flawed those policy prescriptions really were. The inability of most Western economists to imagine that the standard models might well be the source of the problem stands as the principal impediment to a careful assessment of the essential nature of the transition process. And as long as that assessment is flawed, there is little hope that proffered policy prescriptions can come close to the mark.

Acknowledgments

I am indebted to Benjamin Linkow for assistance on an earlier draft of this chapter.

Notes

1 See Liu *et al.* (1998) for a detailed discussion of the array of institutional arrangements prevalent in China's agriculture.

2 One might hope that now, a decade after the decisive collapse of the Soviet empire, the seriousness and intensity of this struggle would begin to dissipate. With that dissipation would come a more honest and dispassionate assessment of some of the issues central to our concerns here.

3 This idea is referred to as the Liberal Creed (Amsden, 1997; Taylor, 1997). The essence of the liberal creed is price "liberalization," free movement of foreign exchange, reduced public debt, lower public expenditures, free trade, and foreign and domestic investment. In other words, the creed insists that all economies must be fully open to world markets and they must be equipped to survive in that unforgiving climate.

4 For examples of this work see Feder (1987), Feder and Onchan (1987), Feder and Noronha (1987), and Feder and Feeny (1991).

5 See Platteau (2000) for an excellent discussion of this problem.

6 See Place and Hazell (1993) for an empirical study showing little if any connection between agricultural productivity and ambitious registration and titling initiatives in parts of Sub-Saharan Africa.

7 Even if tenure security is not found to be decisive in enhancing income, the implication of these models is that it surely *must be* and would reveal itself to be if only more adequate data were available. In this way, the lackluster empirical results are easily blamed on the data rather than on the implicit ideology of the inappropriate model.

8 Indeed, there is a plausible case to be made that much of the serious and persistent economic and social trauma in Central and Eastern Europe and the former Soviet Union is the product of overly simplistic solutions of precisely this sort (Brada 1996; Bromley 2000a; Murrell 1995, 1996; Stiglitz 2002).

9 Determinists are fond of seeing this as "path dependence."

10 It may be worth nothing that a significant percentage of the value of American agricultural output occurs on land that is rented from others. Does the farmer have to be the owner of the land? Not if contracts are crafted to produce the proper incentives.

11 This seems the appropriate place to dispel the notion that private ownership bestows limitless choice and autonomy on the owner. In America, where this myth is most elaborated and refined, the farmer (as full owner) operates under a legislated (and court-supported) institutional structure that controls the range of uses to which "his/her" land may be put, there are restrictions concerning the application of fertilizers and pesticides, and there are prohibitions on a range of other agricultural practices. Ownership does not bestow absolute and comprehensive social autonomy.

12 For theoretical refutation of this fiction see Clark (1973), Page (1977), and Pearce and Turner (1990).

13 One recalls optimistic notions of the day in which it was declared that the "transition" would take several years at most.

14 An additional difference is that much industrial production was traded on favorable terms within the Soviet bloc. As each member country experienced economic collapse, there was less and less to trade, and the terms of trade were necessarily modified. The results produced a cascade effect throughout the community.

15 Wegren (1996) reports that in the late Soviet period total grain imports were approximately equal to harvest losses. He notes that Western sources usually figured that 30 percent of the annual harvest was lost, either in the field or

during post-harvest stages. In addition, Russian sources estimated that between 20–25 million tons of grain were never harvested.

16 It is important to point out that Russia never went through a phase of capitalist/small-holder agriculture. Russian agriculture, at the time of the revolution, was largely feudal in structure. In contrast, Poland had a small-farm/landowning agricultural sector that persisted throughout the Soviet period. Indeed, the ultimate irony of transition is that Poland now finds itself with "too many small and inefficient" farms, while Western-inspired reformers sought to impose this very structure on Russia. We will continue to see farm consolidation in Poland, thereby affirming the wisdom of rural Russians who have so far resisted atomization of their agricultural sector.

17 And with this structure these farms take on the essential traits of a *common property resource.*

18 The irony here is that much of the rationale for aggressive Cold War policies against the Soviet Union was that their industrial might – but especially that part of it located in East Germany – was reported by the CIA to be substantial. At the same time, state and collective farms were dismissed as hopelessly inefficient. We now learn that the degree to which Soviet industrial prowess was *over*estimated seems precisely matched by the degree to which its agricultural prowess was *under*estimated.

19 It also bears mention that the produce from the private plots was the same stuff that urban Soviets obtained from the gardens of their beloved *dachas* – potatoes, tomatoes, cabbage, beets, garlic, onions, and carrots. Why we should expect these particular items to be produced on extensive holdings under state or collective management remains a mystery to those who understand gardening.

20 This point is made by Rozelle *et al.* (this volume).

21 This point is mentioned by Rozelle *et al.* (this volume).

22 Those who advocated the shock therapy defend their approach as the only possible approach since, had they been more gradualist, there was a risk that the transition process would have stalled and many of the nations might have reverted to communism. There are two things wrong with this defense. First, it serves as a mere rationalization without empirical content. Second, evidence at the time suggested that most of the residents of the transition economies had long ago reconciled themselves to the need for political and economic change and therefore the supposition that they would embrace recidivism seems overdone.

23 For example, in Poland and Yugoslavia farm property and operation were never fully collectivized.

24 Taking the transition economies as a whole, 2001 output was only 70 percent of 1990 output.

25 I do not wish to imply that markets for land use are a requirement for creating the incentive structures that will encourage agricultural productivity. Rather, I suggest that land use rights markets can contribute to an institutional structure that promotes socially desirable outcomes.

26 Perhaps an analogy will be useful here. Some private firms emerge from the scientific work of faculty in American universities, particularly in the biological sciences. In these settings the academic department serves as a "collective" firm that nurtures and supports the would-be entrepreneur until economic prospects are adequate to permit complete abandonment of the collective for the harsh reality of market discipline.

References

Amsden, Alice H. (1997) "Bringing Production Back in: Understanding Government's Economic Role in Later Industrialization," *World Development*, 25(4): 469–80.

Besley, Timothy (1995) "Property Rights and Investment Incentives: Theory and Evidence from Ghana," *Journal of Political Economy*, 103(5): 903–937.

Blackorby, Charles and Donaldson, David (1990) "A Review Article: The Case Against the Use of the Sum of Compensating Variations in Cost-benefit Analysis," *Canadian Economics Journal*, 3(August): 471–94.

Bloch, Peter and Rasmussen, Karen (1998) "Land Reform in Kyrgyzstan," in Stephen K. Wegren (ed.) *Land Reform in the Former Soviet Union and Eastern Europe*, London: Routledge, pp. 111–135.

Blum, Jerome (1961) *Lord and Peasant in Russia: From the Ninth to the Nineteenth Century*, Princeton, NJ: Princeton University Press.

Boadway, Robin W. (1974) "The Welfare Foundations of Cost-benefit Analysis," *Economic Journal*, 84: 926–939.

Boadway, Robin W. (1976) "Integrating Equity and Efficiency in Applied Welfare Economics," *Quarterly Journal of Economics*, 90: 541–556.

Boadway, Robin W. and Bruce, Neil (1984) *Welfare Economics*, Oxford: Blackwell.

Brada, Josef C. (1996) "Privatization is Transition – Or Is It?," *Journal of Economic Perspectives*, 10(2): 67–86.

Bromley, Daniel W. (1989) *Economic Interests and Institutions: The Conceptual Foundations of Public Policy*, Oxford: Basil Blackwell.

Bromley, Daniel W. (1990) "The Ideology of Efficiency: Searching for a Theory of Policy Analysis," *Journal of Environmental Economics and Management*, 19(1): 86–107.

Bromley, Daniel W. (1991) *Environment and Economy: Property Rights and Public Policy*, Oxford: Blackwell.

Bromley, Daniel W. (1997) "Constitutional political economy: property claims in a dynamic world," *Contemporary Economic Policy*, 15(4): 43–54.

Bromley, Daniel W. (2000a) "A Most Difficult Passage: The Economic Transition in Central and Eastern Europe and the Former Soviet Union," *EMERGO*, 7(3): 2–23.

Bromley, Daniel W. (2000b) "Can Agriculture Become an Environmental Asset?" *World Economics*, 1(3): 127–139.

Bromley, Daniel W. (2005) *Sufficient Reason: Volitional Pragmatism and the Meaning of Economic Institutions*, Princeton, NJ: Princeton University Press.

Bromley, Daniel W. and Chavas, Jean-Paul (1989) "On Risk, Transactions and Economic Development in the Semi-arid Tropics," *Economic Development and Cultural Change*, 37(4): 719–736.

Bromley, Daniel W. and Hodge, Ian (1990) "Private Property Rights and Presumptive Policy Entitlements: Reconsidering the Premises of Rural Policy," *European Review of Agricultural Economics*, 17(Spring): 197–214.

Chipman, John S. and Moore, James C. (1978) "The new welfare economics: 1939–1974," *International Economic Review*, 19(3): 547–584.

Christman, John (1994) *The Myth of Property*, Oxford: Oxford University Press.

Clark, Colin (1973) "Profit maximization and the extinction of animal species',' *Journal of Political Economy*, 81: 950–961.

Coate, Stephen (2000) "An Efficiency Approach to the Evaluation of Policy Changes," *The Economic Journal*, 110: 437–455.

Commons, John R. (1968) *Legal Foundations of Capitalism*, Madison, WI: University of Wisconsin Press.

Conquest, Robert (1986) *The Harvest of Sorrow: Soviet Collectivization and the Terror-Famine*, New York: Oxford University Press.

Craumer, Peter (1995) *Rural and Agricultural Development in Uzbekistan*, London: The Royal Institute of International Affairs.

EBRD (2000) *Transition Report 2000*, London: The European Bank for Reconstruction and Development.

Feder, Gershon (1987) "Land Ownership Security and Farm Productivity: Evidence from Thailand," *Journal of Development Studies*, 24: 16–30.

Feder, Gershon and Feeny, David (1991) "Land Tenure and Property Rights: Theory and Implications for Development Policy," *The World Bank Economic Review*, 5(1): 135–153.

Feder, Gershon and Noronha, Raymond (1987) "Land Rights Systems and Agricultural Development in Sub-Saharan Africa," *World Bank Research Observer*, 2(July): 143–69.

Feder, Gershon and Onchan, T. (1987) "Land ownership security and farm investment in Thailand," *American Journal of Agricultural Economics*, 69: 311–320.

Gillroy, John Martin (1992) "The Ethical Poverty of Cost-benefit Methods: Autonomy, Efficiency, and Public Policy Choice,' *Policy Science*, 25: 83–102.

Gorman, William M. (1955) "The Intransitivity of Certain Criteria used in Welfare Economics," *Oxford Economic Papers*, (new series), 7(1): 25–35.

Hallowell, A. Irving (1943) "The Nature and Function of Property as a Social Institution," *Journal of Legal and Political Sociology*, 1: 115–138.

Ho, Peter (2001) 'Who Owns China's Land? Policies, Property Rights, and Deliberate Institutional Ambiguity," *The China Quarterly*, 166: 394–421.

Hohfeld, Wesley N. (1913) "Some Fundamental Legal Conceptions as Applied in Judicial Reasoning," *Yale Law Journal*, 23: 16–59.

Hohfeld, Wesley N. (1917) "Fundamental Legal Conceptions as Applied in Judicial Reasoning," *Yale Law Journal*, 26: 710–770.

Lerman, Zvi and Brooks, Karen (1998) "Land Reform in Turkmenistan," in Stephen K. Wegren (ed.) *Land Reform in the Former Soviet Union and Eastern Europe*, London: Routledge, pp. 162–188.

Little, I.M.D. (1950) *A Critique of Welfare Economics*, London: Oxford University Press.

Liu, Shouying, Carter, Michael R. and Yao, Yang (1998) "Dimensions and Diversity of Property Rights in Rural China: Dilemmas on the Road to Further Reform," *World Development*, 26(10): 1789–1806.

Macpherson, C.B. (1973) *Democratic Theory*, Oxford: Clarendon Press.

Macpherson, C.B. (1978) *Property: Mainstream and Critical Positions*, Toronto: University of Toronto Press.

Mellor, John W. (1990) "Agriculture on the Road to Industrialization," in C.K. Eicher and John M. Staatz (eds) *Agricultural Development in the Third World*, Baltimore, MD: Johns Hopkins University Press, pp. 70–88.

Mishan, E.J. (1969) *Welfare Economics: An Assessment*, Amsterdam: North-Holland.

Mishan, E.J. (1980) "How Valid are Economic Evaluations of Allocative Changes?" *Journal of Economic Issues*, 14: 143–161.

Murrell, Peter (1995) "The Transition According to Cambridge, Mass," *Journal of Economic Literature*, 33(March): 164–178.

Murrell, Peter (1996) "How Far Has the Transition Progressed?'" *Journal of Economic Perspectives*, 10(2): 25–44.

Page, Talbott (1977) *Conservation and Economic Efficiency*, Baltimore: Johns Hopkins University Press.

Pearce, David W. and Turner, R. K. (1990) *The Economics of Natural Resources and the Environment*, London: Harvester Wheatsheaf.

Pei, Xiaolin (2004) "The Contribution of Collective Land Ownership to Economic Transition and Rural Industrialization: A Resource Allocation Model," (this volume).

Place, Frank and Hazell, Peter (1993) "Productivity Effects of Indigenous Land Tenure Systems in Sub-Saharan Africa," *American Journal of Agricultural Economics*, 75(February): 10–19.

Platteau, Jean-Philippe (2000) "Does Africa Need Land Reform?" in Camilla Toulmin and Julian Quan (eds) *Evolving Land Rights, Policy, and Tenure in Africa*, London: DFID/IIED/NRI.

Rozelle, Scott, Brandt, Loren, Guo, Li and Huang, Jikun (2003) "Land Rights in China: Facts, Fictions, and Issues," (this volume).

Samuels, Warren J. (1974) "The Coase Theorem and the Study of Law and Economics," *Natural Resources Journal* 14(January): 1–33.

Samuelson, Paul A. (1950) "Evaluation of Real National Income," *Oxford Economic Papers*, (new series) 2(1): 1–29.

Saraydar, Edward (1989) "The Conflation of Productivity and Efficiency in Economics and Economic History," *Economics and Philosophy*, 5: 55–67.

Sen, Amartya (1993) "Markets and Freedoms: Achievements and Limitations of the Market Mechanism in Promoting Individual Freedoms," *Oxford Economic Papers*, 45: 519–541.

Sjaastad, Espen and Bromley, Daniel W. (1997) "Indigenous Land Rights in Sub-Saharan Africa: Appropriation, Security and Investment Demand," *World Development*, 25(4): 549–562.

Sjaastad, Espen and Bromley, Daniel W. (2000) "The Prejudices of Property Rights: On Individualism, Specificity, and Security in Property Regimes," *Development Policy Review*, 18(4): 365–389.

Spoor, Max and Visser, Oane (2001) "The State of Agrarian Reform in the Former Soviet Union," *Europe-Asia Studies*, 53(6): 885–901.

Stiglitz, Joseph E. (2002) *Globalization and its Discontents*, New York: Norton.

Taylor, Lance (1997) "The Revival of the Liberal Creed: The IMF and the World Bank in a Globalized Economy," *World Development*, 25(2): 145–152.

Timmer, C. Peter (1990) "The Agricultural Transformation," in C.K. Eicher and John M. Staatz (eds) *Agricultural Development in the Third World*, Baltimore, MD: Johns Hopkins University Press, pp. 47–69.

Van de Graaff, J. (1957) *Theoretical Welfare Economics*, Cambridge: Cambridge University Press.

Wegren, Stephen K. (1995) "The Development of Market Relations in Agricultural Land: The Case of Kostroma Oblast," *Post-Soviet Geography*, 36(8): 496–512.

Wegren, Stephen K. (1996) "Rural Politics and Agrarian Reform in Russia," *Problems of Post-Communism*, 43(1): 23–34.

Xue-Lascoux, Zhiqun and Bromley, Daniel W. (1996) "Necessity and Purpose in Chinese Agriculture: 1949–95," *Oxford Development Studies*, 24(3): 261–280.

Zettelmeyer, Jerome (1999) *The Uzbek Growth Puzzle*, Washington, DC: IMF Staff Papers 46(3): 274–292.

2 Land use rights

Legal perspectives and pitfalls for land reform

Weiguo Wang

The history of property law shows that property rights are simply institutional forms adopted by a society to confirm and protect people's material interests. According to the rationale of human beings and the cultural traditions of a nation, such institutional forms are subject to change and, arguably, also the result of collective choice in the nation–state. Land tenure is no exception.[1] Under different legal systems, there are various acceptable ways for people to meet their needs for utilizing and transferring land. The creation of land rights is not only the result of legal construction, but also the outcome of socioeconomic development (Wang 1997: 137). In his chapter in this volume, Daniel Bromley frames the basic question for the reform of China's land property rights thus: "What institutional structure will provide the proper incentives to encourage production from a land base that remains under a regime of state (or communal) property?"

This chapter wishes to contribute to the discussion by examining the legal requirements of land use rights and, where directly related, I will also digress on their ownership requirements. Land rights in China are generally classified under two categories: land owned by the state (*guoyou tudi*) and land owned by the collective (*jiti soyou tudi*). However, as Peter Ho has explained in the Introduction, land ownership by the collective is a source of many land-related grievances in China. Western scholars trained in the civil law tradition generally put strong emphasis on ownership as an absolute right and view its protection as a basic right in the liberal democratic state. One outstanding feature – and also a political compromise – of the Chinese land system since decollectivization is that land can only be privately used when there is public ownership. Now and then, within Chinese political and academic circles, discussions have flared up over the need for privatization of ownership *per se* as a precondition for stable economic growth. In particular, in the light of the frequent land allocations by rural collectives, privatization of ownership has been proposed as an ultimate means to provide sufficient security of property rights to the user. However, within the current polity, privatization is not an option. As a result, the transactions in the land market are based on land use rather than ownership rights. To respond to the needs of China's socialist market economy, the focus of the current Land Administration Law (as well of the political debates) has shifted from ownership to the utilization of land and the transfer of those rights to its use.[2]

Land use rights enable citizens to possess, use, and transfer land in the marketplace. These multiple use rights emerged in the 1970s as the heart of the rural economic reforms, and were subsequently enshrined in the 1986 Land Administration Law.[3] Under the present land ownership structure, all urban land is state-owned, while rural land is collectively owned, with the exception of grassland, forest, wasteland, and other land that can be legally proven to be state-owned. For this reason, the inclusion of use rights to state land in the "Provisional Regulation on the Grant and Transfer of Use Rights to Urban State Land" in 1990 was a milestone in urban economic reform. More importantly, with the amendment of the Chinese Constitution in 1988 announcing that "the land use right may be transferred according to the law" (Article 10),[4] a firm legal foundation for the land market and the system of "compensated use" (*youchang shiyong*, a term equivalent to "paid use") was established.[5] The various categories of land rights (or in other words, land titles[6]) in China today are shown in Figure 2.1.

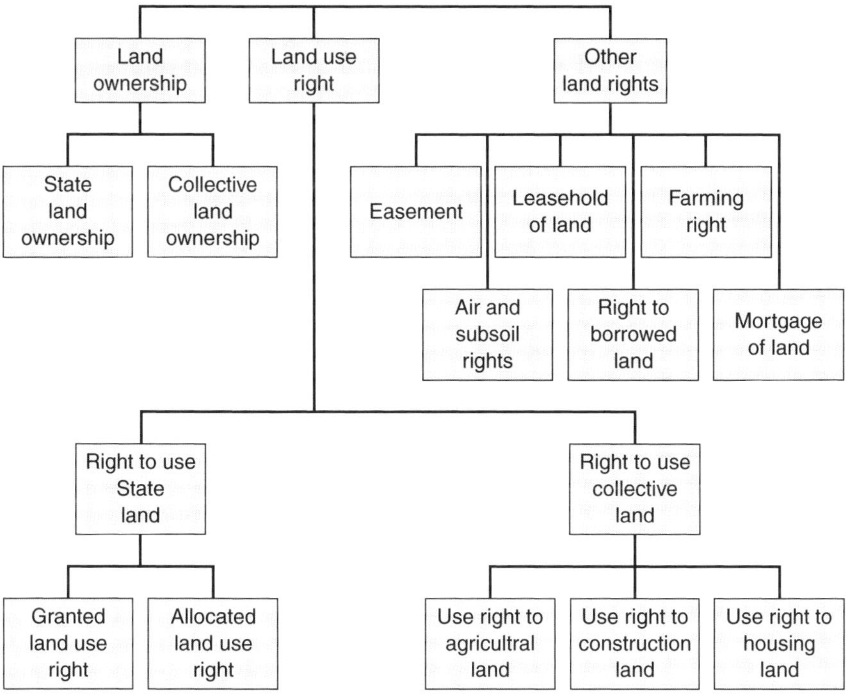

Figure 2.1 Various categories of land rights in China.

In the legal framework of property rights laid down in the General Principles of Civil Law (1986), ownership is defined as an original and major right from which the other property rights (e.g., land use rights) are derived.[7] It is generally understood that ownership has supreme status over other property rights. As a logical result, in case of conflict between land ownership and the right to land use, the former takes precedence over the latter. In such cases, individual land users and the land market are always subordinate to land ownership. In actual practice there have been many instances in which land users were deprived of use rights or their interests were infringed upon by representatives of land ownership, that is, state institutions or rural officials (e.g., village cadres) (Ho 2003a). For this reason, Chinese scholars and the legislature have paid great attention to the development of legal means to protect land users from indiscriminate interference or infringement.

The sensitivity of privatization as a political issue – not merely to pay lip service to the socialist foundations of the Chinese state but, more importantly, to avoid the eruption of social conflict and the potential emergence of a class of landless peasants – has turned the notion of real property rights (*wu quan*, a term in civil law equal to "*jus in re*" in Latin, or "*Sachenrecht*" in German, or "*droit réel*" in French) into a key concern for China. The concept of real rights usually refers to "real property," one of those anomalies of the English land system which the Royal Commission on Land Transfer Acts in 1911 described as "a disgrace to a country which aspires to be numbered amongst civilized nations" (Commissioners of the Land Transfer Acts 1911: 52). And as Sir Arthur Underhill, senior conveyancing counsel of the court, rightfully noted: "The English law of Real Property can only be explained by an elaborate historical analysis. It takes a lifetime to master and when mastered is but lean, wasteful and barren learning."[8]

For the purpose of this chapter, it suffices to say that "realty" or "real property" allows for a "real action" to be brought in court, as opposed to a "personal action." More specifically, a real right is defined as a right *in rem* or a "right against an object" enabling the entitled to possess it exclusively. Contrarily, a personal or obligatory right can be defined as a right *in personam* or a "right against a person," enabling the entitled to demand payment or some other performance from a responsible person under the law, for example, through contract or tort. The word "real" is derived from the Latin *res* meaning "thing." It was applied to actions concerning land, because if an owner had been wrongfully dispossessed of land, the solution was to restore the land (the thing) itself, whereas in a personal action the court would only allow payment of a good's value, instead of compelling its return.[9] In the Chinese civil law system, the terms real and personal or obligatory rights have been respectively translated as *wu quan* and *zhai quan*. The possibility of better legal protection of the land user (the lessee or farmer) versus the land owner (the lessor, that is, the state or collective) by defining land use rights as real rights, was heavily debated in China during the 1990s (see, for example, Chen 1996: 89).

Since land use rights play such a critical role in China today, we will review the current situation and the future development of the legal institutions pertinent to the use rights to rural land (collective land). For many foreign observers and, as a matter of fact, also for many Chinese, China's property rights system is extremely complicated. This is not only due to the fact that the land tenure system is in flux and undergoing rapid change, but also because of inconsistencies within the system itself and political controversies over unresolved issues. It is the aim of this chapter to provide the reader with an overview of the current legal framework for land rights, and address the question of what legal rights are currently held by the state, the collective, and individual farmers. In addition, the chapter demonstrates the direction the government's legal reforms aim to take the land tenure system and what legal changes are necessary to best secure long-term, stable socio-economic development.

The chapter is divided into three sections. The first provides a comprehensive overview of the various use rights to rural, collective land ranging from agricultural land to construction and housing land. The second reviews the general trend of reforms in land property rights, with particular reference to the current debate on land use and ownership rights. In this respect, the political and scholarly discussion on real and obligatory rights is of importance. The final section puts forward several proposals for land use rights reform in China.

An overview of rural land use rights

According to the 1998 Land Administration Law,[10] land in rural areas and suburban areas, except as otherwise provided for by the state, shall be collectively owned by farmers. The "use right to collective land" (*jiti tudi shiyongquan*) refers to the rights obtained by land users in different ways, including (1) the use right to agricultural land (*nongdi shiyongquan*); (2) the use right to housing land (*zhaijidi shiyongquan*); and (3) the use right to construction land (*jianshe yongdi shiyongquan*). The first and second use rights are vested in farm households while the third may be held by either farm households or collective organizations. The stipulations concerning rights to use collective land are provided by a number of laws and regulations, such as the General Principles of Civil Law, the Land Administration Law, the Agriculture Law, the Provisions for Confirmation of Land Ownership and Use Rights, and others. In the sections below, we will review the three use rights to collective land in more detail.

The use right to agricultural land

According to the Land Administration Law, "agricultural land" refers to land directly used for agricultural production, including cultivated land, forested land, grassland, land for farmland water conservancy, and water surfaces for breeding.[11] As a result of the rural reforms since 1978, the use right to virtually all collective land has been allocated to local households through contracts. Even though this right has a contractual basis, it has been recognized as a real right in the General Principles of Civil Law and some other laws.[12]

During the past two decades the State issued a number of regulations to strengthen this use right. Currently, it appears that the use right to agricultural land has obtained a relatively firm position in national law. Land users have a long-term and heritable title provided that they do not leave the land uncultivated or wasted.[13] The use right to agricultural land can be transferred in a variety of ways (Guo and Fang 2002: 936–938, 1053–1061; Schwarzwalder *et al.* 2001). It may be leased or sub-contracted to a third party. Under certain conditions it may be mortgaged. It can also be invested in a joint productive entity such as a partnership or the like. Use rights meant for developing uncultivated land or wasteland can be assigned and mortgaged (Wang and Wang 2001: 184–188). This stipulation provides legal support to the development of the rural land market. In recent years, over 100 million farmers, approximately 12.4 percent of the total rural population, have been transferred to the urban labor market.[14] The main reason for this transfer is because the revenues from agricultural land are comparatively limited.[15] However, the farmers generally do not give up their use rights. Instead, they are kept as security in case of unemployment, disability, or retirement. For these reasons, farmers allow the land to be used by someone else through lease, subcontract, or investment. This in turn may lead to higher economies of scale (for example, when the subcontracted land is leased to fewer farmers) and the promotion of agricultural efficiency. An interesting case study is provided by Frank Pieke in Chapter 3 of this volume.

However, in the existing legal system there are still several problems concerning use rights to agricultural land. First, the use right (generally termed in China "the contractual right to agricultural land" or *nongdi chengbao jingyingquan*) bears more the legal nature of an obligatory right (*zhaiquan*) than that of a real right (*wuquan*). Under these conditions, the use right remains rather weak. For example, since the use right is a contractual right, the lessor (or the leadership of the rural collective) can easily terminate the lessee's contract at will. This is not merely a theoretical consideration, but actual reality. Should the land title not be sufficiently secure, farmers will be reluctant to make investments in the land (in contrast, as Carter and Yao have calculated in Chapter 5, secure tenure would increase investment labor by a total of 40 hours per year per household). Therefore, legal scholars have argued that the agricultural use right should be established as a real right that provides more security against infringement.

Second, there is no sound legal environment in which to regulate transactions for agricultural land use rights. This leads to land fragmentation and inefficient land use. It is obvious that the efficiency and profit from land will rise according to increasing economies of scale. In recent years, the market for land lease and land investment has rapidly developed in certain regions of East and South China.[16] However, the legal rules that should govern such land transactions remain inadequate. In addition, the village or township authorities in some less-developed regions frequently charge extra fees when contract rights for the use of collective land are transferred, thereby infringing upon the interests of the villagers.

Third, a sufficient legal basis for resolving disputes over land use allocation is still lacking. The government proclaimed that "neither the increase nor decrease in the size of a household should lead to changes in the allocated area of land."[17] Yet, to date those or similar stipulations have not been incorporated into law, and legal procedures to deal with disputes over land allocation have not been forthcoming.

Finally, provisions regarding use rights for the development of uncultivated land or wasteland are not unified. The regulations for wasteland development are issued by local authorities and differ from region to region. For instance, terms may vary from 30 to 70 years. Procedural provisions for acquiring use rights, scope of tenure, and restrictions to transactions are also very varied. As China has a tradition of a centralized legal system, such localized and inconsistent provisions lead to ambiguity over the interests of land users and have potential for social conflict. This in turn is also likely to reduce farmers' incentives to develop uncultivated land.[18]

Use rights to construction land: township and village enterprises

According to the Land Administration Law, "land for construction use" refers to land on which buildings and structures are erected, including land for urban and rural housing and public facilities, land for industrial and mining use, land for building communications and water conservancy facilities, land for tourism, and land for military installations.[19]

In the rural areas there are many so-called township and village enterprises (*xiangzhen qiye*) owned by villages, townships, individuals, or combinations thereof. According to the law, any unit or individual that needs land for construction purposes should apply for the use of state-owned land, except in cases when land is owned and used by the collective economic organization (or farmers' collective) for building township enterprises, villagers' housing, and the construction of public and welfare facilities for the township.

Past years have proven that there is a real danger of the loss of agricultural land due to construction activities. For this reason, the law provides some procedural limitations in order to control the loss of agricultural land.[20] For the same reason, the law also imposes certain restrictions on the transactions of use rights for construction land. It is prohibited to transfer or rent the land use rights of farmers' collectives for nonagricultural construction, except when the transaction conforms to the general land use plan or when the transferred land is already in use by an enterprise that has gone bankrupt or has merged. As far as the use of construction land for public facilities is concerned, the situation is not as serious, as public facilities, such as schools and hospitals, are constructed with a nonprofit motive. The amount of land used for such purposes is generally limited by the tight budget of collective organizations.

There are several critical problems concerning the use rights to construction land. First, the regulations governing the original land market for acquiring use rights to construction land are insufficient, and those that do exist are difficult to enforce.[21] The restrictions and procedures set out in Article 60 of the Land Administration Law are often evaded. The key issue is that profit from industrial and trade land use is considerably higher than that from agricultural use, which drives land users to avoid the law. In this regard, much legislative work still remains to be done.

Second, the market transactions of use rights to construction land need to be better regulated. The regulations put forward in Article 63 of the Land Administration Law are contradictory. They state that the land use right of farmers' collectives shall not be assigned, transferred, or rented for nonagricultural construction purposes. Simultaneously, the law makes an exception in cases when land has been legally acquired by an enterprise and is transferred due to bankruptcy or merger. According to this stipulation, a rural enterprise cannot transfer or lease its land use right when it operates normally, but can do so in exceptional cases. This offers opportunities for corruption, as a village could establish an enterprise, then transfer or lease its construction land to it, subsequently pushing it into bankruptcy or a merger.

Use rights to housing land

In Land Administration Law, housing land is regarded as one category of construction land. In rural areas, however, housing land has a special status subject to certain unique, mandatory provisions. In the practical classification of rural land administration, "the use right to housing land" is usually independent from "the use right to construction land." More explicitly, housing land is generally allocated without payment to households by village collectives.

This social welfare characteristic of the housing system has existed since the 1960s. Its guiding allocation principle is "one household, one plot of housing land" in order to protect agricultural land from construction encroachment. The Land Administration Law stipulates that one rural household is allowed to use only one parcel of land for house construction, the area of which should not exceed the standards set by the provincial government.[22] The law also stipulates that housing land shall not be approved for those whose house has been sold or leased. In practice, however, this is extremely difficult to enforce. In the past, a large amount of agricultural land has been converted to housing land. For example, approximately 70,000 hectares of cultivated land was used for building houses in 1986.[23]

With regard to the use rights to housing land, there are also several other problems. First of all, the process for allocation of housing land is insufficiently transparent. Supervision over the allocation process needs to be tightened. The law provides that the use of land for house construction should be examined by the township government and approved by the county government. In practice, however, it is not uncommon that the allocation is entirely controlled by the village leadership, leaving the villagers no recourse in cases of occupation violations or other illegal practices.

Second, the examination and approval system for housing land needs to be master planned. In recent years, housing land in some villages has been abandoned and remains unproductive, as farmers have migrated to towns and cities. In contrast, other villages are in urgent need of additional housing land due to increasing population pressure. However, at present, general plans for township land do not permit sufficient flexibility to adequately respond to such socio-economic and demographic changes.

Third, the practice of paid use of housing land has emerged in certain regions, which is appreciated as a move towards a market system, but such practices do not have the necessary legal underpinnings since existing laws and regulations do not address the issue.

Finally, the existing laws lack clear provisions on the transfer and lease of use rights to housing land. Currently, the rules on the succession of use rights to housing land differ per region. The Land Administration Law does not clearly address such questions as whether the sale or lease of use rights to housing land are included in a transaction where a villager's house is sold or leased, and whether there are restrictions to such a sale or lease. If the answer is positive, how should this be brought in line with Article 63 of the Land Administration Law which states that the land use rights of farmers' collectives shall not be assigned, transferred or leased for nonagricultural construction? If the answer is negative, what would then be the legal basis for prohibiting the transfer of private housing? And suppose the law allows houses to be transferred but restricts the transfer of collective land, how can a compromise be reached? It is also uncertain how to legally deal with a succession case if the successor is not a member of the village. A variety of solutions can be found in common practice, yet none of these have been adopted in legal provisions. To clarify and smooth the way to more effective housing land use, all of these issues must be addressed and clarified within the law.

General trends of reform for rural land use rights

The proposed national legal policy for the institutional reform of rural land use rights can be summarized thus: (1) integrating use rights into the real property system instead of their present inclusion in the system of obligatory rights, and thus establishing a whole body of new legal rules concerning all types of land use rights; (2) strengthening land use rights while "lessening ownership," in other words, avoiding too much emphasis on discussions over ownership reforms. In contrast to other transitional economies, such as East Germany, Hungary and Kyrgyzstan, the Chinese government is not likely to consider the return of land holdings to former owners. For this reason, public and political debates over privatization of ownership are not favoured. Instead, a rudimentary land market has been established through the privatization of land use rights; and (3) developing a transparent and efficient market for land use rights in the rural areas.

The following issues have been put forward in the national political debate over land use reform over the past decades, and will be reviewed in detail in the sections below: refined definition of the legal characteristics of rural land use rights, the reform of rural land ownership, legalities of use rights transactions, and those matters surrounding the distribution of land use rights.

Defining the legal characteristics of rural land use rights

Since the 1980s, there has been considerable debate over the issue of whether use rights to agricultural land should be defined as an obligatory right or a real right. Some politicians advocate what in Chinese is termed the "doctrine of obligatory rights" (*zhaiquan shuo*), focusing on the relationship between land ownership and land use by considering the use right as an obligatory right within a contractual relationship. Their main arguments are as follows:

1 The contractual right to agricultural land is closely related to the "Contract Responsibility System with Remuneration Linked to Output" (*lianchan chengbao zerenzhi*) under which a land user bears a series of duties in relation to the granting of the land use right.
2 The contract between the lessor (contractor) and the lessee (land owner) is an internal relationship, without effect on any third party.

3 In terms of the legal conditions of transfer, a land user cannot transfer his use right without the owner's agreement, which is the condition imposed by law on the transfers of all obligatory rights.[24]

In contrast, many people, particularly legal scholars, promote the "doctrine of real rights" (*wuquan shuo*) and argue that the use rights to agricultural land shall be regarded as a kind of property right protected under a property law. Their arguments are mainly based on the following rationale:

1 The use right to agricultural land has been included in Chapter V of the General Principles of Civil Law, which is commonly deemed as the section dealing with real rights.
2 The contractors have been entitled to possess and use the land directly and exclusively.
3 The contractors' right to use land is characterized by a long, stable term.[25]
4 The contracting method establishing the use right to agricultural land does not necessary imply that the land use right itself is an obligatory right: a contract may have the function of creating, altering, transferring or terminating a property right.[26]

Apart from the two views above, there are other opinions such as the "doctrine of real right concurrent to the contractual right" (*wuquan jian zhaiquan shuo*), arguing that the use right to agricultural land has the nature of a real property right as well as a contractual right,[27] and the "doctrine of multiple ownership" (*fuhe suoyouquan shuo*), which argues that the use right to agricultural land is not only subject to collective land ownership but also bears features of private ownership.[28] These two doctrines have rallied much less political support within the central leadership.

The difference between the doctrines of obligatory rights and real rights is crucial. In legal terms, an obligatory right is located in the contractual realm whereas a real right stands on the bedrock of land registration, which provides more secure protection for land users. The issue here is not merely one of capturing current practices, but also a matter of legal policy, that is, to establish sound guidelines for future developments. It is of the utmost importance for farmers' interests to receive the largest possible legal protection. This will be favorable for the rural economy and the protection of natural resources. The use rights to rural land should become a statutory property right in a future legal framework – directly stipulated and protected by the law.[29]

In contrast, a contract between the land user and the rural collective shall be merely an agreement concerning the distribution of land use and the user's duties, such as contracting fees to be paid to the collective. When a land use right is registered in accordance with the law, nobody can be deprived of it for any reason other than those stipulated in the law. It would then be impossible for village cadres to impose extra charges on farmers to coerce them into terminating their land use rights. It would also become impossible for cadres to sell the village land to a third party without the agreement of the land users. In some instances, the village leadership has decided unilaterally to sell the land and has consequently arbitrarily terminated the contracted land use right. The individual farmers could not seek relief under the law or challenge the decision because they lacked the support of real right provisions and the legal standing to represent their ownership interest.

In August 2002 the Rural Land Contracting Law was promulgated, which provides farmers holding rights to contracted land with stronger legal protection. For example, it is stipulated in Article 26 that during the contract term, the land owner shall not take back the contracted land. However, there is no provision characterizing the right to contracted land as a real property right, even though it has been widely recognized as such in academic circles.[30]

The reform of rural land ownership

The existing rural land ownership structure is the historical heritage of the collectivization movement of the late 1950s. The rural collectives – the commune, brigade and team – were originally designed for a system of collective agricultural production and distribution based on the common ownership of all economic means and resources (such as land, farm tools, livestock and machinery). The decollectivization movement at the end of the 1970s, however, heralded the collapse of the system of collective production and distribution. Consequently, the collective economic organizations have also vanished in most rural areas.[31]

This development has resulted in friction between private management and public ownership, which partly explains the shortcomings of collective ownership to rural land: uncertainty over ownership, low efficiency in land use, and the loss of cultivated land.[32] It has been commonly recognized that the existing system of rural land ownership should be reformed. Following are four of the various viewpoints presently under discussion in China as to how such reform should or could proceed:[33]

1 *Nationalization*, which boils down to abolishing the collective ownership to rural land and granting all ownership of land resources to the state;
2 *Privatization*, in other words, abolishing the collective ownership to rural land and allocating land ownership to individuals or farm households;
3 *Multiple ownership*, by abolishing the collective ownership to a certain part of rural land, and subsequently vesting the ownership of this land

in the state and individual farmers, while the remainder stays in collective ownership; and

4 *Restructuring collective ownership*, which implies maintaining collective ownership to rural land but simultaneously transforming its structure in order to strengthen farmers' land use rights. In this way the market of land property rights would be *de facto* dominated by the use right, while collective ownership would no longer play a significant role in the transfer of land holdings.

Theoretically speaking, each of the above views has its strengths and weaknesses. Each embodies different interests and value-orientations within Chinese society. More critical is the problem of feasibility, which is closely related to the reaction of and interaction between divergent interest groups. Even though the discussions have continued for many years, there has been no real progress towards great changes in rural land ownership, or towards nationalization, privatization, or multiple ownership. For these reasons, the most practical path for future legal reforms is to focus on such questions as: who is the real owner? How should the owner exercise its ownership of (collective) land? According to the Land Administration Law, rural land "shall be collectively owned by farmers."[34] This means that the title of collective land shall belong to the villagers collectively, rather than to a few of them, i.e., the village leaders. It is clear that the future transformation of rural land ownership should be linked simultaneously with political reforms aiming at rural democratization; for instance, revision of the procedures for the election of village leadership and those for decision-making in major village affairs.

Use rights' transactions: conservative or active policy intervention?

History has proven that efficiency and profits from the agricultural use of rural land are usually considerably lower than from industrial and commercial use. Since China has a large population, it is the state's constant concern to preserve the limited amount of farming land to prevent shortages in the food supply. The Land Administration Law has some specific provisions geared to minimize the conversion of arable land into land for construction use or other nonagricultural uses. For example, it stipulates that "the State shall compile general plans to set the usage of land, including those of farming, construction use or nonuse." Strict control is placed on the transformation of agricultural land into construction land "to control the total amount of construction land and exercise special protection over cultivated land," and "the State protects the cultivated land and strictly controls the conversion of cultivated land into noncultivated land." It is also stipulated that "whereas occupation of land for construction purposes involves the conversion of agricultural land into land for construction purposes, examination and approval procedures in this regard are required."[35]

The transfer, lease, or other transactions involving land use rights to cultivated land (for instance, investment in a villagers' partnership) are generally allowed on the condition that the type of land use remains unaltered, albeit the transfer of such rights is usually limited to a large extent. According to a survey conducted by a group of American and Chinese scholars, the current market for transfers of rural land use rights involves 20 percent of the total number of farm households. Most land transfers share the following characteristics: (1) they are limited to a portion of the landholdings of the transferring party; (2) they concern intravillage transactions; (3) they are generally short term, for only a few years; (4) they are uncompensated, with the party receiving the rights assuming the duties for taxes and land fees; and (5) they are informal, and do not require formal approval from the collective landowner. It is important to note that not all transfers conform to these characteristics, and longer-term, compensated transfers do occur in some instances.[36]

In my view, the policy of protecting cultivated land is in conflict with economic growth and social welfare in the rural areas. It compels farmers to use their land in ways that are not economically productive in order to meet the possible long-term needs of the nation. Even though the state has provided increasing opportunities for farmers to obtain jobs in urban areas, a large percentage of rural labor still relies on farming. It is positive that the central government has taken various measures to increase the output and revenues from agricultural production. Yet, despite efforts to spread new agricultural technology and stabilize the prices for grain procurement, the income from farming remains very low. According to official statistics, in 1999 the national average output value of six types of grain, i.e., wheat, maize, rice, soybeans, cotton, and oil bearing crops, was RMB¥[37] 315.47 per *mu*,[38] while the total costs amounted to RMB¥ 235.47 per *mu* (or 74.5 percent of the output value). But when taxes and other fees were added the output–cost ratio became 1.00/1.01.[39]

It is clear that the policy of preserving arable land does not necessarily imply preserving land for agricultural production; in fact an increasing number of farmers – in particular in the wealthier and coastal regions – have left their land fallow. In order to keep the land policy workable it should, apart from strengthening farmers' property rights to land, also relieve their burden of taxation and administrative fees. At the same time, the countryside is urbanizing rapidly as economic development progresses. With the development of new towns and cities, the demand for land for industrial and commercial purposes rises, which necessitates changes in the land use structure. It means that the land market in these areas should be developed, which in turn requires that the law is more active in responding to market needs. For this reason, the legal restrictions to transactions involving land use rights should be more flexible, while at the same time more definitive. In the Rural Land Contracting Law, however, it is stipulated that "no contracted land can be used for nonagricultural construction" and transactions of contracted land use rights shall follow the principle requiring "no change in the nature of land ownership and agricultural use."[40] It seems that further reforms cannot be undertaken until a better legal basis for transactions is provided through, for instance, the enactment of a Civil Code or the Property Law (or Real Right Law), which is currently being drafted.

Distribution of land use rights

In order to provide long-term and stable land use rights for farmers, the Land Administration Law stipulates that "land collectively owned by farmers shall be contracted out to members of the collective economic organizations for use in crop farming, forestry, animal husbandry and fisheries production under a term of 30 years."

The Rural Land Contracting Law requires in Article 20 that the contract term for cultivation purposes shall be 30 years, for grasslands 30–50 years, for forestry 30–70 years, and for special forestry (for example, the production of fruits and nuts), the term could be longer if approved by the forestry administration of the State Council.

To further protect long-term rights, the Land Administration Law provides a strict procedure for land reallocations, stating that

> within the valid term of a contract, the adjustment of land contracted by individual contractors should get the consent from over two-thirds majority vote of the villagers' congress or over two-thirds of the villagers' representatives and then be submitted to the land administrative departments of the township (or town) people's government and county level people's government for approval.[41]

More than 20 years have passed since the implementation of the Household Contract Responsibility System. At the time of the first lease contract, the national government allowed farm households a lease period of five years, which was extended to 15 in 1984, and finally to 30 years in 1993. Initially, there was no law that stipulated the 30-year contract term until the revision of the Land Administration Law in August 1998. At the time, the first term (15 years) of contracts issued since 1978 had expired, and a so-called second round (*di'er lun chengbao*) of land contracting was executed. The central leadership was strongly committed to "long-term, secure rural land use rights," and in order to implement the 30-years' land use right stipulated by law, the rural collectives were required to conclude new contracts with the villagers.[42]

Over time, however, it is inevitable that the size of the majority of rural households has changed and will continue to change. During the process of re-contracting, officials and scholars hotly debated whether land holdings should be readjusted in response to demographic changes.

Furthermore, some also wondered whether it should be made possible to readjust the land *during* the second 30-year term of land use. According to the rural survey mentioned earlier, only 57.5 percent of the villagers support, or do not oppose, a full prohibition on land readjustments, while 42.5 percent are against it. The survey also shows that in the villages that decided to conduct large readjustments during the 30-year term, nearly four out of five farmers (78.8 percent) expressed low confidence in tenure security. Although the chapters in this volume by Bromley and Rozelle *et al.* show that the relationship between tenure security and economic behavior is by no means an unambiguous one, I would argue that the law should expressly prohibit land readjustments during the term of use. As jurists of the Rural Development Institute have stated: "Land readjustments, and the extremely high degree of land tenure insecurity associated with them, currently represent the greatest obstacle to Chinese farmers' ability to compete in the international agricultural marketplace."[43]

Under the current circumstances the enforcement of strict tenure security might be difficult, particularly as land reallocations fulfill the function of a social safety net, as pointed out in my introduction. However, in the long run, both from the perspective of legal as well as agricultural development, the legal protection of the lessee will be critical. In this respect, the government should play a proactive role through the stipulation of new legal norms and values.

Proposed legal reforms for use rights to rural land

During the drafting of the revised Land Administration Law and other laws, proposals for legal reform for rural land use rights have been put forward with regard to three points touched upon earlier: (1) the use rights to agricultural land; (2) the use rights to construction land; and (3) the use rights to land designated for housing. Proposed reform in these three areas of property rights will be discussed in more detail below.

Stable tenure and social security: recommendations for agricultural land use

In order to build an effective legal system for the rights to use agricultural land, it is critical to set three basic objectives: first, maintain the stability of land property rights; second, optimize the utilization of land resources; and third, preserve the social security function of use rights to agricultural land. Within this framework, Chinese legal scholars have proposed several suggestions for reform. In addition to contracting for them, the use rights to agricultural land could be acquired in various ways, for instance, by auction, assignment with payment, and by lease. To date, the use rights to agricultural land can only be acquired by execution of a contract, as set forth by the Land Administration Law[44] and the Rural Land Contracting

Law. Actual practice has already moved far beyond the boundaries of national law, and shows that there are a variety of ways to effectively acquire the use rights to agricultural land.

For example, starting in the late 1980s, Lüliang Prefecture in Shanxi Province issued regulations to encourage the development of wasteland, stipulating that the use rights to wasteland may be granted through public auction. Many local governments ranging from Yunnan to Inner Mongolia have followed suit with regional regulations.[45] This should be further confirmed by national legislation. Moreover, it is even conceivable that the use rights to collective agricultural land over a limited period of time may be granted through direct sale or lease (without supervision from the villagers' committee and township). In some regions such uncontrolled sale and lease of use rights to uncultivated or wasteland would definitely not pose a problem. These transactions do not violate the general prohibition against lease or transfer of rural land tenure for nonagricultural purpose in Article 63 of the Land Administration Law,[46] and could be legally confirmed at the state level.

Moreover, the procedures for the acquisition of use rights to agricultural land must meet the principles of social equity and fairness. The representatives of land ownership, that is the township government or villagers' committee, should have a status equal to that of the land users, the villagers or, in some cases, the nonagricultural populace. A step in this direction has already been made through Articles 14(2) and 15(2) of the Revised Land Administration Law, which require decisions involving land allocation and contracts to be voted for by a two-thirds majority of the villagers or their representatives.[47] But since these voting procedures have not been well complied with, it is necessary to provide more detailed rules to guarantee voting rights and restrict arbitrary land allocation actions by village cadres.

As Carter and Yao argue in Chapter 5, the opportunities for market transactions concerning use rights to agricultural land should be expanded. This implies that the restrictions to the transfer of use rights should be relaxed, allowing villagers to subcontract, lease or transfer their use rights to agricultural land to either members or nonmembers of the collective. There should be a basic policy allowing the transfer of land property rights among different persons, either villagers or nonvillagers, while restricting the conversion from agricultural use to nonagricultural use. In a speech at the 2001 Central Symposium on Population, Resources, and the Environment, former President Jiang Zemin advocated that the land user should be free to transfer, lease or mortgage land based on the legal status of real rights, provided that the transaction shall not convert the type of usage unless formally approved by the relevant authorities.[48]

If the use right to agricultural land is to be protected as a real right, it is essential that a cadastral system (or land registry) be established. With a cadastral system, the individual land user can obtain a certificate of registration for his property from the Land Administration Bureau of the local county government. This ensures that his right cannot be affected unless the registration is legally altered or cancelled. The cadastre will increase the leverage of the individual user versus the township and village cadres, even though the township and village cadres are not barred from unilaterally terminating a contract in some circumstances, for instance, in a case where the land user fails to pay the local fees that have been imposed by them.

It is imperative that the term for the use rights to agricultural land be prolonged. According to existing provisions, the contract term for use rights lasts 30 years. This is generally too short to sufficiently stimulate long-term investments by the farmers. A 50-year term might be more appropriate. If there were sufficient political support, automatic prolongation of the 30-year period might be considered, towards a lease contract in perpetuity (*yongdianquan*, much in the same vein as under British Land Law), provided that the user does not illegally convert land use and needs for community spatial planning can still be met.

Last but not least, there should be legal provisions governing the effects of the termination of use rights to agricultural land. As previously discussed, the second round of leases was initiated as initial 15-year-term lease contracts had expired. As early as 1993 the central government announced that leases would be extended another 30 years on top of the original 15. However, in the current legislation, it is not clear what happens when that 30-year term expires. In fact, there are neither regulations nor legal procedures for the extension of land lease contracts. It is advisable that, upon expiration of his use rights, the user be appropriately compensated for his investments, or allowed to extend his rights of use. Such a law will better stimulate farmers' incentives to keep the land productive, while at the same time securing principles of social equity and fairness.

Safeguarding commercial use: recommendations for construction land

With regard to construction land for commercial use, I believe that three issues need to be stipulated in future legislation and regulations. First, who can acquire construction land needs to be defined. Generally speaking, there are two categories of legal entities that might qualify for this: (1) the enterprise solely invested in and owned by the collective; and (2) the joint venture whereby the collective unit invests by contributing construction land and individuals invest with funds, machinery, and so forth.

A second issue concerns the improvement of procedures for acquiring the use rights to commercial construction land Besides the approval procedure provided in Articles 60 and 61 of the Land Administration Law,[49] there should be an established villagers voting system to avoid abuses of power over land allocation by village cadres. Furthermore, land use rights acquisition should become market-based. Up to now, some regions have carried out the so-called compensated granting (paid transfer) of land use rights. In Guangdong and Zhejiang Provinces, for example, there is a regulation that the land use right to collective construction land shall be granted by way of auction or public bidding. In the cities of Suzhou and Wuhu, local regulations allow use rights to collective construction land to be freely transferred, which has resulted in an active land market and the efficient use of land resources.[50]

Finally, the third critical issue is the necessity for the legal system to provide a regulatory framework for an orderly and effective market for transactions concerning use rights to commercial construction land. The lease of land is generally allowed on the condition that the lease conforms to the general land use plan and the annual land use plan of the township. When an enterprise holding a use right to commercial construction land goes bankrupt or merges, the entity to which the land title is transferred must meet the above qualifications, or otherwise become a transferee through the procedures of land requisition and paid assignment.[51] It is recommended that the use rights to any collectively owned construction land in developed or planned urban areas can be freely transferred through assignment, lease, or investment vehicle.[52] In the case of construction land for public utilities, the fundamental principle should be to prohibit the conversion of such land to commercial use without government approval. This is necessary to control the loss of arable land. Moreover, it should be also forbidden to assign, lease, or mortgage such construction land.

Recommendations for housing land

In this section, four concrete proposals to reform the use rights to housing land will be put forward. Similar to the acquisition of other land use rights, the legal procedures for the acquisition of use rights to housing land need a great deal of improvement. In contrast to current practices, it must be a matter that is determined by villagers collectively rather than village leaders personally. First, the decision to allocate housing land or provide additional housing land should be voted for by more than two-thirds of the total villagers or villagers' representatives, and should subsequently be examined and approved by higher authorities.[53] Procedures for paid acquisition should also follow similar principles of transparency and democracy. Special attention needs to be paid to ensure that the payment for acquiring housing land does not become a financial burden for the farmers in the poverty areas.[54] An appropriate solution is lowering or abolishing payment for housing land within the standard housing land areas as stipulated by the local government in accordance with Article 62 of the Land Administration Law,[55] and substantially increasing payment when the standard area is exceeded.

Second, the law should provide proper rules for transferring the use rights to housing land according to the principle of "one household, one plot of housing land." Households may use housing land not only for a residence, but also for production or commercial activities. This can satisfy multiple land needs of rural households and increase the efficiency of land use. However, industrial or commercial activities shall be subject to other laws and regulations, for instance, the regulations on pollution control, noise nuisance, or the prohibition against illegal business activities. When an enterprise uses housing land in violation of the law, its activities should be halted, although the land use right may be maintained. In practice, the lease of housing land is relatively popular, in particular in the villages near cities. The law does not prohibit villagers from leasing their housing land but imposes some limitations on the lease: the lessee is limited to villagers of the same collective unit;[56] the lease is subject to land registration in accordance with the law (in other words it should be supervised by the county land administration bureau);[57] and the lessor's application for new, additional housing land shall be rejected.[58]

The third proposal concerns the need for more elaborate legal provisions on succession (inheritance) of the use rights to housing land. In particular, the procedures regarding nonmember successors needs to be clarified. One suggestion for such cases is that housing land in principle must return to the collective unit with fair compensation, unless the successor chooses to live in the village and is accepted there. An alternative is to enable the successor to transfer the house together with housing land to a village member. If the collective unit is unable to pay financial compensation and buy the house, the successor should be allowed to keep the house until the collective is able to pay or the house is sold to a third appropriate party. Finally, there should be clear stipulations to deal with over-occupation or leaving housing land fallow. If the over-occupied area can be divided, it should be returned to the collective unit with appropriate financial compensation for its edifices. If it cannot be divided, the user must be allowed to keep it until circumstances permit division, with an extra charge for the over-occupied area during this period.

Conclusion: land property rights with Chinese characteristics?

The use right is a crucial concept in the land system of China, and features certain "Chinese characteristics." Since all land is subject to public ownership held by the state or the rural collectives, private interests in land tenure can only be embodied and protected in the form of land use rights. In addition, as land ownership cannot be transferred, the land use right serves as the sole legal means for transactions in the land market. It is not expected that the Chinese state will abandon the principle of public ownership in the short run. For this reason, the evolution of the land property system relies heavily on the development of land use rights and must keep up with the changes in the degree of commercialization, economic efficiency, and democratic reforms taking place in rural China.

Compared to the Western legal system that features private property rights, the Chinese system of land use rights still has several shortcomings. The land use right is strongly affected by public ownership that is to a great extent controlled by the state and the collectives. It therefore requires sustained effort to establish an institutional framework that will provide land use rights holders with adequate protection against indiscriminate interference by the landowner. Furthermore, it is obvious that the currently stipulated term for land use rights is too limited, and negatively affects land users' economic incentives. The term of use restrains expected returns from land investment, reduces the market value of land, and diminishes both the economic functions of the land market and the growth of the capital market.

Categories of land use rights in China are governed by rules and procedures that are sometimes very laborious and complicated. This situation is, in some ways, comparable to the British system of land tenure and estate, which reflects a historical transition from a predominantly agrarian and feudal society to a society based upon market principles. By way of illustration, in medieval England, there were a number of land tenure types related to particular legal entities. In other words, particular entities of land users were entitled to different kinds of use rights, for example, tenures in chivalry, spiritual tenures, and so-called villein tenure. These have all disappeared in modern times.[59] By comparison, in present-day China, the privilege of state-owned enterprises to obtain allocated land use rights without payment is declining, and the requirement of rural registration (according to the household registration system or *hukou*) to acquire use rights to agricultural land has relaxed in some regions.

Some Chinese scholars have advocated the privatization of land ownership. However, considering the unique cultural and historical parameters of China, certain institutional arrangements – such as state and collective ownership – might be inevitable. China has a vast population but limited developed and cultivated land. Over the centuries systems of private ownership have led to large-scale land mergers, peasants' revolts, and sociopolitical upheaval – with the collapse of entire dynasties as an ultimate result. The public ownership of land might be propitious for a fair allocation of land resources, in particular for agriculture and housing in the rural areas. Moreover, as Xiaolin Pei argues in Chapter 8, the rapid development of capital construction and increase in foreign direct investments might be partially attributed to the public ownership of land. Public land ownership can actually facilitate control over the misuse of land and illegal speculation in the land market. In this way public land ownership might ease the implementation of state economic policies in the areas of social security, environmental protection, and market control.

At present, China is in the midst of drafting the Property Law (*Wuquan fa*) that is going to be a part of the Chinese Civil Code. The draft law aims at consolidating the existing property rights structure. As far as land rights are concerned, present and future developments are barely covered. It goes without saying that the proposed Property Law does provide a basic legal framework for future reforms. However, many issues cannot be dealt with in this law: transfer transactions in the land market, the registration of land rights, the protection of arable land, the development of waste-land, the environmental standards on land use, reallocation of rural land, dispute resolution over historical land titles, and the relationship between land use rights and use rights to buildings, forest, and mineral resources. We should bear in mind that the structure of Chinese land rights is still undergoing a transitional process of reform and evolution. This process cannot be frozen in time or halted through legislation. It is critical that the law should leave ample space for further reforms in the land system, while adapting itself to changes in Chinese society. Socio-economic change results in new institutions that may create new forms of land use rights and rules for land tenure. It can be expected that the future Property Law and revisions of the Land Administration Law will play a critical role in this transformation.

Notes

1 The term "land tenure" used in this chapter refers to possession and use of land in a general sense, based on any legal system. In China, the legal basis of rural land tenure usually falls into the category of "land use rights" (*tudi shiyong quan*).

2 The Land Administration Law is the major legislation on land rights in China. This Law was promulgated in June 1986, and amended in August 1998. The English translation of the Law is available at: http://www.lawinfochina.com/DataBase/LawRegulation/index.asp.

3 Article 12 (1) of the 1986 Land Administration Law reads: "Land collectively owned by farmers, or state-owned land used by units of public ownership or collective ownership, may be contracted out to collectives or individuals for use in crop farming, forestry, animal husbandry and fisheries production." After the amendment in 1998, Article 14 of the Law reads: "Land collectively owned by farmers shall be contracted out to members of the collective economic organizations for use in crop farming, forestry, animal husbandry and fisheries production."

4 The same provision can be seen in Article 2 of the Land Administration Law of 1998.

5 The 1988 amendment of the Land Administration Law stipulates in Article 2: "Land use rights may be transferred by law." "The state introduces the system of compensated use of land owned by the state except for the land that has been allocated for specific use by the state according to law."

6 The term "land title" is more familiar to lawyers in common law countries, referring to ownership of an interest in land. It may confer full rights in a parcel of land, as in the fee simple estate recognized in English and American law, or lesser rights in a parcel of land, such as the mere right to possess a lease or easement (Palomar 2001: 5, 1).

7 See also the discussion of ownership as the absolute and supreme right in Ho (2001).
8 Underhill, cited in Simpson (1976: 24).
9 For more information on real versus personal rights, see Simpson (1976: 24–26).
10 The Land Administration Law was promulgated in 1986 and amended in 1988 and 1998.
11 Article 4, paragraph 3, Land Administration Law.
12 Article 80, paragraph 2, of the General Principles of Civil Law reads:

> The right of citizens and collectives to contract for the management of land under collective ownership or of state-owned land under collective use shall be protected by law. The rights and obligations of the two contracting parties shall be stipulated in the contract signed in accordance with the law.

See also, Articles 14 and 15 of the Land Administration Law (1998), and Article 12 of the Agriculture Law (1993).
13 In Article 37, paragraph 3, of the Land Administration Law it provides: "Whereas a unit or individual that has contracted for land operation has given up cultivation and allowed the land to go wasted for two successive years, the original 'contractee' shall terminate the contract and recover the land."
14 The proportion of the agricultural population has declined from 82.1 percent in 1978 to 69.1 percent in 1999 (National Bureau of Statistics 2000: 95).
15 On average, over 70 percent of the annual income of a rural household comes from agricultural production. In 2000, the general price level of agricultural products had fallen from 1996 by 25.6 percent, indicating that the growth rate of farmers' income has been declining since 1997 (Dong 2001).
16 For example, the Southern Jiangsu model, the Wenzhou model, and the Nanhai model. See Ye Jianping (2000). In the first two models, land tenure was achieved by recontracting or leasing to large-scale farming. In the third, the villagers all agreed to invest the entirety of village land into the Zhoubiao Economic Co-op and received shares in return. The Co-op used the land for industrial and commercial development and the villagers received annual bonuses. See also Zhao Yi (2001).
17 See, *Opinions on Stabilizing and Perfecting the Relationship of Land Contracts (guanyu wending he wanshan tudi chengbao guanxi de yijian)*, issued by PRC Ministry of Agriculture in December 1994.
18 See Tim Hanstad and Ping Li (1997).
19 Article 4, paragraph 3.
20 Article 60 of the Land Administration Law reads:

> In using the land for construction purposes as defined in the general plan for the utilization of the land of townships (towns) to commence enterprises or joint ventures with other units or individuals by utilizing land use rights as shares, the rural collective economic organization shall file an application with the land administrative departments of the local people's governments at and above the county level on the strength of documents of approval. The applications shall be approved by the local people's governments at and above the county level according to the terms provided for by various provinces, autonomous regions, and municipalities whereas the use of land involves the conversion of agricultural land to other uses, the examination and approval procedures provided for in Article 44 of this law shall be followed ... Land for construction purposes utilized by such enterprises provided for in the preceding paragraph shall be put

> under strict control. Provinces, autonomous regions, and municipalities shall determine the standards for land use according to the different trades and scale of operation of township enterprises.

21 The term "original land market" refers to transactions where the land use right is first of all derived from the land ownership and is granted to the user by the landowner (e.g., the State or the village).
22 Article 62 of the Land Administration Law reads:

> One rural household can own one parcel of land for building a house, with the size not to exceed the standards provided for by provinces, autonomous regions, and municipalities ... Construction of rural houses should conform to the general plans for the utilization of the land of townships (towns) and the original land occupied by houses and open spaces of villages should be used as much as possible for building houses. ... The use of land for building houses should be examined by the township (town) people's governments and approved by the county people's governments. Whereas when occupation of agricultural land is involved the examination and approval procedure provided for in Article 44 of this law is required.

23 See Wang Weiguo (1997; 103–104).
24 See Jiang Ping (1999: 308–309).
25 See Guo Mingrui and Fang Shaokun (2002: 137).
26 See Jiang Ping, (1999: 308); Ding Guanliang (1999).
27 Lü Laiming (1995: 201).
28 Ye Hua (1998).
29 See Wang Weiguo (1997: 181–183).
30 For example, reportedly, participants at an international conference on Chinese rural land issues held in January 2002 indicated that, as a consequence of the entitlement with real rights, the "farmers' land use right shall substantially entitle them to retain the land. See Anonymous (2002: 2).
31 During the 1960s and 1970s in China, the society of rural areas was shaped by the "people's commune" system. A people's commune was characterized as a combination of political and economic organizations, structured in three levels: commune, grand production brigades, and small production teams. The basic economic units were small production teams. Peasants worked collectively in their teams and received a distribution of products (foodstuff, etc.). Since the reforms began at the end of the 1970s, the peasants have begun working in their own household and earning income for themselves, while the system of collective production and distribution has collapsed and the collective economic organizations ceased to exist. The former grand production brigades have now become the so-called administrative villages, the grass-roots of rural administration, and the former small production teams have become "natural villages," that is, villagers' autonomous organizations. All of the villages do not have economic functions such as the organizing of production and distribution.
32 See Wang Weiguo (1997; 98–108), Ye Jianping (1999: 67–71).
33 See, among others, Wang Xianjin (1991: 131–132), Du Jun (1989: 100–108), Zhang Quanjiang (1987), Li Zhaodong (1989), Zheng Jinshui (1986).
34 See Article 8 of the Land Administration Law.
35 See Articles 4, 31, and 44 of the Land Administration Law.
36 Schwarzwalder *et al.* (2001).
37 In 2003, US$100 was equivalent to approximately RMB¥ 827.
38 The *mu* is a traditional Chinese unit of land measurement, equivalent to

approximately 667 square meters or one-fifteenth of a hectare. RMB is Chinese currency.

39 These figures are based on statistics from the State Committee of Planning. See Anonymous (2002: 2).

40 See Articles 8 and 33 of the Rural Land Contracting Law.

41 Article 14 of the Land Administration Law. The same provision can be seen in Article 27 of the Rural Land Contracting Law.

42 The Third Plenary Session of the 15th Central Committee of the Chinese Communist Party, "Decisions on Several Major Issues in Rural Work" (*guanyu nongcun gongzuo ruogan zhongda wenti de jueding*), issued in October 1998.

43 Schwarzwalder *et al.* (2001: 20, 43, 60).

44 Article 14(1) of the Land Administration Law provides:

> Land collectively owned by farmers shall be contracted out to members of the collective economic organizations for use in crop farming, forestry, animal husbandry, and fisheries production for a term of 30 years. The contractees should sign a contract with the correspondent contractor to define each other's rights and obligations. Farmers who have contracted land are obliged to use the land rationally according to the purposes agreed upon in the contracts. The rights of operation of land contracted by farmers shall be protected by law.

Article 15(1) reads:

> Land collectively owned by farmers may be contracted out to units or individuals who do not belong to the corresponding collectives for farming, forestry, animal husbandry, and fisheries operations. The contractees and contractors should sign land use contracts to define each other's rights and obligations. The contracted term for operation is to be agreed upon in the land use contracts. Contractors for land use are obliged to protect and use the land rationally according to the usages specified in the contracts.

45 See Peter Ho (2003b: 121–159) and Tim Hanstad and Ping Li (1997).

46 Article 63 of the Land Administration Law reads:

> The land use right of farmer collectives shall not be leased, transferred, or rented for nonagricultural construction, except in the case of legal transfer of the land that conform to the general plan for the utilization of land and have been legally obtained by enterprises due to bankruptcy or acquisition.

47 Article 14(2) of the Land Administration Law reads:

> Within the valid term of a contract, the adjustment of land contracted by individual contractors should obtain the consent by over two-thirds majority vote of the villagers' congress or over two-thirds of villagers' representatives and then be submitted to the land administrative departments of the township (town) people's government and county level people's government for approval.

[Note: here the word "adjustment" refers to reallocation and renewal of the contracts because when the Law was promulgated agricultural land in almost all of the rural areas had to be allocated and contracted. Article 15(2) of the Law reads:

> Whereas land collectively owned by a farmer is contracted out for operation to someone not belonging to the corresponding collective

> organizations, consent must be obtained from over two-thirds majority vote of the villagers' congress or over two-thirds of the villagers' representatives with the resulting contract being submitted to the township (town) people's government for approval.

48 "The administration and, especially, protection of cultivated land shall be earnestly strengthened, and use of cultivated land for construction use shall be earnestly controlled," President Jiang Zemin (2001: 1).

49 Article 60(1) reads:

> In using land for construction purposes as defined in the general plan for the utilization of the land of townships (towns) for start up enterprises or joint ventures with other units or individuals by using land use rights as shares, the rural collective economic organization shall file an application with the land administrative departments of the local people's governments at and above the county level on the strength of documents of approval. The applications shall be approved by the local people's governments at and above the county level according to the terms of reference provided for by various provinces, autonomous regions, and municipalities, whereas concerning the use of land involving the occupation of agricultural land, the examination and approval procedures provided for in Article 44 of this law shall be followed.

Article 61 reads:

> In using land for building public facilities and public welfare facilities, townships (towns) shall file an application with land administrative departments of the local people's governments at and above the county level after being examined by the township (town) people's governments, and the application shall be approved by the local people's governments at and above the county level according to the term of reference provided for by provinces, autonomous regions, and municipalities. Where occupation of agricultural land is involved, the examination and approval procedures provided for in Article 44 of this law are required.

50 Liu Tian (2001: 6).

51 These procedures can be seen in Chapter 5 of the Land Administration Law.

52 Gan Zhangchun and Su Weixing (2001: 11–13).

53 The only approval procedure provided by the Land Administration Law appears in Article 62(2), which states that "construction of rural houses should conform to the general plans for the utilization of the land of townships (towns) and the original land occupied by houses and open spaces of villages should be used as much as possible for building houses." Although there is no voting procedure for allocation of housing land, allocation of housing land must be discussed and decided by meetings of the villagers in accordance with the principle of villager autonomy. See Wang Weiguo and Wang Guanghua (2001: 191).

54 See Ye Jianping (2000): 104).

55 Article 62(1) provides: "One rural household can own one piece of land for building a house, with the area not to exceed the standards provided for by provinces, autonomous regions, and municipalities."

56 This limitation is justified because, first, the allocation of rural housing land bears characteristics of social welfare and, second, the supply of housing land should be controlled for the protection of agricultural land. See Wang Weiguo and Wang Guanghua (2001: 193–194).

57 Article 30 of the Rules of Land Registration provides: "When a land user with rights to sublease does so, the lessor and lessee shall submit the lease contract

and the relative documents for registration within 15 days after the execution of the contract."

58 Article 62(4) provides: "The application for housing land after a party has sold or leased their house shall not be approved."

59 See Simpson (1976: 28–29).

References

Anonymous (2002) *Southern Weekend (Nanfang Zhoumo)*, 7 February.

Chen, Su (1996) "Tudi Chengbao Jingying Wuquanhua yu Nongdi Shiyongquan Zhidu de Queli" (Changing the Contract Right to Land into a Real Right and the Establishment of a System for Agricultural Land User Rights), *Zhongguo Faxue*, 3, 89.

Commissioners of the Land Transfer Acts (1911) *Report of the Royal Commission on Land Transfer Acts*, London.

Ding, Guanliang (1999) "Discussion on the Nature of Contractual Rights to Rural Land," *China Rural Economy (zhongguo nongcun jingji)*, 7: 23–27.

Dong, Shi (2001) "The Burden that Land Cannot Endure," *Caijing Magazine (caijing zhazhi)*, December, 23: 1–3.

Gan, Zhangchun and Weixing Su (2001) "Endeavors to Build Up New Mechanism – On Reform of the System for Use of Farmer-Collective Owned Construction Land," *China Land (zhongguo tudi)*, 3: 35–38.

Guo, Mingrui and Shaokun Fang (2002) "Study on the Property System for Rural Land," in Liming Wang (ed.) *Monographic Studies on Property Law (wuquanfa zhuanti yanjiu)*, Changchun: Jilin People's Press.

Hanstad, Tim and Ping Li (1997) "Land Reform in the People's Republic of China: Auctioning Rights to Wasteland," *Loyola of Los Angeles: International and Comparative Law Journal*, 19: 545–583.

Ho, Peter (2001) "Who Owns China's Land? Policies, Property Rights and Deliberate Institutional Ambiguity," *The China Quarterly*, 166 (June): 387–414.

Ho, Peter (2003a) "Contesting Rural Spaces: Land Disputes, Customary Tenure and the State in China," in Elizabeth Perry and Mark Selden (eds) *Chinese Society: Change, Conflict and Resistance*, New York: Routledge.

Ho, Peter (2003b) "The Wasteland Auction Policy in Northwest China: Solving Rural Poverty and Environmental Degradation?" in Peter Ho, Jacob Eyferth, and Eduard B. Vermeer (eds) "Rural Development in Transitional China: A Special Issue," *Journal of Peasant Studies*, 30: 3/4, April/July: 93-112.

Hua, Ye (1998) "Contractual Right to Agricultural Land Has Similar Nature to Ownership," *China Rural Survey* (*zhongguo nongcun guancha*), 6: 36-40.

Jiang, Zemin (2001) Speech at the Central Symposium on Population, Resources and Environment, Beijing, 11 March. See *China's Land (zhongguo tudi)*, 3: 1.

Jianping, Ye (2000) *Studies on the Rural Land Tenure System in China (zhongguo nongcun Tudi chanquan zhidu yanjiu)*, Beijing: China Agriculture Press.

Jun, Du (ed.) (1989) *Theories and Practice of Land Administration Law (tudi guanli faxue lilun yu shijian)*, Chengdu: Chengdu Science-Tech University Press.

Laiming, Lü (1995) *Land Coming to Market – New Opinions on Land Property Law (Zouxiang shichang de tud – dichanfa xinlun)*, Guiyang: Guizhou People's Press.

Li, Zhaodong (1989) "Rural Collective Land Shall be Nationalized," *Rural Forecast (nongcun zhanwang)*, 2: 18–19.

National Bureau of Statistics (2000) *China Statistical Yearbook 2000*, Beijing: China Statistics Press.

Palomar, Joyce (2001) Land Title Security as a Market Stimulator in China, paper presented at the Chinese Property Law and Real Estate Law Symposium, Beijing, June.

Ping, Jiang (ed.) (1999) *Studies on Land Legislation in China (zhongguo tudi lifa yanjiu)*, Beijing: CUPL Press.

Quanjiang, Zhang (1987) "On Abolishment of Collective Ownership to Rural Land," in *Research Group in China's Rural Economic Law, Selected Theses at the Symposium on Rural Economic Law (zhongguo nongcun jingjifa yantaohui lunwen xuanji)*, Chongqing: Internal publication of the Southwest Institute of Politics and Law.

Schwarzwalder, Brian, Prosterman, Roy, Jianping, Ye, Riedinger, Jeffrey, and Li Ping (2001) *An Update on Rural Land Tenure Reform in China: Analysis and Recommendations Based on a 17–Province Survey*, workshop paper, 21 November.

Simpson, R. Rowton (1976) *Land Law and Registration*, Cambridge: Cambridge University Press.

Song, Hongsong (2001) "Change and Creation of the Contracting System for Agricultural Land," in Liming Wang (ed.) *Monographic Studies on Property Law (wuquanfa zhuanti yanjiu)*, Changchun: Jilin People's Press.

Tian, Liu (2001) "The Vast Wind in March (monthly news review)," *China Land (zhongguo tudi)*, 3: 10.

Wang, Weiguo (1997) *Research on Land Rights in China (zhongguo tudi quanli yanjiu)*, Beijing: CUPL Press.

Wang, Weiguo and Wang, Guanghua (eds) (2001) *A Guide to Land Rights in China (zhongguo tudi quanli zhinan)*, Beijing: CUPL Press.

Wang, Xianjin (ed.) (1991) *Reform of the Land Use System in China: Theories and Practice (zhongguo tudi shiyong zhidu gaige: lilun yu shijian)*, Beijing: China Audit Press.

Yi, Zhao (2001) "Nanhai: An Experiment with the Land System," *Nanfengchuang Magazine* (*nanfengchuang zhazhi*), 204(12): 28–29.

Zheng, Jinshui (1986) "Thinking and Solution to the Problem of Structure of Rural Land Ownership in Our Country," *Study Monthly (xuexi yuekan)*, 11: 16-18.

3 The politics of rural land use planning

Frank N. Pieke

Land is an area of policy-making that is of considerable concern to central and local authorities alike, making land policy a key arena in China where conflicting interests and policy agendas meet. This is particularly true in rural areas, where land is the main asset controlled by village committees and township governments. As Jean Oi has argued, in the collective period the "struggle of the harvest" was the main issue pitting farmers, the national government and local governments against each other (Oi 1989). In the reform period, this conflict over the fruits of the land has increasingly been superseded by the conflict over the land itself. Many of the key challenges that currently confront China, such as rapid urbanization and industrialization, food self-sufficiency, environmental degradation, or the balance of power between local and central government, crucially revolve around the issue of land rights and land use. In many rural areas land is the focal point of often intense conflict between farmers and local government. Farmers consider their use of land the one right that the government should not take away from them, accusing local cadres keen to appropriate agricultural or even residential plots for development of being estranged from the local people they are supposed to serve, or worse, of being self-serving, greedy, or even corrupt (Flower and Leonard 2002; Guo 2001; Zweig 2000).

Whereas Chapter 2 dealt with the institutional and legal aspects of land administration in China, this chapter focuses on the allocation of land for specific purposes detailed in the integrated land use plans (*tudi liyong zong guihua*). These have come into effect across China since 1998. Because of the recent nature of the prominence of rural land use plans, they have been largely ignored in discussions on rural development and agriculture. Other aspects of land policy have played a prominent role in China's rural development strategy for a longer time, and consequently have been much more extensively dealt with in the literature, in particular, tenure and property rights, land ownership, and compensation for appropriated land (Fahlbeck and Huang 1997; Guo 2001; Hu 1997; Kung 2000; Kung and Liu 1997; Li, Rozelle and Brandt 1998; Liu, Carter and Yao 1998; Pennarz 1997; Prosterman *et al.* 1998; Rozelle and Li 1998; Yao 2000; Zhang 2000; Zhang, Huang and Rozelle 1997).

By contrast, the Chinese authorities emphasized urban spatial planning much earlier due to the greater importance attached to urban economic development. This is also reflected in the literature on urban development, in which the issue of urban planning plays an important role (for an overview and synthesis of the literature, see Yeh and Wu 1999). However, since the mid-1990s the issue of spatial planning has gained official attention in rural areas as well. As the Chinese central government relinquishes other, more direct instruments of control over rural areas (in particular, the abandonment of grain quotas), the Chinese bureaucracy assigns to land use plans a leading role in the broader administrative area of land management and rural economic development. In fact, the Ministry of Land and Resources recently went so far as to call for the inclusion of the implementation of land use plans in the targets of the leading cadre responsibility system. Leading cadres were thus made personally responsible for meeting these targets, potentially putting spatial planning on a par with the long-standing core responsibilities of taxation, population planning and public order.[1]

This chapter consists of two parts. The first part presents an analysis of the development of policies on national land use planning since the promulgation of the first Land Law in 1986. This starts with mapping out the main contradictions in national rural development policies. Then the development of rural spatial planning and its role in agricultural development policies is discussed, followed by an analysis of the current procedures and mechanics of rural land use planning. The second part draws on fieldwork data collected in Taicang municipality/county, southern Jiangsu in early 2001, in order to compare the national picture with the role that land has played in policies and practices of economic development there at the county, township and village levels. This case study is not intended to be in any way representative of China as a whole. Quite the contrary, it serves to illustrate two issues. First, over the past ten years administrative reforms have tried to reign in local governments, but at the same time continue to require the same governments to a considerable extent to be self-financing. Land is one of the main resources at the disposal of local governments, who thus find themselves confronted with a contradictory incentive structure in their implementation of land policy. Second, the Taicang case illustrates the lack of fit between blanket national land planning policies and the specific nature of Taicang's highly developed economy. The chapter concludes with the observation that uniform national land use policies do not work. Proscribing the use of designated agricultural land for non-agricultural purposes is arguably vital as a form of social welfare to guarantee the livelihood of the rural population in poorer areas that rely mainly on subsistence agriculture. However, it hamstrings the development of highly commercialized areas such as Taicang in order to provide the poorer members of the rural population with a subsistence guarantee that could be given, at much lesser cost to the overall development of the local economy, by means of specific subsidies or other welfare provisions.

The development of rural land use planning

Despite the passing of two land management laws in a little over ten years, land policy in China continues its uneasy juggle of conflicting policy objectives in rural development. Policy making remains torn between supporting subsistence agriculture and national food grain self-sufficiency on the one hand, and the commercialization of agriculture, industrialization and urbanization on the other.[2] In this part of the chapter I will show how this contradiction has shaped the development of rural land use planning in the last 15 years.

Chinese agriculture between subsistence and modernization

In post-1949 China, the drive for socialist modernization has always been constrained by a need to preserve subsistence agriculture and national food self-sufficiency. China's rural population falls outside the socialist safety net of the work unit system in the cities; instead, the state guarantees farmers access to land or (in the collective period) employment on collective land. Nationally, the government does everything it can in order not to let China slip into the position of a net grain importer: food self-sufficiency was and continues to be a *sine qua non* of national sovereignty. At times, such as under the "take grain as the key link" (*yi liang wei gang*) policy in the 1960s and 1970s, the need to produce sufficient food eclipsed all other concerns, with the exception of military and strategic ones, beyond the point where this seemed reasonable (Lardy 1983: 48–54).

It could be argued that one of the long-term objectives of the post-1978 reform project has been (and continues to be) the reduction and ultimately elimination of the need to be preoccupied with sheer survival caused by poverty, population pressure and backwardness. Indeed, whenever grain crop yields seemed to make this possible (as in 1985, 1993 and again in 1999–2000), the central government has not hesitated to lift the mandatory grain procurement quotas that are the bedrock of China's food self-sufficiency policies. If food production seems reasonably secure, farmers and rural governments are therefore encouraged to de-emphasize food production and to turn to commercial crops, industry or services.

Yet grain and subsistence continue to be major preoccupations. After the relaxation of grain delivery quotas in 1985 and 1993, grain quotas were partially or wholly reinstated as soon as it was clear that farmers would not produce enough to feed China, usually because the relative costs of grain production compared unfavourably with other pursuits, agricultural or otherwise. More spectacularly, 1995 saw the establishment of the "governor's grain bag policy" (*mi daizi shengzhang fuzezhi*), requiring provinces to be self-sufficient in grain.[3] Consistent with the past pattern of policy-making, this did not address the fundamental disincentives of grain production, but dealt with them by administrative fiat.

During the collective period, farmers were tied to the land, prices for agricultural products were kept artificially low and procurement was made mandatory, while industrial products were priced artificially high. The net effect of these "price scissors" was to squeeze funds out of agriculture and to subsidize urban industry. Part of this was made up for by the economies of scale of collective agriculture, collective infrastructural works and, more importantly, the effects of the "green revolution" of the 1960s. Nevertheless, the growth of agriculture throughout the collective period only kept up with population increase (Perkins 1969).

In the early years of the reforms (1979–1984), agriculture received a significant boost when procurement prices for grain were raised dramatically (Ash 1988: 540; Lardy 1983: Chapter 5; Sicular 1988: 684). As grain harvests soared, farmers were increasingly given freedom to grow what they wanted, or even leave agriculture and indeed the countryside altogether.[4] In 1985, prices were reduced and guaranteed state purchase of grain was abolished; immediately, the total sown area and output plummeted (Sicular 1988: 693–695; Walker 1988) and the government quickly re-imposed grain quotas. In 1993, grain quotas were again abandoned, only to be re-imposed a year later due to the sharp decrease in procurement that this caused (Schmidhuber 2001, fig. 1). Quickly, grain production recovered with four years of bumper harvests. In fact, production was so plentiful that grain could no longer be sold, quickly filling up the state granaries. State grain purchases in 1996 and 1997 added up to 115 million tons annually, or 25 million tons more than in 1995. However, in the same period demand plummeted: the state only sold 65 million tons in 1997, down from 70 million tons in 1996 and 90 million tons in 1995. As a result, by 1998 grain stored across China added up to more than 200 million tons. Some 40 per cent of this grain was stored in sub-standard facilities or even in the open air; furthermore, 20 per cent of all stored grain had been kept too long and was simply rotting in storage (Li 2001: 4–5).

Clearly, the long-term problem is not so much that China cannot feed itself, but rather that the comparative disadvantages of grain production are such that only mandatory procurement and/or price subsidies can compel farmers to produce enough.[5] During the 1990s, quotas, import barriers and tariffs, input subsidies and subsidized prices translated into the fact that the unit costs of domestically grown grain have reached and will ultimately even surpass world market levels, although farm-gate price levels have generally remained below world market level (Carter 2001: 80; Du 2001: 56), Yet at best, quotas and subsidies can only postpone the inevitable: the massive abandonment of grain production, with land left fallow, turned to more profitable agricultural uses (orchards, fish ponds, market gardening), or converted altogether to non-agricultural uses. A key question here is for how much longer the Chinese state can and wants to continue subsidizing grain production. The government grain purchasing system is already incurring heavy losses in purchasing the grain that by national regulation it is under obligation to buy at the state's guaranteed prices, a situation not made easier by the re-imposition of the state monopoly on the trade in grain in 1998 (Li 2001).

Given the level of subsidies already paid, and with China's entry to the World Trade Organization, the only direction that grain purchase prices can go is down. In the longer term, grain self-sufficiency is therefore impossible to maintain. However, as Smil concludes, this is not necessarily a problem, given China's high level of export earnings (1999: 428–429). Nationalistic or strategic considerations aside, the logic of comparative costs inexorably pushes China away from national food self-sufficiency, not because the country cannot feed itself, but because it simply does not have the competitive advantage to do so (Du 2001; Schmidhuber 2001).

It has thus become increasingly clear that the long-standing disincentives for basic food production plaguing Chinese agriculture cannot be reversed relying on prices, subsidies, or quotas alone. As a result, policymakers have explored other measures that aim to keep land under grain production, principally land policy and administrative measures. The most important policy documents in this regard are document no. 11 of the State Council and the Party Centre of 1997 and the revised land management law of 1998. The latter incorporates the protection of agricultural land, called for in document no. 11,[6] and makes this part of a package that also includes: (1) the extension of farmers' land use rights to 30 years; (2) the mandatory drafting and implementation of overall land use plans at each level of administration; (3) a policy framework for the confiscation of land; and (4) the regulation of the emerging market in land use rights (Pi 1999: Chapter 1; Xie 2001: 121–122).

Discussing the latter two policy areas would take us far beyond the scope of a chapter that focuses on the second point, land use plans. However, to understand the implications of these plans, a brief discussion is in order on the first point, the lengthening of the land contract period for agricultural land. In the early years of the reforms, land leases given to individual farmers were between one and three years, but soon (1984) were extended to 15 years in the expectation that farmers would invest in the improvement and preservation of land, if they could expect to reap the rewards themselves for a longer period of time. In several policy documents from 1993 onward, the central government committed itself to granting land contracts of 30 years upon the expiration of the first term of 15-year land contracts in 1998. This policy was ultimately incorporated in Article 14 of the revised land law of 1998. However, this has proved a very controversial reform, as it makes it impossible for village cadres to adjust land holdings according to changes in household composition, while simultaneously tempting local cadres to pre-allocate (*yuliu*, see below) amounts of land for non-agricultural uses, leaving farmers with too little land under their new, 30-year leases (Xie 2001: 124).

In this reform the government was bogged down by a fundamental contradiction in its agricultural policies. Thirty-year leases are arguably good for long-term productivity gains in agriculture (although this is by no means an uncontested fact),[7] but run up against an egalitarian counter-discourse in which land is considered the primary means of subsistence that ought to be distributed and redistributed according to current subsistence needs, rather than those of one, two, or three decades earlier (Kung 1994, 1995, 2000; Kung and Liu 1997; Zhu, D. 2001). Yet land is as much a secure asset as a long-term liability to farmers who wish to make use of opportunities for off-farm employment, or the size of whose household has been reduced to the point that they have insufficient labour to farm the land themselves. Stiff penalties for fallowing land or failure to meet grain procurement quotas have forced such farmers to find fellow-villagers or in-migrants from poorer areas elsewhere to sub-contract their land (Kung 2000, 704).[8] The policy of long-term leases thus either ties entrepreneurial villagers to the land, or else devolves to them the responsibility for maintaining agricultural productivity.[9] In this regard, the policy dovetails nicely with the new land use plans that devolve to local governments the task to enforce the farmers' duty to keep their land under the plough.

Agricultural policy and rural land use planning

Since the mid-1990s, national agricultural policy has turned to the new land zoning rules in the integrated land use plans. The land use plans require that specific plots of land be earmarked for specific uses. In the 1980s and 1990s, as villages and townships began to industrialize and became wealthier, increasing amounts of land were taken out of cultivation and used for collective enterprises or other ventures, investment zones, houses, or even tombs.[10] Particularly in rural areas close to cities, the marketization of the economy has not only freed up the application of rural labour and capital beyond subsistence agriculture, but has done the same thing for that third basic production factor, land. Initially, only a very imperfect and limited market in land use rights existed. Even more importantly, the government was ill-equipped to facilitate the growth of such a market and to regulate, monitor and control the resulting changes in land use.

A major step in this direction was taken in 1986 with the passing of the first Land Management Law (*tudi guanli fa*), the establishment of a separate system of land management bureaus (*tudi guanli ju*) at all administrative levels, and the implementation of the first land use plans. Yet, at the time, not agriculture but rural industrialization was at the top of the political agenda. Consequently, the land law and land use plans were designed to regulate rather than limit the conversion of agricultural land to non-agricultural purposes. As a result, the loss of agricultural land continued largely unabated, although this should not necessary lead us to conclude that a crisis of Chinese agriculture was imminent (Ash and Edmonds 1996; Brown, G.P. 1995).

To townships and villages eager to modernize, land was often the chief resource to attract investment and generate revenue. Villagers, villages and townships were all torn between conflicting objectives. Villagers were often keen to enter non-agricultural employment, yet were loathe fully to give up the rights to their land for fear of a political change or an economic downturn. Village cadres not only needed the income from village enterprises and the sale or rent of land use rights, but also had to fulfil the village's grain quota. Township cadres had a range of performance criteria to meet, most importantly having to do with population planning, public order, grain procurement and upward tax remittances, but also with economic performance (Edin 2003; Whiting 2001: 100–110). Profits from township enterprises were the main source of income under their control, providing strong incentives to take land away from agriculture and reallocate it for industrial use. As a result, thousands of county, township and village industrial zones sprang up all across China, as a rule without any central control or planning, and often without any concrete prospects and only on the hope of attracting investment.

These local conflicting objectives have been exacerbated by the fact that, as we saw above, the national government, too, tries to cater for two very different policy agendas. On the one hand, the government wishes to guarantee a minimum subsistence to rural households by granting each a plot of land; on the other, it realizes that there is continuing need to rationalize land use for urban development, industry and commercial agriculture. In the land use and agricultural policies that have come into effect in the latter part of the 1990s, this old contradiction between subsistence and modernization returned with a vengeance when the national government re-emphasized the need to preserve agricultural production, especially of grain.

The most immediately visible aspect of the new conservationist spirit in the area of land management was the requirement imposed on provinces by document no. 11 of 1997 and the 1998 Land Law to make up for any losses of agricultural land by bringing land elsewhere under cultivation (*zhan duoshao, ken duoshao*) in order to bring about "a dynamic equilibrium in the total amount of cultivated land" (*gengdi zongliang dongtai pingheng*).[11] As a consequence, the preservation of cultivated land (*gengdi*) became the chief concern and guiding principle of the integrated land use plans for which the 1998 Land Management Law provides a detailed legal framework. Land use plans are predicated on the principle that the total amount of cultivated land should not decrease[12] and that at least

80 percent of land should be designated basic agricultural land (*jiben nongtian*), i.e. future re-designation of this land as construction land (*jianshe yongdi*) would require direct approval by the State Council itself.[13] Cultivated land may only be used for basic bulk crops (grain, oilseeds, cotton and, more recently, vegetables). Other agricultural pursuits, such as chicken or pig farms, fishponds, flower beds, fruit orchards or commercial forests, are explicitly forbidden and are only allowed on land outside basic agricultural land plots that fall under the broader category of "agricultural use land" (*nongyongdi*).[14]

The Land Management Law is also explicitly concerned with environmental protection. Although the opening up of wasteland is a cornerstone of the preservation of the total amount of cultivated land, the law stipulates that marginal agricultural land may be given up to nature, particularly land with an inclination of more than 25 degrees that is under acute threat of loss through water and soil erosion. Furthermore, although land reclamation is encouraged and the long-term land use rights of individuals or work units that reclaim land are guaranteed, reclamation may only take place in reclamation zones laid down in the land use plans and after proper "scientific assessment." Furthermore, land reclamation should contribute to the protection and improvement of the environment and prevent soil erosion and desertification, while all reclaimed land suitable for cultivation must be used as such. Forests, grasslands, lakes and floodplains may not be reclaimed.[15]

The 1997 document and the 1998 Land Law involve a powerful mix of modern land use planning, environmental protectionism, state socialist economic planning and a Maoist preoccupation with basic food production at the expense of everything else. If strictly, earnestly and fully implemented, this policy would have stifled the development of rural industry and commercial agriculture. However, the recent grain surpluses and unprecedentedly full granaries convinced the government that subsistence is again less of an issue; as a result, from 1999 onward the pendulum has begun to swing back again and the reigns on rural land use and agriculture have been loosened. However, subsistence has by no means disappeared from the policy agenda, and in recent statements the conflict between the two objectives of economic development and basic food production is displayed openly. However, policy has moved on from simply stating that both objectives have to meet. By the year 2000, China was moving in the direction of having two agricultural policies, one for rich, commercialized areas, and quite another for areas where grain production continues to be the mainstay of the local rural economy. The *Opinion of the Party Centre and the State Council regarding Carrying out Agricultural and Rural Work in the Year 2000* formulates this as follows:

> Grain and other major agricultural products have shifted from a long-term [situation] of supply falling short of demand to a successive

> (*jieduanxing*) [situation] of supply exceeding demand ... Agricultural production that in the past mainly strove to increase production in order to meet basic subsistence needs [now] can stress quality and efficiency on the basis of maintaining stability in total production, and develop in the direction of diversification and high quality ... Main grain producing areas will have to stabilize the [sown] area and raise the output per area unit, improve quality, stabilize and raise the level of grain production. Economically developed coastal areas and areas near large and medium sized cities rationally have to adjust the cultivated ratio of grain and economic crops in order to develop a high-efficiency and foreign exchange-earning (*chuanghui*)[16] agriculture.[17]

The bifurcation in agricultural policy translated directly into a major relaxation in land use policy. Multiple agricultural policies require a selective loosening up of the rigid requirement not to encroach on basic agricultural land. A 1999 document from the Ministry of Land and Resources puts it as follows:

> Currently, each locality is carrying out the work of adjusting the designation of protected areas of basic agricultural land, according to the stipulations of the targets for the protection of agricultural basic land in the integrated land use plan. When adjusting the demarcations of protected areas, consideration should be given to the future direction of the use of land, so that the programme of protected areas of basic agricultural land and the structural adjustment of agricultural production are coordinated and in conformity with each other. Under the condition that the area under the programme of basic agricultural land is assured, [land] with a low productive capacity and deficient productive conditions can be adjusted for future use as general cultivated land outside basic agricultural land (*yiban gengdi yuliu zai jiben nongtian wai*) for fishponds, orchards, or other uses.[18]

The document then continues with a warning that any further changes in land use planning in the future will have to be approved at the provincial level. In other words, local authorities are given a one-off chance to undo the strict designation of basic agricultural land they had just been carrying out under the new national land use plan, provided they can come up with a reasonably credible justification of the need for alternative uses in some unspecified future, and if they can find an equivalent amount of other land that can be designated basic agricultural land instead. We will return to this issue in the context of the case study of Taicang, but in order to do so we first discuss the national regulations for land use planning in some detail.

The national administration of land use planning

The 1998 Land Management Law stipulates in considerable detail the nature, role and administration of the new integrated land use plans that formally cover the period of 15 years between 1995 and 2010, although they often were only drafted some years after 1995. The plans are a major tool to beef up the renewed emphasis on agriculture, cultivated land, grain production and environmental protection entailed in the fundamental shift in agricultural policies detailed in the previous section. The new land use plans thus involve a mid-term correction of the first land use plans connected with the first Land Management Law of 1986, which covered the period between 1985 and 2000.[19]

The first land use plans of 1985–1986 differed in two crucial respects from the second land use plans. First, in 1985–1986 the drafting of local and national plans happened simultaneously, making it in practice very difficult to insert national priorities into local plans. One of the problems here is a familiar one of state socialist planning: in order to meet quotas for agricultural land and still have ample land for non-agricultural development, local authorities reported up to twice as much land under use as there was actually available land (Li 2000: 100). To remedy this problem, the second integrated land use plans were hierarchically drafted and implemented, and included extensive land surveys and "scientific land assessments."[20] Article 21 of the 1998 Land Law requires that all land use plans of provinces, cities of more than one million people, and designated cities be vetted by the State Council. The province must in principle approve all other plans, although provinces may delegate the responsibility of township land use plans to the prefectures.

Higher level plans set clear and non-negotiable parameters and targets for local plans; chiefly, a clear ceiling for the conversion of cultivated land into construction land and also, the preservation of the amount of cultivated land. Local plans are thus forced to balance their targets for cultivated land preservation and conversion with the requirements of local development (Li 2000: 86–87; 99–100). The long-term integrated land use plans are further specified in special land use plans for specific purposes and annual land use plans in which land is allocated to specific projects or purposes. The annual plans are subject to the same drafting and approval procedures as the integrated land use plans.[21]

Second, the 1985–1986 land use plans were predicated on the need to *supply* sufficient construction land rather than being based on the need to *preserve* the total amount of cultivated land. The new land use plans are conceived as a key tool for the preservation of long-term interests of the nation, balancing the availability of an adequate supply of land for the needs of the economic and social development (including commercial agriculture) with the requirements of food grain agriculture and the protection of natural resources and the environment.[22] Land use planning thus involves integrated planning: it has to balance the requirements of all land uses and must plan as a whole the relations between reclamation, use, improvement and protection of land. The actual designation of specific use zones (*tudi liyongqu*) mainly takes place at the lowest level, in the integrated land use plans of counties and townships.[23] A land use zone is a piece of land, possibly a large piece of land, designated relatively uniformly to one particular use. In principle, land in a zone used for other purposes will have to be converted to the use stipulated in the plan. However, not all land in a zone has to be used exclusively for the purpose stipulated in the plan: a small amount of land can be used for other purposes that are needed to support its main use. For instance, some land in basic agricultural protection zones may be used for drainage and irrigation, roads between fields, rows of protective trees, etc. When demarcating a particular zone, both restricted and permitted supplementary uses should be detailed (Li 2000: 92).

Land use zones are divided into agricultural use zones (*nongye liyongqu*), construction use zones (*jianshe liyongqu*), human and natural landscape protection zones (*renwen ji ziran jingguan baohuqu*), land adjustment zones (*tudi zhengliqu*), temporary unused zones (*zan bu liyong qu*) and so forth. These zones in turn can be further divided in several grades. For instance, agricultural land use zones can be divided into basic agricultural land protection zones and ordinary cultivated land zones, cultivated land reclamation zones (*gengdi kankenqu*) into forest and pasture land use zones, and construction land use zones into urban construction land use zones, township and village construction land use zones, industrial and mining land use zones, traffic and water resources land use zones and so on (ibid.: 91).

The land use planning system is predicated on the assumption that land is a key resource that needs careful deployment for a broad range of uses, with the Centre assuming the responsibility for national long-term interests. At each level of government, land use planning should balance the land needs of the line departments concerned, and land use planning should be firmly embedded in overall economic and social development planning. In particular, in drafting the annual land use plans hard bargaining is conducted, because here actual plots will have to be allocated for specific projects (ibid.: 101). Land use involves competing interests of different levels of government and many different agencies at the same administrative level (Zhang 2000: 133–134). Land use plans are the outcome of conflicting considerations of national food self-sufficiency, the maintenance of a baseline of rural subsistence, long-term environmental considerations, the commercialization and specialization of agricultural production, urbanization and industrialization, and the need to guarantee an adequate revenue base for local governments.

In analyzing this policy field, it would be a mistake to think of the Ministry of Land and Resources simply as the guardian of the preservation of agricultural land. The Ministry is responsible for the overall use of land, and I read its position more as an outcome of conflicting pressures brought to bear on it from various parts of the administration than as the result of a specific agenda in its own right. Given the current shift in favour of less restrictive land use policies, it should therefore come as no surprise that the Ministry of Land and Resources openly supports a more developmental use of land. In a recent article, Xie Junqi, a researcher at the Ministry, minces no words in discussing the many problems that remain in China's land use policies. Xie affirms that a powerful incentive still exists on the part of local officials to appropriate land for non-agricultural uses, since the proceeds are retained locally. However, Xie goes even further than this perhaps token admission of conflicting policy objectives and outcomes, criticizing local level land management departments, i.e. the local line departments of his own ministry, for their self-interested "leftist" position, for their lack of support for economic construction and for squandering opportunities (2001: 123–124).

Under the current system, the difficulties in implementing the policy of protecting agricultural land are made to rest squarely on the shoulders of local governments, yet it is acknowledged that these governments also have a responsibility for local economic development. This conflict between policy objectives yet awaits adequate institutional arrangements, despite the requirement that township land use plans should be drafted against the background of the interests of landowners and users. Furthermore, when finalized, land use plans should be made public and should specify and guarantee the rights of land users and land owners (Li 2000: 93–94). Still missing are clear procedures for the expression, coordination and mediation of the many different interests regarding land use. A more democratic, or at least accountable, land planning regime in China could potentially provide a way out of the bureaucratic infighting and stalemates that have characterized China's land policies for so long. In this regard, statements at the national legislative work conference of the Ministry of Land and Resources in early July 2001 are of considerable interest. At the conference, Land and Resources Minister Tian Fengshan called for a more open legislative process inviting wide public discussion, which would not only allow people to have their own say in what should be done as far as land use is concerned, but should also serve as a check on officials at all levels of the ministry, "because it will for the first time force them to think more from the point of view of the managed, instead of their usual perspective as managers."[24] Clearly, for those concerned with the use of land, that most precious of resources, this is an area to watch very carefully.

Land use planning: a view from Taicang

The many contradictions in China's national agricultural and land use policies have produced a confusing array of incentives and disincentives across the Chinese administration. However, their full ramifications only become apparent when we observe land use planning in a particular locality and in the context of the implementation of other reform policies, chiefly the reform of the administrative and taxation system and the privatization of China's rural collective enterprises. Below, I will look at the situation in Taicang, one of my long-term field sites.[25]

Rural development and the rise of land use planning

Taicang is a county-level municipality (*xianji shi*) in the easternmost part of southern Jiangsu, bordering on Shanghai municipality in the East and the Yangtze River in the North. Like so many other counties in Shanghai and southern Jiangsu, Taicang took full advantage of the opportunity granted by the reforms and its favourable location close to Shanghai. By the 1990s Taicang had developed a thriving township and village enterprises sector and two county-level foreign investment zones. Already in the mid-1980s some of the more enterprising villages found it increasingly difficult to persuade villagers employed in village and township enterprises to continue growing grain and cotton beyond what they needed to provision themselves. As a result, large-scale farming (*guimo jingying*, literally "scale management") was implemented. By the mid-1990s, in the industrially most successful villages all responsibility land (*zeren tian*) had been divided up in what were locally called "small farms" (*xiao nongchang*) of ten to more than one hundred mu[26] of land, rented out on three- or five-year contracts. Contractors of village land were either local villagers, or, in the richer villages, outsiders from poorer areas in Jiangsu or Zhejiang province. The village food grain land (*kouliang tian*) continued to be cultivated by individual households. Yet on both the household food grain land and the contracted small farms much of the work of ploughing, sowing, irrigating and harvesting was actually done by specialized agricultural service teams (*nongye fuwudui*) of the village. In some of the richer villages these services were provided free of charge, at least until 1999 when new regulations required villages to privatize the agricultural service teams.

The main objective of the small farms was to grow enough grain to fulfil the state procurement quotas, and villages were much less (if at all) interested in any profit that the village might make. Contractors themselves were usually recruited from the ranks of the "floating population" (labour migrants, *liudong renkou*) in Shanghai and southern Jiangsu, to whom contracting agricultural land simply was an alternative to wage labour in construction or industry. As a result, large-scale farming in

Taicang only bore a superficial resemblance to commercial and entrepreneurial agriculture. The "small farms" were the outcome of *de facto* re-collectivization of land by strongly corporatist villages.[27] Contracting was a cheap and labour-efficient way for such villages to ensure that its land remained under cultivation and that its grain quota obligations were fulfilled. The contractors of the land more resembled contract labourers than innovative entrepreneurs. Large-scale agriculture in Taicang is best interpreted as a specific development that continues ownership forms and patterns of agricultural production of the collective period.

As elsewhere in China, from 1995 onward the Taicang Land Management Bureau (later the Land and Resources Bureau, *Guotu Guanli Ju*)[28] and the Department of Agricultural Work of the Communist Party (*Nonggong Bu*) started work on the county and township integrated land use plans, whose drafting and implementation became a national binding requirement with the passage of the 1998 Land Law.[29] As far as agricultural land was concerned, three types of land were distinguished: (1) planning zones (*guihuaqu*) and pre-allocated zones (*yuliuqu*); (2) first-grade agricultural land protection zones (*yiji nongtian baohuqu*); and (3) ordinary agricultural land (*yiban nongye yongdi*). The allocation of land to any of these three categories took the township as unit; the objective was to reach a sensible mix of the three types of land suited to the local economic structure of the township in question.

The pre-allocated land (*yuliudi*) of the planning zones is agricultural or fallow land that has been earmarked for non-agricultural use at some point in time during the 15-year term of the land-use plan.[30] In contrast, the basic agricultural land (*jiben nongtian*) in agricultural land protection zones must remain under crop cultivation and cannot be diverted to other uses, agricultural or otherwise, except for large national projects. However, the establishment of the third category of ordinary agricultural land lends the system a flexibility that is not immediately apparent when we only look at national regulations and laws. Pre-allocated land is, as a rule, located along township roads, while basic agricultural land is mostly village land somewhat removed from roads. Ordinary agricultural land is located adjacent to pre-allocated land, and can be re-assigned to non-agricultural uses if the need arises. Ordinary agricultural land thus provides a buffer against the full impact of the agricultural land protection policy, because it does not require the inhibitive provincial approval that conversion of basic agricultural land does.[31]

The flexibility granted by the category of ordinary agricultural land and the fact that the amount of pre-allocated land is determined on the basis of the developmental needs and potential of the township in question suffice to take off the rough edges from the 1997–1998 restrictive land use policy. Furthermore, as my Taicang informants made clear, the allocation of land to either of the three categories does not take place on the basis of the suitability for agriculture of the plot in question, but on the basis of the suitability of the land for non-agricultural uses, which is what local governments in Taicang are primarily concerned with. In other words, the adequate supply of land for a variety of uses is still the guiding principle in practice, instead of the preservation of cultivated land, as the 1998 Land Law intended.

Moreover, by capitalizing on the indeterminacy of higher-level directives, the government in Taicang has made sure that each township was allocated a planning zone for its own development and as a source of revenue. As one of the two deputy heads of the Taicang National Land Management Bureau said, "The higher levels require that not each and every township set up its own planning zone, but they also have not abolished the township land use plans, although as a rule there are no plans at the level of villages. Concretely, we have acted to suit measures to local circumstances."[32] Arguably, the continued dispersed pattern of land not designated as basic agricultural land will perpetuate the scattered "desakota" pattern of industry and built-up areas (Guldin 1996). While this may constitute an inefficient use of land from a central planner's point of view, locally dispersion also guarantees a more equitable distribution of developmental opportunities.

Revenue, subsistence and land

The government of Taicang in its land use planning seems to have successfully balanced compliance with national desires and developmental needs of the townships under its jurisdiction. Local officials were confident that the amount of pre-allocated and ordinary agricultural land would be more than adequate for the needs of all developmental projects until the expiration of the current plan in 2010. However, not all is well in Taicang, and land and agriculture are very much at the heart of the matter.

Having an adequate supply of non-agricultural land has recently become even more important for local governments. In the mid-1990s, Taicang's once booming rural industries began to share in the woes of collective enterprises across China. First, collective enterprises were increasingly hamstrung by welfare and other obligations to their workforce similar to state-owned enterprises (referred to as "work-unit-ization" (*danweihua*) in one Chinese publication on the subject, Mao 2000). As a result, collective enterprises lost the competitive edge that had made them so successful in the 1980s and early 1990s. Second, as demonstrated by Dan Buck's work in the rural counties of Shanghai municipality (Buck 2002), the boom of rural industry in the area had been heavily dependent on subcontracts with urban state-owned enterprises. These enterprises came under increasing competitive pressure in the 1990s. Seeking ways and means to lower their production costs, state-owned enterprises shifted to private rural subcontractors who did not have to bear the increasingly heavy labour costs affecting the competitiveness of collective rural enterprises.[33]

Consequently, townships and villages found themselves forced to go along with the logic of the continuing process of marketization of the Chinese economy and privatize all but a few successful and usually larger collective enterprises that often also were the main employers of the local peasantry (Buck 2002; Chen, Y. 1998b; Li and Rozelle 2000; Lin and Ye 1998; Putterman 1997; Smyth 1998). Both my own work in Taicang and Dan Buck's work in rural Shanghai show that such large, successful collective enterprises retained their collective identity under shareholding systems that gave management, workers and the village/township all shares in the enterprise. Only later did these shareholding arrangements evolve to give management (quite often former village or township cadres) full control, if not outright ownership of these firms, often at heavily discounted prices (Buck 2002).[34]

Until the first round of privatization of collective enterprises was completed in 1997, land ownership was mainly important to villages and townships in Taicang as an asset which they could use to attract investment, thus generating employment for the local population and revenue from management fees (*guanlifei*), profit sharing (*fenhong*), charges (*tanpai*), loans (*jizi*) and voluntary contributions (*mujuan*) extracted from the enterprises and the local rich. However, with the privatization of their collective enterprises, townships and villages were forced to agree to deals that not only terminated their formal ownership of the enterprises, but also many of their legal or illegal claims on the funds generated by these enterprises. At the same time, village and township budgets were much curtailed and more strictly controlled by higher levels of government as part of the reform of the taxation system.[35]

Tax reform and the crisis and privatization of the TVE sector meant that townships and villages have become much more financially reliant on nationally regulated sources of revenue, chiefly the retention of a stipulated percentage of local taxes, supplemented by the income from the sale or renting out of land use rights. Management fees, charges and voluntary contributions have not disappeared altogether, in fact, the whole state apparatus below the county level would arguably collapse overnight if this were to happen, but have nevertheless been much curtailed. With it, not the enterprises and the local rich themselves, but the land that the enterprises occupy has now become a major source of income for townships and villages. The sale or rent of land use rights now is the main way to share in the fruits of local development, making the allocation of as much land as possible for non-agricultural use a matter of sheer survival to local governments and cadres: their budgets and, even more directly, the payment of their own salaries now depend on their ability to raise revenue from the sale or rent of land use rights.[36]

Accordingly, in the current land use plans in Taicang, industry and infrastructure have been adequately taken care of. However, we should not immediately conclude in the spirit of the 1998 Land Law that this is problematic on the grounds that it threatens China's long-term food supply. Contrary to national concerns about grain production and the preservation of agricultural land, the problem in Taicang is not that there is not enough land or grain, but rather that there is in fact too much cultivated land that is kept under grain rather than having been put to other, more productive uses, agricultural or otherwise.

As we have seen, by the late 1990s, China became caught in the contradiction between increasingly large grain surpluses and new policies that insisted on the preservation of agricultural land. The glut in grain led the state to abolish the mandatory grain quota system across China. Consequently, in 1999 Taicang's grain procurement quotas were much relaxed. They disappeared altogether in 2000, which only left the national requirements to keep designated agricultural land under crop cultivation and to buy all grain produced at fair, i.e. subsidized prices.[37] Yet despite these requirements, grain purchasing prices dropped considerably, although not as much as they would have without subsidies. In Guizhuang township in Taicang, for instance, the state grain procurement department purchased all grain supplied by farmers at a price of 0.05 yuan per *jin* (= 0.5 kilograms) higher than the official state guaranteed price, a subsidy paid for by the township government. Such local grain purchase subsidies (in addition to the national subsidy already built into the state guaranteed price) are much encouraged by the national level. In 2000, in the whole of Taicang 2.2 million jin of grain was bought at this price, compared to 870,000 jin of grain purchases under the old quota system two years earlier. This growth in purchases occurred despite the fact that the current guaranteed price of 0.66 yuan per jin (0.61 yuan state guaranteed price plus 0.05 yuan per jin subsidy from the township) was still substantially below both the old quota price of 0.76 yuan and also marginally lower than the negotiated (over-quota) price of 0.67 yuan per jin in 1998, which in turn had been lower than the equivalent prices in 1997.[38]

The current policies of disallowing fallowing, selling, or transferring basic agricultural land in conjunction with low, but still heavily subsidized grain prices and the new 30-year land contracts granted to farmers in 1998 seem to combine the worst of both worlds, making it almost impossible to break through the developmental stalemate currently confronting Taicang agriculture. Both household village farmers and large-scale contract farmers keep their land under grain simply because they are required to do so and have no other readily available uses for the land. Yet the income that this generates can no longer compare with employment in local industry, the service sector, or, particularly in the case of large-scale contract farmers, a return to employment in Shanghai.[39] Consequently, contract farmers often abandon their farms completely after the expiration of their contract, while both contract and household farmers have given up winter wheat cultivation and concentrate on the summer rice crop which is at least still marginally profitable, a practice that township governments now are beginning to condone despite the national regulations against fallowing land.

Other contract farmers try their hand at vegetable or fruit cultivation. This has only met with limited success: their contracts are too short (three or five years) to make long-term investments, such as planting fruit or other commercial trees, worthwhile. Furthermore, Taicang's long-standing focus on grain and cotton means that it lacks the infrastructure in agricultural extension to provide farmers with suitable crop varieties or agricultural technologies, and only a small part of the land can be brought under intensive vegetable cultivation anyway. Under current policies it is forbidden to use crop land for other purposes, even other agricultural uses such as livestock breeding or fish farming, although local cadres now try their very best to give special dispensation for such ventures if at all possible. On the other hand, state and township grain price subsidies do prevent grain agriculture from becoming so unrewarding that contract farmers and local household farmers simply have no choice but to abandon grain farming altogether. This seems only to postpone the inevitable decline of grain farming in Taicang; indeed, the trend has already been set by the abandonment of winter wheat cultivation.

However, it would be unfair to blame only conservative national policies for this state of affairs. The shake-out, privatization and mass redundancies in the TVE sector between 1995 and 1998 confirmed to many farmers, particularly, the older ones whose chances of finding new non-farm employment were slim, that holding on to their contract land would provide them with at least a minimum subsistence guarantee should they lose their job. In fact, when made redundant between 1995 and 1998, quite a few older TVE employees asked their villages to return their contract land to them. Fortunately, non-agricultural employment, particularly in the private service sector, picked up again after 1998: township officials in Guizhuang claimed in 2001 that almost nobody under 35 years of age works in agriculture anymore. In fact, in 2001 only 20 per cent of the rural households wholly or predominantly depended on agriculture, a figure that still stood at 30 per cent in 1998.[40]

Yet the worst point in the crisis of the TVE sector coincided with the start of the second term of land contracts in 1998, which the national Land Law required to be fixed for 30 years. The renewal of land contracts thus froze an employment and landholding structure of the local economy at the point when it was more depressed than it had ever been since the start of the reforms. Instead of having to deal with a relatively few short-term land contractors, the local authorities are now faced with a much larger number of subsistence farmers than in the past, farmers moreover who in future could only be made to give up their land with great difficulty, yet who also not necessarily put their land to the best possible use, but simply use it for their own subsistence needs and unemployment insurance.[41]

Conclusion

The new land use planning system described in this chapter has been a major step forward in China, putting in place a major administrative instrument to facilitate and regulate land use needs that will help the government to chart a course of long-term sustainable and equitable economic development. However, serious deficiencies in the system remain, specifically the lack of transparency and accountability in weighting conflicting interests in drafting land use plans, but one can at least have some degree of confidence that gradual improvements will be made as the government gains more experience with the administration of land planning.

Yet the outcomes of any administrative system, including land use planning ultimately hinge on the political processes that determine its incentive structure and objectives. Land is both a scarce national resource, a source of local revenue and the final guarantee of subsistence to the rural population. In such a situation there are unlikely to be "correct" solutions to clearly defined "problems." Continuous assessment of the trade-offs between the many aims that have to be catered for, and subsequent adjustments to the plans, are the best one can aim for. In this chapter, I have tried to show how this process of re-assessment and re-adjustment was at work before, during and especially after the passing of the 1998 Land Law, when it became clear that grain production was not the acute problem that the Chinese government and certain foreign observers thought it to be in 1994 and 1995, and the use of land for commercial agriculture and industrial development was again given more leeway, especially in more developed areas.

However, as illustrated by the Taicang experience, this national policy re-assessment and the bifurcation of rural development strategies that followed from it have not gone far enough. The national government's use of land planning to preserve agricultural land has kept land under grain, thus supplementing the incentives provided by price subsidies. Furthermore, the new 30-year land contracts create a powerful constituency of farmers who can keep their land as a final subsistence guarantee, while at the same time giving local governments few instruments to force these farmers actually to grow grain.

This conflicting and contradictory mix of policies has locked a highly developed and commercialized place like Taicang in a sub-optimal and costly land use pattern. In my view, the only alternative for such developed areas would be to bite the bullet and abandon both the current land use plans and land tenure system that fragment agricultural land into innumerable tiny plots and prohibit putting much of this land to non-agricultural uses. As a first step, subsistence grain farmers should be allowed to fallow their land not only in winter but also in summer. Farmers should also be allowed freely to mortgage or sell their land use rights to raise money for commercial ventures, agricultural or otherwise. Discontinuing the price subsidies for grain produced by these subsistence farmers should speed up this process, but simultaneously the government should be given the right to buy up any land fallowed and not put to any other uses for two consecutive years.[42]

Instead of the right to land, the rural population (either as individual households or collectively as villages) should be given the opportunity to use funds raised from mortgaging, renting out, or selling their land use rights to buy themselves into self-funded government-guaranteed social insurance schemes similar to those that currently being set up for much of the urban population. Land thus appropriated from subsistence farmers should then be combined in large, continuous holdings and its use rights sold or leased to entrepreneurs for heavily capitalized, extensive large-scale farms, forests, orchards, fishponds, or indeed non-agricultural enterprises. In order to ameliorate the potentially damaging consequences this might have on social and economic inequality in the countryside, revenue raised in this way ought to be earmarked for funding equal access for the rural population to health care, education, social security, retirement and life insurance. One way this could be done is by subsidizing for the poorer members of the rural population the premiums payable for insurance schemes in these areas; another way would be to provide these services at a reduced rate or even free of charge to people below a certain income threshold.

I do appreciate that there are many issues that have to be carefully considered in implementing these suggestions, not the least of which is the vast opportunities for graft that the sale of land use rights will give to local officials. However, without wishing to deny the seriousness of such matters, I do believe that an important point of principle is at stake here that comes prior to the practicalities of implementation, namely a fundamental reconsideration of what it means to be a Chinese rural citizen and, following from that, what rights and duties such rural citizens should have and how these should be enforced. For the radical changes that have been outlined here to happen, I would argue, the central state will therefore have to make a much more radical break with its conservative agricultural and land use policies. These arguably still make sense for China's poorer areas that still predominantly depend on subsistence agriculture, but are no longer suited to rapidly developing places like Taicang. In other words, the *de facto* dual track agricultural and land policies embarked on recently should be formalized and strengthened. However, for this to happen, the national government will have to accept that access to land in the more developed parts of China should no longer be treated as a right and subsistence guarantee for the rural population. In fact, treating the whole of rural China as an undifferentiated sector locked in a traditional subsistence economy and as somehow fundamentally different from the cities is a legacy of the collective period that was already ill-founded then and has become even more of a political liability with each passing year.

The population of developed rural areas has much more in common with the inhabitants of towns and cities than with subsistence farmers in more isolated parts of the countryside. However, if this fact is to be incorporated in future policy-making, the central government will also have to acknowledge that, apart from strategic considerations, there is no reason why China should wish to feed itself by propping up a grain sector that is not only increasingly costly, but also hamstrings the development of a modern and diversified rural economy. Only if the national government fundamentally reconsiders its rural developmental strategy along these lines can the potential of rural land use planning to promote and guide comprehensive economical development be fully realized.

Acknowledgements

This chapter was first presented at the panel "Rural Land in China: Land Rights and Sustainable Use." Second International Convention of Asia Scholars (ICAS), Berlin, 9–12 August 2001, and subsequently at the Max Planck Institute for Social Anthropology in Halle on 1 March 2002. I would like to thank all those who participated in the discussion on those two occasions, and especially Rick Edmonds, Chris Hann, John Flower and Pamela Leonard. I would also like to thank Peter Ho for a very careful and constructive reading of the manuscript, and Mark Selden for insisting that I never forget about class struggle, persuasively arguing that I address the problems of corruption and inequality that might be caused by my recommendations.

Notes

1 "Tudi liyong guihua shishi guanli gongzuo ruogan yijian", Ministry of Land and Resources (Guotu Ziyuan Bu), 9 May 2000. *Zhonghua Renmin Gongheguo Guowuyuan Gongbao* 2000(34), 27.

2 A further third area of conflicting policy objectives that has become increasingly important in China is the environment. Here, land use planning is caught between, on the one hand, environmental protection and sustainable development, and, on the other, the need to open up land for agriculture, industry and urban development. In the discussion below, I will refer to this area of contradictions where relevant, but in less detail than to the first two areas. The reason for this is that as policy areas land use policy and environmental protection are not connected in my field site of Taicang that is the main case study presented in this chapter. In Taicang, "the environment" refers to the industrial pollution of surface water, the air and specific plots of land. By contrast, "the environment" in the context of national land use policy concerns deforestation, desertification and erosion. This issue simply is not relevant in Taicang that has no forests and hardly any fallow land left. John Flower and Pamela Leonard (2002) present a highly instructive case study of the

complexities of the trade-offs between forest protection, tourism and subsistence agriculture in a remote village in western Sichuan. When read together, the contribution of Flower and Leonard and my own study provide compelling evidence for the main conclusion of this chapter that nationally uniform agricultural and land policies simply do not work in a country as large and diverse as China.

3 This sudden policy change was reportedly also caused by ill-founded worries on China's long-term food supply after the publication of Lester Brown's controversial book *Who Will Feed China?* (1995); see Li (2001: 4). Originally, the policy was intended only to devolve the supply and distribution of grain to the provinces, not to make provinces self-sufficient in terms of production. But this quickly changed when it transpired that provinces with a grain surplus simply reduced their production now that they no longer had to deliver a set quota to the Centre, forcing grain-deficient provinces to grow more and become self-sufficient in terms of grain production. I am grateful to Eduard Vermeer for pointing this out to me in a conversation on 9 August 2001.

4 The first national policies that made it possible for farmers to take up employment in the cities date from 1984–1988 (Huang and Pieke 2003: 32). Likewise, full official endorsement of township and village enterprises (TVEs) dates from 1984, although the importance of such enterprises had already been acknowledged from the onset of the reforms in 1978 (Byrd and Lin 1990: 10–11). A useful source on progressive thinking on policy-making for the development of the rural economy in the 1980s is the collection of speeches delivered by Du Runsheng, the chief advisor of the then premier Zhao Ziyang (Du 1995).

5 In the long term, an important caveat here is that the expansion of the amount of irrigated land keep pace with the projected increase in demand for grain; see Heilig *et al.* (2000).

6 Chapter 3 ("Overall land use planning") and Chapter 4 ("Protection of agricultural land") of the Land Management Law of the People's Republic of China (Zhonghua Renmin Gongheguo tudi guanli fa), adopted at the Fourth Conference of the Standing Committee of the Ninth National People's Congress, 29 August 1998. Reprinted in *Zhonghua Renmin Gongheguo falü fagui quanshu* (Beijing: Zhongguo Minzhu Fazhi Chubanshe, 2000), pp. 229–235.

7 For arguments for and against, see Smil (1999: 428) and Zhang *et al.* (1997: 76). The main issue here seems to be whether or not the limit for gains in bulk grain production has been reached, given China's labour-intensive production and fragmented land holding patterns.

8 In my research on overseas Chinese home areas in Fujian, my co-workers and I have also found ample evidence of such practices. Farmers eager to emigrate even pay the agricultural tax and other charges to in-migrants who sub-contract their land and fulfil their grain quota. Interestingly, this policy has thus led to the growth of a local migration system that supports and complements international migration (Pieke *et al.* 2004; Thunø and Pieke 2005).

9 In direct contradiction with the policy of giving all rural households increasingly longer tenure rights are the frequent calls to allow specialization in large-scale grain farming in the hope of gaining some of the economies of scale found in, for instance, North American grain farming (Wan and Cheng 2001: 184–185; Zhang *et al.* 1997, 74). However, the evidence on large-scale grain farming increasingly points to the fact that there are actually hardly any economies of scale that can be exploited in China's agriculture, given the labour-intensive nature of production, widespread under-employment of labour and a very low land–labour ratio (Li, Rozelle and Brandt 1998; Liu and Zhuang 2000; Wan and Cheng 2001). Its questionable economic gains have contributed to the fact that large-scale farming has never really take off as a

national policy, although it continues to surface in policy documents on agricultural development and is an important feature in many economically highly developed rural areas. I will return to the latter point in section 5 below when I discuss some of the findings of my fieldwork in Taicang county.

10 A particular bugbear in policy documents of the late 1990s was golf links, constructed as part of the booming tourism and leisure industry, particularly in coastal China. Condemnation of the construction of opulent houses, graves and tombs, on the other hand, is a direct leftover from the collective era, when Communist suspicion of private wealth and superstition blended with the need to preserve agricultural land.

11 Articles 18, 19 and 31, 1998 Land Law.

12 Article 31, 1998 Land Law.

13 Articles 34 and 45, 1998 Land Law.

14 See Article 36, 1998 Land Law, which stipulates that no basic agricultural land shall be converted to use for forestry, orchards or fishponds. The distinction between basic agriculture (*nongye*) and non-essential agriculture, considered merely part of "sideline production" (*fuye*), can be traced back a long time and follows directly from the priorities set by the Maoist development strategy, showing that the Chinese Communist Party, when it feels under pressure, quite easily reverts back to old habits.

15 Articles 38, 39 and 40, 1998 Land Law. Article 39 restricting the reclamation of wasteland was inserted at the last minute after disastrous floods in 1998 caused widespread concern in China about soil erosion, water management and climate change. See also Li (2000: 122–125).

16 *Chuanghui* is a term usually associated with spin-off or subsidiary enterprises set up to earn the cash that the main activity of a company, village, or other unit cannot raise. In this context it is used interchangeably with *chuangshou*, "creating income" and does not necessarily entail earning foreign exchange. Using the term in the context of agriculture is unusual, and indicative of the new, enterprising spirit in agriculture that the document calls for. For further details on the terms chuangshou and chuanghui, see Pieke (1996, Chapter 4) and Pieke (1995).

17 "Zhonggong Zhongyang, Guowuyuan guanyu zuohao erlinglingling nian nongye he nongcun gongzuo de yijian" (Opinion of the Party Centre and the State Council regarding carrying out agricultural and rural work in the year 2000). *Zhonghua Renmin Gongheguo Guowuyuan Gongbao* 2000(9), 4–5.

18 "Guanyu gaohao nongyong di guanli cujin nongye shengchan jiegou tiaozheng gongzuo de tongzhi" (Announcement on the correct handling of the work on the management of land for agricultural use and the structural adjustment of the agricultural production structure), document no. 511 (1999) of the Ministry of Land and Resources (Guotu Ziyuan Bu). *Zhonghua Renmin Gongheguo Guowuyuan Gongbao* 2000(15), 35. Similar points are made in a key document of the following year, "Tudi liyong guihua shishi guanli gongzuo ruogan yijian", Ministry of Land and Resources (Guotu Ziyuan Bu), 9 May 2000. *Zhonghua Renmin Gongheguo Guowuyuan Gongbao* 2000(34), 27–29 (see also note 1).

19 Li (2000: 99–100) describes in brief the key policy developments regarding land use planning between 1986 and 1996.

20 Article 28, 1998 Land Law. According to Li Yuan's explanation of this article, land surveys identify plots of land on the basis of ownership type, boundaries, area, use type, grade and level. The latter two criteria refer to the quality of the land relative to the other plots of land in the area. "Grade" refers to the overall quality of a town or city for a particular use of land, while "level" specifies the quality for a particular use of specific plots of land within that city or town.

As far as agricultural use is concerned, grades are assigned within national agricultural areas. Levels are assigned at the county level. The main criteria for grades are land quality, long-term stability of natural conditions, potential development of land productivity and effectiveness of land use. For levels, the criteria are only slightly different, namely land quality, mutability of natural conditions, and the level and effectiveness of use (Li 2000: 106).

21 Article 24, 1998 Land Law.

22 Article 17, 1998 Land Law. Key phrases here are the terms land improvement (*tudi zhengzhi*) and "land adjustment" (*tudi zhengli*), which are elaborated on further in Article 41 of the 1988 Land Law. These terms refer to comprehensive rationalizations of land use patterns and the improvement of the quality of the land in "land improvement zones" designated as such in the integrated land use plans. The mobilizational ethos expressed in Article 17 reveals more than an echo of similar efforts in the collective period, but arguably there is an important difference here in that the new land improvement plans are not limited to agriculture, but cover improvement and rationalization of all types of land for the full range of rural land uses, including irrigation, roads, forests and built-up areas. The overall objective is to increase the effective total acreage of cultivated land, and to improve the conditions of agricultural production and the environment. For a detailed discussion, see Li (2000: 125–128).

23 Article 20, 1998 Land Law.

24 "Public Given Their Say on Land Use", *The China Daily* 7 July, 2001, 2.

25 The Taicang case study is part of a long-term research project on rural China, in which I focus on the intended and unintended outcomes of the interplay of reform of the economy and the administration at the village and township level. Fieldwork in Taicang was carried out in September 1996, March 1998 and most recently in April 2001 together with Professors She (Zhe) Xiaoye and Chen Yingying of the Institute of Sociology of the Chinese Academy of Social Sciences. Professors She and Chen recently published their findings in She (Zhe) and Chen (2000). Each fieldwork trip to Taicang typically took two weeks. Fieldwork entailed the collection of local statistics and printed documentation, in addition to interviews with cadres at the county and township levels that provided the backdrop to interviews with village cadres, entrepreneurs and households in one selected village that was the main field site. During a typical two-week visit, I conducted between 20 and 30 interviews. Returning to the same counties and villages three or four times in the course of several years helped emulate some of the advantages of long-term fieldwork while highlighting changes and processes that take several years to make their impact and consequences fully felt.

26 One mu of land is one-sixth of an acre, or 667 square metres.

27 Corporatism refers to the strength of the village as a local economic and political actor, particularly in terms of investing in and running its own enterprises, see Chen, W. 1998, Christiansen and Zhang (1998), Lin (1995), Oi (1992, 1999), Pei (1998), She (Zhe) (1997).

28 In 1998 or 1999, the National Land Management Bureau was merged with the National Oceanographic Bureau and the the National Bureau of Mapping and Survey, forming the new Ministry of Land and Resources, and their counterparts at lower levels of government followed suit (Zhong 1999: 215).

29 The information below was gathered in an interview with the two deputy heads of the Taicang National Land Management Bureau (Guotu Guanli Ju) on 26 April 2001.

30 The 15-year term of land use plans is stipulated in Article 9 of the Implementation Regulations of the Land Management Law of the People's Republic of

China (Zhonghua Renmin Gongheguo Tudi Guanli Fa Shishi Tiaoli), executive order no. 256 of the State Council of the People's Republic of China, 27 December 1998. Reprinted in *Zhonghua Renmin Gongheguo falü fagui quanshu* (Beijing: Zhongguo Minzhu Fazhi Chubanshe, 2000), 236–240. In actual fact, the current land use plans run from 1997 until 2010 (Zhong 1999: 217).

31 The distinction between agricultural protection land and ordinary agricultural land is based on articles 34 and 45 of the 1998 Land Law. The distinction also features prominently in the 1999 and 2000 documents of the Ministry of Land and Resources referred to above.

32 The latter phrase (to suit measures to local circumstances, *yindi zhiyi*), occurs frequently in national documents, and is a convenient way to allow localities considerable leeway, while at the same time lending them a semblance of conformity to national objectives.

33 From this analysis of events Buck draws the important conclusion that "while the neo-liberal literature argues that clear property rights at the local level thus induce greater economic efficiency, what is really at stake here is the rural labor regime that emerged with the SOE-TVE nexus in the 1980s" (2002: 294)

34 The main reason that this was allowed to happen seems to have been that only in 1998 were multiple ownership forms of township and village enterprises for southern Jiangsu endorsed at the national level with Party Secretary Jiang Zemin's visit to the area in April 1998. See *Jiang Zemin tongzhi zai Jiangsu kaocha xiangzhen qiye shi de jianghua* (Speech of Comrade Jiang Zemin in Jiangsu during His Inspection of Township and Village Enterprises, mimeo, 21 April 1998), pp. 6–7. This followed the national re-affirmation of the theory of the primary stage of socialism and multiple ownership forms at the 15th National Congress of the Chinese Communist Party held between 12 and 18 September 1997. This policy was subsequently re-affirmed at the Third Plenum of the 15th Central Committee of the Chinese Communist Party held in November 1998. The formal sanction by the Centre was important in southern Jiangsu, whose collective model of rural development (the "Jiangsu model") had long been a prominent part in government thinking on the issue of socialism and market reform. Its abandonment in Jiangsu itself was bound to have major ideological and political implications reaching far beyond the area itself.

35 For details on recent tax and budgetary reforms in southern Jiangsu, see Whiting (2001). Additional information was obtained in interviews with the Taicang Finance Bureau (Caizheng Ju) on 30 April 2001, Guizhuang township officials on 29 April 2001 and the party secretary of the village that is my primary fieldsite in Taicang on 27 April 2001.

36 This dependency on land for income would arguably have become even stronger under the "tax-for-fees" (*fei gai shui*) reform of village and township finances, due to be implemented in Taicang in the spring of 2001. However, experiments with this reform in Anhui province have revealed that, despite the fact that such a reform much reduces the "peasant burden" (*nongmin de fudan*), it also make the continuation of village administration and the provisions that come with it almost impossible (Jiang 2001: Zhu, B. 2001a). During a visit to China in July 2001, I was told that for this reason the implementation of the tax-for-fees reform in other provinces, including Jiangsu, had been called off.

37 Taicang lagged behind many other areas in China, where the abolition of grain quotas had happened several years earlier.

38 Interview with the standing head of Guizhuang township, Taicang, 29 April 2001.

39 The minimum income that a large-scale contract farmer expects is around 5–6,000 yuan per year, which at the current grain prices translates into a 35 mu farm.

40 Interview with the standing head of Guizhuang township, Taicang, 29 April 2001.

41 Interview with the standing head of Guizhuang township, Taicang, 29 April 2001.

42 This would in fact not require any new legislation as Article 37 of the 1998 Land Law stipulates just that. The difference will of course be that the land law's intention is to bring the land back under cultivation, whereas the proposal here is to put re-appropriated land simply to its most profitable use.

References

Ash, Robert F. (1988) "The Evolution of Agricultural Policy", *The China Quarterly*, 116: 529–555.

Ash, Robert F. and Edmonds, Richard Louis (1996) "China's Land Resources, Environment and Agricultural Production", *The China Quarterly*, 156: 836–879.

Brown, George P. (1995) "Arable Land Loss in Rural China: Policy and Implementation in Jiangsu Province", *Asian Survey*, 35: 922–940.

Brown, Lester Russell (1995) *Who Will Feed China? Wake-up Call for a Small Planet*, London: Earthscan.

Buck, Daniel (2002) "Constructing China's Capitalism: Connecting Shanghai's Urban and Rural Industries", PhD, thesis, University of California, Berkeley.

Byrd, William A. and Qingsong Lin (1990) "China's Rural Industry: An Introduction", in W.A. Byrd and Qingsong Lin (eds) *China's Rural Industry: Structure, Development, and Reform*, Oxford: Oxford University Press, pp. 3–18.

Carter, Colin A. (2001) "China's Trade Integration and Impacts on Factor Markets", in OECD (ed) *China's Agriculture in the International Trading System*, Paris: OECD, pp. 71–88.

Chen, Weixing (1998) "The Political Economy of Rural Industrialization in China: Village Conglomerates in Shandong Province", *Modern China*, 24: 3–96.

Chen, Yong-sheng (1998) "The Development of Mainland China's Township and Village Enterprises: Is the Third Sector Sustainable?" *Issues & Studies*, 34: 29–55.

Christiansen, Flemming and Junzuo Zhang (1998) "The Village Revisited", in F. Christiansen and Junzho Zhang (eds) *Village Inc.: China's Rural Society in the 1990s*, Richmond: Curzon Press, pp. 1–21.

Du, Runsheng (1995) *Reform and Development in Rural China*, Houndsmills: Macmillan.

Du, Ying (2001) "China's Agricultural Restructuring and System Reform under Its Accession to WTO," in OECD (ed.) *China's Agriculture in the International Trading System*, Paris: OECD, pp. 52–60.

Edin, Maria (2003) "State Capacity and Local Agent Control in China: CCP Cadre Management from a Township Perspective", *The China Quarterly*, 173: 35–52.

Fahlbeck, Erik and Zuhui Huang (1997) "The Property Right Structure of Farmland and Family Farming in China: An Analysis of Developing Options", in (OECD) (ed.), *Agricultural Policies in China*, Paris: OECD, pp. 78–87.

Flower, John and Leonard, Pamela (2002) *Bifeng Gorge Nature Park: The Ownership of Landscape in Postsocialist China*, Halle: Max Planck Institute for Social Anthropology Working Paper no. 41.

Guldin, Gregory Eliyu (1996) "Desakotas and Beyond: Urbanization in Southern China", *Ethnology*, 35: 265–283.

Guo, Xiaolin (2001) "Land Expropriation and Rural Conflicts in China", *The China Quarterly*, 166: 422–439.

Heilig, Gerhard K., Fischer, Günther and van Velthuizen, Harrij (2000) "Can China Feed Itself? An Analysis of China's Food Prospects with Special Reference to Water Resources", *International Journal of Sustainable Development and World Ecology*, 7: 153–172.

Hu, Wei (1997) "Household Land Tenure Reform in China: Its Impacts on Farming Land Use and Agro-environment", *Land Use Policy*, 14: 175–186.

Huang, Ping and Pieke, Frank N. (2003) *China Migration Country Study*, Vol. 3. *Migration, Development and Pro-Poor Policy Choices in Asia*, London: Department for International Development.

Jiang, Guanhuo (2001) "Nongcun shuifei gaige: beili toushi ji qi jiaozheng (Rural tax reform: irrational perspectives and their correction)", *Zhongguo nongcun jingji*, 201: 217–22.

Kung, James Kai-sing (1994) "Egalitarianism, Subsistence Provision, and Work Incentives in China's Agricultural Collectives", *World Development*, 22: 175–187.

Kung, James Kai-sing (1995) "Equal Entitlement versus Tenure Security under a Regime of Collective Property Rights: Peasants' Preference for Institutions in Post-reform Chinese Agriculture", *Journal of Comparative Economics*, 21: 82–111.

Kung, James Kai-sing (2000) "Common Property Rights and Land Reallocations in Rural China: Evidence from a Village Survey", *World Development*, 28: 701–729.

Kung, James Kai-sing and Shouying Liu (1997) "Farmers' Preferences regarding Ownership and Land Tenure in Post-Mao China: Unexpected Evidence from Eight Countries", *The China Journal*, 38: 33–63.

Lardy, Nicholas R. (1983) *Agriculture in China's Modern Economic Development*, Cambridge: Cambridge University Press.

Li, Chenggui (2001) "1998 yilai de Zhongguo lianggai yanjiu (Research on China's grain reform since 1998)", in Zhongguo Shehui Kexueyuan Nongcun Fazhan Yanjiusuo (Institute of Rural Development of the Chinese Academy of Social Sciences) (ed.) *Zhongguo nongcun fazhan yanjiu baogao (Research report on China's rural development)*, Beijing: Shehui Kexue Wenxian Chubanshe, pp. 3–17.

Li, Guo, Rozelle, Scott and Brandt, Loren (1998) "Tenure, Land Rights, and Farmer Investment Incentives in China", *Agricultural Economics*, 19: 63–71.

Li, Hongbin and Rozelle, Scott (2000) "Saving or Stripping Rural Industry: An Analysis of Privatization and Efficiency in China", *Agricultural Economics*, 23: 241–252.

Li, Yuan (2000) *Zhonghua Renmin Gongheguo tudi guanli fa shiyi* (Interpretation of the Land Management Law of the People's Republic of China), Beijing: Falü Chubanshe.

Lin, Nan (1995) "Local Market Socialism: Local Corporatism in Action in Rural China", *Theory and Society*, 24: 301–354.

Lin, Nan and Xiaolan Ye (1998) "Chinese Rural Enterprises in Transformation: The End of the Beginning", *Issues and Studies*, 34: 1–28.

Liu, Shouying, Carter, Michael R. and Yao, Yang (1998) "Dimensions and Diversity of Property Rights in Rural China: Dilemmas on the Road to Further Reform", *World Development*, 26: 1789–1806.

Liu, Zinan and Juzhong Zhuang (2000) "Determinants of Technical Efficiency in Post-Collective Chinese Agriculture: Evidence from Farm-Level Data", *Journal of Comparative Economics*, 28: 545–564.

Mao, Dan. 2000. *Yi ge cunluo gongtongti de bianqian: guanyu Jianshanxiacun de danweihua de guancha yu chanshi* (The changes of a village community: observations and explanations on the work-unit-ization of Jianshanxia village), Shanghai: Xuelin Chubanshe.

Oi, Jean Chun (1989) *State and Peasant in Contemporary China: The Political Economy of Village Government*, Berkeley, CA: University of California Press.

Oi, Jean Chun (1992) "Economic Foundations of Local State Corporatism in China", *World Politics*, 45: 99–126.

Oi, Jean Chun (1999) "Rural China Takes Off: Institutional Foundations of Economic Reform", Berkeley, CA: University of California Press.

Pei, Xiaolin (1998) "Township-Village Enterprises, Local Governments, and Rural Communities: The Chinese Village as a Firm during Economic Transition", in Eduard B. Vermeer, Frank N. Pieke, and Woei Lien Chong (eds) *Cooperative and Collective in China's Rural Development: Between State and Private Interests*, Armonk, NY: M.E. Sharpe, pp. 110–135.

Pennarz, Johanna (1997) "Collective Land Ownership and Sustainable Agriculture: Perspectives on the Diversity of Land Use Rights in China", in OECD (ed.) *Agricultural Policies in China*, Paris: OECD, pp. 88–95.

Perkins, Dwight (1969) *Agricultural Development in China, 1368–1968*, Chicago: Aldine.

Pi, Chunxie (1999) *Xin tudi guanli fa lilun yu shiyong* (Theory and practice of the new land management law). Beijing: Zhongguo Fazhi Chubanshe.

Pieke, Frank N. (1995) Bureaucracy, Friends, and Money: The Growth of Capital Socialism in China", *Comparative Studies in Society and History*, 37: 494–518.

Pieke, Frank N. (1996) *The Ordinary and the Extraordinary: An Anthropological Study of Chinese Reform and the 1989 People's Movement in Beijing*, London: Kegan Paul International.

Pieke, Frank N., Nyíri, Pál, Thunø, Mette and Ceccagno, Antonella (2004) *Transnational Chinese: Fujianese Migrants in Europe*, Stanford, CA: Stanford University Press.

Prosterman, Roy, Hanstad, Tim, Schwarzwalder, Brian and Li, Ping (1998) *Rural Land Reform and the 1998 Land Management Law*, Seattle: Rural Development Institute.

Putterman, Louis (1997) "On the Past and Future of China's Township and Village-Owned Enterprises", *World Development*, 25: 1639–1655.

Rozelle, Scott and Guo Li (1998) "Village Leaders and Land-Rights Formation in China", *The American Economic Review*, 88: 433–438.

Schmidhuber, Joseph (2001) "Changes in China's Agricultural Trade Policy Regime: Impacts on Agricultural Production, Consumption, Prices, and Trade", in OECD (ed.) *China's Agriculture in the International Trading System*, Paris: OECD, pp. 21–51.

She (Zhe), Xiaoye (1997) *Cunzhuang de zaizao: yige "chaoji cunzhuang" de shehui bianqian* (Village rebirth: the social transformation of a 'super-village'), Beijing: Zhongguo Shehuikexue Chubanshe.

She (Zhe), Xiaoye and Yingying Chen (2000) *Shequ de shiji: "chaoji cunzhuang" de fazhan licheng* (The practice of community: the course of the development of a "super village"), Hangzhou: Zhejiang Renmin Chubanshe.

Sicular, Terry (1988) "Agricultural Planning and Pricing in the Post-Mao Period", *The China Quarterly*, 116: 671–705.

Smil, Vaclav (1999) "China's Agricultural Land", *The China Quarterly*, 158: 414–429.

Smyth, Russell (1998) "Recent Developments in Rural Enterprise Reform in China: Achievements, Problems, and Prospects", *Asian Survey*, 38: 784–800.

Thunø, Mette, and Pieke, Frank N. (2005) "Institutionalizing Recent Rural Emigration from China to Europe: New Transnational Villages in Fujian", *International Migration Review*, forthcoming.

Walker, Kenneth R. (1988) "Trends in Crop Production, 1978–86", *The China Quarterly*, 116: 592–633.

Wan, Guang H., and Enjiang Cheng (2001) "Effects of Land Fragmentation and Returns to Scale in the Chinese Farming Sector", *Applied Economics*, 33: 183–194.

Whiting, Susan H. (2001) *Power and Wealth in Rural China: The Political Economy of Institutional Change*, Cambridge: Cambridge University Press.

Xie, Junqi (2001) "Tudi (Land)", in Zhongguo Shehui Kexueyuan Huanjing yu Fazhan Yanjiu Zhongxin (Environment and Development Research Centre of the Chinese Academy of Social Sciences) (ed.) *Zhongguo huanjing yu fazhan pinglun (Review of China's environment and development)*, vol. 1, Beijing: Zhongguo Shehui Kexue Wenxian Chubanshe, pp. 117–130.

Yao, Yang (2000) "The Development of the Land Lease Market in Rural China", *Land Economics*, 76: 252–266.

Yeh, Anthony Gar-on and Wu, Fulong (1999) "The Transformation of the Urban Planning System in China from a Centrally-planned to Transitional Economy", *Progress in Planning*, 51: 167–252.

Zhang, Linxiu, Jikun Huang and Rozelle, Scott (1997) "Land Policy and Land Use in China", in OECD (ed.) *Agricultural Policies in China*, Paris: OECD, pp. 71–77.

Zhang, Tingwei (2000) "Land Market Forces and Government's Role in Sprawl: The Case of China", *Cities*, 17: 123–135.

Zhong, Ziran (1999) "Natural Resources Planning, Management, and Sustainable Use in China", *Resources Policy*, 25: 211–220.

Zhu, Baoping (2001) "Nongcun shuifei gaige shidian de jinzhan: nandian ji sikao (The progress of the rural tax reform test points: problems and reflections)", *Zhongguo nongcun jingji*, 2001: 12–16.

Zhu, Dongliang (2001) "Nongmin yanzhong de tudi yanbao '30 nian bu bian': jiyu xinfang cailiao de fenxi (The extension of land contracts under the policy of 'no changes in 30 years' in the eyes of the farmers: analysis based on petition letters)", *Zhongguo nongcun jingji*, 2001: 27–32.

Zweig, David (2000) "The 'Externalities of Development': Can New Political Institutions Manage Rural Conflict?", in Elizabeth J. Perry and Mark Selden (eds) *Chinese Society: Change, Conflict and Resistance*, London: Routledge, pp. 119–142.

Part II

Land tenure and economic relations

4 Land tenure in China

Facts, fictions and issues

Scott Rozelle, Loren Brandt, Li Guo and Jikun Huang

China's initial reforms triggered an unprecedented acceleration of agricultural growth. From 1979 to 1984, the gross value of agricultural output increased in real terms at an annual rate of 7.6 percent, and grain production rose by 4.9 percent annually (ZGTJNJ, 1989). Empirical studies (McMillan *et al.* 1989; Lin 1992; Huang and Rozelle 1996) attribute a significant part of this increase to the incentives associated with better residual income rights.[1] Growth slackened after 1984, however, especially for grain production. From 1985 to 1994, grain output rose only 0.9 percent per year (ZGTJNJ 1996), despite expanded efforts to further liberalize rural input and output markets.

This deceleration has generated considerable debate about the reasons for the slowdown. Some observers have focused attention on China's land management system, the one dimension of the farm economy that has been least altered since the initial reforms. Some suggest that weaknesses in these institutional arrangements are the fundamental source of the problem. Poor incentives related to tenure insecurity, for example, have reportedly discouraged investment in agriculture and lowered growth (Prosterman *et al.* 1996). The perceived incentive problems have sparked calls for either land privatization or for extending land contracts to 30 or more years (Chen 1999).

The need for privatization or extended tenure has not gone uncontested. By the mid-1980s, low farm-gate prices, not land rights arrangements, were alternatively being blamed for the sagging productivity. In many areas the majority of farmers reportedly oppose privatization (or even extended tenure) because their households enjoy better overall income security under the current form of collective land ownership (Kung 1995; Dong 1996; Kung and Liu 1997). Moreover, it has been argued that China presently lacks the complementary institutions that are required to make land privatization successful. In fact, poorly developed credit markets, the lack of a land registration system, and an incomplete legal system make privatization of land at the current time inefficient, if not socially dangerous (Dong 1996).

Unfortunately, not much support has been presented for either side of the land rights debate, even though the consequences are enormous. The overall goal of our chapter is to lay out the current facts and to describe systematically the organization and utilization of China's cultivated land resources in order to better weigh China's policy options. From a policy perspective, the critical question is how effective these alternative regimes have been in providing households the necessary incentives to ensure rational land use and investment, while simultaneously helping local communities meet distributive objectives. We will try to assess empirically what the effect of China's land system is on the efficiency, equity, and overall development of the rural sector.

Data

The data that we draw on in this chapter come from two main sources. First, in 1996 we collected a community-level data set, which because of its widespread coverage provides a rough estimate of nationwide trends and heterogeneity. We also base some of our insights and findings on a household data set from Liaoning and Hebei Provinces that we collected in 1995. The community-level survey covers 215 villages in eight representative provinces across China. On the coast, the most developed area in China, the sample includes Liaoning, Shandong and Zhejiang Provinces. In the agricultural heartland or inland region of the upper and middle Yangtze River valley, the sample includes Hebei, Hubei and Sichuan Provinces. In the north-west and south-west, China's poorest regions, the sample includes Shaanxi and Yunnan Provinces.

In all of the provinces other than Liaoning and Hebei, counties were stratified on the basis of per capita industrial output. Eight counties per province were randomly selected, two from each of the quartiles of the ranked list of counties. A similar sampling procedure was used in each county to select two sample townships and in each township to select two sample villages. In these six provinces, 32 villages or four in each of eight counties, were sampled, with the exception of Yunnan, where 24 villages were sampled. An additional 31 villages were sampled from a total of six counties in Hebei and Liaoning. The current sample can be regarded as generally representative of China and generates estimates of pertinent variables that are close to those generated from data collected in national surveys by China's statistical bureaux.[2]

In each village, the enumerators elicited a broad array of detailed data from three village leaders: the Party secretary, the chairman of the village committee or the village leader, and the village accountant. The three leaders were chosen because they were generally most able to answer questions about current and past village institutions. The 10–section survey instrument included sections on off-farm labor, land management, local industrial management, local credit markets, periodic markets, agricultural input and output markets, and the local political environment. We asked for information about two years, 1995 and 1988, and for changes since household farming was reintroduced. They answered detailed questions about the frequency, average size, and timing of the village's land readjustment, and about each village's rental activities and related institutions, including local rules concerning renting, how many households rented land in and out, who participated, and how much land was engaged in rental transactions.

To study the impact of tenure types and land rights on production behavior, a survey of 780 households from 31 villages in six counties in Hebei and Liaoning was also conducted in the summer of 1995. Hebei and Liaoning Provinces, located in North and Northeast China, are two of China's major agricultural provinces, and the six sample counties are located in major agricultural regions of the two provinces. Most agricultural producers in the sample counties depend on grain or cash crop production. Farmers primarily grow maize, which accounts for about 70 percent of the total sown area, but also cultivate soybeans, rice, and cotton.

For each of the surveyed households, enumerators recorded detailed information about household characteristics and agricultural production activities. Total landholdings of each household were enumerated on a plot-by-plot basis. After obtaining basic information about each plot, the supervisor of the enumeration team selected two plots from each household to investigate more carefully. An effort was made to ensure that the two plots were being farmed under different tenure forms as discussed below. The enumerators systematically surveyed the two selected plots from each household, eliciting information about the plot's tenure status, specific land rights, all inputs and outputs, and land quality. After data cleaning, the sample consists of 1,073 plots from 612 households.

In the rest of the chapter, we draw heavily on these data sets through a number of different analytical exercises. Although in most cases there is considerable theoretical and empirical work that underlies the findings, we will primarily report the main results of our work as it relates to the topics being discussed. For those interested in more details and the background of the methods, further references are provided in the notes.

Land tenure in rural China

Land tenure types and rights

China has five major land tenure types that are officially sanctioned by the national government: (1) responsibility land (*zeren tian*); (2) ration land (*kouliang tian*); (3) contract land (*chengbao tian*); (4) private plots (*ziliu di*); and (5) reclaimed land (*kaihuang di*). The tenure types, in turn, are packaged into several land tenure systems, including the two-field system (*liangtian zhi*), which combines responsibility and ration land, and the three-field system (*santian zhi*), which adds contract land. In Figure 4.1, we define each of these tenure types in order to establish a consistent vocabulary.

A survey by the State Statistical Bureau in 1992 covering 274 villages provides an estimate of the percentage of land in the first three of these tenure types (Cheng and Tsang 1995/96, Table 4.1, row 1). Responsibility land, the most important, covered 84.5 percent of cultivated land. In contrast, ration land only made up 8.4 percent of cultivated area. Nationwide farmers only cultivated 6.2 percent of their land as private plots.

Our community level survey found similar results (Table 4.1, row 2). The slightly lower percentage of land in responsibility plots (78.1 vs 84.5) is largely explained by the 5.2 percent of land that leaders contracted out to farmers; Cheng and Tsang's survey did not break out this category of land. Our survey estimates that private plots account for 5.9 percent of total area, nearly identical to that reported by Cheng and Tsang (1995/96).

Responsibility Land. Allocated to farm households on the basis of the number of family members, the number of laborers in each family, or desire and/or ability of the household to engage in agricultural production. In exchange for use rights, farmers must deliver a mandatory quota to the state at a price below-market. There may also be restrictions on how they may use the land. Users of responsibility plots also face the possibility that part of this land will be taken away and the use rights reallocated within the community to other households.

Ration Land. Allocated to farm households typically on the basis of household size for the purpose of ensuring that each household is self-sufficient in producing grain. No fees or other obligations are typically tied to use of the land.

Private Plots. Land usually acquired by the rural household during the period of collective agriculture and retained with the implementation of HRS. Today, this is mainly the land in courtyards, and not the private plot under collective times since in many villages private plots are now collectively cultivated. In some villages, newly-formed households are granted private plots. Households enjoy almost complete control over short- and long-term management with the exception of the right of title transfer. In some villages, farmers can bequeath their private plot to their children.

Contract Land. Land contracted out to households by the villages for a fixed fee (*chengbaofei*). Length of these contracts varies considerably from community to community. While the cultivator of contracted land may incur a delivery quota, the defining feature is that a cash rent is paid by the farmer to the village in return for basic use rights. Village leaders may set fees on these plots *ex ante* or farmers may have to bid on the land at a community auction.

Reclaimed Land. Land to which farmers acquire use rights through efforts to reclaim previously uncultivated land. There are not usually obligatory deliveries or fees tied to the use of the land. In some villages, rights to develop wasteland are currently being auctioned off (*huangshan paimai*).

Figure 4.1 Definitions of land tenure types.

Table 4.1 Structure and incidence of land tenure types in China

	Private plots	*Responsibility land*	*Ration land*	*Contract land*	*Misc.*
Share in Total Farmland (% of farmland)					
SSB Survey ($n = 274$)[a]	6.2	84.5	8.4	–	–
Our National Village Survey ($n = 215$)[b]	5.9	78.1	9.5	5.2	0.8
Incidence of Tenure Types (% of villages reporting)					
SSB Survey ($n = 274$)[a]	–	–	23.0	–	–
Our National Village Survey ($n = 215$)[b]	54.0	90.7	19.0	36.7	11.2

Notes

a Adapted from Cheng and Tsang, "Agricultural Land Reform in a Mixed System: The Chinese Experience of 1984–1994." *China Information*, Vol. X, Nos. 3 and 4 (Winter 1995, Spring 1996). Data for 1992.

b Authors' field survey (1995 data).

Tenure types are not uniform throughout China's villages. According to our survey data, 90 percent of villages have responsibility land, making it China's most prevalent tenure type (Table 4.1, row 4). In the remaining 10 percent, this designation is not used since these villages do not have procurement quotas.[3] The second most common tenure type, the private plot, appears in 54 percent of the villages. This exceeds the percentage of those villages that have either ration land allocations (19 percent) or use a system of contracting for a fee (37 percent).

Land Rights

Categorizing land by these tenure types, however, provides a less than satisfactory way of differentiating land rights faced by farmers in different villages. Each tenure type represents a bundle of rights and obligations, and within tenure types, the bundle's composition will not necessarily be the same. Even for villages located within the same region, the residual income and non-residual rights that farmers have on their responsibility land may differ, making it difficult to use tenure type to pinpoint how land organization (tenure types) affects the production or investment behavior of farmers. Compounding this difficulty is the fact that the distinction between land tenure systems can be blurred.[4] A more effective way to examine China's current land tenure system is to disaggregate tenure forms into the residual and non-residual rights households enjoy on their land. Non-residual rights include the security of tenure, freedom of crop selection, rental or transfer rights, conversion to alternative agricultural uses, and the right to inherit. Residual rights are also weakened by taxes and by other obligations.

Heterogeneity of land rights

We focus in this chapter on several rights: security of tenure, transfer or rental rights, and crop selection. The first two rights most likely affect both short- and long-run productivity, while the third may affect the returns to farming more generally.

Security of tenure

Tenure security is typically associated with long-term use rights to land and freedom from the arbitrary loss of these rights without compensation. In most villages, use rights to land are lost (or gained) in the process of village-wide reallocations.[5] Land is taken back from some households, and redistributed to others. For example, leaders shift land from a household that had a daughter marry to one that had a new child born. In this process, households typically are not compensated for investments they may have made in the land. Tenure security will be inversely related to the frequency of these reallocations. The effect of insecurity, however, may be attenuated if the timing and the scope of the reallocations are established ahead of time.

Our data confirm the fact that the right to reallocate land is typically vested in the village.[6] Considerable differences exist among provinces in the average number of reallocations per village since HRS was introduced, with a national average of 1.7 times (Table 4.2, column 1). Local leaders in Liaoning, Shaanxi, and Hubei Provinces make adjustments at higher-than-average frequency, while those in Yunnan and Sichuan Provinces

Table 4.2 Village reallocation behavior in reform-era China

Province	*Average number of reallocations per village*	*Size of most recent reallocation (% of land)*	*Size of most recent reallocation (% of households)*	*Reallocation decision made by township (% of villages reporting)*
Zhejiang	1.2 (1.3)	60.8 (40.6)	91.8 (57.9)	6.2
Sichuan	0.3 (0.5)	28.6 (33.1)	58.6 (36.8)	3.1
Hubei	2.8 (1.6)	55.0 (39.8)	71.1 (33.9)	3.1
Shaanxi	2.8 (1.2)	34.8 (36.7)	62.8 (29.1)	6.2
Shandong	1.9 (1.0)	74.5 (39.8)	71.2 (33.7)	0.0
Yunnan	0.4 (0.6)	31.3 (39.6)	61.4 (45.3)	66.7
Hebei	1.5 (1.0)	75.0 (37.1)	82.5 (23.4)	33.3
Liaoning	3.4 (3.6)	91.1 (22.2)	93.1 (17.9)	25.0
Total	1.7 (1.8)	57.6 (41.3)	74.4 (37.3)	14.4

Source: Authors' field survey.

Note
Standard errors are reported in parenthesis.

intervene relatively infrequently. Examining a histogram for the number of reallocations per village, in 60 of the 215 villages in our survey the land has *not* been readjusted since HRS; in a small number of villages, reallocation occurs almost annually (Figure 4.2). In a quarter of all the villages land has been reallocated once, and in a fifth of the villages reallocation has been conducted two times.

In some parts of China, the decision to reallocate is made at the township level (Table 4.2, column 4). In Yunnan, two-thirds of the villages reported that reallocation decisions were made by higher administrative levels, while in Hebei and Liaoning a third and quarter of surveyed villages, respectively, report that township leaders make these decisions. Overall, however, 85 percent report that these decisions are village-based.

The pattern of reallocations over time is consistent with the idea that villages and townships are making the decisions to reallocate in a decentralized way, without much regard to national policies to maintain land allocations for 15 years. Figure 4.3 shows the percentage of villages in our sample that reallocated land for each year between 1983 and 1995. In any year, slightly less than 10 percent of all villages on average reallocate land. Reallocations differ in their size and scope across China's rural communities. On average, a reallocation entails slightly more than half the village's land, and extends to two-thirds of its households (Table 4.2, column 2). In villages experiencing more than one reallocation, the sizes of the reallocations are highly correlated with each other (i.e., the amount of land reallocated in each of the reallocations is fairly similar). On average, slightly more than half of all cultivated land in our sample of villages (53.4 percent) has been reallocated at least once in the years 1983 to 1995.[7] The distribution is also bi-modal; a nearly equal percentage of village leaders

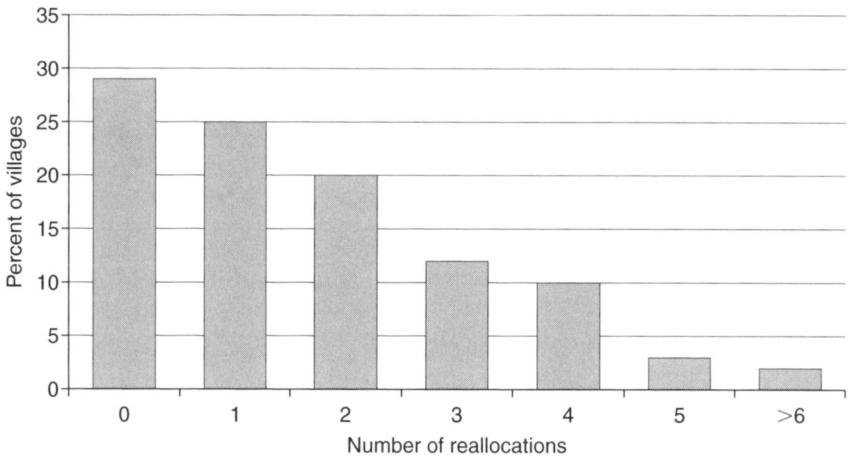

Figure 4.2 Villages carrying out major land reallocations by year in China.

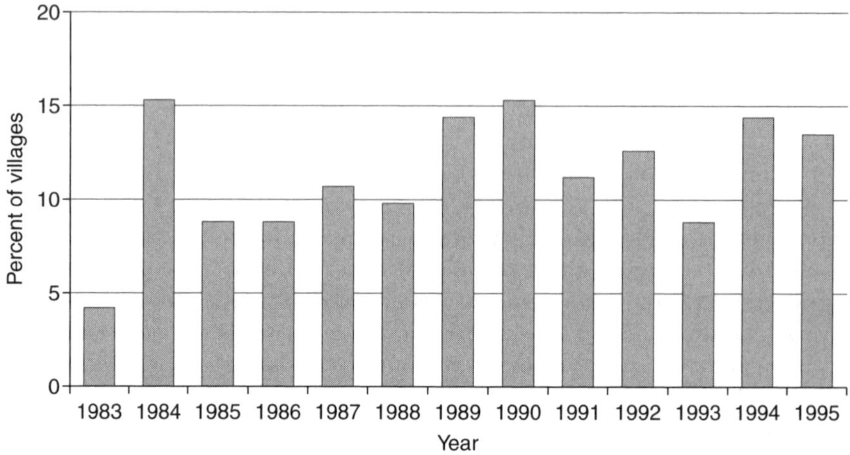

Figure 4.3 Percentage of village's cultivated area that has been reallocated since reform began in 1983.

(about 40 percent) report that nearly all or none of the land was reallocated since HRS.

Insecure tenure is associated with a higher frequency of cultivated land reallocation (Table 4.2, column 3); the more often that land is reallocated in a village, the more likely that a farmer will lose a particular plot of land. Tenure insecurity is also exacerbated if the dates of village-wide adjustment are not known, since it increases the uncertainty that farmers face. From the survey, we know if leaders announced the date of the first adjustment at the time that they implemented HRS. In nearly half of all villages, a date was not announced. A similar percentage of villages also report that households currently do not know the date of the next adjustment.[8] All three factors–the frequency, size, and uncertainty regarding the date of the next reallocation–potentially contribute to farmers' concerns over the security of their use rights.

Transfer or rental rights

Zhuanbao, literally "passing on a contract," refers to the transfer of land-use rights between two households and is comparable to the notion of land rental. The transfer is typically short term and usually entails the payment of a fee and assumption of tax and quota liabilities by another household in return for the use of the land.[9] In 1995, 71.6 percent of villages reported that households had complete freedom to transfer land use rights, about the same as in 1988 (Table 4.3, column 1). In the remaining 28.4 percent of the villages, households faced some sort of constraint,

Table 4.3 Non-residual property rights in China's villages, 1988 and 1995

Province	*Unencumbered right to rent (% of villages)*	*Land rented in 1988 (%)*	*Land rented in 1995 (%)*	*Right to decide crop mix (% of villages)*	*Right to convert land to alternative uses (% of villages)*
Zhejiang	93.8	1.6 (3.3)	6.9 (10.3)	74.1	40.7
Sichuan	93.8	0.2 (0.5)	2.1 (2.6)	93.1	68.9
Hubei	59.4	0.3 (1.1)	3.6 (8.3)	66.7	41.4
Shaanxi	65.6	0.8 (2.1)	2.2 (2.9)	93.3	84.4
Shandong	46.5	NA	1.1 (1.8)	60.0	60.7
Yunnan	66.7	1.3 (0.5)	0.9 (2.2)	66.7	45.8
Hebei	80.0	0.3 (0.6)	2.1 (2.2)	84.6	53.8
Liaoning	62.3	0.1 (0.3)	3.6 (5.0)	93.8	6.3
Total	71.6	0.6 (1.8)	2.9 (5.8)	73.4	53.6

Source: Authors' field survey.

Note
Standard errors are reported in parenthesis.

most often in the form of restrictions on renting to non-villagers, or the need for households to obtain prior authorization from village leaders. Leaders only rarely impose a complete moratorium on rental transactions.

Despite the high percentage of villages reporting that households have unconstrained rights to allow other households to use their land, farmers rent in and out a remarkably low percentage of their land (Table 4.3, columns 2 and 3). In 1988, only one-half of 1 percent of cultivated land was rented in rural China; nearly three-quarters of villages reported no land rental. By 1995, although more than 75 percent of local leaders reported rental activities in their villages, farmers still rented less than 3 percent of their land, most of which occurs between relatives. In Section 5, we will examine several explanations for these observations.

Crop selection and land conversion

Leaders sometimes impose restrictions on how farmers use the land, including their ability to convert it between alternative uses in agriculture. (Table 4.3, column 4). In nearly 75 percent of villages, households freely decide on the crop-mix. In several sample provinces, notably, Hubei, Shandong, and Yunnan Provinces, leaders regulate these decisions. In a survey we conducted in Zhejiang in 1995 farmers showed us a directive from township leaders requiring all farmers in the village to plant two-season (summer and fall crop) rice under threat of a fine, even when the trend in the area was to use one-season varieties or move into horticultural production.

Obligations, such as mandatory grain or cotton delivery quotas, can affect crop choice. In our surveyed villages in Liaoning Province, for example, grain quotas in 1995 averaged nearly 25 percent of gross output, and officials typically did not allow farmers to satisfy their obligations with a cash payment; instead they insisted on delivery of grain. Cotton quotas in parts of Hebei, Hubei, and Shandong Provinces also may have a similar effect on land use. Some of the farmers in areas in which we have surveyed complain that they would rather plant cash crops, but must plant grain or cotton. The level of quotas, however, typically is lower in poor areas, rarely exceeding 10 percent.

Local leaders place even more severe constraints on households with regard to the freedom they have to convert land to alternative uses (Table 4.3, column 5). For example, rules often prohibit farmers from converting cultivated land to orchards, fishponds, greenhouses, or brick kilns. Officials in Liaoning Province are especially strict, and throughout China only about half of the farming population can make significant permanent changes to their land use without the authorization of local leaders.

Land rights formation: identifying the determinants

A popular view expressed in some of the earlier work on land is that rights and land policy are uniformly determined by the central government.[10] Policy pronouncements by the State Council on issues such as tenure security convey this impression. The observed heterogeneity in property rights discussed in the previous section essentially undermines this view. Land security and transfer rights not only differ among provinces, but also from township to township within a county and among villages within a township (Table 4.4). In terms of land reallocations, in 39 out of 44

Table 4.4 Heterogeneity of land security and rental rights within counties and townships

	Reallocation or not	*Frequency of land reallocation*	*Free rental rights or not*
County sample size: 44			
Counties reporting differences in rights between villages within the county	24[a] (55)[b]	39 (87)	30 (68)
Township sample size: 92			
Townships reporting differences in rights between villages within the township)	27 (30)	52 (57)	33 (36

Source: Authors' field survey.

Notes

a Absolute number of counties and townships, respectively.

b Percent of total sample in parentheses.

sample counties (87 percent, column 2), townships within a county reported different frequencies of land readjustment at the village level. In 52 out of 92 townships (57 percent, column 2), villages within a township reported different frequencies in readjustment. Similar patterns appear with respect to land rental rights (column 3). In 30 out of 44 counties (68 percent, column 3), townships within a single county reported different land rental rights at the village level. In 33 out of 92 townships (36 percent, column 3), villages within a township reported different rental rights. In our sample of 31 villages drawn from 6 counties in North-east China, land resources were organized in almost 20 different ways. Qiao (1997) discovered that leaders in 40 Yunnan and Fujian villages managed their forestry land in nearly 30 different ways. Throughout China, heterogeneity is observed at every administrative level, suggesting that central or regional policymakers are not the final arbiters in land management issues.

Instead, the pattern of land rights suggests that the real source of this widely observed heterogeneity is differences at the village level.[11] This interpretation is consistent with several recent studies that find central policy-makers to be less effective in implementing local development programs due to the increased independence of village leaders (Kelliher 1997; Oi, 1999). Some argue that decision-making powers have already shifted from central to local and village authority to such a degree that China is now one of Asia's most decentralized countries (Carter *et al.*1995).

Central policy and laws provide for a considerable degree of decentralization. The *Organic Law of Village Committees* vests village governments with the legal authority over land rights. One of the primary administrative responsibilities of the village leader is to manage this and to guide farmers in their use of local natural resources (Kelliher 1997; ZGNYNJ 1988).[12] To manage land in China's case means to make major decisions about land allocation, the timing and method of land readjustment, and rules regarding land rentals. One consequence is that local leaders in many villages use their authority derived from the Organic Law to invoke decision-making over land and to side-step centrally proclaimed edicts (O'Brien and Li 1999).

If village leaders have discretion in managing land, a fundamental question is on what basis they make land allocation and reallocation decisions. In fact, in the literature there is not a consensus on this issue. One task for the future is to develop a general model of how these interests interact, and to analyze how this interaction is affected by local governance structures. Currently, the literature raises four alternative hypotheses. The explanations are not mutually exclusive and in all likelihood there is more than one motivation for the reallocations of land. The weight of these factors most likely differs across villages and within villages over time.

Demographic change and equal access to land hypothesis

With the introduction of household responsibility system (HRS), local leaders typically allocated land to households in a fairly egalitarian way based on some combination of family size, demographic composition, and labor supply (Putterman 1992). With land collectively owned, a case can be made that *all* villagers, both present and future, are entitled *ex ante* to equal access to this common property resource. This requires village officials to reallocate land on an ongoing basis.[13] This kind of behavior might be reinforced by preferences among villagers (or key constituencies within a village) for an egalitarian land reallocation (Kung 1995) and a village-level decision-making process that reflects villager sentiment. Pressures to redistribute use rights to maintain adequate consumption for all of the households within a village may also be tied to the local economic environment and the extent and security of opportunities outside of farming. If demographic rules are a determinant of land allocation, we can expect to find a strong relationship between household demographics and land allocations, and village reallocation behavior positively correlating with the rate of village demographic change.

Political rent-seeking hypothesis

Johnson (1995) argues that village leaders use their power over villagers to extract rents through the periodic reallocation of land. Rents are often presumed to be pecuniary, but they can be non-pecuniary as well, and can also be collected in the form of cooperation from villagers in other dimensions of village life such as tax remission or family planning. Village leaders may also extract sizeable monetary rents through their control over the sale of village land to non-villagers.[14] There is considerable anecdotal support for this kind of self-interested, rent-seeking behavior on the part of village leaders. Having said that, it is much more difficult to explain differences *across* villages in the pervasiveness of this kind of behavior and the frequency of reallocation. In other words, why does it happen in some villages, but not in other villages?

Missing here is a more complete model of village leader behavior and its effect on the determination of property rights. We expect rent extraction through land reallocation to be tied to leader attributes, career concerns, the potential size of these rents, and other opportunities for rent extraction. Johnson contends that a more open political process at the village level, e.g., village elections, can act as a powerful check on this kind of behavior and reduce reallocations. In all likelihood, honest and open village elections help increase accountability, and provide villagers more of a voice, but it is not clear how this has an impact on land policy (Oi and Rozelle 2000).[15]

Protection of the interests of the state and village leaders

The state entrusts village leaders to implement state policy and to protect the state's interests and resources at the local level. What are these state interests? Through the quota system and the national agricultural tax, the state exercises a claim to agricultural output.[16] Village leaders allocate these burdens among households (and take action to enforce the burden) to ensure that the quota and taxes are fulfilled on time. Village leaders also have a responsibility to ensure that family planning targets are met, and may face other targets, such as maintaining agricultural output growth or drafting corvee labor. Higher level officials can easily measure village leaders' success in meeting these targets, and in principle use the information to evaluate their job performance. Leaders earn job security, promotion opportunities, status, and in some cases bonus payments from village funds by meeting these targets (Ho 1994; O'Brien and Li 1999; Rozelle 1994; Rozelle and Boisvert 1994). More generally, the state has the power to remove cadres who do not succeed in fulfilling the state's interest, and may be able to prevent fired officials from taking advantage of the perks and privileges that otherwise accrue to past and present village leadership.

Control over land may be used by local leaders as an instrument to ensure that the interests of the state are protected and indirectly to protect their own best interests (Kelliher 1996; Rozelle 1994).[17] Using our village data, we can make an argument that the village leader may use land as a bonus or punishment device (or a carrot or a stick), taking away land from villagers who do not fulfill their obligations, and giving it to those who do.[18] Leaders are more likely to use land the more effective it is as an instrument (i.e., when farmers value land higher) and the greater the returns to remaining in office.

While there may be truth in this explanation, it is difficult to generate evidence in support of it. The relatively low incidence of quota default limits the explanatory power of this interpretation.[19] In addition, it is not exactly clear how this kind of behavior maps into the land reallocation behavior we actually observe – especially in the long run. If dispossession is a credible threat, it will rarely be used – especially in areas where land is perceived as being valuable. If it were used, we would expect that reallocations for these purposes will occur fairly regularly and involve a small number of households. The village reallocations that have drawn the attention of many observers, however, tend to be discrete – on average they occur every six to eight years – entail a significant portion of village land and households, and use fixed criteria for reallocating land. As seen above, in many villages, a large part of the turnover of village land is related to larger reallocations.

Even if dispossession is not used to enforce quotas *per se*, our empirical work shows that reallocations can assist in guaranteeing that quotas are fulfilled and that other agricultural targets are met.[20] With the growth of off-farm opportunities and the increase in the returns to labor, quotas will increase the likelihood that the return to labor in agriculture will fall below that offered by other outside employment opportunities.[21] Our observation in China is that if the quota becomes too burdensome, villagers will try to persuade local leaders to have their land-holdings reduced, even as they continue to pay the quotas. Reallocating the land to households for whom farming remains relatively attractive helps ensure that quotas are more easily met, and could help to increase efficiency.

Efficiency gains and missing markets

With the introduction of HRS, land was distributed to households on a fairly egalitarian basis, occasionally adjusted to reflect differences in household demographic composition and the number of family members working outside agriculture. Over time, households change their labor supply in agriculture in response to changes in their off-farm opportunities, changes in household labor endowment or both. Land rental markets and markets for hired farm labor are incomplete in most parts of China. Since under these conditions households cannot easily adjust their land holdings or hiring of labor, a growing inefficiency could emerge in the allocation of land. As land and labor gradually become less well matched, productivity differences arise between households, and village profits in agriculture will fall.

Village-wide reallocations are a way to correct the deterioration. Interviews with village leaders who have carried out reallocations, however, show that the process of reallocation is costly in terms of effort and entails considerable administrative expense. As such, we only expect village-wide reallocations to occur when the land–labor match deteriorates sufficiently and the returns to adjusting land-holdings justify the transaction cost. These costs are likely to differ across villages and reflect differences in village size, land types, and leader attributes. Put more formally, the hypothesis is that administrative land reallocations maximize the discounted present value of agricultural profits, net of the costs to conduct reallocations. Less formally, the hypothesis is that administrative reallocations are a substitute, albeit an imperfect one, for a decentralized exchange of land that would occur if households had well-defined rights to rent their land to each other. Administrative reallocation and a decentralized system of exchange based on land rental among individual households, however, are an imperfect substitute because of informational problems and because the high costs of reallocation prevent reallocations from being carried out more frequently.

There are several reasons why this hypothesis may explain a lot of the reallocations that we observe. First, to the extent that villagers are able to affect reallocations by lobbying village leaders, we expect households that value land more highly to lobby more effectively for favorable reallocations. Second, as the village's agricultural profits increase, it is probably easier for the village leader to collect taxes and agricultural quotas. Since these responsibilities are an important part of the leader's job evaluation, the leader may have an incentive to perform profit-increasing trades. Third, insofar as equity is a consideration, it will involve a reallocation of land from households with low labor-land ratios to those with high labor-land ratios. To the extent that this also equalizes the productivity of land across households, these trades increase farm incomes. All of these forces tend to push reallocated land to households with higher marginal products of land, which increases village profits.

To test how important village profit maximization (excluding profit maximization for cadres) is as an explanation of reallocation behavior (that is that leaders will take actions for the express purpose of maximizing agricultural profits), we formally developed a model that assumes rational village leader behavior and generates predictions for decisions relating to the time between reallocations and the size of the reallocations, and also show how the size of reallocations is related to the timing between reallocations.[22] Our predictions link reallocation choices to village-level changes in family labor supply and demographic composition, transaction costs, the village's prevailing farming technology, and leader attributes. Transaction costs include the costs of carrying out the reallocation, for example, assessing household changes and re-dividing plots, and the potential disruption to agriculture caused by the reallocation.

Central to this interpretation of the role of land reallocations is the fact that farm labor and rental markets are incomplete or relatively thin. There are a number of possible explanations for this. First, the past two generations of farmers and local leaders have grown up with a Communist ideology that regards land rental and hiring of labor as exploitative. Market participation may be low because of a general taboo on this behavior. Alternatively, market participation may be low because households are reluctant to use an unfamiliar method of exchange. While this latter explanation for market thinness is plausible, it is not consistent with the rapid development of factor and product markets elsewhere during the reforms.

Second, households renting land usually must pay the quota on rented land. In the event of default, however, leaders typically hold the household that was originally allocated the land liable for the quota. Administering such a system may require more effort by the leaders and provide them an incentive to discourage actively rental transactions. Data provide some support for this. In 1995, for a village in our national sample without quotas, farmers rented an average of 7.9 percent of land; those with quotas only rented 2.2 percent of the land.

More generally, institutions supporting the enforcement of land contracts are absent. Courts are almost non-existent. Land registration does not exist in most villages. Contracting (transaction) costs may be prohibitive and discourage households from completing exchange. The fact that most rental transactions occur among relatives corroborates such an explanation; we expect transaction costs between relatives to be lower because they have better information about each other and also interact in a variety of economic and non-economic dimensions. In this case, rental markets fail because of factors that are beyond village control: formal institutions supporting contract enforcement are weak.

Finally, rental transactions may signal to leaders that opportunities for gains from the exchange exist. A self-interested village leader will want to appropriate some of these gains. In principle, a leader could reallocate rented land from the rentee to the rentor and demand in return some of the extra income that will now go to the rentor. While few farmers that we have talked to complain about extortion of this type, there is anecdotal evidence that village leaders in some areas regard rental as a signal of land misallocation, and shift land away from households that rent out (Li 1999). In this case, administrative reallocations cause rental markets to fail: Since rental invites dispossession, no one will rent land.

Empirical work on rights formation

Empirical work by us and by others helps illuminate a number of the issues that we raised. This work has focused on several key areas: (1) explaining the criteria by which land is allocated; (2) measuring the extent of static (or allocative) inefficiency resulting from the current land allocation system; (3) identifying the effects of the current property rights regime on dynamic incentives; and (4) explaining village differences in land reallocation policy.

Village land allocation criteria

Most of the village-level survey work that has been done suggests that land is allocated to households on a per capita basis, possibly adjusted for differences in demographic composition (Putterman 1992). Use of household-level data to analyze village allocation rules is limited. Burgess (1997), using SSB data on over five thousand households from Zhejiang and Sichuan for 1990, shows that demographic variables and village dummies explain 75 percent of the variation in household landholdings.[23] All but a handful of households in the sample have land. Allocations are not carried out on a strict per capita basis, but rather reflect the age composition of the household; children and the elderly receive less land. In this respect, the allocations resemble "demogrants," land transfers that are a function of demographic characteristics of the household. Leaders also allocate individuals working off the farm less land (an empirical result also found by Kung and Liu, 1997, and, in fact, in our own data set). Burgess (1997) contends that this universal and egalitarian access to land was central to increasing calorie consumption in regions of China in which residents faced food markets characterized by high transaction costs.

Using our data from Hebei and Liaoning for 1994, we produced results that are consistent with Burgess in many ways, but also differ in a few significant other ways.[24] Out of a sample of nearly 780 households,[25] we found a slightly higher percentage of households that do not have land.[26] Overall, the explanatory power of household demographic variables is significantly less than Burgess finds; they only explain half of the variation in land-holdings between households in these two provinces. One interpretation of this finding is that factors other than demographic and labor supply variables in our sample increasingly matter for household land allocation.

Static inefficiency

Static inefficiency arises because of a misallocation of resources across households, and in the case of China, may arise for a relatively straight forward reason. At the outset of decollectivization, the land was allocated in a fairly egalitarian way to reflect household size and composition, and in some cases, off-farm labor supply. Over time, however, demographic changes, because of births, deaths, marriages, family division, and labor supply shifts, affect the household's demographic structure and would lead to growing inefficiencies.[27]

The key questions are, do these inefficiencies exist and what mitigates or exacerbates them? It is possible that households rent land out or in (or hire farm labor out or in) to offset these differences, but recall that these markets are thin in most of our survey areas. Village reallocations could do the same thing. If land is *not* allocated so that all households have the same land–labor ratio, land–scarce households might be induced to supply more labor per unit of land, a symptom of static inefficiency. In principle, this can give rise to an "inverse relationship" between farm size and land productivity, with output per unit of land higher on smaller farms. In fact, the presence of the inverse relationship is evidence of static inefficiency.

Using our data, we examined the "inverse relationship" as an indicator of inefficiency.[28] And, in fact, we do find that as farm size rises, labor use per unit of land falls and output per unit of labor rises. These findings can only be reconciled by a view there is inefficiency in the use of labor. Constrained farmers apply more labor per unit of land and earn relatively little in return for their extra time. Inefficiencies indeed do exist.[29] Importantly, we also find that well-functioning local labor markets and other sources of off-farm employment help to reduce significantly the inefficiency in farm labor use. Since low productivity is essentially a product of underutilized labor, it appears that less labor is wasted where its opportunity cost is greatest. Together, our findings suggest that there are important efficiency gains to be realized from reallocating land from land-rich households to land-poor ones, a move that equalizes the marginal product of labor across households and enables the same level of output to be produced with less labor.

Are these inefficiencies serious? While the findings also suggest that there is a cost of the current property right regime, a paper by Carter and Yao (1998), drawing on data for 200 rice-farming households in Zhejiang, suggests the cost of allocative inefficiency arising from restrictions on transfer rights is around 2 percent of output. Because of the relatively well developed off-farm opportunities in these areas, the costs are probably lower than they are in other areas where income from farming is much more important.

Perhaps the most important result arising from the work on the impact of reallocation on household welfare is that inefficiency does not have to come at the cost of rising inequality. On the basis of our work (and that of Carter and Yao), it is not unfair to say that there is room for reallocations that improve *both* efficiency and equity. However, this conclusion and any policy implications that might follow are based on the assumption that land rental markets do not operate well. The presumption here is that better-defined rights to rent might alleviate the problem and reduce the need for frequent reallocation of land.

Investment incentives and the dynamic costs of the current property rights regime

The major rationale for calls to extend tenure to 30 years is the anticipated effect of enhanced tenure security on household investment decisions. To date, however, in addition to our own work, only one study has examined the effects of tenure security and related rights on household investment behavior. While the results of our studies are useful, they are done with imperfect data, only address some of the issues, and are based on a small sample in only one region of China.

There are several kinds of investment in which we are interested, all of which can affect land productivity and output growth. On the one hand, there are land quality-augmenting investments, such as expenditures on irrigation, drainage, and wells. There are also investments in long-term soil fertility through the use of organic fertilizers and green manure. Empirically, the key is to link levels of investment to the land rights that households enjoy, notably security of tenure and freedom of rental, while simultaneously controlling for household characteristics and inherent differences in land types and quality that may influence household investment decisions. We used plot-by-plot data collected in Hebei and Liaoning to analyze the incentive effects of property rights on household input use and investment.[30]

In a sub-sample of our data drawn from one county in Hebei Province, we find that farmers had significantly higher yields on their private maize plots than on their responsibility maize fields. On average, private plots yielded 25 percent more than responsibility plots.[31] Also, the difference in output appears to be linked to differences in input use. When cultivating their private plots, farmers applied more labor (11 percent), draft animal input (3 percent), nitrogen fertilizer (5 percent), organic fertilizer (35 percent), and phosphates (22 percent). Note that the greatest differences (which are also significant in a statistical sense) are observed in organic fertilizer and phosphate use, the two inputs with greatest long-term impact on the land.

The key question is how much of these differences in input use can be attributed to property rights? A key difference between private plots and responsibility plots in the sample (both of which are planted to maize) is the length of tenure. For private plots, the average length of tenure was over twice that for responsibility land (21 years versus 9 years) which might point to a more frequent reallocation of this land. Also, for nearly 40 percent of the responsibility plots, the household's contract was expected to expire the following year. Security of tenure as captured by these two variables appears to be much better on private plots. However, several other factors, such as the size of the plot, the quality of the land, and the distance of the plot from the homestead, may also be important.

Inter-plot comparisons are made using regression analysis. Controlling for differences in land quality and other key variables, we find that weaker property rights, either in the form of poorer tenure security or constraints on rental rights, adversely affect incentives of farmers to invest in medium-term inputs such as soil-building organic manure. In fact, these two variables explain much of the difference in organic manure use between the two kinds of plots. The effect of these same variables on other current inputs was insignificant.[32] The relatively low effect of organic fertilizers on output suggests that only a relatively small percentage of the differences in output between the two kinds of plots is related to property rights *per se*.[33]

Our empirical results support the view that heightened expropriation risk dampens investment in rural China, although the impacts may not be large. Farmers living in villages with more frequent land reallocations – or those who are at higher risk of losing a plot, e.g., by virtue of the fact that they have greater landholdings than the average farm household in the village – use organic fertilizer less intensively. The opposite is true of chemical fertilizers, which are known to have no long-lasting effects on soil quality. Despite having a negative impact on investment in soil quality, periodic land reallocations do not appear to entail a substantial cost – only about 5 percent of production, a figure that is above that of Carter and Yao, but still relatively low.[34]

While all studies to date have failed to find a large impact of China's land system in production, we hesitate to make too much of these findings. It may be that soil quality, the focus of our work, is not an important enough input for its under-utilization to matter much. Moreover, to the extent that many of the more capital-intensive agricultural investments are undertaken at the village level, China's system of land management maybe has been able to limit the problem of under investment by households due to the weak land rights. No study has yet presented the data to estimate the impact of China's land management systems on other types of land-augmenting investments and crop choice.

Village reallocation behavior

While previous studies, e.g., Carter *et al.* (1995), try to explain differences in land reallocation behavior across villages using village level data, they focus primarily on the frequency of reallocations.[35] In addition to differences across villages in the frequency of reallocations, the size of reallocations also differs. In our work we believe that tenure security is best thought of as a function *both* of the frequency of the reallocations and the size of the typical reallocation.

Frequency and time between reallocations

The frequency of village reallocation (or number of reallocations since HRS) and the time since the last reallocation are significantly related to changes in the village demographics. For example, in villages where changes in village population are greater, the frequency and elapsed time since the last reallocation rise and fall, respectively. Timing decisions also are sensitive to the rate of change in off-farm opportunities. These findings are consistent with the view that reallocation behavior is tied to the need to accommodate demographic changes and to the view that reallocations help eliminate inefficiency in the allocation of land across households resulting from differential access to off-farm opportunities. It also appears that the effect of population growth is attenuated in villages that have adopted alternative land management practices that deal with population growth in a more systematic way.[36]

The determinants of the size of reallocations

The determinants of the size of land reallocation are more complicated, and depend on other land management practices as well as a number of exogenous factors. For example, the amount of land that is reallocated depends significantly on the length of time since the last reallocation. Estimates suggest that the amount of land reallocated increases by about 6 percent for every additional year since the last reallocation.

Demographic variables, as in the case of the frequency and timing of reallocations, also have an important effect on the size of the reallocation.

This is positively related to the rate of change in the village population and the rate of growth in off-farm opportunities. The significantly larger coefficient on the variable measuring changes in off-farm opportunities and the larger changes in off-farm opportunities suggest that these changes are more important than demographic changes in explaining differences between villages in the size of the reallocations. Insofar as these reallocations entail reallocating land from land-rich to land-poor households, these reallocations also help to lower inequality.

While transaction costs are difficult to identify, our analysis suggests that timing decisions will be influenced by both fixed and variable transaction costs, while the size of the reallocations should only be affected by the variable costs. We estimate that the variable costs of reallocation increase with the average number of plots per household and the percentage of land that is paddy. Apart from the possibility that reallocating paddy reduces investment – paddy requires more ongoing investment – it may be that because of the well-defined perimeter of a paddy field, the cost of sub-division is higher on paddy fields.

Quotas also have an important effect on the size of the reallocations. As quotas increase, the percentage of land that is reallocated increases. Moreover, it appears that quotas are having their greatest impact where off-farm wages are greatest. This finding is consistent with the view that quotas reduce the return to farming and provide both villagers and village leaders with the incentives to try to reallocate the land to other households in the village for whom the quotas do not bind. It is also the case that the effect of quotas on reallocation behavior is significantly reduced when quotas become convertible into cash, a move that helps reduce the distortion related to the quota, and thus the need to reallocate.

Finally, a contested election in the year of the reallocation or the year just prior to a reallocation reduced the time since the last reallocation, and also reduced the size of the most recent reallocation. The overall effect was to reduce the amount of land reallocated. The precise mechanism through which these elections are influencing village behavior is unclear, but the results suggest potentially significant effects.

Administrative versus market exchange

The effect of off-farm opportunities on village reallocation behavior and findings from our work suggest that certain kinds of land reallocations help to eliminate inefficiency in the allocation of land across households, albeit incompletely.[37] In this respect, administrative reallocation is playing a role analogous to that played by land rental markets in the context of decentralized exchange. The questions are, how are these two related and are they substitutes for each other?

When we include measures of land rental activity and the hiring of farm labor in our analysis of the size of the reallocations, we find that reallocations are smaller where markets are more active. Although there may be certain statistical questions that arise in such an analysis, (i.e. the size of the reallocations and freedom to rent may be determined simultaneously), the findings raise the important question: If centralized reallocations are a substitute for decentralized markets, why do villages select centralized over decentralized exchange?

Using the full sample of 215 villages from our village survey, we find that leader attributes, elections, and quotas usually operate in the opposite direction on market and administrative transactions. Specifically, administrative reallocations are more important in villages with higher quotas, older leaders, and non-contested elections; rental, on the other hand, is more prominent in villages with smaller quotas and younger and better-educated leaders. Both administrative reallocations and rental are positively correlated with growth in off-farm opportunities.

Conclusion

The allocation of property rights is widely recognized to have important implications for resource use and the distribution of household welfare. The introduction of HRS in the early 1980s extended to households on a fairly egalitarian basis use rights to cultivated land. In the past two decades, control over the allocation of that land to households has remained in the hands of local leaders. In evaluating China's land tenure system from a policy perspective, the critical question is how effective the system has been in providing households the necessary incentives to ensure rational land use and investment, while simultaneously helping local communities meet distributive objectives. Moreover, looking past 2000, how well does the system fit the needs of China's rapidly evolving economy?

Survey work that we have done suggests enormous heterogeneity at the village level in the rights that household have been extended. In some villages, farmers seem to hold relatively long-term tenure and most of the rights, e.g. right to crop selection, right to convert to alternative agricultural uses, right to rent, typically associated with a private property regime, short of being able to buy or sell the land. In other villages, on the other hand, tenure is more short-term, and farmers' use of the land appears to be constrained in a variety of ways.

We have examined a number of alternative explanations for this heterogeneity. Underlying the reallocation behavior appears to be a number of factors including: quota fulfillment, the desire to maintain equal access to land among villagers, missing rental markets, and rent-seeking behavior on the part of local leaders. The role of reallocations in assuring equal access can only explain a small portion of the reallocation behavior; the other explanations, all of which are linked to the incentives of local leaders, appear to be far more important in explaining decisions with respect to the timing and size of reallocations. These incentives, in turn, are directly tied to their responsibilities for fulfilling state policy, as well as rent-seeking behavior on their part.

So how has China's land management system fared in its effort to increase efficiency and equity? Our work (and that of others) on the impact of the land tenure system on growth, efficiency and distribution is limited, but a number of observations can be made. First, the impact on growth, through tenure security's effect on investment, appears relatively modest. One possibility is that leaders are "internalizing" these costs in making decisions; in other words, in areas in which the potential costs of tenure insecurity are high, reallocation is less likely. Some villages have also invested heavily in agriculture. Since we do not have the basis for estimating investment, crop choice, and output under a counterfactual in which households enjoy all of the rights associated with private property, we hesitate to push this conclusion too far.

Land allocation also has important distributive implications. In the 1980s, equal access to land played an important role in enabling households to meet basic nutritional needs at minimum cost in an environment in which food markets were highly imperfect and off-farm opportunities were limited. This feature of the system, however, has probably become less important as grain markets have developed, as off-farm opportunities have expanded, and as rural incomes have risen. All of these developments in some sense have taken pressure off the land. In the changing economic environment in China, the current land tenure system may actually be adversely affecting income distribution. Households differ considerably in terms of their ability to access rapidly emerging off-farm opportunity. This ability is linked to the age of individuals and human capital. Hence, it is likely that poorly developed rental markets have prevented households limited in terms of their ability to access off-farm opportunity from more fully utilizing their labor and earning more income through expanding the size of the farm operations. More generally, the land system may have discouraged households from specializing in agriculture. This issue will become more important over the next decade as the farm labor force continues to shrink both in absolute and percentage terms, and as a reorganization in farm structure is required, and as competitive pressures in food markets grow.

In the long run, most economists believe that China needs a land tenure system that provides long-term security of tenure and promotes the efficient use of land. The current policy to provide households with security for 30 years and only allow small adjustments to accommodate population changes is a step in that direction. In the meantime, however, keeping the door open for small adjustments may be enough to meet distributional concerns. As we noted above, only a small percentage of the land that is reallocated appears related to the desire to maintain equal access, and so small adjustments can likely meet this need. Secure use rights and the expansion of rental markets are one way to help facilitate the reorganization that is required in the farm sector.

If the past is any clue, however, this policy will only be effective if the incentives of local leaders are aligned in this direction, (i.e., when there is less incentive for leaders to undertake major reallocations). Interestingly, during the past several years the decline in farm prices and the conversion of the quota-tax into a subsidy have worked in that direction by reducing the "rents" and other benefits that local leaders originally had from maintaining control over land. Rental activity appears to have increased as a consequence, with potentially important benefits for both efficiency and distribution. Without secure land rights, however, the propensity of leaders to have increasingly less interest in land reallocations could be short-lived. A rise in farm prices and a reintroduction of the quotas would once again put a premium on the control over land, and likely reverse the recent trend. As long as land is not privatized – and that raises a separate set of issues – additional reforms, including an elimination of the quota, and additional checks on leader behavior such as that provided through genuinely contested elections, are likely needed to sustain the current trends. This highlights once again how embedded the property rights households enjoy are in the local political economy, and how reform of the local political economy is required to provide farmers the kinds of property rights a rapidly growing economy requires.

Notes

1 The growth rate was so fast that some policy-makers even began to worry about how to deal with the problem of surplus grain in China.

2 For example, compare our estimates of the areas covered by different land tenure types (see below). The survey also collected data on labor movement and labor market participation, and our estimates are nearly identical to the point estimates released by the State Statistical Bureau – see Rozelle *et al.* (1999).

3 These are poverty areas, largely mountain or disaster area villages.

4 The distinction between responsibility and ration land is a case in point. For example, in some villages, quotas are allocated on the basis of a combination of household size and the amount of responsibility land that the household has. If we assume that there are no other differences, the distribution of quota obligations across households in a village with only responsibility land (and the quota allocated on the basis of land and household size) will look exactly the same to the distribution in a village with both ration land and responsibility land in which the quota was tied only to the amount of responsibility land.

5 According to our household-level data, roughly three-quarters of all changes in land-holdings are related to village-wide reallocations. Expiration of contracts on land contracted from the village, family division, as well immediate village accommodation of increases in household size appear to make up much of the remaining quarter.

6 Even in villages in which ownership is with the small group and land reallocation occurs among households within the small group, decisions regarding the timing and nature of the reallocations appear to reside in most cases with the village.

7 The survey question asked for the percentage of land that has not been reallocated since HRS. One minus this percentage is the amount of land that has been reallocated *at least once*.

8 In almost 60 percent of the villages that have previously reallocated, the date of the next reallocation has been announced. In contrast, in only 15 percent of the villages that have not reallocated has a date of the first reallocation been announced. These percentages are open to several interpretations, but villages that have not yet reallocated do not appear to be facing a higher probability of reallocation in the near future. Although no reallocation date has been given, these villages likely are experiencing more secure tenure.

9 A related concept is that of *zhuanrang*, which usually refers to a permanent transfer of use rights between households and often carries the connotation of a "quasi-sale" (as opposed to the rental) of use rights. Unfortunately, the terms *zhuanrang* and *zhuanbao* are not used consistently throughout China.

10 See, for example, Prosterman *et al.* (1996). Carter *et. al.* (1995) is an exception.

11 An analysis of variance (ANOVA) highlight the role of local factors: Inter-provincial differences only explain 31.5 percent of the variation in the frequency of land reallocations across villages; inter-county differences are the source of 44.6 percent, while inter-township differences explain 71.3 percent. This leaves almost 30 percent to within township or village-level differences alone.

12 According to the Organization Law of the Village Committee, the responsibility of the village committee is "to manage the land and other assets belonging to the collective, to guide villagers to use natural resources properly, and to guide villagers to protect and improve the natural environment" (Article 4, Organization Law of the Village Committee of PRC, *China's Agricultural Yearbook* (ZGTJNJ 1988: 459–460)).

13 There are ways to ensure access to new households other than through village reallocations. In some villages, a portion of village land, *jidong tian*, was retained at the time of the introduction of HRS to accommodate these future demands. Other villages use land returned by out-migrating households or adjust tax and quota obligations, and newly formed or newly enlarged households "line up" for land as it becomes available.

14 This occurs to be increasingly common as suggested by comments by Chen Xiwen and Du Ying in presentations made at a recent conference in Beijing on land policy, although such sales were rarely observed in any of the 215 randomly selected villages in our sample.

15 Implicit in Johnson's analysis is the assumption that villagers universally prefer secure tenure. If Kung and Liu (1997), Carter *et al.* (1995), and others are correct, however, a majority of villagers favor reallocations. The size of the constituency in support of reallocations differs among villages and is tied to household demographics, the local economic environment, and the extent and security of opportunities outside of farming (Kung and Liu 1997).

16 In absolute terms, government grain procurement increased during the early 1980s, fell and then remained more or less fixed at around 50 million tons in the late 1980s. In the 1990s, procurement gradually fell to around 40 million tons. This currently represents about 10 percent of grain output. The government's monopsony in cotton is more pervasive, and in the mid-1990s more than 80 percent of cotton was procured by the government. See Sicular (1995).

17 It is interesting to note that local leaders frequently point out that the willingness of higher officials to overlook local policy deviations on such things as tenure security is directly linked to requests for local leaders to meet these other more crucial targets.

18 See Rozelle and Li (1998).

19 Our survey data suggest that less than one percent of households default on their quotas. Non-compliance of other forms may be higher however.

20 See Turner *et al.* (2000).

21 This also implies that the "rent" associated with the land is effectively negative or at least quite low.

22 See Turner *et al.* (2000).

23 The village dummies or "fixed-effects" help absorb cross-village heterogeneity in farm size that might also be correlated with family size.

24 See Benjamin and Brandt (2000), for a more in-depth analysis.

25 A total of 50/780 households do not have land. Most of these households are involved exclusively in non-agricultural activity, and in fact returned their land to the village to avoid having to farm it.

26 Nonetheless, controlling for systematic differences across villages, we cannot reject the hypothesis that cultivated land is allocated on average in direct proportion to family size. The coefficients on the variables capturing the demographic composition of household, on the other hand, are usually insignificant. However, when we add a variable representing the number of household members participating in off-farm opportunities, we found that households with members working off-farm receive less land per capita. Apparently, villages are taking into account the importance of farming to the household, reallocating land from the partly non-agricultural households to those solely engaged in agriculture.

27 Deaths of the elderly and births do not affect the number of individuals of working age in the household, but can affect how much other members of the family decide to work through a variety of channels, e.g. the number of individuals that need to be fed.

28 Benjamin and Brandt (2000). Burgess (1997) in a related paper also utilizes the inverse relationship, but only looks at output and not also at labor input and labor productivity because of data limitations. He finds support for a fairly severe inverse relationship in Sichuan but only a small one in Zhejiang, which he attributes to differences in off-farm opportunities in the two provinces.

29 We also examined if the severity of the relationship is correlated with key institutional factors, such as the nature of village land reallocation. We find that villages that undertook larger and more comprehensive village land reallocations eliminated some of the labor inefficiency. One interpretation of this result is that reallocations are partially mimicking the outcome of a functioning land rental market. However, even after the reallocations, we still find that inefficiency remains.

30 Out of a total of 735 households in our survey who farm, 664 have more than one plot. After obtaining basic information about each plot, two plots, of different tenure types when possible, were selected from each household to investigate more carefully. Enumerators systematically surveyed the two selected plots from each household, eliciting information about the plot's tenure status, specific land rights, all inputs and outputs, and land quality. See Li *et al.* (1998). Because of the nature of our data, we are limited to analyzing only one household investment decision, the use of organic fertilizer. Other kinds of land quality-improving investments are excluded from the analysis.

31 These differences are actually small when compared to the gaps existing between private and collective fields in the pre-reform period. Burki (1969), for example, observed that private plots had a yield averaging more than twice the collective yield. This can likely be attributed to the fact that the differences in the residual income rights between private and collective plots were much greater than that between private and responsibility plots.

32 This is as expected given that the impact of these other current inputs on productivity does not extend past the current agricultural year.

33 One problem with the above results is that the length of time that a household has held a plot may not be a perfect measure of tenure; it could be that the longer one has held a plot, the more likely the land will be taken away.

34 Carter and Yao (1998) consider several investment activities in the context of a structural econometric model that allows for three kinds of effects of property rights. These include: (1) the effect of tenure security on the household's investment; (2) the effect of the right to rent the land on the households investment incentives; and (3) the effect of rental rights on the equalization of the returns to labor and other current inputs across households. Drawing on a two-year panel of data for 214 households in Zhejiang, they estimate the effect of these property rights on investment and labor supply decisions conditional on households' decision regarding land rental. They find that the most important effect comes through the influence of tenure security on the household's investment. The right to rent does not have a significant effect on investment, while neither tenure security nor the right-to-rent appear to be affecting labor intensity. Simulations suggest that reducing the number of reallocations by one would result in an increase in investment sufficient to support an increase of output by about 5 percent, an impact about the same as our study.

35 The papers on this subject, including ours, differ in their methodological sophistication and their attention to a number of econometric issues that arise in analyzing duration-type behavior of this sort. Empirical problems are compounded by the fact that the regressions are often of highly reduced form, which leaves their results open to a number of alternative interpretations. At a minimum, however, the papers as a group suggest that land reallocation is tied to village population growth; to the growth of off-farm opportunities; to the need to eliminate inefficiencies in the allocation of land across households; and to quota fulfillment. In the rest of this section, we draw heavily on Turner *et al.* (2000). We believe that this work that examines the broadest number of institutional factors.

36 For example, villages can use land set aside explicitly for these purposes, or it can readjust the household's farm quotas. In addition, A number of non-demographic factors also appear to affect the timing decisions surrounding reallocations. Variables capturing the size of the fixed costs associated with reallocation have a significant effect on timing decisions related to reallocation: Reallocations are less frequent where fixed costs are higher. Village leaders also reallocate land more frequently in areas with higher quotas, a finding consistent with alternative interpretations about how quotas may affect village behavior that we examined earlier. Finally, reallocation is less likely in villages where decisions about reallocations are made by the township. In fact, in areas in which townships have rights over reallocation, reallocation is rare, a finding that may mean that township-level involvement in land policy helps enforce the earlier fifteen-year tenure security provision of the HRS Law. Interestingly, in villages with contested elections, in other words, in those village elections that have two or more candidates vying for the village leadership position, the time between reallocations is shorter.

37 See Benjamin and Brandt (2000) for more details.

References

Alchian, A. and Demsetz, H. (1973) "The Property Rights Paradigm," *Journal of Economic History*, 33(1): 16–27.

Benjamin, D. (1995) "Can Unobserved Land Quality Explain the Inverse Productivity Relationship," *Journal of Development Economics*, 46 (1 February): 51–84.

Benjamin, D. and Brandt, L. (2000) *Property Rights, Labor Markets and Efficiency in a Transition Economy: The Case of Rural China*, working paper, Toronto: University of Toronto.

Benjamin, D., Brandt, L., Glevve, P. and Li, G. (2000) *Markets, Human Capital and Income Inequality in Rural China*, WDI Working Paper.

Benjamin, D., Brandt, L. and Rozelle, S. (2000) "Aging, Well-being, and Social Security in Rural North China," forthcoming, *Population and Development.*

Besley, T. (1995) "Property Rights and Investment Incentives: Theory and Evidence from Ghana," *Journal of Political Economy*, 103(5): 903–937.

Binswanger, H. and Rosensweig, M. (1986) "Behavioral and Material Determinants of Production Relations in Agriculture," *Journal of Development Studies*, 22: 503–517.

Burgess, R. (1997) *Land, Welfare, and Efficiency in Rural China*, London: London School of Economics.

Burki, S. J. (1969) *A Study of Chinese Communes*, Cambridge, MA: Harvard University Press.

Carter, M. (1984) "Identification of the Inverse Relationship between Farm Size and Productivity: An Empirical Analysis of Peasant Agricultural Production," *Oxford Economics Papers*, 36(1 March): 131–146.

Carter, M., Liu, S., Roth M., and Yao, Y. (1995) *Property Rights Evolution and Induced Institutional Change in Post-Reform Rural China*, working paper, Madison, WI: Department of Agricultural and Applied Economics, University of Wisconsin-Madison.

Carter, M., Liu, S. and Yao, Y. (1995) *Dimensions and Diversity of Property Rights in Rural China*, working paper, Madison, WI: Department of Agricultural and Applied Economics, University of Wisconsin-Madison.

Carter, M. and Yao, Y. (1998) *Property Rights, Rental Markets, and Land in China*, working paper, Madison, WI: Department of Agricultural and Applied Economics, University of Wisconsin-Madison.

Chen, X. 1999. "Issues in Land and Management of Land Rights in China," paper presented in the 1999 conference on Land Rights, China Institute of Reform, Haikou, China, January 15–16.

Cheng, Y. and Tsang, S. (1995/1996) "Agricultural Land Reform in a Mixed System: The Chinese Experience of 1984–1994," *China Information*, 10(3/4): 44–74.

Demsetz, H. 1967. "Toward a Theory of Property Rights," *American Economic Review*, 57(2): 347–359.

Dong, X. 1996. "Two-Tier land System and Sustained Economic Growth in Post-1978 Rural China," *World Development*, 24(5): 915–928.

Giles, J. 1998. "Off farm Labor Markets, Insecurity, and Risk Aversion in China." Mimeo, Department of Economics, University of California, Berkeley.

Ho, S. (1994) *Rural China in Transition*, New York: Oxford University Press.

Huang, J. and Rozelle, S. (1996) "Technological Change: Rediscovering the

Engine of Productivity Growth in China's Rural Economy," *Journal of Development Economics*, 49(2): 337–67.

Jacoby, H.G., Li, G. and Rozelle, S. (2002) *Hazards of Expropriation: Tenure Insecurity and Investment in Rural China*, working paper, Washington, DC: World Bank, Research Department.

Johnson, D.G. (1995) *Property Rights in Rural China*, working paper, Chicago: Department of Economics, University of Chicago.

Johnson, D.G. (1996) *China's Rural and Agricultural Reforms in Perspective*, working paper, Chicago: Department of Economics, University of Chicago.

Kelliher, D. (1997) "The Chinese Debate over Village Self-Government," *The China Journal*, 37 (January): 63–86.

Kung, J. K. (1995) "Equal Entitlement versus Tenure Security under a Regime of Collective Property Rights: Peasants' Preference for Institutions in Post-reform Chinese Agriculture," *Journal of Comparative Economics*, 21: 82–111.

Kung, J.K. and Liu, S. (1996) "Land Tenure Systems in Post-Reform Rural China: A Tale of Six Counties.," working paper, Hong Kong: Division of Social Sciences, Hong Kong University of Science and Technology.

Kung, J.K. and Liu, S. (1997) "Farmers' Preferences Regarding Ownership and Land Tenure in Post-Mao China: Unexpected Evidence from Eight Counties," *The China Journal*, 38 (July): 33–63.

Li, G. (1999) "Land Rights, Tenure, and Leaders in China," unpublished Phd dissertation. Food Research Institute, Stanford University, Stanford, California.

Li, G., Rozelle, S. and Brandt, L.(1998) "Tenure, Land Rights, and Farmer Investment Incentives in China," *Agricultural Economics*, 19: 63–71.

Lin, J.Y. (1992) "Rural Reforms and Agricultural Growth in China," *American Economic Review*, 82 (1): 34–51.

McMillan, J., J. Whalley, J. and Zhu, L. (1989) "The Impact of China's Economic Reforms on Agricultural Productivity Growth," *Journal of Political Economy*, 97: 781–807.

O'Brien, K.J. and Li, L. (1999) "Selective Policy Implementation in Rural China." *Comparative Politics*, (January): 167–186.

Oi, J. and Rozelle, S. (2000) "Elections and Power: The Locus of Decision Making in Chinese Villages," *China Quarterly*, 162: 300–325.

Prosterman, R., Hanstad, T. and Li, P. (1996) "Can China Feed Itself?" *Scientific American*, (November): 90–96.

Putterman, L. (1992) *Continuity and Change in China's Rural Development: Collectives and Reform Eras in Perspectives*, New York: Oxford University Press.

Qiao, F. (1997) "Property Rights and Forest Land Use in Southern China," unpublished Master's thesis, Graduate School of Chinese Academy of Agricultural Sciences, Beijing, China.

Rozelle, S. (1994) "Decision-Making in China's Rural Economy: The Linkage between Village Leaders and Farm Households," *China Quarterly*, 137: 99–124.

Rozelle, S. (1996) "Stagnation Without Equity: Changing Patterns of Income and Inequality in China's Post-Reform Rural Economy," *China Journal*, 35 (January): 63–96.

Rozelle, S. and Boisvert, R. (1994) "Quantifying Chinese Village Leaders' Multiple Objectives," *Journal of Comparative Economics*, 18 (February): 25–45.

Rozelle, S. and Li, G. (1998) "Village Leaders and Land-Rights Formation in China," *American Economic Review*, 88(2): 433–438.

Rozelle, S., Li, G., Shen, M., Hughart, A. and Giles, J. (1999) "Leaving China's Farms: Survey Results of New Paths and Remaining Hurdles to Rural Migration," *China Quarterly*, 158 (June): 367–393.

Sicular, T. (1995) "Redefining State, Plan and Market: China's Reforms in Agricultural Commerce," *China Quarterly*, 144: 1020–1046.

Turner, M., Brandt, L. and Rozelle, S. (2000) *Local Government Behavior and Property Right Formation in Rural China*, working paper, Toronto: Department of Economics, University of Toronto.

ZGNYNJ (Zhongguo Nongye Nianjian, *China Agricultural Yearbook*) (1985–1997) Beijing: China Statistical Publishing House.

ZGTJNJ (Zhongguo Tongji Nianjian, *China Statistical Yearbook*) (1989–1997) Beijing: China Statistical Publishing House.

5 Market versus administrative reallocation of land

An econometric analysis

Michael R. Carter and Yang Yao

China's household responsibility system (HRS) created a hybrid property rights system. While it decisively individualized residual income rights, land use, transfer and reallocation rights were divided between the individual land users and their villages that remained the legal custodians of land.[1] As Peter Ho points out in the Introduction to this volume, the result of the HRS reforms was a socially credible land tenure institution that apparently managed to successfully mediate between competing equity and productivity goals.

However, much has changed in the quarter century since the adoption of the HRS. China has seen spectacular industrial growth and increasing urban and rural incomes. As both Ho (Introduction, this volume) and Rozelle *et al.* (Chapter 4, this volume) argue, China's rapid growth has challenged the HRS along many dimensions, including: (1) its ability to bring land and labor together in efficient combinations in the face of massive outflows of labor from agriculture; (2) its ability to provide adequate investment incentives in the face of rising value of labor; and (3) its ability to secure the basic land rights of villagers against encroachment as economic growth pushes up the value of land, especially in peri-urban areas. Given these new challenges, it is not surprising that China's land tenure system is once again under scrutiny.

The aim of this chapter is to better understand the functioning of the HRS as a way to clarify reform options for the future. In particular, we try to clarify how well periodic administrative land reallocations have maintained egalitarian land access goals, and at what cost in terms of foregone production and investment. To achieve these goals, we rely on household- and village-level panel data collected during the middle of the HRS period. Fortunately, these data show substantial variability across time and space in the allocation of rights between individuals and their villages. As Rozelle *et al.* (this volume) review, in some areas of China, villages have periodically redistributed land between households based on economic and demographic changes among households, while in others areas households were granted much greater immunity against redistribution of any sort. Similarly, villages have differed in the degree to which individual households could trade land among themselves, with some villages not regulating the practice at all, whereas others required village approval or simply prohibited land rental relationships. By econometrically exploiting this local variability in land tenure practice, we are able to identify strengths and weaknesses of the hybrid HRS.

At the time of the HRS reform, most villages allocated land to households based on the size of the household and its labor force (Graynor and Putterman 1993; Liu *et al.* 1998). Given this distributional mechanism, the initial post-HRS distribution of factor endowments – defined as the ratio of contract land to family labor – across households must have been fairly compressed. Moreover, with limited opportunities for off-farm jobs or for urban migration, there must have been relatively little scope for land and labor exchange between households. Even with limited exchange of these factors, and irrespective of the definition of tenure security and transfer rights, the intensity with which land was cultivated must have also been quite similar across households.

However, the rapid growth and industrialization of the Chinese economy since 1980, with its concomitant withdrawal of labor from agriculture, have put new pressure on the fluidity and efficacy of the institutions that allocate rural land and labor. In this new environment, the absence of further administrative reallocation of endowments, with no increase in private land or labor transactions, would imply an increasing dispersion in both the factor endowment and the factor intensity distributions. An increased dispersion in the latter distribution would signal a potentially costly (static) allocative inefficiency problem of under- (and over-) utilized land. Moreover, as we have argued elsewhere (Carter and Yao 2002), in an environment of rapidly growing off-farm employment, imperfectly transferable rights may discourage investment by households that expect to exit or reduce their participation in agriculture in the near future.

While either market or administrative mechanisms could in theory resolve the new challenges posed by rapid industrialization, this chapter turns to empirical data to gauge how these mechanisms actually function in practice. Using panel data on a sample of 80 villages drawn from across rural China in 1988 and 1993, we will first clarify the extent of these new land tenure problems. We will empirically study how well administrative reallocations and market transactions have responded to the potential efficiency gains. One possibility might be that administrative reallocations do, to some extent, take care of the allocative efficiency because they bring closer a household's land and labor endowments. Accordingly, the function of market transactions might be weakened because they only take care of residual transaction needs that are not fulfilled in administrative reallocations. However, the allocative efficiency thus obtained is only a side product of the land reallocation system whose major concern is equity of land-holding. In addition, the reallocation system may entail a substantial dynamic loss due to lost investment. We will also provide an empirical assessment of the size of the loss.

The chapter is organized as the following. The second section looks at the evolving distributions of endowments and factor proportions in production over the 1988 to 1993 time period. We find that these distributions have statistically changed over time and that the land–labor endowment distribution has become more disperse, revealing the uneven impact of industrial employment growth and other demographic shifts. At the same time, we find that the factor intensity distribution (in rice production) has, if anything, become slightly less disperse over this time period, indicating that either centralized or decentralized mechanisms are at least keeping pace with the challenge of demographic and industrial change.

How, then, do these two competing mechanisms work and at what cost? Addressing this first issue, the third section explores how administrative and market-mediated land reallocations respond to evolving opportunities to improve the efficiency or the endowment equality of the rural economy. We use panel data and appropriate econometric methods to estimate the factors that lead to land reallocations and land rentals. Our strongest finding is that administrative reallocations respond primarily to increasing dispersion in endowment ratios (i.e., to equity concerns) and hence can be seen to play a social insurance function.[2]

The fourth section then turns to see if this social insurance is indeed costly by exploring whether or not the tenure insecurity implied by centralized powers of administrative reallocation significantly dampens investment sunk into land. Using panel data methods to control for the likely correlation between tenure regime and unobserved factors that influence returns to investment, the analysis in this section shows that tenure insecurity does significantly reduce investment.[3] Whether or not this price is one worth paying for this insurance is an issue that will require additional research, as discussed in the chapter's final section.

Changes in factor endowment and factor intensity distributions, 1988 to 1993

A well-functioning economy that obtains maximal output from the resources that it utilizes will allocate inputs such that their marginal productivities are equal across different uses and production units. Were this not the case, total output could be increased by shifting inputs from lower to higher productivity locations. Under fairly general assumptions about the nature of technology, dispersion in the ratio of labor allocated to production per-unit area cultivated is a good indicator of the degree to which an agricultural economy has succeeded in equating factor productivities across farm units. While it is unlikely that any real-world economy will perfectly equalize factor intensity across households,[4] panel data from a sample of households that were surveyed in 1989 and again in 1994, permits us to explore whether the dispersion in factor proportions has increased over time. These same data also provide a window through which to view how the endowment distribution (defined as the ratio of household contract land per-family member) has evolved under hybrid property rights and the pressure of rapid industrialization.

The overall survey covered 800 households spread across 80 villages drawn from four provinces.[5] In our study, we only use data on about 400 households in four counties in Zhejiang and Jiangxi Provinces that primarily cultivate rice. We do this because we have to confine our study to a sample with fairly homogenous production technology and cropping pattern. Zhejiang is an advanced province located in China's south-east coast, Jiangxi is a neighboring province to the west of Zhejiang and is primarily an agricultural province. The coverage of the sample is limited but encompasses the income spectrum in rice-producing areas. One measure of dispersion is the coefficient of variation, defined as the standard deviation of a variable normalized or divided by the variable's mean. Table 5.1 shows the 1988 and 1993 coefficient of variations for both the household land–labor endowment ratio (family members per *mu*[6] of land owned or contracted) and the factor proportions ratio (labor hours of work in rice per *mu* of rice cultivated). As can be seen, both the endowment and factor proportions distributions became more disperse over time for the sample as a whole. The coefficient of variation for the endowment distribution rose from 74 percent to 100 percent, while this variation measure increased from 46 percent to 50 percent for the factor proportions ratio.[7]

The increase in both of these dispersion measures is not surprising given China's rapid rate of industrialization over this time period. It signals the sort of economic losses mentioned above. Some of the increase in overall dispersion is likely to result from differences that have emerged between, rather than within, villages. For example, we might expect that more rapidly growing regions will experience an increase in wage rates and a matching fall in the labor intensity of rice production. In order to distinguish this source of increased variation from that which occurs because of, say, faulty allocative institutions within the local village economy, Table 5.1 also presents an intra-village coefficient of variation that permits us to see whether or not local level dispersion has increased.[8] As can be seen, the intra-village coefficient of variation of factor endowments rose from 43 percent to 54 percent, whereas the intra-village measure for the distribution of factor proportions actually declined slightly (34 percent from to 32 percent). This latter finding suggests that on average at least, village institutions and rules are doing a good job at preventing the increased endowment dispersion from spilling over into the sorts of productivity losses that would be signaled by increasing dispersion in factor proportions. However, it is not clear whether this relatively

Table 5.1 Descriptive statistics, 1988–1993

	1988		*1993*
Endowment distribution of paddy land			
Mean (*mu*/family member)	0.72		0.85
Coefficient of variation			
Overall (%)	74		100
Intra-village (%)	43		54
Factor proportions in rice paddy production			
Mean (hours/*mu*)	239		309
Coefficient of variation			
Overall (%)	46		50
Intra-village (%)	34		32
Village level data			
Percentage of land rented	9.2		8.7
Percentage of land reallocated (1988–1993)		11.3	
Intra-village variation in non-farm income (standard deviation)	947 yuan		2,775 yuan
Structural indicators			
Quotas (% expected yield)	23		21
Non-farm employment (% of total)	34		38
Property rights indicators (% villages)			
Unrestricted rentals	73		55
Immune to reallocation	65		53
Household level data			
Fixed investment (hours/*mu*)	6.3		6.4
Average household age	32		35
Average household schooling years	5.4		5.8
Fragmentation (number of parcels)	9.1		9.9
Land quality (% flat land)	84.0		81.0

positive result on average has been produced by increasingly effective centralized administrative reallocations or by decentralized, market-based adjustments.

Before turning to that issue, it is useful to develop a more refined picture of the shifts in the underlying endowment and factor proportion distributions. Figure 5.1 displays distribution functions for these variables that have been estimated using our data.[10] Figure 5.1 graphs the estimated land–labor endowment distributions for 1988 and 1993, showing that greater dispersion in this distribution that has emerged over time reflects increased density in both the upper and lower tails of the distribution. That is, some households have become relatively land abundant (those in the upper tail of the distribution), while others have become increasingly land scarce (those in the lower tail of the distribution).

Figure 5.2 displays the estimated distribution of the labor to land (or factor proportions) ratio for the sample of rice producers. Already by 1988, the distribution of factor intensity appears relatively disperse.

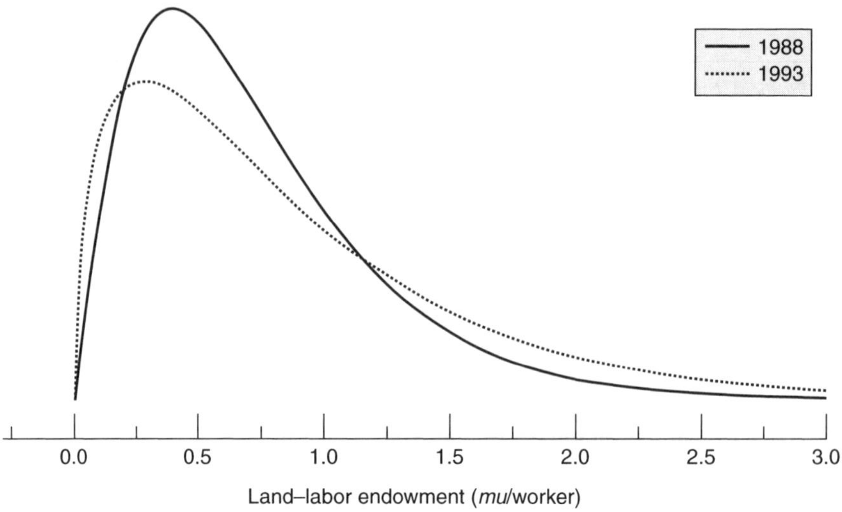

Figure 5.1 Estimated land–labor endowment distributions, 1988 and 1993.

The mode for the estimated 1988 factor proportions distribution is about 200 hours of labor per-*mu*. However, as can also be seen, there is a not inconsequential number of farms that apply as few as 100 hours of labor per-*mu*, acting as if labor is very scarce or dear. Similarly, there are a number of units that behave in the opposite way, allocating as many as 400 hours of labor per-*mu* of cultivated rice. Either reallocation of land from the land-abundant to the land-scarce farms, or reallocation of labor from labor-abundant to labor-scarce farms would be expected to increase total agricultural output from the same resource base. Assuming constant returns to scale, an output labor elasticity of one-third and equal use of non-labor inputs per-*mu* on all farms, this estimated dispersion in labor intensity implies a 2.2 percent yield loss (that is, yields would average 2.2 percent higher if all farm units produced at the average labor intensity of 240 hours per-*mu*). Compared to the 1988 distribution, the 1993 distribution has shifted right. While the upper tail of the distribution has increased (indicating that there is a greater proportion of farms that are cultivating their land more intensively in 1993), the lower tail has actually shrunk over the 1988 to 1993 period. Calculated under the same assumptions described above, the yield loss implied by this 1993 distribution of labor intensity is 2.4 percent, slightly higher than the 1988 value. Note that because average labor intensity was higher in 1993 than in 1988 (309 versus 240 hours per-*mu*), the physical losses implied by this labor intensity dispersion are greater than the 0.2 percent yield loss difference would imply.

To summarize the findings of this section, we see that as expected

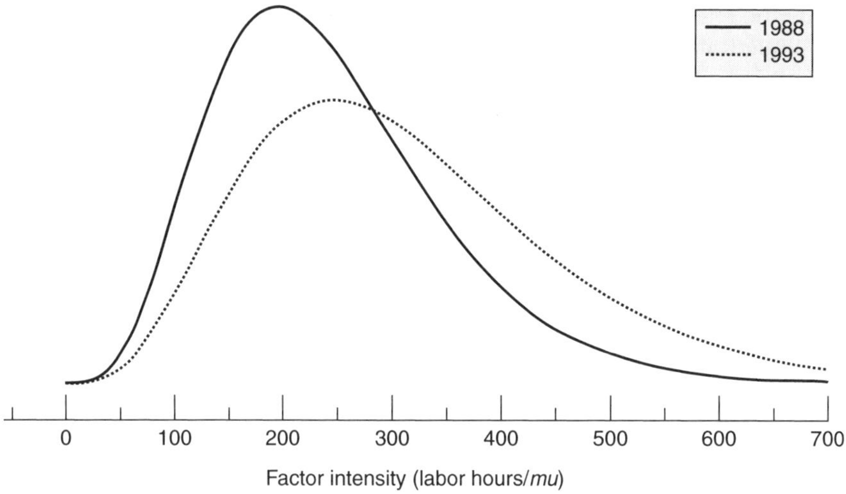

Figure 5.2 Estimated land–labor distribution for rice producers.

under the pressure of an industrializing economy and ongoing demographic change, the overall endowment distribution has spread out over time, both across and within villages. However, the impacts on distribution of labor intensity in production have been much more muted. While the overall level of allocative inefficiency in the rural, rice-producing economy seems to have increased slightly (to about a 2.4 percent yield loss), most of that change seems to have occurred between rather than within villages. There is thus some evidence that local institutions and mechanisms are coping relatively well with the challenges of continuing industrialization and labor outmigration.

The responsiveness of market and administrative reallocations to social and economic forces

As described above, the endowment and factor proportions distributions in rural China have been evolving under a variety of locally determined institutional mechanisms. While considerable controversy surrounds the relative merits of decentralized, market-based mechanisms versus centralized administrative mechanisms, empirical analysis of how either functions is scarce. An important exception is the study by Turner *et al.* (1998) who estimate the determinants of administrative land reallocation in China. Their theoretical ruminations suggest that cadre (and the village political process) may reallocate land for a variety of reasons, ranging from equity goals to concerns to maximize the productivity of village resources (which they term the "rational village" hypothesis). In the analysis here, we will follow their theoretical lead and test for the significance of both equity and efficiency factors in motivating administrative reallocations.

While finding evidence in favor of what they term the "rational village" hypothesis, Turner *et al.* (1998) also note that market and administrative mechanisms are alternative means of achieving the same goal. Unfortunately, their data do not permit them to adequately explore the determinants of both market and administrative reallocations. Using the panel data available for this study, we are able to study this question using the model developed in the remainder of this section.

Administrative and market-mediated land reallocation: a regression model

The panel data available here suggest a resolution to statistical identification problem and open the way to an exploration of the responsiveness of market and administrative reallocation to socio-economic forces. We begin by noting that the percentage of land that the village cadre would desire to administratively reallocated in village i PRIOR to the commencement of agricultural production in year t (denoted A^*_{it-}) may respond either to inequitable intra-village dispersion in the endowment distribution, or to inefficient intra-village dispersion in the factor proportions distribution that were observed to have occurred in the prior production period, $t-1$. Dispersion in the former distribution would signal the potential for equity gains from reallocation, while dispersion in the latter would indicate that reallocation would create efficiency gains. The intra-village coefficients of variations defined above suggest themselves as natural measures of this dispersion. In addition, the percentage of village grain output that must be delivered to the state quota system is likely to signal the severity of the pressure upon village cadres to attend to productivity-dampening inefficiency.

These considerations suggest the following base regression model for the amount of land we would expect cadre to desire to reallocate in village i in year t:

$$E[A^*_{it-}] = \beta^A_0 + Q_{it-1}\beta^A_1 + \sigma^T_{it-1}\beta^A_2 + \sigma^\ell_{it-1}\beta^A_3 \quad (5.1)$$

where $E[A^*_{it-}]$ denotes the expected amount of land reallocation, Q_{it-1} is the quote obligation for village i in year $t-1$ (*i.e.*, the period prior to the redistribution); σ^T_{it-1} is the intra-village coefficient of variation in village land-labor endowment; and, σ^ℓ_{it-1} is the intra-village coefficient of variation in factor proportions. As discussed above, we would expect the three key parameters, β^A_1, β^A_2 and β^A_3 all to be positive. For simplicity we will compactly write the regression function for administrative reallocation as $E[A^*_{it-}] = z^A_{it-1}\beta^A$, where z^A_{it-1} is simply the set of explanatory variables in equation (5.1) above and β^A is the set of regression parameters for the administrative regression.

Turning now to the land rental market, we denote the percentage of village land that villagers would desire to transact through rental contracts in period t as R_{it}^*. Note that market transactions take place AFTER any administrative reallocations and thus respond to residual opportunities for mutually beneficial exchange. Such opportunities are created by intra-village dispersion in the contemporaneous distributions of endowments and in off-farm, wage labor opportunity, where the latter is measured as the standard deviation in household off-farm earnings and is denoted σ_{it}^w.[10] We posit the following regression model for the expected percent of in village i in time t to be reallocated through rental transactions:

$$E[R_{it}^*] = \beta_0^R + \beta_1^R \sigma_{it}^w + \beta_2^R \sigma_{it}^T \tag{5.2}$$

where σ_{it}^w is the intra-village variation in off-farm earnings, and as before σ_{it}^T is the intra-village variation in households' land–labor endowment. We would expect the key regression parameters, β_1^R and β_2^R, both to be positive. Analogously to the simplification for the administrative reallocation equation, we will compactly write the regression function for market mediated land reallocation as $E[R_{it}^*] = z_{it-1}^R \beta^R$.

Table 5.1 presents descriptive statistical indicators of these dispersion measures, as well as measures of the amounts of land reallocated by both administrative and market-based mechanisms. To calculate both these latter two measures, we first estimated the total land stock in a village using the information on household land allocation together with reports of land set aside by the village for future redistributions. The reported rental variables were calculated by summing up the absolute value of all rental transactions (both land rented in and land rented out) and dividing by the estimated village land stock. The administrative reallocation variable is the sum of all land reallocations (positive or negative) reported by surveyed households over the 1988 through 1992 period.[11] As can be seen, on average just under 10 percent of the village land base was affected by rental transactions in both 1988 and 1993.[13] The total amount of land administratively reallocated over the 1988 to 1992 period was about 11 percent of the village land base. Unfortunately, we do not have data on the administrative allocations that took place in the wake of the 1993 cropping season.

Consistent with the data from the rice-producing villages analyzed above, the intra-village coefficients of variation measures show on average an increase in the variation in the endowment distribution, and a decrease in the dispersion of the factor proportions distribution.[13] Intra-village variation in off-farm income (as measured by the intra-village standard deviation in non-farm earnings) increased markedly over the 1988 to 1993 period. In 1988, the standard deviation was 947 yuan (fully 93 percent of mean household off-farm earnings). By 1993, this figure had risen to 2,775 yuan (or 98 percent of mean off-farm earnings that had grown rapidly over this time period from 1,350 to 4,000 yuan). The changes in these figures reflect the rapid growth of the non-farm economy and the modest increase in household specialization between agricultural and non-agricultural sectors.

While the dispersion measures reflect opportunities for gains from administrative reallocation as well as gains from rental trades, the desired levels of these transactions would be expected to depend on the permissiveness of the village-level property rights regime. As Liu *et al.* (1998) analyze in detail, in some villages the power of the cadre to administratively reallocate land is greatly hampered by regulations that grant individuals considerable tenure security and immunity against reallocation. There is also significant variation across villages in the degree to which individuals are permitted to engage in rental transactions. For the analysis here, we have defined two binary property rights variables, D^A_{it} and D^R_{it}. The first takes on the value of 1 when individuals are protected from or immune to administratively dictated redistribution. The second takes the value of 1 when individuals are at liberty to rent land out to others with no or minimal restrictions.

In conformity with the preceding observations about how property rights regimes constrain the ability of both cadre and villagers respectively to use administrative and market-based reallocation mechanisms, we consider the following switching regressions specification for the desired administrative reallocation:

$$E[A^*_{it-}] = \begin{cases} z^A_{it-1}\beta^A, \; if \; D^A_{it} = 0 \; (\textit{redistribution not limited}) \\ z^A_{it-1}(\beta^A + \delta^A), \; if \; D^A_{it} = 1 \; (\textit{redistribution limited}) \end{cases} \tag{5.3}$$

where δ^A are the parameters that give the dampening effects that occur when individuals are relatively immune to redistribution by village cadre. We would expect all the δ^A terms to be negative.

Paralleling equation (5.3), we express expect land transacted through markets as:

$$E[R^*_{it}] = \begin{cases} z^R_{it}\beta^{RA}, \; if \; D^R_{it} = 0 \; (\textit{transfer rights limited}) \\ z^R_{it}(\beta^R + \delta^R), \; if \; D^R_{it} = 1 \; (\textit{transfer rights not limited}) \end{cases} \tag{5.4}$$

where the δ^R parameters again give the additional effects expected to occur when individual rights are less restricted. We would expect all the δ^A terms to be positive.

A number of statistical difficulties confront the estimation of the parameters in equations (5.3) and (5.4), including those induced by the possibility that the property rights regimes are themselves endogenous, as Liu *et al.* (1998) discuss. A technical appendix available from the authors details the simulated maximum likelihood methods that are used to estimate equations (5.3) and (5.4) using panel data methods that should eliminate potential biases resulting from this endogeneity and other problems.

Estimation results

Table 5.2 presents our estimates of the parameters for the regression functions equations (5.3) and (5.4).[14] Turning first to the estimates of expected administrative land reallocation, we see that the variables related to both quotas and endowment dispersion are significant (statistically and economically). These results imply that village cadre respond to both equity concerns in reallocating land (in the absence of property rights forbidding reallocation, a 10 percentage point increase in the intra-village coefficient of variation for the endowment distribution brings an estimated reallocation of 2.4 percent of village land), and that they reallocate more frequently when quota delivery pressure is higher. Individual immunity against such redistributions ($D^A = 1$) seems to block further reallocations for equity purposes, though interestingly, it has no dampening effect on quota-driven reallocations as the interaction between the property rights variable and quotas is small and statistically insignificant. While both of the quota and endowment dispersion results are consistent with a rational village model of reallocation, the coefficient on dispersion in the land–labor factor intensity variable is significant and counterintuitively negative in the regression.

The regression estimate of the land rental equation failed to confirm any of the hypotheses concerning the factors expected to increase the amount of land in a village that is rented. Indeed, the only significant coefficient in the equation is that for the endowment dispersion measure. However, the negative sign of this coefficient is again counterintuitive.

Table 5.2 Econometric estimates of determinants of rental/administrative reallocations

	Administrative reallocation	*Market rental*
Structural factors		
Constant	0.51** (0.25)	–
Rights indicator, D^A, or D^R	−0.12* (0.07)	−0.21 (0.13)
Time effect	–	0.11 (0.07)
Quota	0.78** (0.26)	–
$D^A{}_*$Quota	0.01 (0.06)	–
Dispersion measures		
Endowment, σ^T	0.24** (0.10)	−0.63** (0.26)
$D^{A(R)}{}_*\sigma^T$	−0.61** (0.19)	0.42 (0.28)
Factor intensity, σ^ℓ	−0.42** (0.16)	–
$D^A{}_*\sigma^\ell$	0.13 (0.08)	–
Off-farm earnings, σ^w	–	0.13 (0.48)
$D^R{}_*\sigma^w$	–	−0.38 (0.49)

Notes

* Significant at the 10% level.

** Significant at the 5% level.

Regional dummy variables, variance terms and nuisance parameters not reported.

A simpler, but less reliable estimation procedure[15] yielded an estimate of the coefficient of the interaction between property rights and endowment dispersion that was large and significantly negative (indicating that more land passes through rental markets when property rights are permissive and the endowment dispersion in a village is large). These same estimates also identify a positive effect of off-farm earnings on land rented. While these pooled results are sensible, they are likely to be biased as they do not control for unobserved factors that may simultaneously increase the demand both for rental transactions and for less restricted property rights.

To summarize, the statistically conservative panel data approach used in this section has provided uncertain inference concerning factors that shape market and administrative reallocation of land. The data in general offer little insight on the factors that increase land rentals.[16] A clearer picture emerges about administrative reallocation, however, with both equity and production-minded (if not precisely allocative efficiency) concerns driving these reallocations.

Costs of administrative reallocation: tenure insecurity and investment disincentives

The analysis in the prior section found evidence that administrative land reallocations respond to emerging inequality in endowments. A potential cost of this sort of social insurance is that by attenuating the security with which individuals hold their property rights, it may reduce incentives for investments that are attached to land. The fact that insurance (or any other good) is costly does not by itself mean that it is bad public policy to provide it. The more relevant question concerns how costly that insurance is relative to its benefits and to other ways of providing it. As a first step toward answering this question, this section turns to the household data from the rice-producing villages in an attempt to determine whether or not the prospect of administrative reallocations dampens fixed investment.

The kinds of fixed investments observed in the data include wells, irrigation and drainage ditches, ponds, land leveling, soil improvement, and application of organic fertilizers whose fertility effects persist for several years. The major cost associated with all these investments is the labor hours devoted to producing them. For each of the rice-producing household in the sample, we calculated the total hours devoted to such activities in both 1988 and 1993. We specify the regression function for the desired level of investment as:

$$E[k^*_{ht}] = z^k_{ht}\beta^k, \tag{5.5}$$

where k^*_{ht} is the desired level of fixed investment by household h in year t. The factors likely to influence desired investment that we include in the vector z^k of explanatory variables include a measure of land quality (percentage of land that is flat and can be irrigated) a measure of farm fragmentation (the number of parcels held by the household), measures of household endowments (age and education of household head, and household contract land endowment per family member) and measures of the opportunity cost of labor (non-agricultural employment opportunities). Regional and time dummies are also included in z^k to capture the effect of otherwise unmeasured factors. Finally, the property rights variable defined earlier, D^A_{ht}, that signals individual immunity against administrative land reallocation is included as a measure of tenure security. Table 5.1 presents mean values for these explanatory different variables.

Consistent and reliable estimation of the parameters of the regression function (5.5) must again confront the problem that the property rights regime and the degree of tenure security are endogenous, and perhaps are themselves caused by the same factors that make investment more profitable. Panel data methods and simulated maximum likelihood estimation were again used to deal with these problems.[17]

Table 5.3 presents the estimates of the parameters in equation (5.5).[18] The statistically significant coefficient on the land fragmentation variable indicates that as a farm shifted from only 1 parcel to the sample average of about 10, investment would decrease by about 1.5 hours per *mu* (or 25 percent of the sample average investment level). In addition, the tenure security variable has become large and statistically significant. The quantitative magnitude of the coefficient is such that it says that providing a household of immunity against administrative land reallocation would increase investment attached to land by nearly 4 hours per-*mu*, an amount equal to about 60 percent of the sample average investment level. For an average farm comprised of about 10 *mu*, this estimate suggests that the provision of tenure security would increase investment labor by a total of 40 hours a year for the farm in its entirety. Whatever its benefits, these

Table 5.3 Administrative reallocation, tenure insecurity and investment

Parameters	*SML panel estimates*
Year	0.47 (0.96)
Education	0.88 (0.73)
Age	0.08 (0.13)
Fragmentation	−0.13* (0.08)
Land quality	0.05 (1.2)
Endowment ratio	0.07 (0.19)
Non-ag employment	0.90 (7.6)
Tenure security, D^A	3.9** (0.96)

Notes
* Significant at the 10% level.
** Significant at the 5% level.
Regional dummy variables and nuisance parameters not reported.

results indicate that the current mixed system of property rights has economic costs in terms of foregone investment.[19] Tempering this finding is both the mixed findings in the literature in general (see the review in Rozelle *et al.*, this volume), as well as our own related work that estimates that these investment costs may be more related to restricted land transfer rights than they are to conventional tenure insecurity per se.[20]

Conclusion

This chapter began with the observation that while the HRS reforms in China resolved labor effort incentive problems, they left the rural economy vulnerable to increasing allocative inefficiency, especially as the non-farm economy began to boom and pull labor out of the farm sector (Putterman, 1992, describes this inter-sectoral labor reallocation in terms of the logic of the dual economy literature). Comparing 1988 with 1993, we indeed see that the distribution of household land to labor endowments has become more disperse. Reactions to this increasing dispersion could either come through administrative reallocations that operate directly on the endowment distribution, or through factor market trade that prevents the increasingly disperse distribution from spilling over and generating the sorts of allocative inefficiency that would appear as an increasingly disperse distribution of factor proportions in production. While these two mechanisms are potential substitutes for one another, they have nearly opposite implications for the post-HRS evolution of the property rights system. As Liu *et al.* (1998) argue, there is evidence that the local evolution of property rights in rural China is in fact heading off in two disparate directions, one where private rights are secured and made more marketable, and another where individual rights become increasingly restricted and subject to more regulation and reallocation.

Our efforts to use village-level panel data to gauge the forces that shape the amounts of land reallocated administratively and via the rental market have been only partially successful. While Turner *et al.* (1998) find evidence of a "rational village" model in which administrative land reallocations respond directly to efficiency concerns (and indirectly to equity concerns), we find strong evidence that equity concerns dominate. Note, however, that to the extent that access to local off-farm job opportunities in township and village enterprises is rationed in an egalitarian fashion (a possibility consistent with the labor market analysis in Yao 1999), administrative reforms that maintain an egalitarian endowment distribution will also tend to preserve agricultural allocative efficiency.

Our analysis of private rental transactions was unable to satisfactorily identify the factors at the village level that shape the activeness of the rental market, and hence we have not been able to definitively compare the relative efficacy of an administrative versus a market=based resolution of the post-HRS agrarian question in China. Interestingly, our comparison of the 1988 factor proportion distribution with that in 1993 shows that the latter is slightly more compressed, indicating that in the aggregate at least, rural allocative inefficiency is not increasing. In both years, the cost of allocative inefficiency is roughly estimated as 2.5 percent of agricultural production.

While our results make it difficult to compare the responsiveness of administrative versus market-based reallocations to village level disequilibria, one clear difference between the two mechanisms is their impact on household tenure security. Panel estimates suggest that increasing household tenure security by providing households' immunity against administrative reallocations boosts investment in land by four hours per-*mu*. While seemingly modest, this figure amounts to over 50 percent of the average total labor time invested in land improvement. Given the earlier evidence that administrative reallocations tend to maintain egalitarian land access (and hence function as a social safety net as Dong, 1996 and Kung, 1994 and others have argued), this finding suggests that the foregone investment and income are the implicit insurance premium paid for this social insurance embedded in the land tenure system. Whether or not this embedded insurance is reasonably priced for what it delivers, and whether it constitutes good social policy are important questions that will require additional research.

Despite these uncertainties, there is a clear trend in the Chinese policy arena to undo the hybrid HRS and more fully privatize land rights. Two new laws address the land tenure issue. One is the *Land Contracting Law*. The other is the *Property Law*, which was still under discussion when this chapter was written. The first law proposes the termination of all periodic administrative land reallocation. If implemented, this law will drastically change land tenure in China. While it will definitely enhance land investment incentives, the motivation of the law is not purely economic. Rather, the law intends to empower farm households to counter the village cadre who are believed to use land reallocations for personal gain.

This apparent move to use land law in this way is an interesting reflection on problems of village governance. While the present *Organic Law on the Villagers' Committee* provides for free village election, continuing concern about the abuse of power by cadre signals that the electoral guarantees and village democracy have by themselves proven inadequate. Interestingly, the state appears to be trying to solve the governance problem by empowering individual farmers with more private property rights. Clearly, the state authority either does not have the faith in the current village politics, or is unwilling to change it, and instead turns to economic decentralization, which has been proven to be a successful tool in the past 20 years of the Chinese reform history.

While there are thus multiple motivations for the new property law, its adoption will raise the problem of finding substitutes for the social insurance function embedded in the current land tenure. After 20 years of rapid economic growth, the social security system in rural China has not improved and, indeed, has most probably deteriorated. The Chinese pension system and unemployment insurance only cover those who live in cities. In addition, the rural primary healthcare system that existed in the commune era has collapsed, leaving most of the rural population relying on own savings to pay for their hospital costs. While family savings are likely to dominate in the foreseeable future, organizational and financial inputs from the state should also be strengthened. Currently, all urban residents are going to be covered by a comprehensive social security system that ranges from pension and healthcare to unemployment benefits, but rural residents have none. This inequality cannot be justified on any grounds, and potentially constitutes an explosive factor to China's social stability. As the new land contracting law is going to take effect soon, the need for a new social security system in rural China becomes pressing.

Acknowledgments

The authors thank the World Bank and the Ford Foundation for their support of this research. We would also like to thank Klaus Deininger and Pedro Olinto for their extensive comments and help, and Weiping Chen for her research assistance. All views expressed in this chapter are the authors' responsibility and should not be attributed to the funding agencies.

Notes

1 See Rozelle *et al.* (Chapter 4, this volume) and Ho (2001) for complete description of the HRS and the associated system of property rights.

2 Rozelle *et al.* (this volume) question whether rural income growth, and the deepening of rural food markets, have reduced the social safety net value of the sort of egalitarian land access that our analysis shows has been partially maintained by administrative land reallocations. While this question clearly has merit, analyses of the wide-ranging impacts of egalitarian land access (e.g., Burgess 1997 and Birdsall *et al.* 1995), as well as the dearth of alternative rural social safety nets, caution against a premature dismissal of the value of land.

3 The review by Rozelle *et al.* (this volume), as well as some of our other work (Carter and Yao 2002), suggest that these investment costs may be even more modest than these results indicate.

4 In the measurement sense we have trouble with unmeasured factor quality differentials that may make it efficient to have different factor proportions. Also we should expect some time of adjustment such that at any moment there will be some variation.

5 The data used in this study come from two comprehensive surveys administered in Zhejiang, Jiangxi, Henan and Jilin in 1988 and 1993 for studies of land tenure evolution and its implications to agricultural productivity. These provinces were chosen to represent different regions and different agricultural technologies. Both surveys have a household and a village questionnaire. Vil-

lages and households were chosen from the Rural Survey Base maintained by the Rural Survey Organization of the National Bureau of Statistics of China. A household questionnaire was administered to ten randomly selected households in each village and they were asked questions ranging from land rights, land transactions and annual agricultural production to off-farm employment. The village questionnaire asked questions about land tenure arrangements at the village level both in the surveyed years and in history. In order to eliminate extraneous noise, the analysis of investment and changing dispersion in factor proportions in production relies only on the subset of villages where rice is the predominant crop. For an in-depth introduction of the data, see Liu *et al.* (1998) and Carter and Yao (2002).

6 Fifteen *mu* = one hectare.

7 As judged by the Kolmograv-Smirnov test, the 1998 and 1993 distributions are statistically different from one another for both endowments and factor proportions.

8 Defining τ_{hit} as the contract land-family labor ratio for household h in village i in year t, the intra-village coefficient variation is:

$$\sigma_{it}^{\tau} = \sqrt{\left(\sum_{h=1}^{n_{it}} (\tau_{iht} - \bar{\tau}_{it})^2 / n_{it}\right) / \bar{\tau}_{it}}$$

where n_{it} is the number of sampled households in village i in year t; and, the mean endowment ratio for village i in year t is $\bar{\tau}_{it} = \sum_{h=1}^{n_i} \tau_{iht} / n_{it}$. A similar expression was used to calculate the intra-village coefficient of variation in factor proportions in rice production.

9 Maximum likelihood methods were used to estimate distributions under the assumption that variables are distributed according to a gamma distribution. The gamma distribution was chosen for this analysis because it is a flexible distribution form that can take on a wide variety of shapes, from normal to skewed to exponential, depending on the value of the parameters of the distribution. The underlying parameters are estimated to be statistically significant, including those which tested for shifts in the distribution from 1988 to 1993.

10 In one of the few studies that focuses on private rental transactions in China, Carter and Yao (2004) use standard household models to show that households become more likely to undertake land rental transactions as their land–labor factor endowment ratio becomes more extreme and as the household enjoys specific factors and skills that encourage it to specialize in either agricultural or non-agricultural activities. The intra-village dispersion measures hypothesized here to influence the activeness of the village land market capture in a simple way the forces identified by Carter and Yao.

12 A multi-year measure was used on the grounds that administrative reallocations are costly and therefore take place only periodically. A single-year measure would thus be likely to understate the frequency and amount of administrative reallocations.

12 As measured in the survey, land rentals include both transactions between individuals and temporary lease transactions between villages and households in those villages that did not initially distribute all land to households.

13 Factor proportions was here measured as the total household input of labor into agriculture divided by the household's cultivated land area.

14 The table does not report variance and various 'nuisance' parameters related

to the panel data estimation technique. Full results are available from the authors.

15 The simpler procedure ignored the panel structure of the data and estimated a standard Tobit model using the pooled data. These results are available from the authors.

16 These disappointing results suggest that household-level analysis is necessary to gain insight on the forces driving rental transactions, such as that in Carter and Yao (2002) discussed in note 10 above.

17 Estimation also had to deal with censorship problems, as 19 percent of the households in the sample did not dedicate any labor to these investment activities.

18 The table again does not present variance and nuisance parameters. In addition, the regression included regional dummy variables, which were by and large statistically significant. Full results are available from the authors.

19 An economic evaluation of this investment would require knowledge of the marginal returns to investment as well as an estimate of how much *less* the investing household might do of other activities. The study of tenure security by Carter and Olinto (2003) finds that for capital-constrained households in Paraguay, tenure security indeed boosts investment in fixed or attached capital, but it comes at the cost of reduced investment in other types of capital.

20 Carter and Yao (2002) show from a theoretical perspective that limited land transfer rights may reduce investment via what they call an "investment regret effect." After controlling for land transfer rights in a structural econometric model, they show that a conventional tenure security variable has no independent effect on investment.

References

Birdsall, Nancy, Ross, David and Sabot, R. (1995) "Inequality and Growth Reconsidered: Lessons from East Asia," *The World Bank Economic Review*, 9: 477–508.

Burgess, R. (1997). *Market Incompleteness and Nutritional Status in Rural China*, working paper, London: London School of Economics.

Carter, Michael and Olinto, Pedro (2003) "Getting Institutions Right for Whom? Credit Constraints and the Impact of Property Rights on the Quantity and Composition of Investment," *American Journal of Agricultural Economics*, 85: 173–186.

Carter, Michael and Yao, Yang (2002) "Local versus Global Separability in Agricultural Household Modesl: The Factor Price Equalization Effect of Land Transfer Rights in China," *American Journal of Agricultural Economics*, 84(3) (August): 702–715..

Carter, Michael and Yao, Yang (2004), "Specialization without Regret: Land Transfer Rights, Agricultural Productivity, and Investment in an Industrializing Economy," *World Bank Policy Research Working Paper 2202* (revised).

Dong, Xiaoyuan (1996) "Two-tier Land Tenure System and Sustained Economic Growth in Post-1978 Rural China," *World Development*, 24: 915–928.

Graynor, M. and Putterman, Louis (1993) "Productivity Consequences of Alternative Land Division Methods in China's Decollectivization: An Econometric Analysis," *Journal of Development Economics*, 42: 357–386.

Ho, Peter (2001) "Who Owns China's Land? Policy, Property Rights and Deliberate Institutional Ambiguity," *The China Quarterly*, 166: 387–414.

Kung, James K. (1994) "Egalitarianism, Subsistence Provision and Work Incentives in China's Agricultural Collectives," *World Development*, 22: 175–188.

Liu, S., Carter, Michael and Yao, Yang (1998) "Dimensions and Diversity of Property Rights in Rural China: Dilemmas on the Road to Further Reform," *World Development,* 26: 1798–1806.

Putterman, Louis (1992) "Dualism and Reform in China," *Economic Development and Cultural Change* 40:467–493.

Turner, Matthew, Brandt, Loren and Rozelle, Scott (1998) *Property Rights Formation and the Organization of Exchange and Production in Rural China,* working paper, Toronto: Department of Economics, University of Toronto.

Yao, Yang (1999) "Rural Industry and Labor Market Integration in Eastern China," *Journal of Development Economics,* 59: 463–496.

6 Regional differences in land holdings and land use

Analyzing the First Agricultural Census

Roberto Fanfani and Cristina Brasili

Rapid economic development and the transformation of Chinese society have meant that China is receiving greater attention for their impact on future global affairs. However, many aspects of the current development are not well understood; not only the size of the country and its large population of almost 1.3 billion people, but also the scarce availability of information. In particular, knowledge of rural China, until recently, was incomplete and fragmented. This lack of knowledge has caused, among other issues, controversial and incorrect estimations of the agricultural sector's capacity to meet the growing food demands of the nation. This in turn may have significant effects on world prices and the international agricultural market.

For the first time in history, the First National Agricultural Census (1997) in China gives a detailed and, in many respects, a new picture of rural China. The census represents the greatest statistical survey ever carried out in the world with over 214 million rural households surveyed and over 890 million people involved. The new figures on Chinese agriculture are important for our understanding of the structural characteristics of agriculture and the differences at a provincial and county level. Furthermore, these data allow evaluation of the role that agriculture will play in the future development of the Chinese economy, as well as the potential impact of China on global food markets. The recent availability of the census data, particularly the greater availability of arable land, has led to the revision of previous estimates of Chinese food deficits (Abbassian 2001; FAO 2000; USDA 2000).

The census on agricultural and non-agricultural households, and land use, gives a better understanding of the massive changes launched by the agrarian reforms of 1978 and the resulting structure of Chinese agriculture. The boom in agricultural production since 1978 has stimulated considerable academic attention and analysis. A review of the numerous studies completed during the 1990s on the effects of the agrarian reform is reported by Carter (1999). Carter states that the increasing agricultural production in China, due to the agrarian reforms, ranges from 35 per cent to 60 per cent according to the different authors and methodologies reviewed. However, recent analysis of agricultural development in China has focused attention on the importance of other variables, such as land fragmentation, technological change, off-farm employment, and rural industrialization (Carter and Estrin 2001; Fan 2001; Giovannini 2000; Mead 2000; Zhang *et al.* 2001).

The increase in agricultural production and productivity in most recent studies is based on the previous official statistics collected by the SSB (State Statistical Bureaux). The Agricultural Census gives new, and more complete figures, at the national and provincial level. The new figures on land availability, land use, and land quality are now more relevant, allowing a better definition of resource endowments at various levels. In fact, the differences between the 1997 Census data and previous statistics on land use, at the local level, are often amplified at the national level. The new figures on land use will be useful to improve the assessment of agricultural productivity, and will contribute to revision of the recent, and numerous, analyses on the trends of China's land use (Fisher *et al.* 1998; Hubacek and Sun 2001; Vermeer 2001).

The first part of this chapter examines the main features of over 214 million rural households. The analysis will highlight the substantial differences in the structure and characteristics of the households across China's 30 provinces. The differences in land use between the main agricultural and non-household holdings (state, collective, co-operative, private, and joint venture), allow us to fully assess the impact of the agrarian reforms. The figures on cultivated and sown area of the 1997 Census are compared with previous statistics and it is found that there is a more pronounced disparity, at both the national and the provincial level. The differences in farm structure and resource endowments are strongly correlated to the regional development of agriculture.

In the second part of the chapter, the geography of Chinese agriculture at the provincial and county level is redefined. This is done by identifying four main agricultural areas of rural China at the provincial level, and considering the data of more than 2,100 Chinese counties. The new geography of Chinese agriculture substantially differs from the typical regions used to describe the recent economic developments and growing regional disparities. We aim to show, through this analysis, that the new regional and territorial image of Chinese agriculture will allow for an improved design of agricultural and rural development policies in China.

Chinese agriculture today

The data used in empirical studies of the Chinese agricultural sector, to date, are mainly based on the "scheme of statistical reporting on farming, forestry, animal husbandry and fishery" carried out by the Rural Social–Economic Survey Organization of the State Statistical Bureau. Considering the critical role of agriculture in the Chinese economy, the

Chinese government, in collaboration with the Food and Agriculture Organization of the United Nations, decided to execute the First National Agricultural Census.[1] The census of 1997 covered over 214 million rural households, more than 356,000 non-household holdings, and about 1.4 million non-agricultural town and village enterprises. The census is considered a milestone as it allows for a better understanding of the Chinese rural system. In this chapter we mainly rely on data from the 1997 Census, although we also use some other general macroeconomic statistics.[2]

General characteristics of agriculture: labor and economic development

To fully understand the relevance of the information collected through the Agricultural Census, we first review some general data. Rural China counts about 214 million rural households, with more than 193 million agricultural households and more than 20 million non-agricultural households. There are more than 873 million people living in rural households, of which 451 million (51.66 per cent) are male and 422 million are female. There are over 561 million people engaged in production activities, of which 42.5 million are in non-agricultural households and about 519 million are in agricultural households. The number of workers is higher than the previous official statistics on the rural labour force (453 million, SSB 1997: 363).[3]

The 193 million agricultural households are found across all regions of China. There are relatively few (358,000) non-household holdings in agriculture (state, collective, co-operative, private), which involve less than 10 million people.

According to the 1997 Census, the number of people engaged in agriculture is very high. Of the 561 million active people in rural households, over 75 per cent (about 425 million) are active in agriculture, while a mere 25 per cent are engaged in other productive activities. It is important to emphasize that the current Census reports a greater share of agricultural labor force than the SSB statistics (less than 70 per cent). It is also relevant to observe that in agriculture, unlike other non-agricultural activities, the number of active women (221 million) is much higher than the number of active men (203 million). As shown below, this is related to the growing importance of non-agricultural activities and part-time farming. In the six economic-geographical regions shown in Table 6.1, the share of the labor force engaged in agricultural activities is lower in the East region (66 per cent), and higher in the North-West (86 per cent), the North East (83 per cent) and the South West (83 per cent) regions.

The differences between these macro areas are not a suitable measure for the larger variation among provinces. At one end of the spectrum, is Shanghai (31 per cent) and Beijing (39 per cent), while at the other end is Tibet with a share as high as 95 per cent. As a result of this wide range, we analysed the correlation of the share of agricultural labour force with

Table 6.1 Rural households: number of persons engaged in agricultural/non-agricultural activities per province and geographic region

	Total number of persons	*Persons engaged in*			
		Agricultural activities	*%*	*Non-agricultural activities*	*%*
China, total	561,479,490	424,995,487	75.7	136,484,003	24.3
North region	57,982,103	43,900,561	75.7	14,081,542	24.3
North-east region	32,519,454	27,058,206	83.2	5,461,248	16.8
East region	172,649,034	115,306,768	66.8	57,342,266	33.2
Central-south region	155,998,864	118,519,012	76.0	37,479,852	24.0
South-west region	104,568,029	87,664,988	83.8	16,903,041	16.2
North west region	37,762,006	32,545,952	86.2	5,216,054	13.8

Source: Our analysis of the Abstract of the National Agricultural Census of China (1999).

the per capita GDP (1996) in order to arrive at a more general indicator of economic development per province. The results (Figure 6.1), show a very high inverse correlation between these two variables, with a high correlation coefficient (−0.81).

Chinese provinces can be divided in two main groups. The first group includes the provinces with a high percentage of labour engaged in agricultural activities (more than 75 per cent) and a low level of GDP per capita (less than 6,000 yuan). This group includes almost all the Western and Middle provinces – the main rural provinces. The other group features high levels of GDP per capita and lower levels of people engaged in

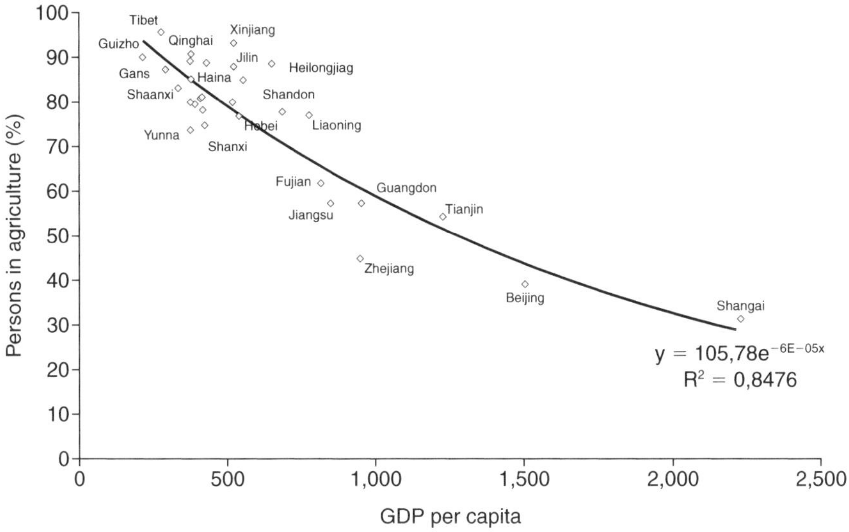

Figure 6.1 Share of agricultural labour force correlated with per capita GDP.

agricultural activities, and includes the municipalities of Shanghai and Beijing, and the coastal provinces in the East (Tianjin, Jiangsu, Zhejiang, Fujian, and Guangdong). The only provinces with high levels of agricultural activities and a relatively high level of GDP per capita are Shandong and Liaoning on the north-eastern coast.

Household typology

The 1997 Census gives important information on household classification according to the prevalent activity (agricultural and non-agricultural), and the typology of agricultural households (purely agricultural, mainly agricultural, mainly non-agricultural). The main findings show that the extent of integration of agriculture with other economic activities is an important variable that characterizes the differences between provinces. Of the 214 million rural households, about 193 million (over 90 per cent) are agricultural. The agricultural households are then divided into three classes:

1 *Purely agricultural households* accounting for 126.7 million (65.6 per cent of households) and over 500 million people (62.1 per cent);
2 *Mainly agricultural households* accounting for 39 million (20.2 per cent) and more than 179 million people;
3 *Mainly non-agricultural households* accounting for 27.3 million (14.2 per cent) and 120 million people.

There are substantial differences between the agricultural households in terms of people engaged in economic activities, in relation to the number of active people in agricultural activities, and especially in relation to the number of active women (see Table 6.2). In fact, the purely agricultural households have more than 311 million active people (60 per cent of total people active in agricultural households), of which there are more active men than women. In the mainly agricultural households there are 126.7 million active people (24.4 per cent of the total), but only 80.8 million of them (64 per cent) are active in agriculture. Among the people active in agriculture, there is a higher proportion of active women (33 million men and 48 million women). In the mainly non-agricultural households there are 80.8 million active people (15.6 per cent of the total), yet in this case only 32.6 million (40 per cent) people are active in agriculture with more than 25.3 million women (more than 77 per cent) compared to only 7.3 million men.

The importance of active women in agricultural households (HH) increases consistently as the household's involvement in agriculture declines. These data show the rise of part-time farming, in which women play an increasingly important role as the men remain primarily involved in non-agricultural activities. The fast growth of non-agricultural activities in rural areas, in particular the employment generated by town and village

Table 6.2 Persons engaged in economic, agricultural and non-agricultural activities by household type and gender (aged 7 years and older, in millions)

Type of households	*Persons engaged in*								
	Economic activities			*Agricultural activities*			*Non-agricultural activities*		
	Total	*Male*	*Female*	*Total*	*Male*	*Female*	*Total*	*Male*	*Female*
Rural households	561.5	295.4	266.0	425.0	203.6	221.4	136.5	91.8	44.6
Non-agricultural households	42.5	23.3	19.2	0.0	0.0	0.0	42.5	23.3	19.2
Agricultural households	518.9	272.2	246.8	425.0	203.6	221.4	93.9	68.5	25.4
Pure agricultural	311.5	163.4	148.1	311.5	163.4	148.1	0.1	0.08	0.06
Mainly agricultural	126.7	66.7	60.0	80.8	32.9	48.0	45.8	33.8	12.0
Mainly non-agricultural	80.8	42.1	38.7	32.6	7.3	25.3	48.1	34.8	13.3
Non-household holdings	9.8	6.2	3.6	8.5	5.4	3.1	1.3	0.8	0.5
All agricultural holdings	528.8	278.4	250.4	433.5	209.0	224.5	95.3	69.4	25.9

Source: Abstract of the First National Agricultural Census in China, China Statistics Press (1999).

enterprises, will increase the relevance of part-time farming in China in the near future.

The different types of agriculture HH shed some light on the importance of family members who work in the non-agriculture sector. In the *purely agricultural* HH all family members work in agriculture (or if one of them works in non-agricultural activities he gains less than 10 per cent of the household income). In the *mainly non-agricultural* HH (where more than half of the family income comes from non-agricultural activities), there are more than 48 million people working in non agricultural activities, of which about 35 million are men (73 per cent) and only 13 million are women (27 per cent). In the *mainly agricultural* HH (where the family income coming from non-agricultural activities is more than 10 per cent but less than half), there are more than 45.8 million family members who work outside agriculture, of which a higher proportion are men. Across China, in agricultural HH, there are in total about 94 million of family members who work outside agriculture, of which more than 68.5 million are men and 25.5 million are women.

In these agricultural HH it is not possible to know which sector the family members are working (industry, construction, transportation, retail and services, or other activity), or where their jobs are located (home town, county, province, or out of province). This information is, however, available for the total rural households, which include the non-agricultural HH. If it is assumed that all the workers of non-agriculture HH (about 42.5 million), work primarily in their home town, and that the women of the agricultural HH, with a job in non-agricultural activities (25.5 million), work in their home towns, we could estimate the distance from home that the men, in the agricultural HH, work. With this assumption we could estimate that of the 68.5 million men working outside the agricultural HH, approximately 25 million (36 per cent) work out of their town but within their home county; about 44 million work out of their home counties; and of these, 23 million (about 33 per cent of the total) work out of their province. The men of these households who work outside their home province are employed primarily in the construction industry, and services.

Size and land-holdings of agricultural households

As Tan, Qu and Heerink show in Chapter 7 in this volume, the rural reforms have led to the emergence of a huge number of small households. On average, the amount of active labour (that is, labour engaged in economic activities), per rural household is 2.6 people. This value shows that the size of rural families is not particularly large. This could be due to birth control and family planning policies. It is also important to note that there are no significant differences between provinces. Beijing has a minimum value of about 2 people per household, and in Tibet and

Qinghai the maximum value is 3 people per household. The differences in household size between provinces are strictly related to the differences in the number of people engaged in agriculture and in non-agricultural activities as described in the previous section.

More interesting information can be obtained in terms of land holdings, as the farms are small, fewer people are remaining in the agriculture sector. The 1997 Census shows that the land holdings of rural and agricultural households are indeed very small. More than 30% of agricultural households cultivate less than 3 *mu* of land (1 *mu* is $\frac{1}{15}$ ha), and about 53 per cent tend 3 to 9 *mu* of land. The agricultural households with less than 1 ha (or 15 *mu*) account for 93 per cent of total households (SSB 2000) (see Figure 6.2). The distribution of agricultural households by area of cultivated land highlights discrepancies between the main typology of households. In the *purely* and *mainly agricultural* households the distribution is similar to the one described above, whereas the mainly non-agricultural households are much smaller in size (49 per cent of the households have less than 3 *mu*, and 48 per cent have 3 to 9 *mu* of cultivated land).[4]

Land use in Chinese agriculture

National and provincial figures

According to the First Agricultural Census, the total cultivated land in China is more than 130 million hectares, with more than 123.3 million hectares of sown area cultivated by household holdings. The data on total cultivated land are relevant because this figure is substantially higher than the previous SSB statistics of 95 million hectares in 1995. Although there was an awareness of the under-estimation of agricultural land in China, as this topic had attracted wide scholarly attention, (Wu and Kirke 1994; Ash and Edmonds 1998), the new value of cultivated area was not officially reported until the publication of the *2000 Statistical Yearbook*. The

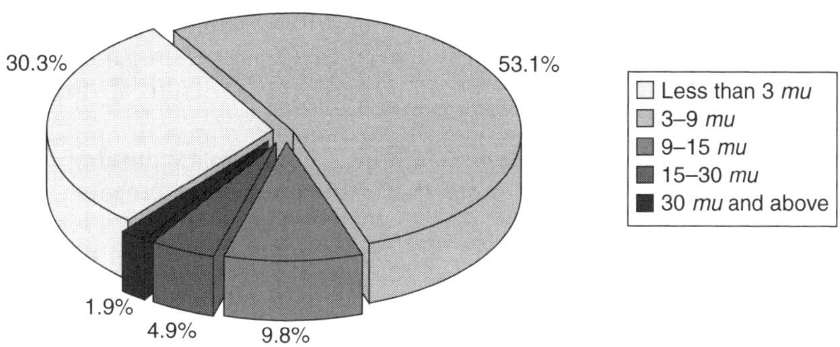

Figure 6.2 Land holdings of rural and agricultural households.

increased availability of cultivated land implies that average yields of crops are lower than previously reported in official figures. There is, therefore, the opportunity in China for productivity and yield increases with a higher intensity of agricultural production per capita and per unit of land.[5] As many analyses have suggested, this consideration has influenced the recent downward estimates of China's future food deficit (Abbassian 2001; FAO 2000; USDA 2000).

Obviously, the figures of the 1997 Census are more accurate than the previous official estimates. In particular, they are more detailed on land use at the provincial and county level. Given the importance of the data on cultivated land, more in-depth analysis is needed, not only to clarify the differences between the new census data and the previous statistics, but also to explain the differences in the reported cultivated land figures from the various questionnaires of the census. The so-called A606 questionnaire for the map of agricultural land reported 130 million hectares of cultivated land, whereas the total cultivated land registered for the agricultural households (A601 questionnaire) and non-households holdings (A602 questionnaire) only reports 86.3 million hectares, that is, 51 per cent less than the A606 record. The map for agricultural land has been conducted by village with the support of the National Land Administration (since 1998 the Ministry of Land Resources), which provided the data in the previous land use survey. The villages updated this survey, which took place in October 1966. According to Zhu Xiandong (2001), the Census data on cultivated area are more accurate because of the use of standardized measurements and statistical standards for quality control.[6]

The main explanation for the upward bias discrepancy, between the amount of cultivated land reported by questionnaire A606 and those of questionnaires A601/2, is dependent on the different definition of cultivated land. In fact, the cultivated land determined by the agricultural map consists of land with steep slopes (of over 25 degrees), and stone rifts. These land categories are not included in questionnaires A601/2, or in any previous official statistics. Furthermore, the land map data refer to "gross" cultivated land which includes ditches, field roads and ridges with a width of 1 metre in southern China and a width of 2 metres elsewhere. As suggested by Vermeer (2001), it is crucial that these discrepancies are fully understood so as to accurately determine the agricultural productivity in China

In order to analyze the differences between the types of cultivated land across provinces, Vermeer suggests that "the average discrepancy for China masks considerable differences in provincial discrepancies". Hence, a comparison of the three sources of data on cultivated land can be used to demonstrate the provincial differences (Table 6.3). It is important to highlight that the greatest differences between types of cultivated land within the questionnaires are reported for all the southern provinces from the East (Shanghai 75 per cent, Zhejiang 76 per cent, Fujian 62 per cent),

Table 6.3 China's cultivated land derived from three sources, 1997 (in 1,000 ha)

Regions	*A606*	*A601 + A602*	*SSB*	*Ratio 1/2*	*Ratio 1/3*	*Ratio 2/3*	*Differences (1–2) ha*
China, total	130,039.2	86,317.3	95,466.5	1.51	1.36	0.90	43,721.9
North region							
Beijing	343.9	254.0	395.9	1.35	0.87	0.64	89.9
Tianjin	485.6	327.8	425.8	1.48	1.14	0.77	157.8
Hebei	6,883.3	5,194.5	6,498.8	1.33	1.06	0.80	1,688.8
Shanxi	4,588.6	3,017.2	3,624.0	1.52	1.27	0.83	1,571.4
Inner Mongolia	8,201.0	5,607.1	5,923.6	1.46	1.38	0.95	2,593.9
North-east region							
Liaoning	4,174.8	3,243.3	3,383.7	1.29	1.23	0.96	931.5
Jilin	5,578.4	3,748.7	3,958.5	1.49	1.41	0.95	1,829.7
Heilongjiang	11,773.0	9,095.2	9,174.6	1.29	1.28	0.99	2,677.8
East region							
Shanghai	315.1	180.2	287.3	1.75	1.10	0.63	134.9
Jiangsu	5,061.7	3,452.9	4,435.4	1.47	1.14	0.78	1,608.8
Zhejiang	2,125.3	1,208.4	1,613.8	1.76	1.32	0.75	916.9
Anhui	5,971.7	3,909.7	4,280.3	1.53	1.40	0.91	2,062.0
Fujian	1,434.7	886.3	1,196.2	1.62	1.20	0.74	548.4
Jiangxi	2,993.4	2,221.5	2,301.7	1.35	1.30	0.97	771.9
Shandong	7,689.3	5,744.6	6,679.4	1.34	1.15	0.86	1,944.7
Central-south region							
Henan	8,110.3	6,116.5	6,786.3	1.33	1.20	0.90	1,993.8
Hubei	4,949.5	3,161.3	3,349.2	1.57	1.48	0.94	1,788.2
Hunan	3,953.0	3,092.1	3,239.4	1.28	1.22	0.95	860.9
Guangdong	3,272.2	1,844.0	2,304.4	1.77	1.42	0.80	1,428.2
Guangxi	4,407.9	2,221.4	2,632.3	1.98	1.67	0.84	2,186.5
Hainan	762.1	344.9	429.4	2.21	1.77	0.80	417.2
South-west region							
Sichuan	9,169.1	5,641.3	6,165.2	1.63	1.49	0.92	3,527.8
Guizhou	4,903.5	1,979.6	1,839.4	2.48	2.67	1.08	2,923.9
Yunnan	6,421.6	3,050.2	2,889.4	2.11	2.22	1.06	3,371.4
Tibet	362.6	223.7	227.9	1.62	1.59	0.98	138.9
North-west region							
Shaanxi	5,140.5	2,822.0	3,359.0	1.82	1.53	0.84	2,318.5
Gansu	5,024.7	3,408.9	3,486.4	1.47	1.44	0.98	1,615.8
Qinghai	688.0	554.0	589.9	1.24	1.17	0.94	134.0
Ningxia	1,268.8	834.8	813.5	1.52	1.56	1.03	434.0
Xinjiang	3,985.7	2,931.3	3,175.8	1.36	1.26	0.92	1,054.4

Sources: Vermeer E. (2001), Questionnaires A606 and A601/2: Abstract of the First National Agricultural Census of China (1999); State Statistical Bureau, China Statistical Yearbook 1997.

Central (Guangdong 77 per cent, Guangxi 98 per cent, Hainan 121 per cent) to the West regions (Sichuan 63 per cent, Guizhou 148 per cent, Yunnan 111 per cent, Tibet 62 per cent). Another province showing a large difference is Shaanxi with an 82 per cent discrepancy. These provincial discrepancies can be attributed to several different factors. First, the weighty importance of ditches, field roads and ridges in the southern provinces and, second, to the higher pressure on cultivated land as a result of the greater rural population growth in these frontier, western and mountainous provinces. As presented in the next section, the census reports more cultivated land in the provinces where land utilization is dominated by woodland which covers over 50 per cent or 80 per cent of the total agricultural land.

The cultivated land of the households and non-households (86.3 million hectares) is lower (10 per cent) than previously reported by the official statistics (95.5 million). The geographical distribution of these differences between provinces requires an alternative explanation. In the most developed provinces, the cultivated land belonging to households and non-households is lower than previously reported by the official statistics: 64% in Beijing and Shanghai, and more than 75 per cent in Jiangsu, Zhejiang and Fujian. On the contrary, in almost all the provinces in the West the amount of cultivated land owned by HH and NH are virtually equal. These differences may be attributed to the delay in the registration of land use which changed from agricultural to industrial or urban land utilization, as well as the significant losses in arable land due to construction activities in the wealthier urban regions.

Since the total area of agricultural land has not been reported directly in the Abstract of the First Agricultural Census, we made some estimations of the value of the total agricultural land using the data on cultivated land and the distribution of agricultural land use. We conclude that there are more than 301 million hectares of agricultural land, of which 130 million hectares are cultivated land, more than 97 million hectares are woodland, 62 million hectares are grassland, more than 7 million hectares are permanent crops and 4.8 million hectares are land used for fisheries (see Table 6.4).

The cultivated land in China only composes 43 per cent of the total agricultural land, whereas woodlands cover more than 32 per cent, and grasslands more than 20 per cent. Permanent crops take up only 2.3 per cent of total agricultural land and the area devoted to fisheries is 1.6 per cent. The differences in land use vary greatly among the provinces (see Figure 6.3). In many provinces the cultivated land is more than 70 per cent of the total agricultural area, whereas in other provinces it is lower than 30 per cent. There is a high percentage of cultivated land in all provinces of the North Region (except Inner Mongolia), in the provinces of Shanghai (85 per cent), Jiangsu (85 per cent) and Shandong (83 per cent) in the East Region, but also in Henan province (84 per cent), Chongqing (66 per cent) and Ningxia (75 per cent). In some North-

Table 6.4 Land use by type of land in all agricultural holdings (1,000 ha)

	Agricultural land (ha)	*Cultivated land (ha)*	*Permanent crops (ha)*	*Woodland (ha)*	*Grassland (ha)*	*Fisheries (ha)*
China, total	301,156.1	130,039.2	7,016.9	97,122.8	62,158.6	4,788.4
North region	39,994.3	20,502.4	605.3	8,858.2	9,716.7	314.4
North-east region	43,523.4	21,526.2	372.2	19,441.5	1,367.7	819.4
East region	50,146.8	25,591.2	2,447.5	20,327.9	56.2	1,725.9
Central-south region	55,313.6	25,455.0	2,270.5	25,441.3	549.8	1,598.3
South-west region	49,281.4	20,856.8	841.0	19,363.2	7,989.5	212.5
North-west region	64,624.0	16,107.7	876.8	8,772.0	38,773.3	93.8

Source: Our estimation on data from Abstract of the First National Agricultural Census of China (1999).

Note
The total agricultural land differs from that of the regions for 1.7 million hectares, due mainly to a higher value of 5.1 million woodland and a lower value of 3.7 million grassland.

western provinces the lower share of cultivated land is due to the presence of grasslands, such as in the provinces of Xinjiang (86 per cent of grassland), Qinghai (67 per cent), Tibet (62 per cent) and Inner Mongolia (40 per cent). Woodlands are dominant in several provinces. In the East Region the proportion of woodland is high, 70 per cent in Fujian, 67 per cent in Jiangxi and 59 per cent in Zhejiang respectively. The provinces of the Central-south are heavily forested with woodlands accounting for around 50 per cent to 60 per cent of total agricultural area. A relevant aspect in the land utilization is the importance of the land devoted to fisheries, which is more than 4.7 million hectares (in some provinces such as Tianjin, Shangai and Jiangsu, it reaches 7–8 per cent of the total agricultural land).

Land use by farm typology (households and non-households)

The utilization of land in China differs widely between the various types of farms, in particular between the agricultural households holdings (over 193 million), and the agricultural non-households holdings (about 358,000 holdings). The latter includes: state, collective, co-operative, private, individual and joint venture holdings (Table 6.5).

According to our calculations the total agricultural land belonging to the agricultural holdings is distributed as 63 per cent (more than 189 million hectares), to household holdings, and 37 per cent to non-household holdings (112 million hectares). A higher proportion of the cultivated land is held by households (120 million hectares or 92.5 per cent), than by the non-household holdings (10 million hectares or 7.5 per cent).

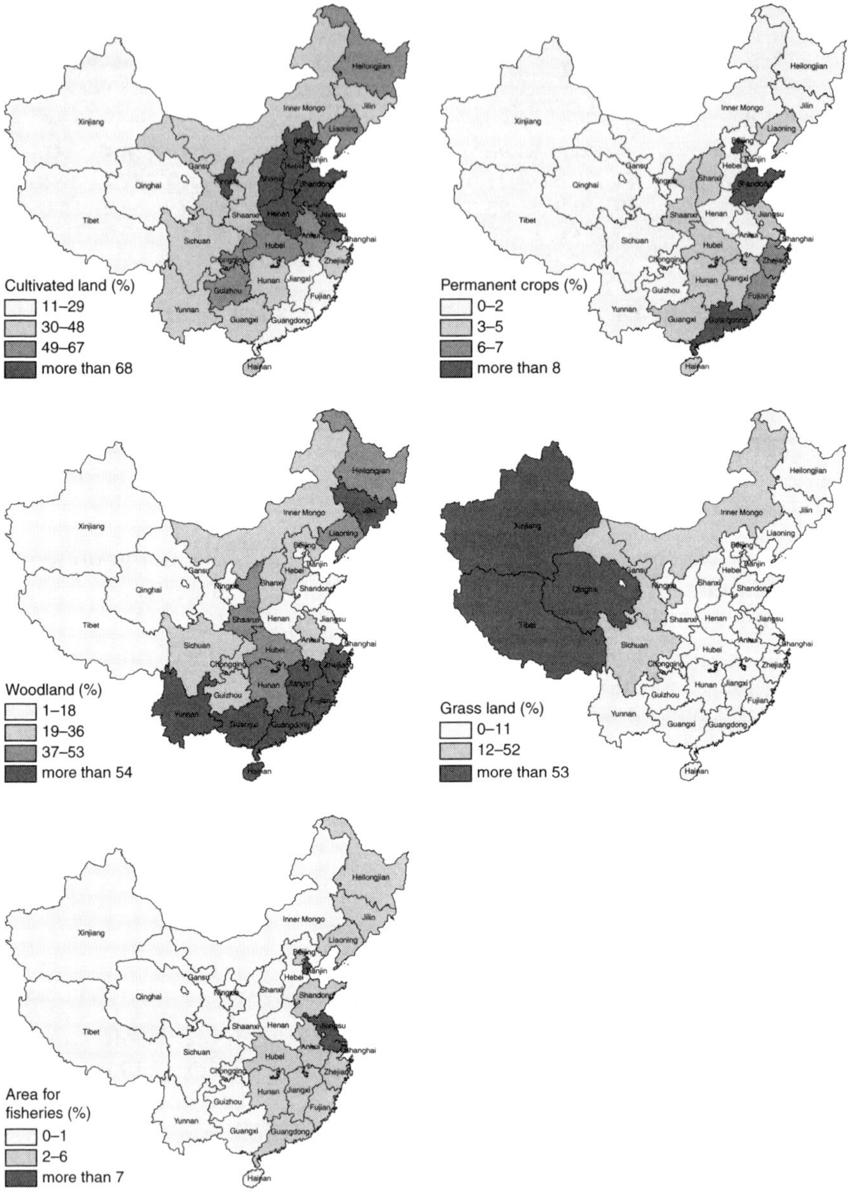

Figure 6.3 Distribution of land use in China.

Table 6.5 Main typologies of agricultural households (number and persons, in 1,000s)

Agricultural holdings	*Number*			
	Holdings	%	*Persons*	%
Household holdings	*193,088*	*99.8*	*799,673*	*98.8*
Pure agricultural	126,719	65.6	500,391	62.6
Mainly agricultural	39,011	20.2	179,168	22.4
Mainly non agricultural	27,358	14.2	120,114	15.0
Non-household holdings	*358*	*0.2*	*9,845*	*1.2*
State	37	10.3	6,294	63.9
Collective	213	59.7	2,690	27.3
Private	6.0	1.7	78	0.8
Individual	69	19.3	388	3.9
Cooperatives	31	8.7	332	3.4
Foreign businessmen	1.3	0.3	61	0.6
Total	193,446	100.0	809,518	100.0

Source: our processing on Abstract of the First National Agricultural Census of China (1999).

From Figures 6.4 and 6.5 we can see that agricultural households are characterized by the prevalence of cultivated land which is over 63 per cent (120 million ha) of the total agricultural area, whereas grassland and forestry is limited to 17 per cent and 15 per cent respectively. Permanent crops and fisheries are only 2.8 per cent and 0.8 per cent respectively. The land use of the non-households holdings (belonging mainly to the state, collectives, and cooperative holdings), is completely different when compared to the land use of the household holdings. In the non-HH holdings forestry covers more than 60 per cent of agricultural land, with grassland accounting for over 26 per cent. In the non-household

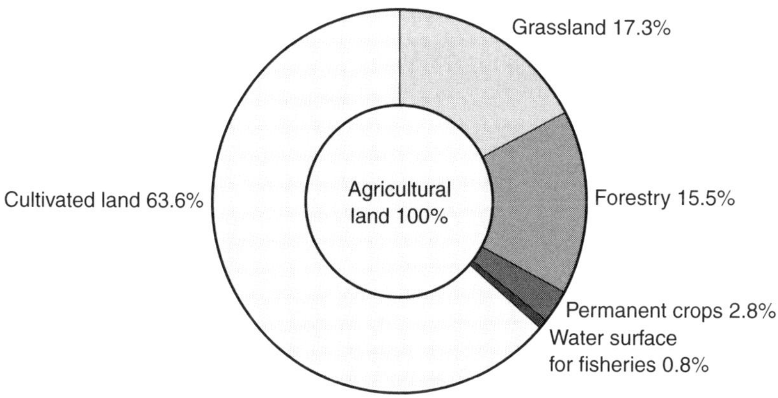

Figure 6.4 Distribution of land use of agricultural households.

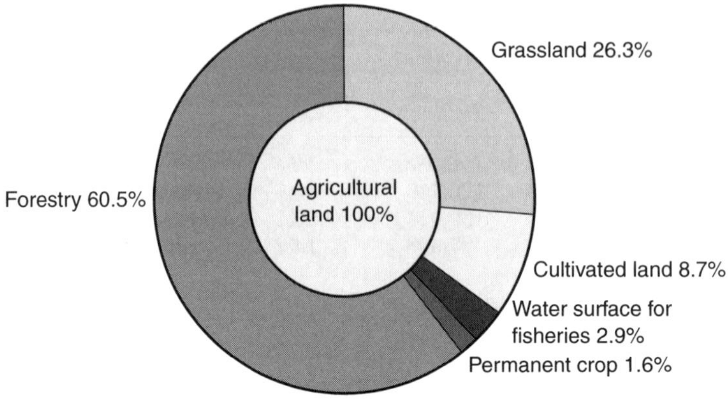

Figure 6.5 Distribution of land use of non-households.

holdings the presence of cultivated land is minimal, only 8.7 per cent of the total agricultural land. We have to note that in state and cooperative holdings there is a large amount of land devoted to fisheries (more than 3.2 million hectares), which in this case covers about 2.9 per cent of agricultural land and more than two-thirds of the nation's total agricultural land.

The large divergence in land use between household holdings and non-household holdings is clearly evident as a result of the agrarian reforms: almost 96 per cent of the total area of cultivated land is now tilled by more than 193 million farm households. Land in the hands of non-household holdings is extremely low in terms of cultivated land, but is much higher in less-intensive land uses like forestry and grassland.

Sown area and the intensity of land utilization

The data on sown areas available from the census are not easily comparable with that of the previous statistics supplied by the SSB. The total sown area according to the SSB was about 150 million hectares in 1995 and more than 156 million in 1999. The changes in the composition and trend of the sown areas are relevant, and show a consistent reduction in cereals (except for corn), a reduction in cotton acreage, and an increase in oilseed crops. In general, there has been a reduction in crops in favour of a steady increase in vegetables and orchards (Feng 2001).

The Agricultural Census reports for 1996 a sown area of 123.3 million hectares tilled by agricultural households. This sown area accounts for 94.7 per cent of the total sown area of all holdings. The total sown area of households and non-households in China is about 130.2 million hectares, this is approximately 14 per cent less than the official figure of 1996

(Vermeer 2001). It is important to consider the different definitions of the 'sown area' between the Agricultural Census and the SSB statistics. In the previous official statistics (SSB) the sown area included: tea plantations (1.1 million ha in 1996) and orchards (more than 8.5 million ha in 1996). The census, however, includes these crops (tea and orchards) as permanent crops rather than as "cultivated land" or "sown area". The discrepancies between these definitions are considered, as the differences between the census data and the previous official statistics are not substantial: the inconsistency within sown area is less than 10 per cent, while it is more or less the same for the cultivated land.[7]

Considering the more homogeneous data of the agricultural census, which refers to all agricultural holdings (households and non-households) from the A601/2 questionnaire, the intensity of land utilization is high. The multi-cropping index for all agricultural holdings is around 151 (130.2 million hectares of sown area divided by 86.3 million of cultivated land). This index is considerably lower than the index of 160 reported by the Ministry of Agriculture (Vermeer 2001). The lower intensity of crop use may be even lower if we presume the sown area of agricultural holdings also includes non-cultivated land (courtyards of the houses and other areas primarily devoted to permanent crops, woodland or grassland). Unfortunately, we do not have up-to-date information on the importance of these types of sown areas. In summary, the census results show that the intensity of land use in Chinese agriculture is much lower than for previous estimates. However, one should take care when using the multiple cropping index at the provincial and county level without first checking the quality of the data. As a result of critical differences in the sown area, recorded by the census and the SSB for various crops at the national level, large regional variations may remain hidden.[8]

It is also worth noting the figures of the sown area in relation to the different agricultural holdings (see Table 6.6). According to our estimation

Table 6.6 Cultivated and sown area by farm typology (in million ha)

Type of land	*All agricultural holdings*	*Households holdings*	*Non-households holdings*
Agricultural land	*301.2	*189.2	*112.0
Cultivated land (A606)	130.1	*120.2	*9.8
Cultivated land (A601/2)	86.3	79.8	6.5
Sown area (A601/2)	*130.2	123.3	*6.9
Multi-crops index (A601/2)	*151	*155	*106
Sown area SSB- 1996	152.4	–	–
Cultivated land SSB- 1996	95.5	–	–
Multi-crops index (SSB 1996)	160	–	–

Source: Our estimation (*) of data from Abstract of the First National Agricultural Census of China (1999).

of the cultivated and sown area, the intensity of land use (expressed by the multiple-cropping index) is higher in the household holdings (155) than in the non-household holdings (106).

Figure 6.6 shows the distribution of the sown area by the size of household holdings in hectares. We can see that over 50 per cent of the sown area is concentrated in the households with land between 0.2 to 0.6 hectares (3 to 9 *mu*). The smaller households, with less than 0.2 hectares, only account for 10 per cent of the sown area, whereas those between 0.6 and 1 hectare have more than 15 per cent of the sown area. In China, 75 per cent of the sown area is held by households with less than 1 hectare, whereas the other 25 per cent of the sown area is distributed among the remaining households with more than 1 hectare of land.

Regional differences and a new geography of Chinese agriculture

Macro-agricultural areas at provincial level

The differences in Chinese agriculture that exist at the provincial level do not necessarily correspond to the usual regional geography used to describe the rural economy and recent agricultural development trends. The numerous and recent analyses on regional development and socio-economic inequality focus on the different trends between three regions – the East, Central and West – and subsequently classify provinces in these three macro-regions, see Raiser (1998), Yao (2000), Zhang I *et al.* (2000), Dèmurger (2001), Yao and Zhang (2001). With the Agricultural

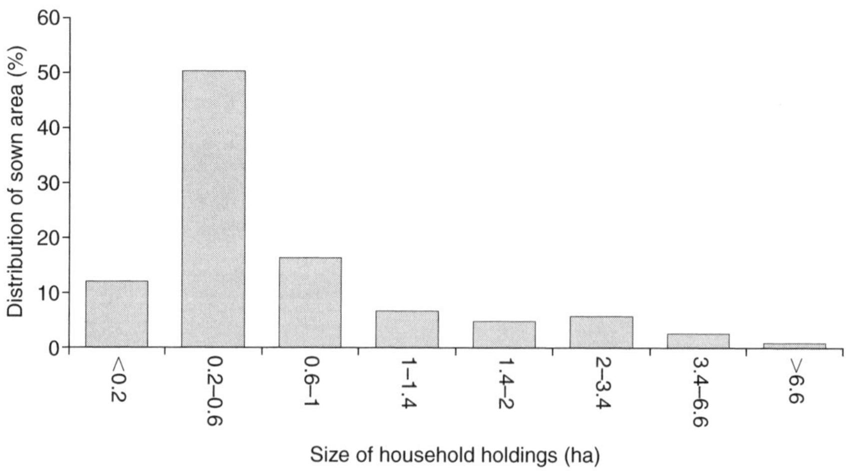

Figure 6.6 Distribution of the sown area by size of household holdings.

Census Data in hand, we have an excellent opportunity to gain an improved understanding of the differences existing at the provincial level, thus laying a basis for a renewed definition of China's agricultural geography. The knowledge on these geographical differences will allow for a better comprehension of the development of farms and the patterns of land use, and thus enable better design of agricultural and development policies.

In the analysis of the geographical differences of Chinese agriculture, we used more than 30 variables from the Agricultural Census including: labour engaged in agricultural and non-agricultural activities; the main agricultural activities; the level of education in the households; the land use in all agricultural holdings; and the use of machinery, (see Table 6.7). The analysis of geographical differences was conducted across 30 provinces and municipalities of China, while the selected variables data analysis used more than 2,400 counties. To define the main macro-agricultural areas, the analysis was performed in three different steps using statistical multivariate analysis. In the first step we carried out a Principal Component Analysis (PCA) on the 30 selected variables. The PCA is a multivariate technique (an analysis of many variables). The aim of the PCA is to reduce the number of the original variables (for example, rainfall, evaporation and temperature; price, demand and supply) by creating a smaller set of related variables (e.g. climate and economy).[9] The price paid for the PCA is a loss in the original variance of the variables explained. However, the gain is a clearer insight into complex phenomena, as one has reduced it to its bare essentials. In the second step we employed a Cluster Analysis (CA) on the data at the provincial level, to identify the four main macro agricultural areas of China. Finally, in the third step, we conducted a preliminary cluster analysis at the county level inside each macro agricultural area.[10]

The four Chinese agricultural macro areas are quite different from the generally accepted agricultural classification, in terms of both the number of provinces involved as well as the main characteristics of agriculture and land use (see Figure 6.7). The four macro-agricultural areas emerging from our analysis are ranked by the different levels of agricultural development and resource endowment, with particular reference to land utilization. The macro areas show different numbers of people engaged in agricultural activities, associated with different levels of education. Land utilization differs mainly in the relative importance of cultivated land, but also the relevance that woodland and grassland adopt in the different areas. The four macro areas derived from our analysis describe the geography of Chinese agriculture in a substantially different way than the three macro-economic regions defined by the SSB (East, Central and West). These also differ from the SSB's more disaggregated six economic geographic regions (North, North East, East, Middle and South, South West, North West). The four agricultural macro areas are:

Table 6.7 Cluster analysis of the Chinese provinces

	Gray – Cluster 1		*Blue – Cluster 2*		*Pink – Cluster 3*		*Green – Cluster 4*	
	Mean	*Var*	*Mean*	*Var*	*Mean*	*Var*	*Mean*	*Var*
1 Persons in agricultural households/persons in non-agricultural households	191.26	13,785.62	36.02	184.72	2.49	2.00	14.20	35.62
2 % of persons aged 7–25 years in rural households	37.53	0.56	28.61	17.04	15.94	6.70	23.89	10.94
3 % of persons aged 36–61 years in rural households	35.39	0.42	42.78	9.06	54.26	19.28	46.69	9.60
4 Rural households – % of persons aged 7 and over engaged in crop planting	67.80	15.05	84.24	13.07	41.40	124.57	70.27	130.51
5 Rural households – % of persons aged 7 and over engaged in animal husbandry	25.00	40.72	3.11	3.57	1.54	0.35	2.52	3.14
6 Rural households – % of persons aged 7 and over engaged in non agricultural activities in rural area	6.99	6.17	12.21	10.35	54.60	114.64	25.61	107.53
7 Rural households – % of persons aged 7 and over engaged in non agricultural activities in urban area	0.78	0.01	0.92	0.08	0.33	0.01	0.91	0.17
8 Rural households – % of persons aged 7 and over engaged in economic activities in home township	95.70	3.71	93.07	5.87	82.56	23.64	86.08	17.88
9 All holdings – persons engaged in economic activities, female/male.	0.98	0.00	0.88	0.00	0.92	0.00	0.89	0.00
10 All holdings – persons engaged in non-agricultural activities/ persons engaged in agricultural activities	0.07	0.00	0.12	0.00	0.51	0.01	0.25	0.01
11 Households holdings – % of persons illiterate and semi-illiterate	61.06	216.53	21.24	96.71	13.22	28.19	12.37	12.90
12 Households holdings – % of persons with educational level of primary school and junior middle school	37.40	177.30	73.86	87.68	79.16	21.28	82.17	13.92
13 Households holdings – % of persons with superior educational level	1.54	1.96	4.91	2.16	7.61	3.82	5.45	1.80
14 Households holdings – % of male with superior educational level	2.09	3.48	6.61	3.86	9.10	2.09	7.64	4.03

15 Households holdings – % of female with superior educational level	0.97	0.82	2.99	1.30	6.06	7.92	3.04	1.01
16 Households holdings – male/female with superior educational levels	2.71	0.36	2.45	0.65	1.72	0.36	2.69	0.7
17 Households holdings – % of persons engaged in agricultural activities 6 months and over	82.68	6.42	75.56	104.53	50.00	17.12	66.47	128.51
18 All Holdings – Hettar/number of rural households	1.06	0.00	1.60	0.67	0.36	0.01	0.53	0.04
19 All Holdings – Percentage of Agricultural Land (area) for cultivated land	24.31	22.52	48.44	441.02	82.25	33.41	47.19	332.04
20 All Holdings – Percentage of Agricultural Land (area) for woodland	10.84	5.31	28.59	370.58	5.68	34.66	42.92	333.36
21 All Holdings – Percentage of Agricultural Land (area) for grassland	64.78	6.03	21.10	787.30	0.12	0.00	3.44	80.65
22 All Holdings – Percentage of Agricultural Land (area) for fisheries	0.01	0.00	0.72	0.36	6.70	7.49	2.24	2.37
23 All Holdings – Percentage Distribution of Sown Area for grain	78.28	62.88	79.99	114.75	79.14	51.34	79.01	53.64
24 All Holdings – among cultivated land tractor plughed area (%)	20.68	163.71	39.34	830.81	82.17	6.30	27.27	451.46
25 All Holdings – among cultivated land electro-mechanelly irrigated area (%)	2.26	0.11	13.01	213.78	74.28	58.12	25.37	353.59
26 All Holdings – among harvested area mechanelly harvested area (%)	9.62	45.70	12.35	143.59	30.24	213.85	6.07	69.65
27 All Holdings – number of large animals for 100 persons engaged in agricultural activities	369.21	13,831.25	55.07	440.63	12.61	66.69	22.46	116.68
28 Large and medium tractor/persons engaged in agricultural activities	5.90	15.57	8.40	45.11	34.34	843.68	7.58	52.11
29 Small/persons engaged in agricultural activities	4.59	5.82	4.14	4.59	3.35	1.55	1.95	2.31
30 All Holdings – persons engaged in agricultural activities/ persons engaged in economic activities	93.51	4.99	89.74	6.67	66.54	20.71	80.40	41.13

Source: Authors' processing on Abstract of the First National Agricultural Census of China (1998).

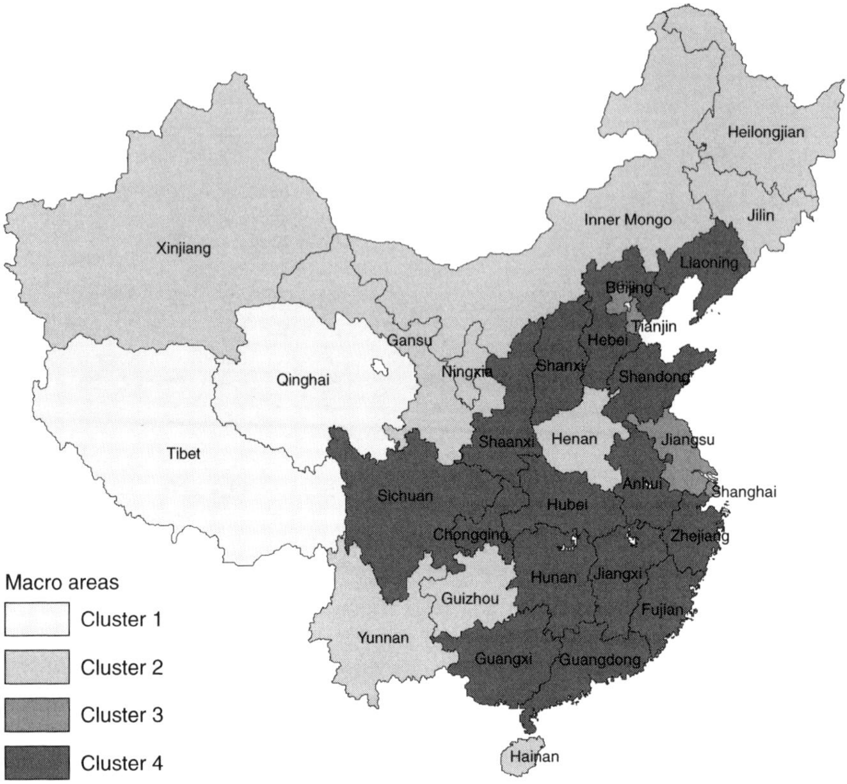

Figure 6.7 The four clusters of the agricultural macro areas.

1 *Cluster 1 – Mountain area.* This involves only two provinces (Qinghai and Tibet) which cover a vast, mainly mountainous area. This cluster has little traditional agriculture, but features high levels of animal husbandry practices (25 per cent of persons over age 7) and also a relatively low use of machinery. There are a large number of young people in this region which has the highest rate of semi-illiteracy (61 per cent). The holdings encompass a relatively large area, and land use is characterized by the lowest percentage of cultivated land (less than 25 per cent) in comparison to the total agricultural land of the area. The most prevalent land use is grassland covering about 65 per cent of the total agricultural area. The level of mechanization is low whereas the presence of large animals (yak) is significant. In these two provinces there are no fishery activities.

2 *Cluster 2 – Peripheral area.* This cluster includes nine provinces from the Northern part of China and also from the South (Yunnan and Guizhou). It is the largest cluster in terms of size and it is character-

ized by holdings with the largest area (1.6 hectares). The people engaged in agricultural activities account for approximately 90 per cent of the total number of people occupied in economic activities. The level of education is not high, with 21 per cent of the population being semi-illiterate. The prevalent agricultural activity is crop cultivation (about 85 per cent of people are involved in this). Cultivated land occupies less than half (48 per cent) of the agricultural land whereas the forest covers about 29 per cent and the grassland more than 21 per cent of the land area. The mechanized areas (tractor ploughed) are about 40 per cent of the cultivated land, and the numbers of large livestock are low.

3 *Cluster 3 – Urban area.* This cluster includes four provinces and municipalities (Beijing, Jiangsu, Shanghai, and Tianjin). It is the smallest cluster in area, but represents the largest urban region with substantive food consumption. It features the smallest percentage of people engaged in agricultural activities (66.5 per cent), and the highest level of education (only about 13 per cent of the population is semi-illiterate and 7.6 per cent have higher education). The households are the smallest in size among all four clusters. In this area the cultivated land is more than 82 per cent of the total agricultural area, whereas the presence of forestry and grassland is insignificant. Instead, fisheries are of great importance in this cluster (6.7 per cent of agricultural land). The agriculture of this area shows the highest level of mechanization: 82 per cent of tractor ploughed areas, and 30 per cent of mechanically harvested areas.

4 *Cluster 4 – Principally agricultural area.* This area includes the highest number of provinces (16), all located in the East-southern and Middle and South Region of China. This cluster also includes the Sichuan province. This area is relevant in terms of people engaged in agricultural activities (80 per cent), which is lower than the second cluster (peripheral area). Generally, there is a good level of education with the smallest proportion of semi-illiterate people (12 per cent). The prevalent agricultural activity is crop cultivation with more than 70 per cent of labour involved. The distribution of land use is 47 per cent of cultivated land, 42 per cent forest, and an irrelevant area of grassland and fisheries. As in the other clusters, the largest part of sown area (79 per cent) is used for grain. The level of mechanization of this area is low with only 27 per cent of tractor-ploughed land. This large area represents the "core" of Chinese agriculture.

Inside the macro-agricultural areas of China

The four agricultural macro areas are not homogeneous and can be further differentiated if we consider the internal conditions within each province. Only the "urban cluster" is well defined, small and uniform.

Employing the available data at county level allows further geographical differentiation of Chinese agriculture. The Abstract of the First National Agricultural Census in China reports only seven maps representing data at the county level. The seven variables represented in the maps are: (1) per-capita possession of cultivated land; (2) agricultural machinery power possessed by 100 people engaged in agricultural activities; (3) proportion of non-agricultural households to rural households; (4) proportion of total population engaged in agricultural activities to rural people engaged in agricultural activities; (5) proportion of irrigated area to agricultural land; (6) proportion of number of towns to total number of towns; and (7) the educational level of rural labour force in years. These data, presented by the maps in the Abstract, were made available by courtesy of SSB.

We performed the same type of cluster analysis for each of the four macro-agricultural areas described in the previous section. Each cluster (representing a group of counties inside each macro area) is arranged as follows: five for the mountain macro area, five for the peripheral macro area (cluster 2), four for the principally agricultural macro area (cluster 4), whereas the urban macro area (cluster 3) remains uniform. Through this analysis we found that there is a big difference in the number of counties in each cluster (see Table 6.8).

These results immediately highlight how relevant it is to further differentiate within each macro-agricultural area (Fanfani and Brasili 2001a). It falls beyond the scope of this chapter to deal with this issue in detail. However, in brief, within the largest principally agricultural macro area there is a large homogeneous sub-area which includes 1,050 counties. These counties account for 40 per cent of all Chinese counties and are characterized by a low per-capita possession of cultivated land (0.03). Furthermore, this group of counties has a higher share of non-agricultural households (state, collective, cooperative, private, and so forth), compared to the number of rural households (16 per cent) in the other macro areas (except for the urban area). These counties have the highest proportion of people employed in agricultural activities compared to the other four groups of counties within the principally agricultural area (80 per cent). This large group of counties is characterized by less irrigated

Table 6.8 County clusters in the macro areas

Macro areas/clusters	*Number of clusters*	*Number of counties inside the cluster*	*Total*
1 Mountain area	5	24, 16, 8, 21, 46	115
2 Peripheral area	5	427, 206, 15, 14, 75	737
3 Urban area	1	100	100
4 Principally agricultural area	4	42, 333, 15, 1,050	1,440

Source: our processing on Abstract of the First National Agricultural Census of China (1998).

land (36 per cent of agricultural area). The counties included in this large cluster (1,050 counties), appear to be so homogenous that we could not make any further distinction with the given indicators. This group of counties can be considered characteristic of Chinese agriculture. Inside the principally agricultural area there is another important group of 333 counties that seems to be more developed than the previous larger group. The share of non-agricultural holdings is much higher (38 per cent) and the proportion of people engaged in agricultural activities is lower (60 per cent). The proportion of irrigated land is significantly higher (more than 62 per cent), and within this group there are a larger number of towns.

Conclusion

The results of the First Agricultural Census of 1997 provide a better knowledge of the structure of Chinese agriculture and land use by different farm typologies and provinces. The Agricultural Census shows that the number of rural households is very large, more than 214 million, with 871 million people involved in the rural sector. The data on the availability of land and land use differ significantly from previous data. The Agricultural Census shows a larger availability of cultivated land in China, over 130 million hectares against the 95 million of the previous official estimates of the State Statistical Bureau. These results indicate greater possibilities for future increases in agricultural productivity and a higher intensity of land use per capita and per surface area. In addition, the census has substantiated the recent downward revision of earlier alarmist predictions of huge food deficits in China (FAO 2000; OECD 2000; USDA 2000). Even though the census does not provide complete data on land availability, the results so far have provided empirical evidence for the great relevance of cultivated land, and the importance of woodland and grassland (more than 97 and 62 million hectares respectively, according to our estimates). The importance of permanent crops is increasing, with more than 7 million hectares (2.3 per cent of agricultural land) planted, and the area set aside for fisheries is also growing in importance (about 4.8 million hectares, 1.6 per cent of the total agricultural land). This acts as an indicator for recent shifts in the structure of food consumption (towards protein-richer foods), as economic development progresses in China.

Land distribution and land use are quite different according to the types of agricultural holdings. The main types of farms show the prevalence of the agricultural household holdings (over 193 million), whereas non-household holdings (state, collective, cooperative, private) only account for only 358,000 farms. The agricultural households use a large part of China's cultivated land, whereas the non-household holdings are mainly involved in forestry, grassland (animal husbandry), and fisheries. Households own most of the cultivated land in China, more than 120 million hectares (92.5 per cent), while less than 10 million hectares

(7.5 per cent) are distributed to non-household holdings. Land use in agricultural households encompasses cultivated land (over 63 per cent of total agricultural land), with a limited presence of grassland and forestry (17 per cent and 15 per cent respectively). Alternatively, land use of the non-household holdings is characterized by woodland (more than 60 per cent of total) and grassland (28 per cent of total), with less than 10 per cent devoted to cultivated land. The non-households play a significant role in fisheries, with more than 67 per cent of the nation's total agricultural land.

The presence of such a great number of small agricultural households that till a high proportion of cultivated land is a measure of the degree of fragmentation of the land triggered by the 1978 agrarian reforms. In some ways, it explains the social and economic stability of rural China in the last decade of rapid economic development. A contribution to social stability in rural China is also given by the growing presence of part-time employment in households where some family members, almost exclusively male, have off-farm jobs. Part-time farming occurs in about 35 per cent of the agricultural households. This means that one-third of rural households have one or more income earner outside agriculture, whether they are working in local enterprises, construction, peddling, or living and working far from home, often out of their counties and provinces and perhaps in cities. The large availability of workers and mobility of people (between villages, towns, counties and provinces) who are presently active in agricultural households could be the main force for future developments of non-agricultural activities in China. Further, more relevant changes will manifest in the future when entire families, as opposed to a single family member, choose to migrate from agricultural areas.

The area of cultivated land in China is 43 per cent of the total agricultural land, whereas woodlands cover more than 32 per cent and grasslands more than 20 per cent. Permanent crops (2.3 per cent) and fisheries (1.6 per cent) are less significant. The new figures of the Agricultural Census show a profound diversity in land use among the provinces. There are many provinces where the cultivated land is over 70 per cent of the total agricultural area, whereas in other provinces it is less than 30 per cent. There is a high percentage of cultivated land in all provinces of the North Region (except Inner Mongolia) and in the East Region, and in Henan (84 per cent), Chongqing (66 per cent) and Ningxia (75 per cent) provinces. In some North-western provinces the lower share of cultivated land is due to the large presence of grasslands, Xinjiang (86 per cent), Qinghai (67 per cent), Tibet (62 per cent) and Inner Mongolia (40 per cent). Woodlands dominate the Eastern regions in the provinces of Fujian (70 per cent of woodland), Jiangxi (67 per cent) and Zhejiang (59 per cent); but also in all provinces of the Centre-south, where woodlands comprise around 50–60 per cent of total agricultural land. A relevant aspect in land use is the importance of the proportion devoted to the fisheries, more than 4.7 million hectares; in some provinces such as Tianjin, Shanghai and Jiangsu, it reaches between 7 and 8 per cent of the total agricultural area.

The data on the sown areas reported by the census are relevant to evaluate crop distribution and the intensity of land use. These data are not easily comparable with the previous official statistics because they do not include permanent crops (mainly tea and orchards). In fact, the total sown area according to the official statistics was about 150 million hectares in 1995 and more than 156 million in 1999, whereas the agricultural census gives for 1996 a sown area of 123.3 million hectares for the agricultural households alone. The total sown areas of households and non-households was estimated at about 130.2 million hectares, with a difference of less than 10 per cent with respect to the previous official statistics, and taking into account the different definitions of the sown area.

The intensity of land use calculated on the basis of the census data is higher than the world average, but lower than the previous official estimates of the State Statistical Bureau: 151 versus 160. The lower intensity of crop use that results from the 1997 census data can be even lower if we consider that the sown area of the agricultural holdings also includes the sown area in non-cultivated land (courtyards of the houses and other areas primarily devoted to permanent crops, woodland or grassland). The use of multiple cropping indices at provincial and county level requires more attention and extreme caution when interpreting the data.

The data on the sown area of the Agricultural Census gives interesting information about the intensity of land use of, and distribution over, the different farm types. The multiple-cropping index is much higher in the agricultural household holdings (155) than in the non-household holdings (only 106). The agricultural household holdings index is also closer to the total cropping index derived from the previous official statistics. The distribution of the sown area of the household holdings by size shows that more than 50 per cent of the sown area is concentrated in the holdings of 0.2 to 0.6 hectares. The smaller holdings with less than 0.2 hectares have only 10 per cent of the sown area, whereas those with 0.6 to 1 hectare have more than 15 per cent of the sown area. In China 75 per cent of the sown area is in holdings with less than 1 hectare of land, whereas the other 25 per cent of the sown area is distributed among the holdings with more than 1 hectare of land. The changes in the agricultural population and rural urban migration could heavily influence the distribution and dimension of land among the main farm types in the future.

The differences between the data of the Agricultural Census and the previous statistics suggest a new framework for agricultural geography in China. For this purpose, we applied a principal components and cluster analysis to more than 30 variables of the First Agricultural Census at provincial and county level. From this analysis, four new macro agricultural areas were determined: *mountain area*; *peripheral area*; *urban area*; and *principally agricultural area.* Different levels of land use, agricultural development and resource endowment characterize these areas. The macro areas show different proportions of the population employed in agricultural activities; this is associated with the different levels of education seen across the macro areas. The land use is different across each of these areas, the importance of cultivated land is of primary importance, but the value of the woodland and grassland in the different areas should not be underestimated. The four macro areas derived from our analysis are quite distinct from the widely accepted three main economic regions (East, Central and West) which are currently used to describe the Chinese economy. Our definitions also differ compared to the more disaggregated six economic geographic regions of China (North, North-East, East, Middle and South, South-West, North-West).

The publication of the complete results from the First Agricultural Census in China, particularly the data on land use and land distribution, will contribute to a more sound analysis of rural China, with specific reference to the intensity of agricultural production and the productivity of land and labour. It is hoped that this information will help to define policy issues crucial to the future economic and social development of China. The availability of more comprehensive data in the future will continue to provide the necessary information to redefine China's shifting agricultural geography.

Acknowledgements

We thank Mirko Bonetti for his valuable help in preparing the chapter.

Notes

1 The Agricultural Census involved 7.2 million numerators; 140,000 training courses; 90,000 TV commercials; 1.7 million radio programmes, and 36 million posters. The Chinese National Agriculture Census Office presented the preliminary results in 1998. The main results and tabulation of the First Agriculture Census in China were published at the end of 1999.

2 For the quality of the Chinese agricultural statistics prior to the First Agricultural Census, see Taylor and Bannister (1989), Zhang Sai (1990) and the explanatory notes of the *Chinese Statistical Yearbook* (SSB, 2000, and previous years). For a description of the problems in designing the Agricultural Census and data collection, see Biggeri (2001) and an initial comparison of the previous official statistics and the census results are in Zhu Xiangdong (2001).

3 However, the larger labour force estimated by the census could also depend, at least partly, on the different definitions used. For instance, the census definition considers those working less than two months a year as active participants.

4 The small size of the agricultural households in China is also evident by the size of the livestock. There are more than 128 million large animals (cattle, buffalo, yak, and so forth) in more than 73 million of agricultural holdings, with an average of 1.7 head per holding, but more than 55 per cent of large animals are draught animals. The census reports more than 335 million pigs in

more than 130.3 million agricultural holdings, mainly in the household holdings (95 per cent), with an average of about 2.5 pigs per household. The large number of pigs and poultry in the household is important in relation to meat consumption in rural areas. There are more than 2.6 billion poultry across China in more than 143.8 holdings involved. Over 90 per cent of poultry are in household holdings, with an average of more than 16 animals per household. See SSB (2000).

5 In his first comments on the Agricultural Census results, Zhu Xiandong (2001) reports that on the basis of the new figures of cultivated land, the yields of cereal in China are about 3,900 kg per hectare, 994 kg less than previous statistics. However, the yields of cereals still remain larger than the world's average of 900 kg per hectare.

6 A comparison of the current survey for rural households with the Agricultural Census results has been done by Steine *et al.* (2001).

7 For example, the census reports about 7 million hectares of permanent crops; if we consider that half of this could be cultivated, the sown area is approximately 3.5 million hectares. If each household within the 193 million has a courtyard of 0.1 *mu,* the total sown area will be about 1.3 million hectares. As a result, the multiple crop index will fall to 145.

8 According to the census, the sown area devoted to total grain crops is a little more than 100 million hectares, less than 11 per cent of the SSB estimate of 112.5 millions. If we consider single crops, there are larger disparities: the grain crops have large differences (more than 30 per cent) for beans and tuber. For all other crops, the differences in sown areas are relevant: around 30 per cent for oil-bearing crops, cotton, fibre crops, and tobacco. Even larger differences in the sown area are registered for sugar (970,000 hectares, about than 47 per cent) and in particular for vegetables with 5.9 million hectares compared to the 10.5 million of the SSB estimate (−43 per cent). The differences in the sown areas for rice, vegetables, beans, tuber, and oil-bearing crops are responsible for the main quantitative differences in the sown area registered by the Agricultural Census and the official SSB statistics. On the contrary, among cereals, the sown area of rice is 10 per cent lower (27.9 million hectares against 31.4), whereas that of wheat (28.2 million) is only 5 per cent lower than the SSB data. The sown area for corn (24.3 million) is almost equal to that of the SSB. See SSB-1996 from *China Statistical Yearbook 1999*; the census data are from the Abstract of the First National Agricultural Census of China (1999), questionnaire A601. Note that the definition of the sown area is not the same between the SSB survey and the Agricultural Census (tea plantations and orchards are included in permanent crops in the census).

9 The newly created variables are Principal Components and the total variance explained by a Principal Component is the Eigenvalue.

10 A more detailed description of the analysis of this section can be found in the previous work Brasili and Fanfani (2000).

References

Abbassian, A. (2001) "China's Food and the World: the Revised Perspectives", IV International Symposium on "Perspective of the Agri-food System in the New Millennium" Bologne, 5–8 September.

Alexandratos N. (1996) "China's Projected Cereals Deficits in a World Context", *Agricultural Economics*, 15(1): 1–16.

Alexandratos, N., Bruisma, J. and Schmidhuber, J. (2000) "China's Food and the

World", paper presented at International Seminars on China Agricultal Census Results, Beijing, 19–22 September.

Ash, R. and Edmonds, R.L. (1998) "China's Land Resources, Environment and Agricultural Production", *The China Quarterly*, 156(December): 836–879.

Biggeri, L. (2001) "China Agricultural Census Design and Data Collection: Issues and Lessons", *Proceedings of the International Seminar on China: The Agricultural Census Results*, Beijing: China Statistics Press

Biggeri, M. (1998) I fattori dello sviluppo dell'agricoltura cinese dopo le grandi riforme, analisi empiriche su un panel di dati a livello provinciale, Phd thesis, Università degli Studi di Siena.

Biggeri, M., Brasili C. and Fanfani, R. (1998) "Perspectives of the Chinese Agricultural Sector from the First Agricultural Census and from an Analysis of the Structure of Farm Households", paper presented at AIEA2 – Fondation Polar – Université des Andes, "Mondialisation et systèmes alimentaires" 15, 16, 17 July.

Brasili, C. and Fanfani, R. (2000) "The new geography of Chinese Agriculture", paper presented at International Seminar on China Agricultural Census Results, Beijing, 19–22 September.

Brown, L. (1995) *Who Will Feed China? Wake-up Call for a Small Planet*, New York: W.W. Norton.

Carter, C. (1999) "Institutional Reform and Agricultural Productivity Growth in China", in C. Findlay and A. Watson (eds) *Food security and economic reform*, London: Macmillan.

Carter, C. and Estrin, A. (2001) "Market Reform Versus Structural Reform in Rural China", *Journal of Comparative Economics*, 29: 527–541.

Choe, C. and Yin, X. (2000) "Contract Management Responsibility System and Profit Incentives in China's State Over Enterprises", *China Economic Review*, 11: 98–112.

Chu Xuejin and Li Wenhai (1992) "Method and Quality Control for Data Processing", in Shao Zongming, Zhu Xiangdong and Wang Jili (eds) *Proceedings of the International Expert Consultation on Agricultural Censuses*, Beijing: Agricultural University Press,.

Dèmurger, S. (2001) "Infrastructure Development and Economic Growth: An Explanation for Regional Disparities in China?", *Journal of Comparative Economics*, 29: 95–117.

Fan, S. (2001) "Infrastructure and Regional Economic Development; New Evidence from the Agricultureal Census" in *Proceedings of The International Seminar on China Agricultural Census Results*, Beijing: China Statistics Press.

Fanfani, R. and Brasili, C. (2001a) "The New Geography of Chinese Agriculture", *Proceedings of the International Seminar on China: the Agricultural Census Results*, Beijing: China Statistics Press.

Fanfani, R. and Brasili, C. (2001) "Land Use in China: Regional Differences from the 1997 Agricultural Census", paper presented at the 2nd International Convention of Asia Scholars (ICAS 2), Berlin, 9–12 August.

Fanfani, R. and Brasili, C. (2001) "The Economic and Social Structure of the Chinese Agricultural Sector", paper presented at the IV International Symposium on "Perspective of the Agri-food System in the new Millennium", Bologna, 5–8 September.

FAO (2000) *Agriculture: Toward 2015/30, Technical Interim Report*, Rome: FAO, Global Perspective Studies Unit, April.

FASC (1991) *The Concise Aggregate Data of the Pilot Agricultural Census in Wei County*, Food and Agricultural Statistics Center, China State Statistical Bureau, Beijing: Agricultural University Press.

Feng Haifa (2001) "Chinese Agricultural Production Factor Movement and Substitution Analysis", in *Proceedings of the International Seminar on China Agricultural Census Results*, Beijing: China Statistics Press.

Findlay, C. and Watson, A. (1999) *Food Security and Economic Reform*, London: Macmillan.

Fisher, G., Chen, Y. and Sun, L. (1998) *The Balance of Cultivated Land in China during 1988– 1995*, Report 98–047, Luxemburg: International Institute for Applied System Analysis (IIASA).

Giovannini, E. (2000) "The Chinese Rural Non-Agricultural Enterprises: The Evidence from the Agricultural Census", in *Proceedings of the International Seminar on China: The Agricultural Census Results*, Beijing: China Statistics Press.

Hubacek, K. and Sun, L. (2001) "A scenario analysis of China's land use and land cover change: incorporating biophysical information into input-output modelling", *Structural Change and Economic Dynamics*, 12: 367–397.

Mead, R.W. (2000) "China's Agricultural Reform: the Importance of Private Plots", *China Economic Review*, 11: 54–78.

Maddison, A. (1998) *Chinese Economic Performance in the Long Run*, OECD, Paris; Development Centre.

Maddison, A. (2001) *The World Economy, a Millennial Perspective*, Paris; OECD Development Centre.

National Agricultural Census Office of China (1999) *Abstract of the First National Agricultural Census in China*, Beijing: China Statistics Press.

National Bureau of Statistics (2000) *Introduction to Rural Household Survey in China*, Beijing, National Bureau of Statistics.

Raiser M. (1998) "Subsidising Inequality: Economic Reform, Final Transfers and Convergence across Chinese Provinces", *Journal of Development Studies*, 34(3): 1–26.

SSB (2000) *China Statistical Yearbook 2000*, Beijing: Agricultural University Press.

Steiner, M., Bailey, J., Beranek, J. (2001) "Improvement of Sample Design by Using Results from the Agricultural Census", in *Proceedings of the International Seminar on China: The Agricultural Census Results*, Beijing: China Statistics Press.

Taylor, J.R. and Bannister, J. (1989) *Statistical Reliability in China*, Washington, DC: US Bureau of the Census.

USDA (2000) "China WTO Accession Would Boost U.S. Agricultural Export and Farm Income", *USDA Agriculture Outlook*.

Vermeer, E.B. (2001) "Determinants of Agricultural Productivity in China: A Comparison of the New Provincial Census Data with Official Figures, and Some Implications", in *Proceedings of the International Seminar on China: The Agricultural Census Results*, Beijing: China Statistics Press.

Weber, M. (2001) *Il miracolo cinese, perché bisogna prendere la Cina sul serio*, Bologne: Il Mulino.

Wu, Z. and Kirke, A.W. (1994) "An Assessment of Some Key Chinese Agricultural Statistics", *China Information*, 9(1): 42–76.

Yao, S. (2000) "Economic Development and Poverty Reduction in China over 20 years of Economic Reforms", *Development and Cultural Change*, 48(3): 447–474.

Yao, S. and Zhang, Z. (2001) "On Regional Inequalities and Diverging Clubs: A

Case Study of Contemporary China", *Journal of Comparative Economics*, 29: 466–484.

Zhang, I., Liu, A. and Yao, S. (2000) "Convergence of China's regional incomes 1952–1997", *China Economic Review*, 12: 243–258.

Zhang, L., Rozelle, S. and Huang, J. (2001) "Off-farms Jobs and On-farm Work in the Period of Boom and Bust in Rural China", *Journal of Comparative Economics*, 29: 505–526.

Zhang Sai (1990) 'Statistical Activities of China', ISTAT Conference paper, ISTAT, Rome.

Zhu Xiangdong (ed.) (1995) *The Concise Aggregate Data of National Pilot Agricultural Census*, Beijing: Food and Agricultural Statistics Centre (FASC).

Zhu Xiangdong (2001) "A Concise Analysis of the Main Results of the First National Agricultural Census in China", in *Proceedings of the International Seminar on China: The Agricultural Census Results*, Beijing: China Statistics Press.

7 What drives land fragmentation?

Theoretical approaches and empirical analysis

Shuhao Tan, Futian Qu, and Nico Heerink

The existence of fragmented landholdings has long been regarded as a characteristic feature of less-developed agricultural systems (Blarel *et al.* 1992). It can be a major obstacle to agricultural development because it hinders modernization, causes inefficiencies in production, and involves large costs to alleviate its effects (McPherson 1982). In view of these considerations, land consolidation and land reform policies have been implemented to reduce fragmentation in Europe, including the Netherlands and France, Africa, for example, Kenya, Tanzania, and Rwanda, and elsewhere. But in China, with its high population pressure and limited availability of arable land, landholding fragmentation remains most problematic. China's fragmented landholdings cause a loss of farmland area due to use of land for marking boundaries, and a low efficiency in irrigation water management because of the irregular shape of numerous plots (Zhang *et al.* 1996). They also cause time loss in travel and form an obstacle to mechanization and agricultural management (Nguyen *et al.* 1996).

In order to eliminate fragmentation, village-level land consolidation and land redistribution programs to increase plot sizes have been implemented in China since the mid-1980s. In some areas it is comparatively easy to implement such programs, while in other areas it involves high transaction costs to consolidate land plots contracted to individual households. Farmers have to meet frequently to discuss how to implement the policy so as to balance the interests of each household. This causes a loss of labor time both on-farm and off-farm. In addition, government funds are needed to assist in the engineering part of the programs. A good understanding of the causes of land fragmentation may help policy-makers decide which areas are suitable to undertake land consolidation and what the extent of land consolidation should be.

Although land fragmentation is a recognized problem in China (Qu *et al.* 1995; Hu 1997), little is known about its origins and driving forces, and the knowledge needed to design appropriate policies to eliminate land fragmentation therefore still remains rudimentary. Unfortunately, China's First National Agricultural Census carried out in 1997 is not very helpful in this respect, as data on the number and sizes of individual plots per household were not collected.

A better understanding of the causes of land fragmentation in China is needed, especially now that the country is faced with the challenge of agricultural modernization resulting from its entry into the World Trade Organization (WTO). New technologies are urgently required to reduce the production costs and to improve farm households' well-being. This chapter examines the causes of land fragmentation at two levels: the village and the household, in present-day China. The village is the actual decision-maker on many factors affecting land fragmentation; the household is the basic unit with respect to production decisions. Hence it is important to understand the factors that are responsible for differences in land fragmentation between villages and households.

The chapter is organized into several sections, the first of which briefly reviews available studies on the origins and causes of land fragmentation in various countries. Next follows a discussion of the situation and background of land fragmentation in China since the implementation of the household responsibility system (HRS), focusing on the introduction of the HRS and the land distribution process under this system. An analytical framework is then derived that will form the basis for the empirical analyses, and the results of the village- and household-level regression analyses are presented and discussed. The chapter ends with a conclusion and policy implications.

Review of the literature

Land fragmentation is defined as the existence of a number of spatially separate plots of land that are farmed as single units (McPherson 1982). Many studies have examined land fragmentation in different countries and areas (Birgegard 1993; Heston and Kumar 1983; Jabarin and Epplin 1994; Najafi and Bakhshoodeh 1992; Nguyen *et al.* 1996; Parikh and Shah 1994; Simons 1988; Soltow 1983). The topics covered in these studies include explanations of land fragmentation, cost estimates of fragmentation, effects of land fragmentation on agricultural production, and methods used to test the effects of land fragmentation on agricultural production.

Two broad viewpoints can be distinguished with regard to the emergence and persistence of land fragmentation, namely, "supply-side" explanations and "demand-side" explanations (Bentley 1987; McPherson 1982). The former treats fragmentation as an exogenous imposition on farmers. One major factor is land scarcity caused by inheritance and population pressure. Many authors with this viewpoint claim that partible inheritance in a growing population logically leads to fragmentation when farmers want to provide each of several heirs with land of similar quality (Anthony *et al.* 1979; World Bank 1978). Likewise, extreme land scarcity may lead to fragmented holdings as farmers seeking additional land will tend to accept any available parcel of land within reasonable distance of their house. Another supply-side factor is the breakdown of common property systems under the pressure of population growth. This breakdown has led to increased fragmentation in many developing countries, such as Kenya (King 1977) and eastern Nigeria (Udo 1965).

Supply-side explanations cannot always fully explain land fragmentation. When plots differ with respect to soil type, water retention capability, slope, altitude, and agro-climatic conditions, or when alternative risk-reducing mechanisms are absent, demand-side factors may play a role as well. Demand-side explanations view fragmentation primarily as a positive choice made by farmers. This viewpoint presumes that the private benefits of fragmentation exceed its private costs. Some researchers argue that when alternative risk-spreading mechanisms such as insurance, storage, and credit are not available or are more costly, land fragmentation will persist as a means for risk reduction (Charlesworth 1983; Ilbery 1984). In less-developed areas, farmers need land as a safeguard. When land quality is not homogenous, the scattering of parcels can reduce the risk of loss from flood, drought, fire, or other perils, and farmers can diversify their cropping mixtures across different growing conditions. When food commodity markets fail, land fragmentation may be beneficial for crop diversification, allowing farmers to grow (nonmarketed) subsistence crops. Another demand-side explanation was developed by Fenoaltea (1976). He argued that scattered parcels enable farmers to better allocate their labor over the seasons. If a labor market is missing, agricultural labor supply is determined by household size, and the need for spreading labor requirements over time is greater.

Several studies have examined land fragmentation in China in the past and at present (e.g., Buck 1937; Chao 1986; Nguyen *et al.* 1996). Two theories have been used to explain the existence of fragmented landholdings before the foundation of the People's Republic of China in 1949 (Chao 1986). One is the Chinese *fenjia*, that is, the system of dividing the family property equally among the sons, whenever one of them married. The married son could get his own share of family property (among which land was the most important), which was separated from his parents' family. The other explanation is the shortage of farmland that emerged with the increase of population after the eleventh century. Given the serious shortage of land, demand for it was immense relative to the supply. A so-called seller's market emerged, leading to land fragmentation. Remembering that China was an agricultural country, what we call off-farm activities today were very limited at that time. Most people had to make a living by cultivating land. The land accumulation rate was so slow in traditional China that a landowner could add only a small piece to his holdings every few years. By the time he was ready to buy, he had little choice in terms of location and had to settle for the size of plot he could afford. As a result, a typical landowner ended up holding small plots scattered not only throughout the same village but also sometimes throughout neighboring villages. Because most buyers could afford only small plots, large plots were often cut into small pieces when they were sold.

Some researchers examined the factors causing land fragmentation in contemporary China. Kung (1994), Chen *et al.* (1997), and Lin (2000) have argued that the system of land distribution is responsible to a great extent for the current fragmentation in China. Detailed empirical analyses that test the relevance of this hypothesis and prevailing land fragmentation theories for explaining the causes of land fragmentation in present-day China are lacking. In order to provide concrete suggestions for land fragmentation alleviation policies, there is a strong need for such in-depth studies of the causes of land fragmentation.

The background of land fragmentation

Land fragmentation since the 1980s

Land fragmentation in China finds its origin at the end of the 1970s and the beginning of the 1980s with the introduction of the household responsibility system (HRS). Before the HRS, rural land was owned and managed collectively; land was only divided into plots to match the soil type and irrigation and drainage condition, and for the convenience of management. Under the HRS, land use rights were assigned to individual households for a period of 15 years. As a result, land fragmentation became more pronounced.

Figures 7.1–7.3 show the degree of land fragmentation in China since

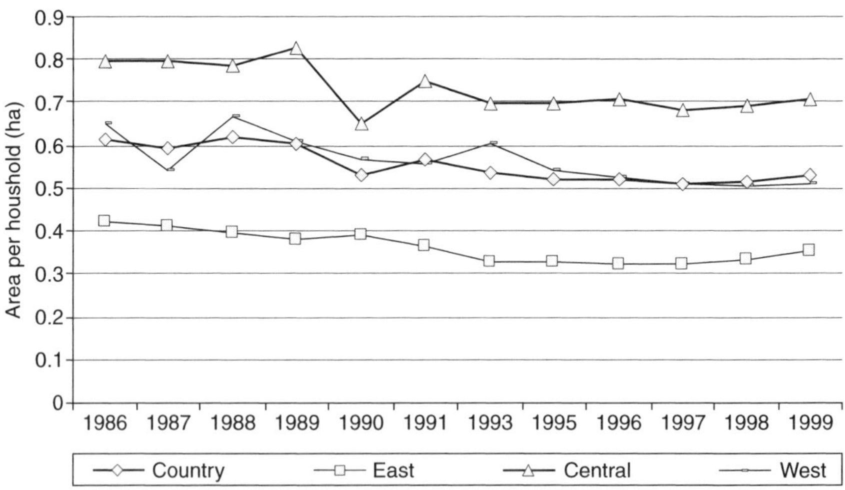

Figure 7.1 Area per household (in ha), 1986–1999.

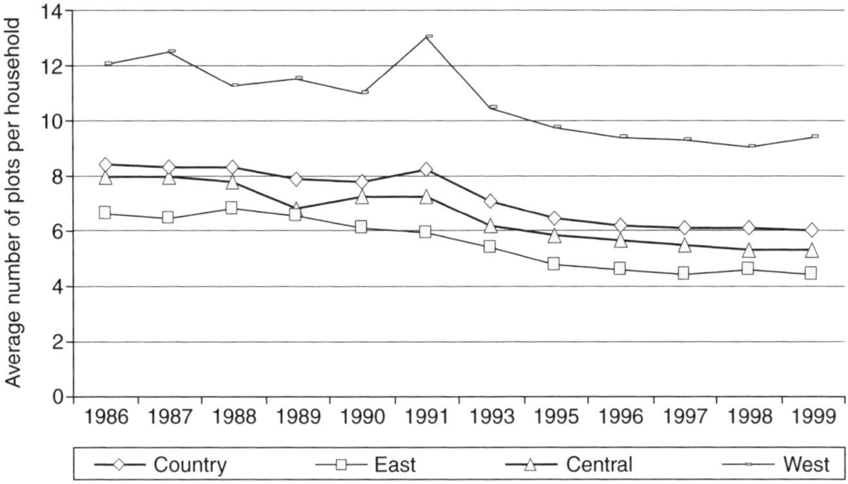

Figure 7.2 Average number of plots per household, 1986–1999.

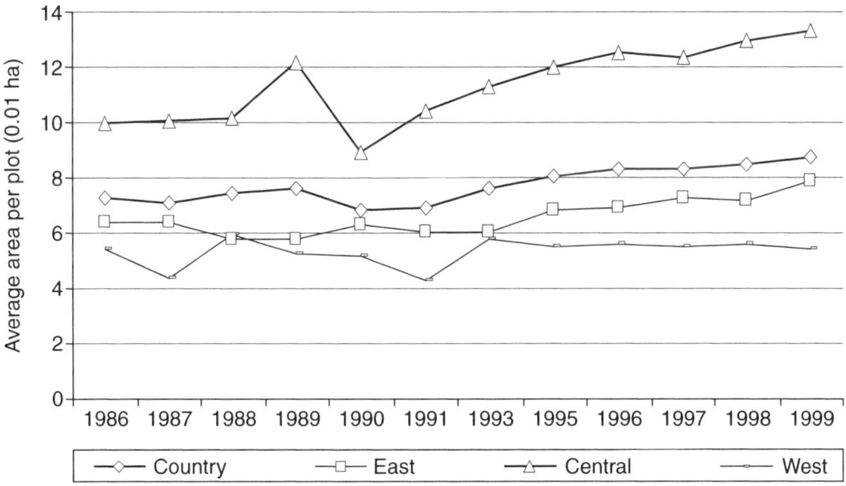

Figure 7.3 Average area per plot, 1986–1999.

1986, when systematic data collection on this issue started.[1] Figure 7.1 shows that the area per household has decreased from 0.61 ha in 1986 to 0.53 ha in 1999.[2] It decreased most before 1996 and remained roughly constant afterwards. There was a very small increase since about 1996 in the eastern part of China.

Figure 7.2 shows the average number of plots per farm household for China as a whole and for the eastern, central, and western parts of the country.[3] It confirms that a few years after the start of the HRS, land fragmentation was high in China. In 1986, farm households had on average 8.43 plots. In the course of the 1990s, land fragmentation slightly decreased, with a 1999 average of 6.06 plots. The average area per plot shown in Figure 7.3 slightly decreased until the beginning of the 1990s but increased afterwards. Throughout the entire 1986–1999 period, the number of plots per household was highest in the west and lowest in the east. It has been decreasing over time in all three regions, although some small fluctuations can be observed. The average area per plot was lower in the west than in the other two regions at the beginning of the period, and it remained roughly constant over time in the western region. In the east of China, this average steadily decreased until 1993, at which point it began to increase. In contrast, it increased in the central region since the beginning of the 1990s. The next section will discuss some of the major underlying causes of these trends.

Causes of land fragmentation

The introduction of the HRS had a large impact on land fragmentation. The goal of the HRS was to improve agricultural productivity through increasing individual incentives. Under this system, although land was still controlled by the collectives, the farmers were allocated land for production management in the sense that they were allowed to keep the surplus they produced over the contracted output. In return, farm households had to pay an agricultural land tax and some fees. Every person with rural registered permanent residence (*hukou*) could claim land. The distributed land area, however, differed from village to village and from hamlet to hamlet within the same village, mainly depending on the availability of land. The land of a village or hamlet could only be allocated to households within the same hamlet or village. The larger the number of households in a village, the more the farmland would be divided. Traditional villages and hamlets still control their own land. They actually have the legal rights of land ownership. They determine the land distribution, the reallocation of land, and the conversion of land from agricultural use to nonagricultural uses within their villages or hamlets; they are also responsible for the collection of grain quotas imposed by the state (Yao 2000).

Land fragmentation induced by the HRS was to a great extent determined by the rules and patterns of the land distribution process. According to Liu (2000) and Kung (2000), there were three main types of land distribution. The first is where all land was simply assigned to households based upon the family size. A nationwide survey of 300 villages conducted by China's State Council in 1988 confirmed this. Nearly 70 percent of the villages used this land assignment rule (State Council 1992). The second is where *kouliangtian* was equally distributed per person, and *zerentian* was allocated according to the number of laborers in a household.[4] The third is where all land was allocated according to the number of laborers.

Plots that were homogenous in soil and irrigation and drainage conditions, and where the same type of land use was possible, were grouped into one land class within a hamlet. Where necessary, as required by farmer consensus on the degree of homogeneity, a land class could be further divided into several subclasses, depending on variations in the conditions of the land within the class itself. Each class and subclass was used as an area unit where at least one plot was allocated to each household. In principle, each person should get an equal share of each class of land. If, for example, four classes of land are distinguished in a village, then a family of five persons could get five shares of each class of land. To reduce the number of plots, the land within the same class for the five members was kept in one place as much as possible. In this way, the household obtained at least four plots. The location of a plot allocated to each household was done by lottery. Differences in family sizes made the plot sizes within each class different. The more varied the water and soil conditions, the higher the number of land classes and the higher the number of plots would be in this process.

Traditional conceptions have a major influence on land allocations and thus on fragmentation. The land reform of 1951 realized land privatization based on the principle of equality. Because land was considered both a production factor and a social welfare security, land became the common property of the collective, with each villager having equal rights to claim it. In other words, land was shared equally in the farmers' understanding (Zhang 2001). This notion was strengthened in the period of the people's community when land was owned and managed by the collectives. Since the introduction of the HRS, this attitude has resulted in frequent land reallocations to correct for demographic changes within villages. After all, the rural population is quite large, and land is relatively scarce. In this situation, an equal distribution of land is still considered a very effective social security.

Results of a nationwide survey show that by the beginning of the 1990s around 95 percent of the villages had adjusted the land distribution at least once since the adoption of the HRS; on average, land reallocations had occurred 3.1 times (Yang 1995). The research by Yao (2000) and Kung (2000) of 83 villages in eight counties within four typical provinces (Jiangxi, Zhejiang, Henan, and Jilin) offers some interesting conclusions on village characteristics that affect land reallocations and thus land fragmentation. About 70 percent of the reported land reallocations were partial; they involved only households whose membership had changed (Kung 2000). With respect to the frequency of reallocation, Yao (2000) has shown that per capita net income, agricultural taxation (state grain quotas on the land), and presence of a land-leasing market have had a significant negative impact. In addition, he sees an inverse U-shape relationship between land endowment and land adjustment frequency. Kung (2000), in contrast, has found that income from non-farm sources negatively affects the frequency of land reallocations and that land endowment has a negative impact on both the frequency and the magnitude of land reallocations. What is clear, however, is that land reallocations are not mechanical adjustments to demographic changes. Demand factors such as income, off-farm employment, and agricultural taxation seem to play a role as well.

In order to prevent further fragmentation, land consolidation programs started to be implemented during the mid-1980s in some coastal areas (eastern provinces) and a few years later also in some central areas of China. Land consolidation refers to the exchange of spatially dispersed fragments of farmland to form new holdings at one place, or at as few places as possible (Oldenburg 1990). It has become an important element of so-called comprehensive agricultural development projects. Their purpose is to improve the agricultural infrastructure (roads, irrigation, drainage conditions, etc.) so as to strengthen the agricultural development capacity in the future, as well as to enhance farmers' incomes. For consolidation, plots have to be taken back by collectives first. Then a program is conducted to make each plot between 0.13–0.20 ha in plain areas and around 0.07 ha in hilly areas. After that, land is reallocated to individual farm households.[5] These projects are normally conducted in areas with medium or low crop yields.

Although the government called for land consolidation for several years, the response was often slow. An important reason for this may be that consolidation involves lots of transaction costs. In present-day China, the consolidation process involves many households in each village. Moreover, in order to implement it successfully and to keep it balanced, farmers have to participate at all stages of the process (including decision-making) to find appropriate solutions for all the farm households concerned. In the western provinces, farm households and their farmland are spread over a much larger area compared with the eastern and central parts. Land consolidation therefore involves relatively more transaction costs in west China.

The new Land Administrative Laws issued in 1998 in China also have had some impact on land fragmentation. According to these laws, farm households can use their contracted land for an additional 30 years.[6] Land was again redistributed within a few years of the laws' implementation, with the goal of being more considerate and equitable than ever. To achieve this, the land was divided into several plot classes in terms of soil type, water access, drainage condition, road access, and any other conditions the farmers consider to affect agricultural yield and land management. As a result, China's land became even more fragmented after the implementation of the 30-year contracts (Zhu 2001).

Another factor resulting in land fragmentation is the re-emergence of land markets. As described earlier, the combination of land scarcity with land markets (and the system of partible inheritance) in a largely agricultural society led to a high degree of land fragmentation in China before the foundation of the People's Republic. In present-day China, farm households cannot buy or sell agricultural land, but in many villages it is possible nowadays to hire land from other households or the village collective. Particularly farm households involved in off-farm employment outside the village are often inclined to rent their land to other households in the same village. In case of unemployment, the households that rented their land out can fall back on it to make a living.

The emergence of a rental market for land does not necessarily lead to an increase in land fragmentation. When there are no major bottlenecks in markets for risk insurance, food commodities, or agricultural labor, farmers are likely to prefer an increase in the scale of their plots by hiring land neighboring their own plots. Hence, they are willing to pay a higher rent for such neighboring plots than for other plots. Whether or not the emergence of rental markets for land has decreased the degree of land fragmentation in present-day China is an empirical question.

An analytical framework

From the preceding discussion, it follows that land fragmentation in China is mainly determined by: (1) the land allocation by central policies (with the introduction of the HRS and land contracts for 30 years in recent years); (2) the frequency of land reallocations by villages or hamlets; (3) the presence of land consolidation programs, and (4) the presence of a land rental market.

Figure 7.4 shows the four main determinants of land fragmentation in

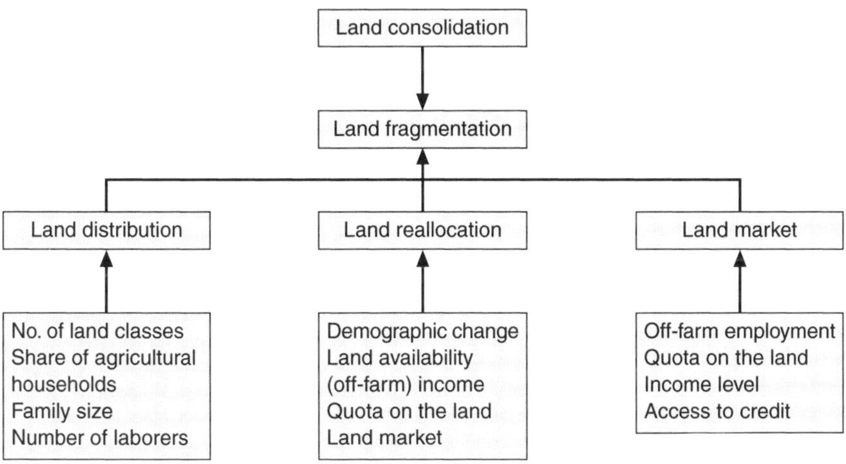

Figure 7.4 The determinants of land fragmentation in China.

China and the underlying factors that affect these determinants. The number and size of land plots assigned during the land distribution process depend on the number of land classes that are distinguished, the share of agricultural households in a village, and family size and/or the number of laborers in a household. The number of land classes mainly depends on supply-side factors such as topography, soil types, water and drainage conditions, and access to roads (Zhu and Jiang 1993), but demand factors may also have some impact. When there are imperfections in the labor market, the food market, or the market for insurance, households in a village may push to increase the number of soil quality classes in order to spread labor requirements and increase the number of crops that are grown. For example, a survey conducted by China's State Council found that egalitarian tendencies in land distribution were stronger in villages poorly endowed with land and lacking off-farm employment opportunities (Liu *et al.* 1998). And Zhu (2001) has argued that the duration of the contract matters in determining the number of land classes. This also suggests that land fragmentation is partly a demand-driven process.

Land reallocation, according to Kung (2000) and Yao (2000), depends on demographic pressure, land availability, income level, off-farm employment, quotas on the land, and availability of a land market. Participation in the land market depends on factors that affect the hiring out of land (particularly off-farm employment opportunities) and the hiring in of land (income level, access to credit, quotas on the land). Finally, land consolidation is initiated and conducted to a large extent by local governments. It may therefore be considered exogenous to villages and households.

Model specification

The analytical framework derived in the previous section suggests several factors that can potentially affect the degree of land fragmentation in China. It is used in this section to derive a structural model of factors affecting fragmentation. Due to problems with data availability for some of the driving factors, it is not possible to empirically estimate the whole set of structural equations. Through substitution, however, reduced-form equations will be obtained that can be estimated.

The factors influencing fragmentation differ considerably between the village level (where household-level factors may cancel out) and the household level (where village-level factors are exogenous). Separate models are therefore specified for the analysis at the village level and at the household level. The structural models and the reduced-form models used for the regression analyses at the village level and at the household level are also presented.

The structural models

Our earlier analysis indicated four factors that were directly responsible for land fragmentation in China. Each of these four factors is affected by a different set of variables (see Figure 7.4). It may be useful to distinguish between hiring in and hiring out of land, since different sets of considerations lead farmers to either hire land in or hire land out, while their impact on land fragmentation is also expected to differ. We also saw that the number of land classes plays a crucial role in land distribution decisions at the village level. Therefore, a separate equation can be added to the model to describe (supply and demand) factors that are expected to influence the number of land classes distinguished in a village. This gives a model consisting of six equations to describe the factors that drive land fragmentation at the village level.

The first equation gives the factors directly affecting village-level land fragmentation (Fv):

$$Fv = f_1(Dv^{+}, Rv^{+}, HOv^{+/-}, HIv^{+/-}, Cv^{-}) \qquad (7.1)$$

where

- Fv = land fragmentation indicator (e.g., average number of plots per household or average plot size) at village level;
- Dv = fragmentation resulting from land distribution process (either the HRS or 30-year contract system);
- Rv = frequency and/or magnitude of (partial) land reallocation since HRS or 30-year contract system;
- HOv = average size of hired-out land per household;
- HIv = average size of hired-in land per household;
- Cv = presence of land consolidation program.

The expected effects (+, increase, or –, decrease) are shown immediately after each variable; f_1 is a functional relationship that needs to be specified. By definition, the fragmentation resulting from land distribution (Dv) has a positive impact. The frequency and size of land reallocations (Rv) can in principle lead to both higher and lower fragmentation. In practice, it tends to increase fragmentation, since land is taken away from households that have become smaller and added to the land of "generally nonneighboring" households that have expanded. In order to meet with the equality principle, land plots may need to be subdivided. The impact of the land market (HOv and HIv) can be positive as well as negative, depending on where the hired-in and hired-out land is located and whether or not farm households split their plots if they want to rent out part of their land. Land consolidation (Cv) by definition has a negative impact on fragmentation.

The second and third equations describe the process of land distribution:

$$Dv = f_2(NCv^+, LAv^+, SNv^-) \tag{7.2}$$

$$NCv = f_3(TPv^{+/-}, LQv^+, CLv^+, MAv^-, LAv^-, OFv^-) \tag{7.3}$$

where:

NCv = number of land classes distinguished during the land distribution process;
LAv = indicator of land availability (e.g., arable land per capita);
SNv = share of nonagricultural households in the village;
TPv = indicator of topography (e.g., plain, hilly, or mountainous area);
LQv = indicator of variation in land quality (soil types, water access, drainage conditions, road access, and so on);
CLv = length of land use contract (in years);
MAv = indicator of degree of market access;
OFv = share of off-farm income in total village income.

The fragmentation caused by the land distribution process is positively linked to the number of land classes (NCv) that is distinguished during this process. Within each land class, the number of plots assigned per household is positively related to the availability of land, that is, per capita availability of arable land (LAv). In many cases, no land is distributed to households involved more or less permanently in off-farm employment. Hence, the land assigned to households within each land class is also positively related to the share of nonagricultural households in a village (SNv).

The number of land classes distinguished during land distribution depends partly on topography (TPv) and on the variation in land quality (LQv) within a village. The duration of the contract (CLv) affects the number of land classes positively, as Zhu (2001) indicates. The need to distinguish more classes is expected to be lower when a village has better access to markets for labor, food, and insurance (MAv), has more land available (LAv), and when more income is obtained from off-farm employment (OFv).

The fourth equation explains the process of (partial) land reallocations due to demographic factors:

$$Rv = f_4(DCv^{+,} LAv^{+/-}, ILv^-, OFv^-, QUv^-, HIv^-) \tag{7.4}$$

where:

DCv = indicator of demographic change (e.g., birth rate, death rate, or indicator of migration) in the village;

ILv = average income level of the village;
QUv = quota on the land (e.g., size of the quota or dummy variable for presence of quota).

The frequency and magnitude of land reallocations are positively related to demographic changes in a village (DCv). But, as the studies by Kung (2000) and Yao (2000) indicate, the income level (ILv), involvement in off-farm employment (OFv), presence of grain quota on the land (QUv), and possibility to hire land (HIv) all negatively affect the demand for such reallocations. The availability of land in a village (LAv) may affect the demand for reallocations as well; according to Yao (2000), its impact can be positive as well as negative.

The final two equations explain the hiring out and hiring in of land:

$$HOv = f_5(OFv^+, CRv^{+/-}) \tag{7.5}$$

$$HIv = f_6(QUv^-, ILv^{+,} CRv^{+/-}) \tag{7.6}$$

where:

CRv = access to credit (approximated, e.g., by total value of assets).

The share of land hired out (HOv) is expected to be higher when a larger share of the village income is earned outside the farms (OFv). Since land can be important collateral, access to other sources of credit (CRv) can promote the hiring out of land; however, access to credit may reduce the need to obtain cash by renting the land. The share of land that is hired in (HIv) will be lower in the case of state grain quotas on the land (QUv). A higher income level (ILv) allows more hiring in of land. Likewise, access to credit (CRv) may allow more hiring in of land, but it also reduces the need to obtain more land (as collateral or as a source of income).

Land distribution, land reallocation, and land consolidation are processes that are decided at the village or higher levels. Hence, they are exogenous for the households in a village. What matters for land fragmentation at the household level (Fh) is mainly household size (or share of laborers), because it determines to a great extent the amount of land that a household will receive from the village. Possibilities to rent land in or out also play a role. The structural model at the household level therefore specifies land fragmentation (Fh) as a function of the degree of fragmentation for the village as a whole (Fv) and these household-specific factors:

$$Fh = f_7(Fv^+, HSh^+, LFh^+, HOh^{+/-}, HIh^{+/-}) \tag{7.7}$$

$$HOh = f_8(OFh^+, CRh^{+/-}) \tag{7.8}$$

$$HIh = f_9(QUh^-, ILh^+, CRh^{+/-}) \tag{7.9}$$

where:

Fh	= land fragmentation indicator (e.g., number of plots or average plot size) at household level;
HSh	= household size;
LFh	= share of laborers in household;
HOh	= size of household land that is hired out;
HIh	= size of household land that is hired in;
OFh	= share of off-farm income in total household income;
CRh	= household access to credit (approximated, e.g., by total value of assets);
QUh	= quota on land managed by household (e.g., size of the quota or dummy variable);
ILh	= level of household income.

The degree of fragmentation at the household level depends to a large extent on the fragmentation at village level (Fv), which by definition has a positive effect. Households with a relatively large size (HSh) or a large share of laborers (LFh) are expected to obtain more and larger plots. The hiring out of land (HOh) will reduce either the number of plots or its average size (if a share of a plot is hired out), or both. The average plot size may also increase, namely when relatively small plots are hired out. Conversely, the hiring in of land (HIh) may increase the number of plots and either increase or decrease the average size. The factors influencing the hiring in and out of land are similar to those specified at the village level.

The two models specified here describe the land fragmentation processes in China at village and household level in general terms. In order to obtain empirical estimates of the relative importance of each factor, choices have to be made with respect to the selection of the appropriate indicators and functional forms of the relationships. Moreover, data may not be available on some of the factors listed in the models, implying that some adjustments will have to be made. The next two subsections discuss the choices that we made for estimating the two models from two data sets for 40 villages and 863 households, respectively.

Model specification at the village level

We used a data set of 40 villages in three provinces, Guangxi, Hubei, and Jiangxi, in the year 1999 to examine the factors affecting land fragmentation at the village level. The data were obtained from the Office of Fixed Rural Observation Locations in Guangxi, Hubei, and Jiangxi Provinces. Of these villages, 14 are from Guangxi, 15 from Hubei, and 11 from Jiangxi. Criteria used by these provincial offices for the selection of villages were that they should reflect differences in topography (plain, hilly, or mountainous areas), in distance to the (provincial or county) capital, and in economic development level.

Guangxi Province is located in the south of China, bordering Vietnam. Total land area covers 236.6 thousand square kilometers. At the end of 1995, the total population was 45.43 million people. Population density of the whole province was 192 people per square kilometer. Jiangxi Province is located along the connection of the mid- and lower streams of the Yangtze River, covering 166.9 thousand square kilometers of total land area. The population in 1995 was 40.63 million, of which the nonagricultural population accounted for 20.3 percent and the agricultural population was 79.70 percent. The population density was 243 people per square kilometer. Hubei Province is located further north along the mid-stream of the Yangtze River and covers 185.90 thousand square kilometers of land. The population in 1995 was 57.72 million, of which the nonagricultural and agricultural populations accounted for 26.23 percent and 73.77 percent, respectively. Population density within Hubei Province was 310 people per square kilometer (Chinese Agricultural Resource Zoning Office 1999). Mountainous or hilly terrain in these three provinces varies from 71 to 78 percent. The results obtained are assumed to be representative for a much larger mountainous and hilly area in central and eastern China. Moreover, because some important policies related to land fragmentation – such as the HRS and the 30-year contract policy – have similar characteristics in the whole country, some of the insights gained may be relevant for the rest of China as well.

The village-level data set provides information on land fragmentation and some of the major explanatory variables described above. Unfortunately, no information is available on the left-hand variables LDv, LRv, and NCv. This means that reduced-form equations, that can be empirically estimated, need to be derived. Substituting equations (7.2), (7.3), and (7.4) into the first equation gives the following village-level reduced-form equations:

$$\begin{aligned} \mathrm{Fv} = g_1(&\mathrm{TPv}^{+/-}, \mathrm{LQv}^{+}, \mathrm{CLv}^{+}, \mathrm{MAv}^{-}, \mathrm{LAv}^{+/-}, \mathrm{OFv}^{-}, \mathrm{SNv}^{-}, \\ &\mathrm{DCv}^{+}, \mathrm{ILv}^{-}, \mathrm{QUv}^{-}, \mathrm{HOv}^{+/-}, \mathrm{HIv}^{+/-}, \mathrm{Cv}^{-}) \end{aligned} \tag{7.10}$$

$$\mathrm{HOv} = g_2(\mathrm{OFv}^{+}, \mathrm{CRv}^{+/-}) \tag{7.11}$$

$$\mathrm{HIv} = g_3(\mathrm{QUv}^{-}, \mathrm{ILv}^{+}, \mathrm{CRv}^{+/-}) \tag{7.12}$$

An important question is how land fragmentation should be measured. Potential indicators are the number of plots, average plot size, average distance from plots to dwellings, and the so-called Simpson index[7]. The choice between these indicators depends on the researcher's interest and on data availability. In this research, the number of plots per household and the average plot size are chosen as indicators. The village- and household-level data sets that are used for the analysis do not contain data on the other two indicators.

For four explanatory variables in equation (7.10), length of contract, land quality, demographic change, and presence of land consolidation program, no information is available in the data set. Hence, they had to be left out of the model. Provincial dummies are added to the model to correct for factors that are not included in the model and may systematically differ between the three provinces (such as agro-ecological or political factors). Assuming linear relationships and adding a random disturbance term to the equations gives the following regression equations at the village level:

$$\begin{aligned}
\text{NPv} &= C_{10} + C_{11}{*}\text{D_GX} + C_{12}{*}\text{D_JX} + C_{13}{*}\text{D_NP} + C_{14}{*}\text{D_MO} + \\
&\quad C_{15}{*}\text{D_NS} + C_{16}{*}\text{D_RE} + C_{17}{*}\text{LAv} + C_{18}{*}\text{OFv} + C_{19}{*}\text{SNv} + \\
&\quad C_{110}{*}\text{ILv} + C_{111}{*}\text{QUv} + C_{112}{*}\text{HOv} + C_{113}{*}\text{HIv} + u_1 \\
\text{PSv} &= C_{20} + C_{21}{*}\text{D_GX} + C_{22}{*}\text{D_JX} + C_{23}{*}\text{D_NP} + C_{24}{*}\text{D_MO} + \\
&\quad C_{25}{*}\text{D_NS} + C_{26}{*}\text{D_RE} + C_{27}{*}\text{LAv} + C_{28}{*}\text{OFv} + C_{29}{*}\text{SNv} + \\
&\quad C_{210}{*}\text{ILv} + C_{211}{*}\text{QUv} + C_{212}{*}\text{HOv} + C_{213}{*}\text{HIv} + u_2 \\
\text{HOv} &= C_{30} + C_{31}{*}\,\text{D_GX} + C_{32}{*}\,\text{D_JX} + C_{33}{*}\text{OFv} + C_{34}{*}\text{CRv} + u_3 \\
\text{HIv} &= C_{40} + C_{41}{*}\,\text{D_GX} + C_{42}{*}\,\text{D_JX} + C_{43}{*}\,\text{QUv} + C_{44}{*} \\
&\quad \text{ILv} + C_{45}{*}\text{CRv} + u_4
\end{aligned}$$

Cij denotes the unknown coefficients, while u_i denotes a random error term with standard properties. The definitions of the variables and the expected signs of unknown coefficients in each of the four equations can be found in Table 7.1. The impact of topography is approximated by distinguishing whether a village is located in a plain, in a hilly area, or in a mountainous area. Two dummy variables, one for nonplain area (equals one when a village is located in a hilly or mountainous area) and one for mountainous area, are included in the model. The degree of market access is approximated by distinguishing whether a village is located in a suburban area rather than a remote or not remote rural area. Again two dummy variables are included in the model, one for nonsuburban (that is, not remote rural or remote) villages and one for remote villages. The indicator used to approximate access to credit in the model is the size of fixed assets in the village. The regression results for this model will be discussed in the next section.

Descriptive statistics of the (nondummy) variables used in the analysis are presented in Table 7.2. It can be seen from Table 7.2 that there is a wide spread in land fragmentation between the villages. The average number of plots per household for the 39 villages in the sample varies from 2.2 to nearly 24, with an overall average of almost 9.3. It should be remembered that the villages are located in relatively hilly and mountainous provinces, where fragmentation tends to be relatively high. For one village in Guangxi, the average number of plots per household equals

Table 7.1 Variables used in the village-level analysis and their predicted effects

Variable name	*Unit*	*Symbol*	*Predicted effects*			
			NPv	*PSv*	*HOv*	*HIv*
Dependent variables						
Average number of plots per household		NPv				
Average plot size	*mu*	PSv				
Average size of land hired out per household	*mu*	HOv				
Average size of land hired in per household	*mu*	HIv				
Explanatory variables						
Guangxi Province dummy		D_GX	+/−	−/+	+/−	+/−
Jiangxi Province dummy		D_JX	+/−	−/+	+/−	+/−
Nonplain area dummy		D_NP	+	−		
Mountainous area dummy		D_MO	+	+/−		
Nonsuburban area dummy		D_NS	+	−		
Remote area dummy		D_RE	+	−		
Arable land area per capita	*mu*	LAv	+/−	+/−		
Off-farm income share	%	OFv	−	+	+	
Share of non-agricultural households in village	%	SNv	−	+		
Grain quota on land (in terms of rice)	Jin	QUv	−	+		−
Average annual net income per household[1]	10^4 yuan	ILv	−	+		+
Average size of fixed assets per household	10^4 yuan	CRv		+/−	+/−	
Average size of land hired out per household	*mu*	HOv	−/+	+/−		
Average size of land hired in per household	*mu*	HIv	+/−	−/+		

Note

1 The income that can be directly used for production, for nonproductive construction investment and for improving life. The annual net income = (total annual income − subside − gift income from rural relatives − income from selling assets) − (farm management costs + taxation + fees to village).

Table 7.2 Descriptive statistics of village-level analysis on land fragmentation

	N	*Minimum*	*Maximum*	*Mean*	*Standard deviation*
NPv	39	2.20	23.64	9.27	5.87
PSv	39	0.20	1.89	0.74	0.40
HOv	39	0.00	1.31	0.16	0.23
HIv	39	0.00	1.23	0.17	0.30
LAv	39	0.34	2.55	1.24	0.53
OFv	39	2.16	77.80	25.24	19.85
SNv	39	0.00	17.00	3.29	4.06
QUv	39	0.00	844.00	140.00	210.00
Ilv	39	0.42	14.11	1.25	2.13
CRv	39	0.48	5.06	2.20	1.10

Source: Rural Fixed Observation Office, Central Policy Research Division and Agricultural Ministry, PRC (2001).

153.[8] Because this seems rather unrealistic, this village was deleted from the data set. In some villages, no hiring in or hiring out of land takes place. Some villages have agricultural households only (SNv = 0), while the share of nonagricultural households in the village reaches up to 17 percent in other villages. Per capita land availability ranges from 0.34 to 2.55 *mu*, which indicates that there exists a large difference in population pressure between the villages. Likewise, there is a considerable spread in the data set in the average net income level, the share of income obtained from nonfarm sources, the average grain quota (equals zero in some villages), and the size of fixed assets.

Model specification at the household level

For the 11 villages in Jiangxi that are in the village-level data set, household-level data for the year 2000 are available as well. The 11 villages are spread across each prefecture in the whole province. From the 950 households that are in the data set, 863 provided enough information to be included in the data set. Information is available for all the variables listed in equations (7.7)-(7.9). The resulting regression equations at the household level can be expressed as:

$$\text{NPh} = C_{50} + C_{51}{*}\text{NPv} + C_{52}{*}\text{HSh} + C_{53}{*}\text{LFh} + C_{54}{*}\text{HOh} + C_{55}{*}\text{HIh} + u_5$$
$$\text{PSh} = C_{60} + C_{61}{*}\text{PSv} + C_{62}{*}\text{HSh} + C_{63}{*}\text{LFh} + C_{64}{*}\text{HOh} + C_{65}{*}\text{HIh} + u_6$$
$$\text{HOh} = C_{70} + C_{71}{*}\text{OFh} + C_{72}{*}\text{CRh} + u_7$$
$$\text{HIh} = C_{80} + C_{81}{*}\ \text{D\_QU} + C_{82}{*}\ \text{ILh} + C_{83}{*}\text{CRh} + u_8$$

The definitions of the variable names, and the expected signs of their coefficients in each of the four equations, can be found in Table 7.3.

Table 7.4 shows the main characteristics of the households in the data

Table 7.3 Variables used in the household-level analysis and their expected effects

Variable name	*Unit*	*Symbol*	*Predicted effects*			
			NPv	*PSv*	*HOv*	*HIv*
Dependent variables						
Number of plots managed by household	NPh					
Average plot size	*mu*	PSh				
Size of land hired out	*mu*	HOh				
Size of land hired in	*mu*	HIh				
Explanatory variables						
Average number of plots per household in village	NPv		+			
Average plot size in village	*mu*	PSv		+		
Household size (number of rural persons in household)		HSh	+	+		
Share of labor force members in household	LFh		+	+		
Off-farm income share	%	OFh			+	
Quota on land dummy		D_QU				−
Annual net income	10^4 yuan	ILh				+
Value of fixed assets	10^4 yuan	CRh			+/−	+/−
Size of land hired out	*mu*	HOh	−	+/−		
Size of land hired in	*mu*	HIh	+	+/−		

+, increase
–, decrease

Table 7.4 Main characteristics of villages used for household-level analysis

Village number	*Topography* *1 = plain* *2 = hilly* *3 = mountainous*	*Village type* *1 = agricultural area* *2 = forestry area* *3 = grazing area* *4 = fishery area* *5 = others*	*Location* *1 = suburban* *2 = non-suburban*	*Economic level* *1 = best* *2 = less best* *3 = middle* *4 = bad*	*Annual net income per capita*	*Percentage of non-agricultural households*
1	3	1	2	4	1,351	0.00
2	2	1	2	1	2,220	0.56
3	2	1	1	4	2,027	0.00
4	1	1	2	3	1,303	0.00
5	1	1	1	2	2,067	0.84
6	1	1	2	3	2,812	2.56
7	1	1	2	3	2,160	0.00
8	3	2	2	4	1,922	0.00
9	2	5	1	2	2,966	1.08
10	2	2	2	4	1,840	2.54
11	2	1	1	3	3,289	2.47

Source: Rural Fixed Observation Office, Central Policy Research Division and Agricultural Ministry, PRC (2001).

set, disaggregated for the 11 villages. Table 7.4 reflects the wide variation in topographic and economic features that made these villages belong to the sample.

Descriptive statistics of the main variables used in the analyses at the household level are presented in Table 7.5. The number of plots per household ranges from 1 to 80. The average number of plots is 9.06, which is close to the average for the village-level data set. Likewise, the average plot size of 0.73 *mu* is close to the village-level average. The mean level of land hired in is substantially larger than the mean of land hired out. This may reflect either that a substantial share of the land is hired from the village collective or that a large share of the households hiring out are not included in the survey (for example, because they are involved in employment outside the village). Household sizes vary from 1 to 17, while the share of labor force members in a household varies from 20 to 100 percent. The average net income level is about 30 percent lower than the average for the village-level sample, while the value of fixed assets is about 20 percent higher. Both variables vary considerably between households.

Regression results

Village-level results

The results of the regression analyses for the village level are shown in Table 7.6. All coefficients in the equations for number of plots and plot size have the expected signs, but several of them do not differ significantly from zero. Around 70 percent of the variation in number of plots and 56 percent of the variation in average plot size are explained by the regressed variables.

The dummy variables for Guangxi Province (D_GX) and for nonplain

Table 7.5 Descriptive statistics of household-level analysis on land fragmentation

	N	*Minimum*	*Maximum*	*Mean*	*Standard deviation*
NPh	863	1.00	80.00	9.06	7.04
PSh	863	0.01	2.90	0.73	0.41
HOh	863	0.00	10.40	0.19	0.98
HIh	863	0.00	11.00	0.32	1.22
HSh	863	1.00	17.00	4.39	1.83
LFh	863	20.00	100.00	67.37	21.78
OFh	863	0.00	100.00	19.87	28.83
ILh	863	0.01	8.38	0.89	0.66
CRh	863	0.02	26.42	2.67	2.70

Source: Rural Fixed Observation Office, Central Policy Research Division and Agricultural Ministry, PRC (2001).

Table 7.6 Regression results for land fragmentation at the village level

Explanatory variables	*Dependent variable*			
	NPv	*PSv*	*HOv*	*HIv*
Constant	−0.91 (−0.27)	0.45 (1.62)	0.21*** (2.81)	0.16 (1.41)
D_GX	9.59*** (5.32)	−0.38*** (0.57)	0.07 (0.89)	0.14 (1.16)
D_JX	2.19 (0.98)	−0.27 (−1.42)	0.35*** (4.10)	0.33*** (2.53)
D_NP	5.01*** (2.97)	−0.42*** (0.97)	–	–
D_MO	0.64 (0.30)	0.11 (0.62)	–	–
D_NS	4.60** (1.65)	−0.13 (−0.57)	–	–
D_RE	4.51*** (2.33)	−0.21* (−1.32)	–	–
LAv	0.51 (0.28)	0.50*** (3.34)	–	–
OFv	−0.003 (−0.08)	0.01** (1.60)	−0.00 (−0.14)	–
SNv	−0.14 (−0.64)	0.01 (0.64)	–	–
QUv	−0.001 (−0.48)	0.00 (0.75)	–	–
IIv	−0.27 (−0.77)	0.02 (0.62)	−0.00 (−0.21)	–
CRv	−0.08** (−2.12)	−0.06 (−1.12)	–	–
HIv	3.29 (0.89)	−0.35 (−1.15)	−0.00 (−0.07)	–
HOv	−0.12 (−0.03)	0.38 (1.04)	–	–
F-statistic	4.54	2.44	4.90	1.32
R^2	0.70	0.56	0.37	0.17
Adj. R^2	0.55	0.33	0.29	0.04

Notes
t-values are reported in parentheses.
* Significant at the 10 percent level.
** Significant at the 5 percent level.
*** Significant at the 1 percent level.

areas (D_NP) have a significant positive impact (at the 1 percent testing level). The coefficients indicate that, controlling for differences in topographic and economic variables between the villages, the number of plots in Guangxi is on average 9.59 more (and the average plot size is 0.38 *mu* smaller) than in the other two provinces. Hence, farm households in Guangxi Province are faced with a higher degree of land fragmentation. As expected, households in hilly and mountainous areas are confronted with a higher degree of land fragmentation degree than those in plains areas; their number of plots is on average five more (and the average plot size is 0.42 *mu* smaller). No significant difference exists, however, between households in hilly areas and in the mountains; the dummy variable reflecting this difference (D_MO) does not differ significantly from zero.

The two dummy variables for market access, D_NS and D_RE, have a significant positive effect on the number of plots (at the 10 percent and 5 percent testing levels, respectively). These results indicate that in villages that are relatively isolated from external markets, there exists some demand to increase the number of plots during land distribution and land reallocations. The underlying reason – whether households want to spread risk, crop types, or household labor – cannot be obtained from the regressions. Additional research is needed to discover these motives. Lack of market access is also found to decrease average plot size, but the estimated coefficients differ significantly from zero (at the 10 percent level) in the case of D_RE only.

Land availability (LAv) is found to affect positively the average plot (at 1 percent testing level) but not the average number of plots. Hence, population pressure leads to smaller plots, but not to a larger number of plots per household. This result indicates that only the sizes of plots allocated within each land class during land redistribution or land reallocation depend on land availability, not the number of plots. Likewise, a high share of off-farm employment is found to increase the amount of land allocated per plot but does not affect the average number of plots.

The other variables in the regressions do not have a significant impact on either plot size or number of plots. This comprises the two land market variables, HIv and HOv. A potential explanation is that farm households who rent out (part of) their land do so because they join in off-farm activities. In modern China, however, owing to some institutional problems like *hukou*, it is almost impossible for farmers to obtain formal or permanent off-farm employment.[9] In order to reduce potential disputes, off-farm households mainly rent land to their relatives or other people they trust in the same village, in case they have to come back for cultivation some day. Evidently, this does not contribute much to land consolidation at the village level.

The last two columns in Table 7.6 show the regression results for land market participation. Contrary to expectations, the results indicate that villages with a higher share of households involved in off-farm employment (OFv) do not have a more active land rental market (HOv). The results of the equations for the land rental market are not very satisfactory. Only a small share of the variation is explained by the variables in the equations, especially in the case of renting in (HIv). Apparently, other factors than the ones included explain the emergence of village rental markets for agricultural land in China. The results do show, however, that hiring out/in of land is significantly greater in Jiangxi than in Hubei and Guangxi Provinces. The possession of fixed assets, which is used as a proxy for the access to credit, is found to have a negative impact on the hiring out of land. One possible explanation is that access to credit reduces the need to rent the land to other households as a source of cash income. An alternative explanation is that the possession of fixed assets adds to other productive assets in rural areas, which are regarded as "sunk cost." Households with more such costs tend to make use of them and are not inclined to rent out their land.

Household-level results

The regression results for land fragmentation and land market participation by households are shown in Table 7.7. The results for land fragmentation show a relatively good fit for such a micro-level data set (R-squared equals 0.43 for number of plots and 0.47 for plot size). As expected, the degree of land fragmentation at the village level is a major determinant of the degree of fragmentation at the household level, with the estimated coefficients close to one for both the number of plots and the average plot size.[10] Hence, land fragmentation at the household level is to a great extent determined by the characteristics of the village that the farm household belongs to.

Household size has a significant positive impact on the number of plots and on the average plot size. Each additional household member results, on average, in an increase of 1.15 in the number of plots and an increase of 0.02 *mu* in average plot size. So, the results confirm that large families tend to receive more plots within each land class (and larger plots) than small households do, as explained earlier in this chapter. Distribution on the basis of labor force seems to play a role as well. The share of labor force members in a household has a significant but small effect on the number of plots that households receive, but it does not affect the average plot size. When the share increases from 67 percent (the mean in the sample) to 100 percent, households receive on average 0.66 additional plots.

Table 7.7 Regression results for household level

Explanatory variables	*Dependent variable*			
	NPh	*PSh*	*HOh*	*HIh*
Constant	−5.81*** (−5.97)	0.03 (0.56)	0.21*** (4.24)	0.40*** (5.31)
NPv	1.02*** (21.7)	–	–	–
PSv	–	0.90*** (27.0)	–	–
HSh	1.15*** (10.6)	0.02*** (2.86)	–	–
LFh	0.02** (2.10)	0.00 (−0.01)	–	–
OFh	–	–	0.00 (0.03)	–
D_QU	–	–	−0.23** (−1.94)	–
ILh	–	–	0.13** (1.81)	–
CRh	–	–	−0.01 (−0.48)	−0.06*** (−3.46)
HOh	−1.03*** (−5.45)	−0.02* (−1.70)	–	–
HIh	0.81*** (5.47)	0.03*** (3.11)	–	–
F-statistic	131	151	0.12	5.30
R^2	0.43	0.47	0.00	0.02
Adj. R^2	0.43	0.47	0.00	0.02

Notes
t- values are reported in parentheses.
* Significant at the 10 percent level.
** Significant at the 5 percent level.
*** Significant at the 1 percent level.

An interesting finding is that hiring out (HOh) and hiring in of land (HIh) significantly influence land fragmentation degree at the household level. Each additional *mu* of hired-out land reduces the number of plots by an average of 1.03 plots and reduces the average plot size by 0.02 *mu*. Each additional *mu* of hired-in land increases the number of plots by 0.81 and average plot size by 0.03 *mu*. These results indicate that each *mu* of land that is transferred will, on average, decrease the number of plots by 0.22 and increase average plot size by 0.01 *mu* for the household involved in the transaction.

The last two columns of Table 7.7 show the regression results for the land rental market. No satisfactory results are obtained for the hiring out of land. Neither the degree of involvement in off-farm employment nor access to credit seems to have a significant effect on the size of land hired out. In contrast, the hiring in of land is found to be positively related to the income level of households and negatively related to the presence of a quota on the land. Access to credit is found to have a significant negative effect on the hiring in of land. In other words, the need to obtain additional land as collateral or as an income source seems to become less when households possess more fixed assets.

Conclusion

This study advances previous empirical analyses of land fragmentation in China by providing a more detailed analysis of the processes underlying land fragmentation and by using available Fixed Rural Socio-economic Observation data from three provinces to obtain empirical estimates of the major factors that drive land fragmentation. The major empirical finding is that land fragmentation is to a large extent driven by supply factors. Higher population pressure reduces the average plot sizes in a village but does not affect the average number of plots. In addition, topographic features play an important role in land fragmentation. On the demand side, market access is found to have a significant impact on land fragmentation. This suggests that in areas with less access to markets, farm households prefer fragmented plots so that they can spread risks, crop types, or household labor; however, which of these motives play the strongest role in land fragmentation needs further research. The household-level results for 11 villages in Jiangxi Province further indicate that the hiring in and out of land can make a modest contribution to land consolidation. One *mu* of land that is transferred reduces the number of plots of the households involved by 0.22. Another important finding is that larger households have a larger number of plots as well as larger average plot sizes. Each additional household member increases the number of plots by 1.15 on average, and the average plot size increases by 0.02 *mu*. This indicates that the rules used for assigning land to households during land distribution and reallocation (where land within each land class is assigned on the basis of household size) are an important cause of fragmentation.

The driving factors of land fragmentation that were found, together with the prevailing imperfections of the land market and the insecurity of off-farm opportunities, imply that land fragmentation will remain pervasive and persistent in China. The small and highly scattered land plots are likely to remain an important obstacle to cost reduction and productivity improvement, and thus they will continue to be a source of rural poverty. In recent years, land fragmentation has slightly decreased as a result of favorable demographic factors (reduced household sizes, migration), the emergence of a land market, and government-initiated land consolidation programs. But land fragmentation throughout China still remains very high.

Based on the results of the analyses, four proposals for alleviating land fragmentation are offered. The first is to reform the land distribution system so that land is assigned in terms of value instead of physical units. This can substantially reduce land fragmentation and at the same time maintain equity among households. The second is to give tradable land use rights to all farmers, so that they can freely transfer their agricultural land in the market. The land market currently makes a limited contribution to land consolidation due to institutional limitations. With the development of the economy, the liberalization of the *hukou* system, and the increase in off-farm employment, tradable land user rights can provide an important contribution to the consolidation of land plots. The third is to promote the establishment of non-state-owned small enterprises that will absorb large numbers of rural laborers throughout the country, so as to reduce the demographic pressure on the arable land and to increase average plot sizes. Fourth, the results indicate that land consolidation policies should focus on regions and villages with relatively good market access. In remote areas, farm households have an interest in having many different plots so that they can spread their risks, crop types, and household labor. Policies focusing on improved market access may help to reduce land fragmentation in such areas while contributing to poverty reduction at the same time.

Acknowledgements

The authors are grateful to Arie Kuyvenhoven, Robert L. Edmonds, Gideon Kruseman, and Marijke Kuiper for their comments on this chapter, and for the financial support provided by the Netherlands Ministry of Development Co-operation (SAIL program) and the European Union (INCO program).

Notes

1 In his monumental study of land utilization in China, Buck (1937) noted that land fragmentation was an important characteristic in the 1930s. On average, farm households had 0.34 hectares of land dispersed over 5.6 plots at that time.

2 The Agricultural Census of China conducted in 1996 shows that available statistics under-report the size of cultivated land. Its results indicate that agricultural households occupy around 0.61 hectares of land. Data on the number of plots per household are notoriously lacking in the Agricultural Census.

3 According to the gradient difference in regional economic development level, three economic regions are distinguished in China, namely, the eastern part, the central part, and the western part. The eastern part includes Liaoning, Hebei, Beijing, Tianjin, Shandong, Jiangsu, Shanghai, Zhejiang, Fujian, Guangdong, Guangxi, and Hainan. The central part covers Heilongjiang, Jilin, Neimeng, Shanxi, Henan, Hubei, Hunan, Jiangxi, and Anhui. The western part includes Shaanxi, Gansu, Qinghai, Ningxia, Xinjiang, Sichuan, Yunnan, Guizhou, and Xizang.

4 *Zerentian* refers to the farmland assigned by a village to a household to pay agricultural taxes and state quotas, the remaining land assigned to a household is called *kouliangtian*.

5 According to discussions held in 1999 with individuals responsible for land consolidation in Jiangxi Province, the government invests around 250 *yuan* per *mu* in such programs; farm households have to supply the labor.

6 The extension of land use rights for an additional 30 years aims to increase land tenure security and thus stimulate land conservation investments (Ye *et al.* 2000; Zhu 2001). Frequent land reallocations are forbidden. But recent evidence from areas that have already implemented this arrangement in 1995 shows that land is still readjusted every three to five years (Zhu 2001).

7 The Simpson index is defined as $S = 1 - \sum_{i=1}^{i} A_i^2/A^2$, where A_i is the area of plot i, and A is the total land area.

8 The descriptive statistics in Table 7.3 refer to the data for the remaining 39 villages.

9 Nowadays, the *hukou* system has been changed in some provinces like Zhejiang. But in the surveyed year of 1999, it had some restrictions on off-farm employment.

10 The difference between the estimated coefficients and unity is probably caused by the exclusion of some 10 percent of the households from the data set.

References

Anthony, R., Kenneth, M., Johnston, B.F., Jones, W.O. and Uchendu, V.C. (1979) *Agricultural Change in Tropical Africa*, Ithaca: Cornell University Press.

Bentley, J. (1987) "Economic and Ecological Approaches to Land Fragmentation: In Defence of a Much-Aligned Phenomenon." *Annual Review of Anthropology*, 16: 31–67.

Birgegard, L.-E. (1993) *Natural Resource Tenure: A Review of Issues and Experiences with Emphasis on Sub-Saharan Africa*, Lund: Swedish University of Agricultural Sciences International Rural Development Centre.

Blarel, B., Hazell, P., Place, F. and Quiggin, J. (1992) "The Economics of Farm Fragmentation: Evidence from Ghana and Rwanda." *The World Bank Economic Review*, 6: 233–254.

Buck, J.L. (1937). *Land Utilisation in China*, London: Oxford University Press.

Chao, K. (1986) *Man and Land in Chinese History: An Economic Analysis.* Stanford, CA: Stanford University Press.

Charlesworth, N. (1983) "The Origins of Fragmentation of Landholdings in British India: A Comparative Examination," in *Rural India*, London: Carson Press Ltd.

Chen, F., Davis, J. and Wang, L. (1997) *Current Issues in China's Land Reforms*, working paper No. 1/97, Belfast: Centre for Rural Studies, Queen's University of Belfast.

Chinese Agricultural Resource Zoning Office, Geographic Science Institute of Chinese Academy of Science (1999) *Chinese Rural Economic Zoning: Chinese Rural Economic Regional Development Research.* Beijing: Scientific Press.

Fenoaltea, S. (1976) "Risk, Transaction Costs, and the Origin Of Medieval Agriculture." *Exploration in Economic History*, 13: 129–151.

Heston, A. and Kumar, D. (1983) "The Persistence of Land Fragmentation in Peasant Agriculture: An Analysis of South Asian Cases," *Exploration in Economic History*, 20: 199–220.

Hu, W. (1997). "Household Land Tenure Reform in China: Its Impact on Farming Land Use and Agro-environment," *Land Use Policy*, 14: 175–186.

Ilbery, B.W. (1984) "Farm Fragmentation in the Vale of Evesham." *Area*, 16: 159–165.

Jabarin, A.S., and Epplin, F.M. (1994) "Impact of Land Fragmentation on the Cost of Production Wheat in the Rain-fed Region of Northern Jordan," *Agricultural Economics*, 11: 191–196.

King, R. (1977) *Land Reform: A World Survey*, London: G. Bell and Sons.

Kung, J.K. (1994). "Egalitarianism, Subsistence Provision, and Work Incentives in China's Agricultural Collectives." *World Development*, 22: 175–187.

Kung, J.K. (2000) "Common Property Rights and lAnd Reallocations in Rural China: Evidence From a Village Survey." *World Development*, 28: 701–719.

Lin, Q. (2000) "Sharing Ownership and Leasing Use: A lAnd Tenure Innovation Model for Sustainable Agricultural Development," in Huang Zhenfu (ed.) *Sustainable Development and Eco-economics*, Beijing: China Environmental Scientific Press (in Chinese).

Liu, S. (2000). "Structure and its Changes in Farmland Collective Ownership of China." in Chi Fulin (ed.) *China's Rural Land System Reform after the Entry into 21st Century*, Beijing: China Economic Press (in Chinese).

Liu, S., Carter, M. and Yao, Y. (1998) "Dimensions and Diversity of Property Rights in Rural China: Dilemmas on the Road to Further Reform." *World Development*, 26: 1789–1806.

McPherson, M.F. (1982). *Land Fragmentation: A Selected Literature Review*, Development Discussion Papers, Cambridge, MA: Harvard Institute for International Development, Harvard University.

Najafi, B., and M. Bakhshoodeh (1992) "The effects of land fragmentation on the efficiency of Iranian farmers: A case study." *Journal of Agricultural Science and Technology* 1: 15–22.

Nguyen, T., Cheng, E. and Findlay, C. (1996) "Land Fragmentation and fArm Productivity in China in the 1990s," *China Economic Review*, 7: 169–180.

Oldenburg, P. (1990) "Land Consolidation as Land Reform in India." *World Development*, 18: 183–195.

Parikh, A. and Shah, K. (1994) "Measurement of Technical Efficiency in the

North-West Frontier Province of Pakistan." *Journal of Agricultural Economics*, 45: 132–138.

Qu, F., Heerink, N. and Wang, W. (1995). "Land Administration Reform in China: Its Impact on Land Allocation and Economic Development." *Land Use Policy*, 12: 193–203.

Rural Fixed Observation Office, Central Policy Research Division and Agricultural Ministry, People's Republic of China (2001) *National Rural Social-Economic Survey Data Collection (1986–1999)*. Beijing: Chinese Agricultural Press (in Chinese).

Simons, S. (1988) "Land Fragmentation in Developing Countries: The Optimal Choice and Policy Implications." *Explorations in Economic History*, 25: 254–262.

Soltow, L. (1983) "Land Fragmentation as an Index of History in the Virginia Military District of Ohio." *Explorations in Economic History*, 20: 263–273.

State Council, People's Republic of China (1992) *Changes in the Land Institution at the Village Level: A Preliminary Report on a Survey of 280 Villages in China*. Beijing (in Chinese).

Udo, R.K. (1965) "Disintegration of Nucleated Settlement in Eastern Nigeria," *Geographical Review*, 55: 53–67.

World Bank (1978) *World Development Report 1978*, New York: Oxford University Press.

Yang, Z. (1995) "To Further Ascertain Peasants' Land Use Rights," *Problems of Agricultural Economy*, 2: 48–52 (in Chinese).

Yao, Y. (2000) "Inducing Institutional Transition Under the Decision-making of Collective: A Case Study of the Evolution of Land Tenure Stability in Rural China." *China Rural Survey*, 2: 11–19 (in Chinese).

Ye, J., Prosterman, L., Xu, X. and Yang, X. (2000) "Research on 30 Years Chinese Rural Land User-rights Investigation: Results and Policy Suggestions from 17 Provinces." *Management World*, 2: 163–172.

Zhang L., Huang, J. and Rozelle, S. (1996) "Land Policy and Land Use in China," paper presented at OECD Conference on Agricultural Policies in China, Paris, 12–13 December.

Zhang, X. (2001) "Dilemma of Chinese Rural Land Property Rights," *Takungpao* (Hongkong), D3, 17 January.

Zhu, D. (2001) "Re-recognization on Extension of Land User-right to Additional 30 years." *Agricultural Economic Problem*, 1: 37–41 (in Chinese).

Zhu, L. and Jiang, Z.Y. (1993) "From Brigade to Village Community: The Land Tenure System and Rural Development in China," *Cambridge Journal of Economics*, 17: 441–461.

8 Collective landownership and its role in rural industrialization

Xiaolin Pei

The other contributions in this part of the volume have mainly focused on questions within the agricultural sector itself: the impact of property rights on farm production and investments; the newly emerging agricultural geography in terms of land use, land ownership, and household type; and the increasing problem of land fragmentation and its hampering effects on mechanization and agricultural operation. However, this chapter will take a different perspective. It attempts to find the key to China's rapid rural industrialization in the specific lay-out of collective land ownership, which has allowed a swift and massive transfer of agricultural surplus labor out of the primary sector into the secondary sector.

The high growth of output of township and village enterprises (TVEs)[1] is a remarkable feature of China's transition to a market economy. Therefore, many researchers regard TVEs as the major force driving China's high growth and its transition. They hotly debate the reasons for TVE growth, supplying various explanations for why China's transition has been more "successful" than that of the East European countries. These explanations (e.g., Che and Qian 1998; Lin, N. 1995; Oi 1992) fall into two schools, exemplified by the debate between Andrew Walder (1995) and Victor Nee (1992): one emphasizes statism and the other, neoclassical liberalism. The debate considers nothing outside the state market, and neither side believes in the existence of a "third alternative." While Walder claims that local governments that directly control the collective TVEs act as efficient industrial firms, Nee argues that the organizational form of TVEs – a hybrid between state and private ownership – makes them more efficient than state-owned enterprises (SOEs) in China's mixed economy.

Both arguments are too general and fail to address two basic reasons for TVEs' growth in output: the specific roles played by China's rural institutions and the quantitative expansion of the TVE sector. Local governments and hybrid organizational forms are found everywhere in the world, and an argument that they suddenly became most "efficient" only in rural China strains belief. Moreover, because China's urban collective enterprises are also controlled by local governments, they could similarly be regarded as hybrid organizational forms, yet their output has grown much more slowly than that of TVEs. Barry Naughton (1994: 266) correctly points out that

> the success of TVEs is due largely to a set of external conditions to which TVEs are an effective adaptation. TVEs are responses to one of the most distinctive characteristics of the Chinese transition as a whole: the early creation of product markets, which had existed for a prolonged period without well-developed markets for factors of production or assets.

About 110 million surplus laborers moved from farm to rural industries between 1978 and 1996, a unique expansion that occurred only in the TVE sector. The question arises: how could the vast labor surplus shift from one sector to another without factor markets? Nobody has answered this key question, because the two schools described above cannot deal with it. This chapter will try.

In so doing, I adopt a different approach from that taken in previous studies of TVEs. A metaphor borrowed from botany will illustrate the difference. While other studies describe the forms of the plants and how they are cultivated, I examine the ecological environment in which the plants grow. In the absence of an appropriate environment, particular plants, no matter how carefully nurtured, cannot flourish. If an appropriate environment exists, then sooner or later plants suited to that environment will naturally appear, even if they were initially absent. In short, specific plants are products of a specific environment. TVEs are the specific product of the resource allocation model developed here, which is based on collective landownership. Land, labor, capital, and their interconnections are the focus of this study; they, more directly than organizational analysis, relate to growth. I argue that collective landownership can be the third alternative in between the two extremes of statism and neoclassical liberalism, and describe how it reallocates resources in ways different from the planned and market systems.

In the following section, I show that TVE growth was predicated on the rapid increase in the number of TVE workers. China's high growth in the reform era has resulted not so much from "efficient organizations and management" as from utilizing the world's largest pool of surplus labor better than during the pre-reform era. The primary mechanism that moved this vast rural labor surplus from the farm to the TVE sector was neither the planned system nor markets, but collective landownership. After briefly introducing China's collective landownership in the second section, I present a model of resource allocation that it creates in the third. The fourth section shows that all the types of capital investment in and employment of China's rural industry are the products of this model. The fifth section explores how the model makes land rents a big part of profits of the collective TVEs, and explains why the collective TVEs developed faster than private enterprises from the early 1980s to the mid-1990s. Finally, a conclusion is presented.

What is the mechanism for reallocating resources?

In 1978, when China's reform started, there were three sectors in the Chinese economy: state, urban collective, and rural collective. At that time, 82 percent of China's population were living and working in the rural collective sector; because of their number, the nature of this sector shaped China's economic transition as a whole (Pei 1994; Pei and Gunnarsson 1996). TVEs were a subsector in the rural collective sector. They were then called commune and brigade enterprises (CBEs), and their share of outputs in China's economy was small. However, this subsector has since grown extremely rapidly, and its share is now a large part of the economy.

Economic growth is a relation of input and output. According to growth theory (Solow 1956), in the absence of technological progress, output is determined by the growth rate of the labor force; thus returns are constant, to scale. TVE growth fits this model exactly. TVEs are typically labor-intensive industries. Their technology is less advanced than that used in the state and urban collective sectors, and clearly is not the reason for TVEs' relatively higher growth. Even in the transition period, growth in employment still basically explains why TVE output has grown faster than that of China's state and urban collective sectors. Figure 8.1 and Figure 8.2 show this very clearly. At the start of China's reform, the

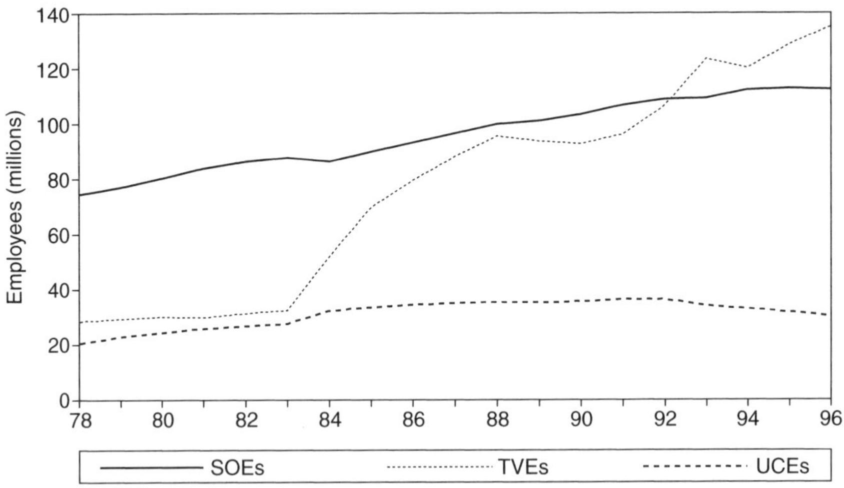

Figure 8.1 Number of employees of SOEs (state-owned enterprises), UCEs and TVEs, 1978–1996.

Note
Central, UCE.
East, TVE.

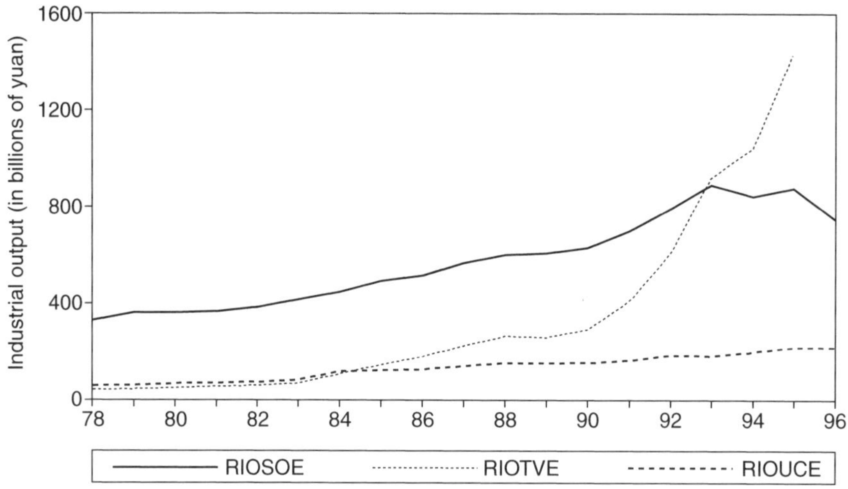

Figure 8.2 Industrial output of SOEs, TVEs and UCEs, 1978–1996.

number of employees of urban collective enterprises (UCEs) was very close to the number of employees of TVEs (more precisely, CBEs). Between 1978 and 1996, the former held steady while the latter grew rapidly, so that by the end of the period there were 4.5 times as many TVE as UCE employees. Thus the outputs of TVEs have grown much more quickly than those of UCEs, although local governments at the bottom of the hierarchy administer both.

In 1978 the number of employees in the state sector was 2.6 times that in TVEs; ten years later their numbers were nearly equal, and by 1993 TVE employment had overtaken that in the state sector. As Figure 8.1 shows, TVE employment caught up with the state sector's in merely five years (1983–88). It would be most surprising if its sudden expansion in scale did not result in a higher growth rate of output than in the state sector. In fact, sudden expansion of production scale always generates high economic growth, even if the property rights of enterprises are vaguely defined (Weitzman and Xu 1994) and the firms are poorly managed. We should not forget that China also successfully launched rapid economic growth under its planned system by expanding state industry in the First Five-Year Plan of the 1950s. The growth of collective TVE output declined in the second half of the 1990s when its expansion of scale slowed, even though TVE property rights were better defined than earlier (for example, the share-holding system was introduced in the collective TVEs in the mid-1990s).

The quantitative expansion of TVEs meant that rapid rural industrialization was the product of a large-scale reallocation of resources. As Figure 8.1 indicates, some 110 million laborers moved from the farm to the TVE sector from 1978 to 1996. This huge number, close to one-half of the entire US population, constitutes one of the largest sustained industrializing movements in history. The resource reallocation it represents has far-reaching historical significance beyond powering China's high economic growth in the reform era. As Philip Huang's (1990) rigorous study argues, it has reversed China's 600-year-long pattern of economic stagnation caused by an overpopulation of labor relative to land. Real development requires not just the quantitative growth of output but structural change in labor. When millions of laborers move from a less productive sector (labor-intensive/labor surplus agriculture) to a more productive sector (rural industry), this structural change not only can suddenly increase the productivity of these laborers but also greatly improve overall productivity, as happened in China, thereby promoting the growth of the overall economy.

The large-scale reallocation of resources is the key to understanding the so-called Chinese gradual transition model. In the Eastearn European transition model, factor markets created by rapid privatization replace the planned system as the mechanism to reallocate resources. However, it takes time to develop well-functioning factor markets and there may be no bridge between the two systems. This lack of a bridge is one of the reasons why reforms throughout Eastern Europe and particularly in the former Soviet Union have led to economic collapse and disarray. The Chinese reform did not begin with privatization creating factor markets, but a large-scale reallocation of resources did occur early in the transition. The feature of this reallocation of most interest, theoretically and empirically, was that it resulted from neither the planned system nor factor markets – a feature that is critical for understanding how China could achieve high economic growth at a time of transition between the two systems.

W. Arthur Lewis (1954) and Gustav Ranis and John Fei (1961) present a two-sector model as they investigate the expansion of the industrial sector by supplies of cheap labor from the agricultural sector. This theory does little to explain the success of TVEs. First, in general, China failed to meet the precondition for this model to work: a well-functioning labor market. An embryonic labor market gradually appeared in the 1990s as the transition progressed, but none was visible during the early reform of the 1980s. Lewis as well as Ranis and Fei would suggest that the transfer of labor to industry should have been faster in the 1990s, when a labor market had taken shape, than in the 1980s, when it was lacking. Similarly, the argument of Nee (1992: 2) that marketized firms represent an intermediate form of property, which is shaped by new pressures for efficiency and flexibility in rapidly changing environments as market forces incrementally replace the state redistributive mechanism, suggests that the transfer should have accelerated in the 1990s. However, Figure 8.1 shows that the reverse is true. The transfer of labor was far more rapid at the early stage, with the most rapid growth occurring between 1983 and 1988. The labor transferred during those five years was 60 percent of the total transfer from 1978 to 1996. The peak of the entire 18-year period was in 1984, when 20 million laborers shifted from agriculture to industry and the growth rate of the TVE labor force was 61 percent, a level far higher than in any other year. This was at the very beginning of the reform, when the household responsibility system (HRS) of agricultural production was just being set up. Here, Ranis and Fei's emphasis on the role of increasing agricultural productivity in promoting the shift of labor to industry indeed makes sense, but the rapid shift was surely not enabled by a labor market.

Second, the Lewis model hinges on not just the reallocation of labor but also on its mass migration to urban industry through a labor market. Yet the large-scale reallocation of labor linked to TVEs involved little permanent migration. The TVE pattern of labor transfer is, as the slogan has it, "leaving the land but not the village, entering the factory but not the city." According to China's Ministry of Agriculture, the agency responsible for TVE statistics, 1 percent of TVEs were set up around county seats, 12 percent in townships, 7 percent in administrative villages, and 80 percent in natural villages. No firms opened factories outside their own communities (Lin 1997: 328), which is why they are called "township-village" industry.

The large-scale reallocation of resources did not occur through the planned system (Pei 1996: 45–46). In fact, China's planners tried to protect SOEs and criticized the development of TVEs. Attacking the enterprises as "duplicative constructions" and a "waste of resources," they tried to stop TVEs from competing with SOEs in obtaining raw materials and markets for the finished goods. They thought that the limited supplies of energy and raw materials in China could be efficiently used only by state industry and not by TVEs. As China's leader, Deng Xiaoping, admitted in 1987, the amazing growth of TVEs was completely unexpected, and he called TVEs a new force suddenly coming to the fore (*yijun tuqi*).

No one has yet asked, let alone answered, a crucial question: what was the mechanism that made possible the large-scale reallocation of resources between the two planned and market systems? This mechanism is the key to the success of both TVEs and China's transition model. As shown above, most studies of TVEs are micro explanations of organizational form and firm management, whose arguments bear no relation to the macro features of China's transition model; furthermore, neither school allows for the possibility of a third mechanism to reallocate resources. The analysis of Figure 8.1 and Figure 8.2, joined to the recognition that no firms establish factories outside their communities, provides evidence that suggests where to start looking for an answer. Why was the quantitative expansion unique in TVEs in the rural collective sector, while the state and urban collective sectors lagged far behind?

The first prerequisite for setting up a factory is a plot of land. In China, land is owned by only two entities: rural collectives, which own most of China's agricultural land, and the state, which owns the rest. Construction within the state sector is highly controlled by the state plan, which must ratify the land use of new SOEs. The urban collective sector also finds expansion difficult because it does not own land. The only exception to the constraint on land use is in the rural collective sector. The *China Agricultural Statistical Yearbook* shows that in every year since the early 1980s, a portion of agricultural land has been used by villages for construction, mainly for building more and more TVEs. Thus, by studying the rural land system we should be able to find the mechanism of resource reallocation.

The redefinition of collective landownership rights

Ownership is a bundle of rights, including the right to use a resource, the right to benefit or derive income from the resource, and the right to transfer the resource. These rights can be assigned to individuals, groups, or communities. Furthermore, the rights should be exclusive (Umbeck 1981: 3). During China's planned era, when the rights assigned to rural communities were not exclusive, the so-called collective landownership existed more in name than in reality. But even nominal assignment of rights made it possible for them to be redefined effectively within the existing framework of collective landownership in the reform era.

Mark Selden and Aiguo Lu (1993) view China's collective landownership rights as consisting of five elements: (1) formal landownership rights; (2) use rights over cultivation, investment, industry, mining, and construction on the land; (3) transfer rights over the purchase, sale, rent, contracting, or inheritance of the land; (4) product rights over the consumption and sale of products of the land; and (5) labor rights over the labor power of those attached to the land. The last two can be grouped together as the right to benefit or derive income from the land. Selden and Lu show that in the framework of collective landownership, these rights are indeed much better defined by the reform.

Formal ownership rights to the land have been vested in the collective from the collectivization of the 1950s to the present. Following the collapse of the Great Leap Forward in 1960, a three-level organization was devised for the commune system: collective ownership rights were divided among the commune (the township since 1984), the brigade (the village since 1984), and the production team. The team, consisting on average of 20 to 30 households and farming 15 to 20 hectares of land, was the primary unit of ownership, production, distribution, and accounting from the early 1960s to the early 1980s. The team members worked jointly on the land, and their remuneration was solely based on the labor they contributed to team production.

This team system was replaced by the household responsibility system in the early 1980s. Under the HRS, land is contracted to individual households and the rights to use it are separated from collective landownership, which is retained by the village. Households became the basic units of production and accounting. The production team disappeared and its administrative function was assumed by the village (in many instances, the former brigade). Contracts between the village and households give a household the right to use land independently for 30 years,[2] and to keep or sell whatever surplus output remains after paying its share of agricultural tax, selling a quota of the output to the state, and meeting its obligation to the village's public accumulation fund and welfare fund. The village retains other rights associated with collective ownership. It manages land contracts, in many instances is responsible for the supply of seeds and irrigation to households, for marketing and technological diffusion, for periodic redistribution of land, and so on.

In the planned system, the state plan determined how the land should be used, and what and how much the collective should produce. Despite its formal ownership of the land, the collective had no right to decide how to use it. The state gave orders to the collective leader, who in turn gave orders to the farmers. For the command principle of the planned system, the HRS substituted the principle of contracts with those at the bottom of the hierarchy. The household negotiated with the village, whose sole responsibility was simply to deliver the state share and the collective share that had been provided by the plot of land that the household now used. In all other matters, such as what and how much should be produced, how to produce, and how to deal with the remainder of the crop, the household itself made decisions. A single contract therefore redefined the distribution of property rights among the household, the collective, and the state.

Another key difference between the planned and reform periods lies in the rights to residual income and residual control, which are closely tied to use rights. Before reform, the state claimed all farm surpluses, squeezing residual harvests out of villages through the state monopoly for purchasing and marketing farm products, planned low purchase prices, encouraging "over quota sales," and so on. During the HRS reform, these practices changed considerably, and households and villages partitioned the rights to residual income and control.

Rural collective industry is an integral part of the rural collective sector. Before reform, state policy as a whole restricted its development: it was illegal for rural collective industry to buy raw materials and energy controlled by the planned system. Moreover, its activities were narrowly limited to making farm tools, processing the farm products remaining after the state purchase quotas had been fulfilled, and the like. In short, only production for agricultural and local demand was allowed, and it was called "making good the omissions and deficiencies of state industry." In the process of redefining collective ownership rights, these rules and state macro policy were largely changed. Rural industry immediately started to compete with the state sector in supplying goods and services, and successfully extended its production in the 1980s to meet the demand of the whole society and even of international markets.

The above changes clearly differentiate the pre-reform "collective" and the post-reform collective. Before reform, the collective had to adhere strictly to the state plan and state control, but after reform it became relatively independent. This difference largely explains the sudden and rapid expansion of TVEs after the HRS was set up in 1984. However, the state still tightly controls land transfer rights: the collective has no right to sell its land, and no entity except the state itself is allowed to purchase collective land. Nor is the inheritance of land allowed. According to China's Land Law, all residents of a village own the village land collectively. That is, anyone registered as a village member receives a share of the collective land without making any payment (Zhou 1994). These "owners" are mainly the original villagers, those newly born there, and newly married women who move into their husbands' residences. If the sale, purchase, and inheritance of land were unfettered, such a system of collective landownership would collapse. However, the transfer of use rights among households in a given village and the rental of land to outsiders are allowed.

In sum, the institutional root of the changes sketched above is the original exclusive right to collective land. The collectivization of the mid-1950s made the collective, not the state, the owner of the land. Although property rights of members of the collective were not defined as well as those of the "mutual-aid teams" and "elementary cooperatives" of the early 1950s, they remained, like those of the other groups named, putatively exclusive. When the exclusive right to collective land came to be respected and protected by the village through the HRS in the early 1980s, rural collectives had better defined rights to use and derive income from the collective land. To prevent the collapse of collective landownership, the state still does not allow the unfettered sale and purchase of land.

A model of resource allocation based on collective landownership

The resources discussed in this chapter are classical: namely, land, capital, and labor. Capital and labor can flow but land cannot. Therefore, the first prerequisite for setting up a factory is a plot of land, to which capital and labor flow. In planned economies, the state plan directly allocates resources. The state uses its own land or purchases collective land to invest capital, and then employs workers. In short, the state plan determines the flow of capital and labor. In market economies where factor markets exist and capital can purchase land, the owner of capital plays a leading role in allocating resources. The owner decides where to invest capital, and then hires workers through labor markets. The investments are often highly concentrated at a number of points, such as big cities where capitalists can take advantage of superior infrastructure and can benefit from economies of scale. Laborers often move from traditional agriculture to modern industries. As Figure 8.3 shows, this is the well-known two-sector model or dual economy proposed by W. Arthur Lewis. It and the planned system have three features in common. First, investments tend to be highly concentrated in cities. Second, laborers follow the flow of capital, whether determined by the state plan or by the capitalist. Third, the laborers are employed either by the state or by the capitalist, not by themselves or by the collective.

As Figure 8.4 shows, as long as collective land cannot be purchased or sold, laborers' rights to use and derive income from the land cannot be transferred; at the same time, capital can never purchase land, though the ownership rights of capital are transferable.[3] The result is a mechanism that makes possible capital but not labor flow in the process of allocating resources. The condition for its success is a surplus of labor relative to land, which inherently attracts capital to the land but keeps out external labor. When the labor surplus is exhausted, outside laborers may move in and a labor market may gradually emerge. This is a micro model. It is also a macro model if land is collectively owned, there is a surplus of labor relative to land everywhere, and all the villages have homogeneous institutions, conditions, and behavior. Such was indeed the case throughout rural China in the era prior to decollectivization.

In this model, the owners of collective land play the leading role in allocating resources. When industry is labor-intensive, the demand for capital is not high. The owners of land can use the agricultural surplus as their original industrial capital or they can borrow from banks, using land as collateral. They can also use surplus from former collective industries as well as personal savings. Thus resource allocation can begin even without

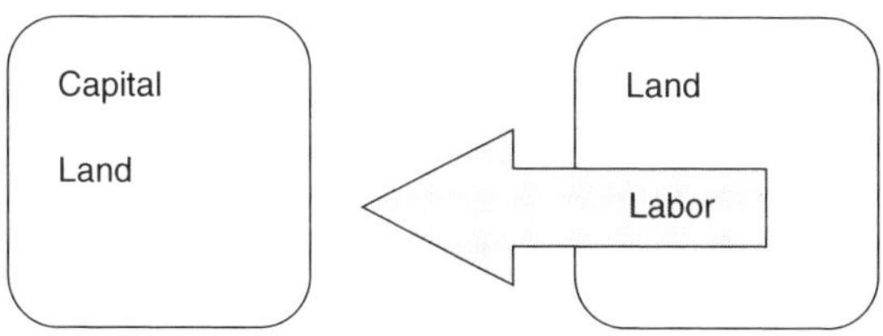

Figure 8.3 The Lewis model.

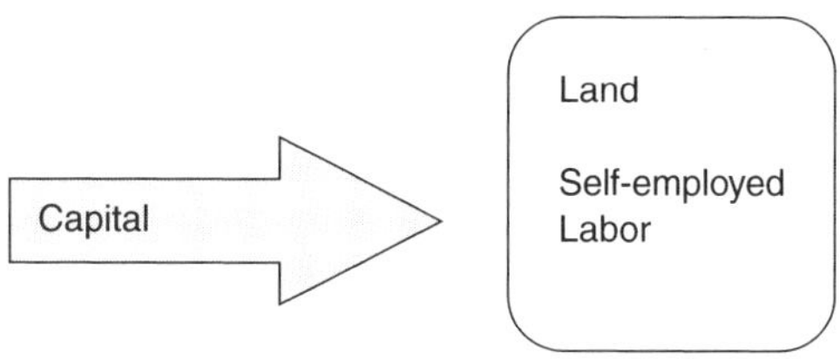

Figure 8.4 The TVE model.

well-developed capital markets. Furthermore, when thousands of rural collectives use this method, large-scale reallocation of resources is not difficult, but the investments may be thinly diffused throughout the rural collective sector. The most important point to note is that laborers, as members of the collective, are often owners of both the land and the factory established on that land, and they may provide the labor force, too.

I will emphasize again the main features of the TVE model. First, if capital cannot purchase collective land, capital flows but labor does not. Second, investments are thinly diffused. Third, the transfer of millions of laborers from agriculture to industry does not need labor markets if it occurs within the borders of collective land and the workers are self-employed.

Collective landownership, capital investments, and employment

According to the *China Township Enterprise Statistical Yearbook,* there are three types of investment associated with the system of collective landownership. First, collectives themselves invest. Second, an individual household or several households in partnership set up enterprises on collective land, that is, on land leased to these individuals or partnerships. Third, external capital flows into collective land. This section will examine each, showing that none of the three types of investments and the employment associated with them can be excluded from the specific outcomes of the model outlined above.

Collective investment of local capital

As long as the purchase and sale of collective land are not allowed, the ownership relations involving villagers and collective land remain intact. Of the three classical resources, land becomes the one in shortest supply for those who have no land, and the most valuable resource (even an oligopoly-producing resource) for those who have land. External investors, no matter how much capital they have, cannot purchase collective land. Only when the owners of collective land themselves invest in it is there no need to purchase or rent land. Furthermore, external investors can never own the enterprises completely or exclusively if they invest in collective land, because they cannot own the land on which they set up their factories. These are institutional constraints on external investors. Only owners of collective land who themselves invest can own the enterprises exclusively, a circumstance that explains why the early investors in TVEs were nearly all rural collectives (Bao 2000: 11). It also explains why I elsewhere define the collective TVEs as both products of collective landownership and internal reinvestments in the collective land (Pei 1998: 112).

Collectives that directly invest draw on three sources of capital: collective accumulation funds, bank loans, and household capital. Household capital can be invested in either collective TVEs, private enterprises, or joint enterprises; the latter two cases will be discussed below. The early investments of TVEs did not depend on bank loans and household capital. Instead, most of the capital came from early collective accumulation, meaning that the land as well as labor invested mainly in the land generated the original capital. It is rare for a village to invest in other villages (including neighboring villages) and cities (Bao 2000: 56), for two reasons. First, every village has its own land on which to invest capital. Second, the property rights to two neighboring villages' land are exclusive even though both parcels of land are collective. A village can never purchase other land and own a factory exclusively if it invests externally. Only when the investor and owner of land is the same collective are the rights to use and derive income from both the land and factory consistent. In other words, the benefits of industrialization can be almost totally internalized in the village only in this way. Thus, investments are widely diffused rather than concentrated in a few communities.

For example, in Fuyang prefecture, Anhui Province, each TVE is on average 2.94 km from the township, 4.04 km from roads, and 24.43 km from county government (Du Ying 1997: 328). This diffusion is caused by three interrelated factors. First, about 800,000 rural collectives own land. Second, these collectives are relatively autonomous and are dispersed throughout rural China. Third and most important, the purchase and sale of land are not allowed. If factor markets develop and capital can purchase land, the Lewis model – investment concentrated mainly on a number of special points (cities) – may appear. In the absence of factor markets, only the Chinese state can purchase land. China's planners often criticize the diffusion of investments as "small and complete" (i.e., unable to take advantage of economies of scale), "duplicative constructions," and a "waste of resources." However, in the early days of reform it was precisely the diffusion of small-scale investments that made possible the transfer of surplus labor rapidly and widely, thereby providing an alternative to the labor transfer approach of the Lewis model and of the planned economy. Whatever the inefficiencies associated with dispersed small-scale industry, the "waste of resources" would be larger if China's vast labor surplus could not be utilized. Under collective landownership only five years were required to increase the number of TVE workers from 32.35 million (in 1983) to 95.45 million (in 1988), a scale of job creation that has few precedents in history. It took the planned system 25 years to increase the number of SOE workers from 33.07 million (in 1962) to 96.54 million (in 1987).

Community governments, the inheritor of the collective, often take responsibility for resource reallocation, or they are founders of collective TVEs. However, local villagers are shareholders of the collective TVEs because they are owners of collective land, collective accumulation funds, and household capital that are used to establish the collective TVEs.[4] According to Armen A. Alchian and Harold Demsetz (1973), the bundle of rights is divisible in that one party may hold some of these rights while delegating other rights to another party. Such divisibility occurs whenever an asset is owned by a group of individuals. While each of them owns a share of the asset and hence has the corresponding rights, it is impossible for each to directly control the use of the asset. Thus, the shareholders (the principals) must find a much smaller party as their agent, to whom the rights of control are delegated. That is why community governments get the rights to directly manage investments and allocate resources owned by villagers, and why researchers regard the villagers as "nominal" owners (Weitzman and Xu 1994) and the community governments as *de facto* owners of collective TVEs (Walder 1995).

Shareholders naturally have the right to use and derive income from collective TVEs when the TVEs are set up; the right to get jobs originates from the use rights of shareholders. It is in this sense that we say local villagers are self-employed, because the employment is a result of realizing their use rights. However, a use right cannot ensure that every shareholder gets a job. The actual practices of collective ownership vary widely, ranging from genuine shareholding to vaguely defined "communal ownership" to control by the village leaders. When collective ownership is vaguely defined communal ownership or family control by the village leader, then friends, relatives, and family members of the leader in the village may be assigned jobs earlier than other shareholders. Therefore, deciding who gets a job and who does not is not totally up to the shareholders.

However, villagers' status as shareholders explains why they have priority in getting jobs in local collective TVEs and receive better treatment than outsiders. Although shareholders in a village may not all get jobs, there is a clear difference between them and hired labor. Even the external managing and technical labor cannot enjoy the same rights as the local villagers. During the period of industrial formation in the late 1970s and the 1980s, collective TVEs had to hire managers and technical personnel from the state sector, because villagers previously had little industrial experience. However, those hired had no right to make decisions about the enterprise, only to advise, even though they were better educated, had a technological edge, and were experienced in industry. The directors and decision-makers of collective TVEs were always selected from local villagers despite their relative lack of education (Bao 2000: 56), simply because outsiders are always hired labor and a collective can easily fire them when it does not need them. Only local villagers are shareholders of collective TVEs and are self-employed, and thus they have more rights and benefits. As Huang points out, "Like the family farm, the collective could not fire its surplus labor" (1990: 317). Because the sale of collective land is not allowed, the laborer is always an owner of the land. Thus the collective is forced to attract capital to the land and keep away external labor.

If the purchase and sale of collective land are not allowed, and labor is scarce relative to land in a village, then both capital and external labor may move in. It should be easier for capital to flow in if capital is relatively cheaper than labor. This has never been the case in China, with its virtually unlimited supply of labor but relatively limited capital. It should be easier for labor to move in if labor is relatively cheaper than capital. But in China, while it is true that labor is relatively cheaper than capital, labor is not relatively scarce compared to land. The reality is that local labor supply exceeds local labor demand throughout the country. Therefore, the state-imposed household registration (*hukou*) system is not the only factor checking migration between urban and rural areas and among villages. The labor surplus in every village naturally blocks the inflow of outside labor. Here we should note that not only is it impossible for a collective to fire its surplus labor but also the laborer has nowhere to go. Thus, attracting capital to create off-farm jobs for local surplus labor becomes the only option, even though capital is relatively much dearer than labor.

In the process of reallocating resources, two areas, south Guangdong and south Jiangsu, have typically been extremely successful, and a local labor shortage has appeared in both places. A large and sudden inflow of capital from Hong Kong led to a labor shortage that first appeared in Guangdong, and cheap labor from poor areas moved in. Still, local workers benefit much more from collective TVEs than do outside laborers. Local villagers enjoy subsidies for pig raising, grain production, medical care, pensions, and so on. Outside laborers receive only wages and cannot benefit from the welfare provisions. Villages contract with them once a year: while local villagers are self-employed, external laborers are hired.

Unlike Guangdong, Jiangsu mainly depends on its strong collective institutions to accumulate capital. Its development of commune and brigade enterprises, the predecessors of collective TVEs, was rapid and well known as early as the 1970s. Because its collective tradition was stronger, it reacted differently than Guangdong. When a labor shortage gradually appeared, it tried to change its collective TVEs from labor-intensive to capital-intensive, increase local wages, and block the inflow of outside labor (Wang 1990). Because capital accumulation and labor shortages result from long-term local collective efforts, collectives do not want outsiders to share the benefits; poor areas and collectives are thus forced to transfer their surplus labor to industry by their own efforts. Therefore, both the investment and wage patterns of the TVE model differ from those of the Lewis model. The latter is an open economy; the former is an economy with many relatively closed units created by collective landownership. The dispersion in average pay level is substantial among different collectives and areas, but the income distribution within a collective is egalitarian (Byrd and Lin 1990: 276). This equality further demonstrates that all the landowners are also shareholders of the collective TVEs and have equal rights to the income distributed in a collective; outsiders cannot share those rights.

However, Guangdong's experience indicates that it is possible for labor markets to develop from collective landownership when a labor shortage appears. In fact, there is a huge "floating population" in China today. But two points must be noted. First, no such population existed in the 1980s. As the model in the previous section would suggest, labor indeed did not move in the early stage of reform. Second, when the floating population appeared in the 1990s, it was an indirect product of the model. Although there was no factor market and the 70 million laborers who shifted from farm to industrial sector in the 1980s did not leave their villages, they had to create product markets so that they could buy machines, energy, and raw materials as well as sell their products. Such markets were not provided by the planned system for the huge number of new workers. Nearly all raw materials and energy were produced by the state sector or under the control of the planned system. To obtain the products, TVEs offered to pay more than the prices set by the planners. And to make profits, the state enterprises preferred to sell their products at market prices rather than at planned prices. Moreover, TVEs competed with each other as well as with the state sector in supplying goods and services. This competition, together with the consumer demand that generally could not function in the planned economy, gradually created goods and service markets as well as market prices. Therefore, the planned system broke down largely because 70 million workers unexpectedly and suddenly came to the fore in the Chinese economy in the 1980s. Thus Naughton finds that

> TVEs are responses to one of the most distinctive characteristics of the Chinese transition as a whole: the early creation of product markets, which exist for a prolonged period without well-developed markets for factors of production or assets.
>
> (1994: 266)

When the planned system lost its balance and product markets developed, factor markets could also gradually appear. Profits accumulated from the product markets could lay the foundations for creating capital markets, and labor markets could emerge from the most rapidly growing areas of the product markets where labor shortages first appeared, as happened in Guangdong. Thus, the conditions were ripe for the rise of the floating population, which I therefore call an indirect product of the model. In sum, most workers of the collective TVEs are self-employed in the sense that the employment stems from their use rights as shareholders. Only when a local labor shortage appears is there a possibility of hiring outside laborers, but they cannot enjoy the same rights as the local collective members.

Private investment of local capital

Individual household enterprises and partnerships are private enterprises built on collective land. Under the HRS, every household has a plot of land to farm. Without the permission of the collective a household cannot set up a private factory on that land, because the collective as a whole owns it and it is designated for agricultural use. Private and joint enterprises therefore have two choices. One is to occupy the yard of the founder's home. In this case, the factory is certainly very small and cannot develop further (Pei 1998: 24). The other is to rent collective land designated for nonagricultural purposes. Household capital is the primary source for private investments. Enterprises may also borrow from banks, relatives, and friends, and the risk is borne by the founders and by the providers of capital. Because the amount of capital in a household or joint enterprise is typically limited, these enterprises tend to be even more labor-intensive and smaller scale than collective TVEs. By and large, collective enterprises dominate rural industry; private enterprises dominate the rural service sector, with businesses such as shops and restaurants. Workers in individual household and joint enterprises are typically family members and relatives.

Individual household enterprises and partnerships have two basic features in common with collective TVEs. First, they are also typically located on collective land. Second, their workers are also largely self-employed in the sense of being investors or family members of investors. Undoubtedly, both are largely the result of collective landownership. The most serious problem private enterprises face is how to acquire land: because capital cannot purchase it, rental is the only option. But in the early 1980s, China had no general market for individual household enterprises and partnerships to rent land. To the extent that such markets existed in some special areas, they were few and undeveloped. Thus, most individual household and joint enterprises rented land from their own collectives. Furthermore, the market price of land rent is very high when there is a surplus of labor relative to land, but the capital available to an individual household enterprise or partnership is often limited. If they had paid rents at market prices, most would not have been able to establish their enterprises in the early 1980s.

When private enterprises chose factory sites in the 1980s, the first factor considered was the cost of land (Lin, Q. 1990: 179). Rural collectives provided land to their own villagers at very low rents. In Houji village, Liangshan county, Shandong Province, the rent paid by village entrepreneurs was 200 yuan per *mu* in 1984 (Dang-zhibu 1985: 286). However, in the same year the market rate per *mu* in Jieshou county, Anhui Province, was

1,962 yuan (Du, H. 1990: 53), which was big money in China then. Both counties were in poor, remote areas at the same level, and no factor was present to explain the differential rent. Few individual household enterprises and partnerships could bear the high cost of market rent in the 1980s. Moreover, villages were eager to support local entrepreneurs as well as to create jobs in the community – providing another important reason why nearly all such enterprises were located in the entrepreneurs' own villages.

It may seem odd that private entrepreneurs in a village must pay rent when they are owners of the collective land. This is not a real rent, if by "real" we mean a rent determined by market factors. In exchange for access to collective land to farm in the HRS, households are obliged to contribute management fees, public accumulation funds, and welfare funds to their village. They have the same obligation to contribute to the collective if they use land for nonagricultural activities. Here, the big gap between the payment they make and the market rent is the benefit derived from their identity and rights as landowners. Outsiders have neither the right to use village land nor the right to benefit from the big gap. They have to pay rent at the market price.

The collective TVEs already had a strong base in the pre-reform era, but it is remarkable that without land privatization, the number of workers in individual household enterprises and partnerships increased from zero in 1983 to 12.3 million in 1984. Four factors explain their emergence almost overnight. First, the sudden increase of household income from the HRS and the rise in state-purchasing prices of farm goods provided household capital at the right time. Second, collectives immediately provided land at very low charge. Third, workers were family members and were thus available immediately rather than being transferred by the labor market in a lengthy process. Fourth, investment was diffused. There were about 930,000 villages in 1984, and the average number of laborers per village who moved to industry was only about 13. It is thus not difficult to understand how a new force could suddenly come to the fore.

Although individual household enterprises and partnerships are private enterprises, they, like collective TVEs, enact the slogan "leaving the land but not the village, entering the factory but not the city." In both cases, collective landownership produces this outcome. It thus is reasonable for China's official statistics to track household enterprises and partnerships as TVEs, an inclusive category that illustrates the flexibility of collective landownership in the reform era. Private economy can easily grow on this base as long as landownership is not privatized, and thus collective and private economies coexist. Household farming and private nonagricultural enterprises constitute the private economy; the collective economy mainly consists of collective TVEs. This mix lays a foundation for the later stage of economic transition. In fact, since the mid-1990s private enterprises rooted in collective landownership have overtaken collective TVEs in size of output. The three waves of high growth created in turn by the HRS, collective TVEs, and private enterprises followed one after the other, and all took place within the framework of collective landownership. That framework and the preponderantly rural population have shaped China's continued high growth and smooth transition to a market economy.

Inflow of external capital

Seeking profit is the nature of capital. It has to invest somewhere, even if it cannot purchase land. Conversely, rural collectives by instinct compete fiercely with each other to attract external capital. Villages with more external capital often become rich faster. When external investors need land and collectives need capital, and both can benefit, they cooperate. There are two types of collaboration. In one, collectives and external investors set up joint ventures. In the other, collectives lease land to external investors. Such leases, which may be long-term, are permitted though the sale of land is prohibited.

In the case of joint ventures, capital investments are of two types: investments from state enterprises and from private capital, both domestic and international. Investment by state enterprises is common in areas around industrial cities, where land constraints and environmental regulations may prevent them from expanding production on an existing site in the city. Thus, collectives often contribute land and self-built workshops as their shares in the joint venture, while state enterprises supply equipment and technical expertise. The director and workers are always local villagers, and the state enterprise provides only a small number of technicians and a vice director. In this voluntary contract between the collective and the state enterprise, the state itself is not involved. It plays a direct role only when the project is big and state-planned, requiring the purchase of land (Pei 1998: 125). Private capital has come from private investors in China, and from Hong Kong (since the mid-1980s), Taiwan and South Korea (since the early 1990s), and elsewhere. Still, the same pattern holds: the collectives' shares are land and self-built workshops, the private investors' shares are equipment and technical expertise, and workers are always selected first from local villagers.

The reason for relying on local villagers for labor has often been misunderstood. In the case of investment from state enterprises, Bao Yongjiang (2000: 11) argues that city workers do not like to move to rural villages. This may be true, but it is not the main reason. In the case of private capital, analysts frequently point to the cheapness of rural labor. Yet labor is cheap everywhere in China. What I saw during my fieldwork was that private investors in a village could easily find cheaper and more qualified laborers nearby, but they could not hire them and fire local villagers. The reason is very simple. Since all the villagers are owners of the land and the land is a share of the joint venture, they are also shareholders.

The outsiders have no such identity and related rights. By contrast, if capital could purchase land, the original owners would have no standing, and workers could be hired and fired at will; even if the original landowners were hired, they would no longer be self-employed.

Collective land can be leased for both service and industrial use. Leasing to the service sector is popular in areas around cities. For example, a village in Shijin township, a suburb of Guangzhou city, leases four plots of its land to four vegetable wholesale firms. The firms not only invest in buildings on the land but also pay the village substantial rent: more than 20 million yuan every year. The four plots of land total 150,000 square meters, and in 1996 their monthly rent was 11 yuan per square meter. The contract between the village and the firms is renegotiated every two years, and thus the rent may increase every two years as the value of urban and suburban land rises. In fact, when the deputy village head (*fu cunzhang*) guided me on a visit to the vegetable wholesale market, the managers of the market called him landlord (in jest), a title he did not dispute.

External tenants seeking land for industrial use can rent collective land alone, or both land and workshops, or land, workshops, and equipment. Again, local villagers have first claim on jobs. This may seem strange, as tenants normally have the exclusive right to use the land during the period of their contract, and therefore have the right to choose workers according to their interests. However, when acquiring land is not easy, landlords are always the final arbiters in deciding who should be tenants and on what terms. By the 1990s prospective investors, including international investors and investors from cities, would look at a variety of sites and they were in a very strong bargaining position: local communities were eager to have them rent land and hire workers. If surplus labor is a village's biggest problem, then leasing land with the proper conditions can solve it. If its requirement for employing villagers is not met, the collective can simply choose another tenant: the villagers always possess the long-term use right, to which the temporary use right of the tenant must be subordinate. In this way, local villagers can be assured of the first opportunity to become workers. Outsiders have no such right. Furthermore, the factory is on village land and is surrounded by villagers. To make business go smoothly in this environment, the tenant has to build good relations with villagers. Of course, the tenant can hire workers from outside when a village begins to suffer a labor shortage.

The above cases show that even though the general model of TVE investment is thinly diffused, the inflow of external capital is relatively greater in areas around industrial cities. Suburban TVEs benefit much more than TVEs in remote areas from urban capital and technical spillovers, as well as easy access to transportation and markets. Although external capital hires mostly local villagers, the number of outside workers employed in these areas may grow faster than in other areas.

All the types of investments, enterprises, and employment examined in this section are products of collective landownership, which makes capital but not labor flow, making investments diffused and workers basically self-employed. The only exception, which has not been discussed, is the case in which the state purchases collective land when it carries out big projects. It often pays a very low price, but it also provides jobs for the villagers who have been deprived of the land needed to make a living. Since this is a relatively rare function of the planned system, and results in the land being no longer collective-owned, it falls outside our purview here.

Land rents and the profits of collective TVEs

From the early 1980s to the mid-1990s, the output of the collective TVE sector grew the most rapidly of all China's sectors. While this growth has been widely noted, an important reason for it has been ignored: namely, the transfer of land rent into profits of collective TVEs, as a result of collective landownership encouraging townships and villages to build factories on their own land. Under those conditions, the landowners pay rents neither to others nor to themselves. Such landowners may be village collectives that invest in their own land or, if we regard collective TVEs as a whole, townships that invest in collective land. Townships generally do not own land, although there are exceptions, such as land used by commune enterprises prior to the reform era. Townships that need more land to build township enterprises generally take one of two approaches to acquiring it. In the first, they enter into joint ventures with villages that supply land while they supply capital. In the second, townships buy the use rights of village land for some years, often paying very little because they have administrative oversight over the villages. The specific number of years and amounts paid depend on relations between the particular townships and villages involved and can differ widely. Both the state and townships pay low prices when appropriating land from villages, but there is a basic difference. When the state purchases collective land, the land becomes state-owned. When townships buy use rights of village land, the land remains collective-owned, for townships are another level of rural collectives.

In short, the collective sector as a whole does not pay rents to other sectors when it builds collective TVEs on collective land. Therefore, the production costs of private enterprises always include land rents; the production costs of collective TVEs do not. This does not mean that TVEs incur no land rent, for rent always exists; but in the case of collective TVEs, it becomes a part of their profits. This point is substantiated by data that I collected during fieldwork in July and August 2000, which are presented in Table 8.1 and Table 8.2. Village A is regarded as the most prosperous village in the suburbs of Shenyang city, Liaoning Province. Enterprise A is a township enterprise in a suburb of Tianjin city and a

Table 8.1 Land rent as share of profits of collective TVEs, I

	Village A, Shenyang						*Township enterprise A, Tianjin*				
	N	*Area (mu)*	*Rent (r)*	*Profit (p) (1,000 yuan)*	*Real p (p − r)*	*Share (r ÷ p) (%)*	*Area (mu)*	*Rent (r) (1,000 yuan)*	*Profit (p)*	*Real p (p − r)*	*Share (r ÷ p) (%)*
1986	15	140	549	221	−328	248.0	–	–	–	–	–
1987	17	140	622	304	−318	205.0	60	266	433	167	61
1988	22	140	654	1,237	583	53.0	60	280	1,235	955	23
1989	22	140	673	1,442	769	47.0	60	288	1,400	1,112	21
1990	24	140	686	780	94	88.0	60	294	1,630	1,336	18
1991	18	140	809	624	−185	130.0	60	347	2,030	1,683	17
1992	16	140	1,096	917	−179	120.0	60	441	3,005	2,564	15
1993	14	200	1,563	3,643	2,080	43.0	60	469	4,009	3,540	12
1994	15	200	1,695	4,292	2,597	39.0	60	508	4,504	3,996	11
1995	8	200	1,747	5,892	4,145	30.0	60	524	4,520	3,996	12
1996	8	200	1,773	7,908	6,135	22.0	60	532	4,030	3,498	13
1997	8	200	1,807	17,200	15,393	11.0	60	542	3,500	2,958	15
1998	8	200	1,852	14,040	12,188	13.0	60	556	3,210	2,654	17
1999	8	200	1,961	36,060	34,099	5.4	60	588	3,509	2,921	17

Source: Author's fieldwork.

Note
N = number of enterprises.

Table 8.2 Land rent as share of profits of collective TVEs, II

	Village B, Wuqing County, Tianjin					
	N	*Area (mu)*	*Rent (r) (1,000 yuan)*	*Profit (p)*	*Real p (p − r)*	*Share (r ÷ p) (%)*
1994	5	12	59	700	641	8.4
1995	6	92	532	3,050	2,518	17.0
1996	7	92	676	1,300	624	52.0
1997	8	92	719	1,530	811	47.0
1998	8	92	780	2,900	2,120	27.0
1999	8	100	873	3,400	2,527	26.0
1–6/2000	8	100	444	1,600	1,156	28.0

Source: Author's fieldwork.

Note
N = number of enterprises.

model enterprise as well. Village B is a moderately prosperous village in Wuqing county, Tianjin municipality (I was not given access to its pre-1994 data).

Table 8.1 and Table 8.2 show, first, that more than 50 percent of the enterprises' profits initially came from land rents. If the rents were taken away from village A's profits, the village enterprises would have lost money in the early period; the same is true of Houji village, as its own account makes clear (Dang-zhibu 1985). Houji's collective enterprises were relatively inefficient and for a long time were unable to repay the bank loans borrowed by the village to invest in them. Thus, it leased its enterprises, including land, workshops, and equipment, to the villages' private entrepreneurs. From 1984 to 1985, the village received rent of more than 2 million yuan, enabling it not only to repay its debts but also to establish a large new factory. As we saw in the previous section, collectives sometimes lease land, workshops, and equipment to private entrepreneurs, both external and internal. However, the rents paid by external entrepreneurs are higher; in their absence, collectives often lease to local villagers at lower rent. Leasing to private entrepreneurs in the village is often more profitable than using the land, labor, workshops, and equipment in collective TVEs because collective TVEs are less efficient than private enterprises. The bottom line of TVE production is to get land rent. If the profit produced by a collective TVE is less than the rent, then the TVE is leased to private entrepreneurs.

Such leasing is particularly frequent in the case of small collective TVEs, and less common in the case of big collective TVEs. That is the story I heard of village A in its early years. In fact, the profits of private enterprises in village A and Houji also came in part from land rents, because they paid rents lower than market rates. Only when outsiders rent both land and collective TVEs can the collective collect the full rent. However, external investors may not be interested in renting small and less profitable TVEs. As even the most prosperous suburban village of Shenyang initially had no profit or lost money if the rents were subtracted from profits, the same may be true in the early stages of many other collective TVEs. Since more than 50 percent of the profits came from land rents in all three cases I studied, and two of them were models in their areas, early collective TVEs probably followed a similar pattern; if so, TVE profits from land rents must be huge in rural China.

The second point to be deduced from Table 8.1 and Table 8.2 is that land rent can provide a relatively stable portion of collective TVE profits, thereby making them less risky than private businesses. Village A's data show this clearly. For China's rural industry as a whole, 1990 and 1991 were difficult years; reform stopped after the Tiananmen Square crackdown, and the real profits of village A became negative again. However, it still enjoyed some "profits" because it did not pay others land rents. Their freedom from rent payments makes bankruptcy far less likely for collective TVEs than for private enterprises. Yet it could also lead to complacency as access to an easy source of profits from land rents means that collective TVEs feel less pressure to run their enterprises efficiently.

Third, in the long run, the relative contribution of land rent to the profits of collective TVEs has declined. All three cases clearly show this trend. They also suggest a reason why collective TVEs and private enterprises demonstrate a different pattern of expansion. Collective TVEs could develop faster than private enterprises at the early stage of reform largely because land rents made up a bigger share of TVE profits. The previous section listed three sources of TVE capital: collective accumulation funds, bank loans, and household capital. An important source not mentioned is available only after collective TVEs have been established: enterprise capital from the profits of collective TVEs pooled by community governments. According to William Byrd (1990: 201), these retained profits provided 60 percent of the funds invested in large-scale collective TVEs from 1984 to 1986. We have seen that these profits were largely from land rents. Private firms generally had no such profits to reinvest, and thus were unable to expand as rapidly.

Local governments can siphon off profits from collective TVEs and reinvest not because they own collective TVEs but because collective TVEs, like households in the HRS, are obliged to contribute to the collective when they use collective land. However, the collective owns both the land and collective TVEs and cannot charge itself rent for using land. Therefore, the contribution takes the form of TVE profits. When the share of land rent in TVE profits declined sharply in the 1990s, the relative advantage of collective TVEs over private enterprises also decreased. This change played an important role in enabling private enterprises to overtake collective TVEs in the mid-1990s.

Another important reason for the advance of private enterprises and relative decline of collective TVEs in the 1990s is that the Chinese economy was a shortage economy from the early 1980s to the mid-1990s, and aggregate demand always exceeded aggregate supply. Under those conditions, it was easier for collective TVEs to expand; but the conditions no longer held after the mid-1990s.

Fourth, the differential rents play an important role in capital accumulation for TVE investment. Land rents are higher in suburbs of cities, areas near highways, and coastal areas than in remote and inland areas. Thus capital accumulates at different rates in different areas. The land rent of village A in 1986 was about 3,900 yuan per *mu*, which was twice the rent of 1,962 yuan per *mu* in Jieshou county, a relatively remote area. The land rent of the village in the suburb of Guangzhou was 88,044 yuan per *mu* in 1996 – ten times the rent of village A then (8,865 yuan).

Although land rents can accumulate funds for TVE investment, those funds are not automatically transformed into industrial profits. As noted above, TVEs grow around cities to benefit from urban technical and capital spillovers and from easy access to markets and transportation. This process creates the high land value, which provides more funds for TVE investment. This pattern supplies another reason why TVE investment tends to be more concentrated in areas with higher land rents, though the general model is diffused investment in rural China.

From Table 8.1 and Table 8.2 and the preceding discussion, we can deduce three interrelated factors. First, collective TVEs benefit more from collective landownership than do private enterprises. Second, collective ownership enables their scale to expand more rapidly in early stages of development. Third, their output can grow faster in the early period of the model of resource allocation sketched above. This phenomenon has nothing to do with local governments and markets, because local governments cannot generate land rent, and the transfer of land rent into TVE profits is a result of resource allocation that typically does not follow market principles. In sum, the data do not support the argument of many researchers that the higher growth of TVE output can be explained by their having more efficient organization and management than SOEs and private enterprises in the transitional environment. We simply cannot accurately compare the efficiency of collective TVEs with other enterprises if the transfer of land rents into TVE profits is not recognized. The mistake is in confusing efficiency of resource allocation with efficiency of firm management. The high economic growth achieved when state industry expanded in the 1950s cannot directly prove that SOEs are more efficient than other kinds of enterprises; the same is true of TVEs.

China is still a developing country. Its general growth pattern is less likely to depend on improvements in management than on better resource allocation. What is clear and interesting is that except for the short period after the failure of the Great Leap Forward, China's expansion has not stopped. Before 1978, the state sector expanded most rapidly and led the country's growth, which was supported by the large transfer of agricultural surplus into state investment. From 1978 to the mid-1990s, the collective TVE sector expanded most rapidly and led the country's growth. Since the mid-1990s, the most rapid growth has been located in the private sector, including international and joint investment, which will continue to play a leading role in China's economic expansion in the near future. The continuity of this expansion is no doubt due to collective landownership, which served to bridge these different periods. Because the TVE model described above was already at work under Mao, commune and brigade industry experienced high growth as early as the 1970s and there was a mechanism at hand to allocate resources at the very beginning of reform.

Today, scholars often talk about the role of institutions and property rights in China's transition. What is forgotten is that the land system is always the most deeply rooted institution in any agrarian society. In fact, collective landownership centered on the village community is both the deepest root of China's transition model and the most fundamental reason why China is having such difficulty developing factor markets. Another large-scale reallocation of resources can start from land privatization, but it takes time to build a new mechanism; moreover, privatization will put a halt to expansion based on scale. If land were privatized, all the rural collective organizations and collective industries would collapse, because they are based on collective land ownership. Both land and capital markets would appear if capital purchased land; and once privatization led millions of laborers to lose land, labor markets then appear. Then the factor markets would start to reallocate resources. The Eastern European countries show the high social cost of such a transition – a cost that necessarily must be much higher in China, where most of the population depends on land to make a living.

Conclusion

China's high economic growth in the reform era has been driven by better utilization of the world's largest supply of surplus labor. About 110 million surplus laborers moved from farm to rural industrial sectors, a resource reallocation that succeeded largely because it was based on collective land ownership. By transferring the surplus labor broadly and massively, this model not only promotes growth but also plays a historic role in connecting the planned system and market system models of resource allocation. This "third mechanism" makes the Chinese transition different from that in Eastern Europe.

When capital cannot purchase collective land, capital flows but labor does not. The mechanism works only when there is an excess of labor relative to land, which attracts capital to the land but blocks the inflow of external labor. Because all the villages are homogeneous in their institutions, conditions, and behavior, the capital investments are thinly diffused everywhere. And because labor does not flow and investments are diffused, the transfer of labor to industry is localized in villages – and those villages are spread across rural China. The uniform system of collective landownership has several important consequences. First, the number of transferred laborers is vast. Second, the micro cost of the transfer is low, because rural collectives do not purchase land and even use land rents to shift more surplus laborers to industry. Third, the macro cost is also low, because the original social resources – the land system and collective organizations – are directly utilized to transfer surplus labor. Fourth, without a labor market the transfer can proceed rapidly, because laborers do not move but build factories on their own land; moreover, they are largely self-employed, in the sense that their employment stems from their use rights as shareholders.

This model can quickly collapse if laws change to freely permit the sale and purchase of land. Its mechanism could not have reallocated resources between the planned and market systems if land had been privatized in the early 1980s. Like the production teams and team leaders in the early 1980s, all China's rural collectives and TVEs, as well as the Chinese style of rural local governments and the gradual transition model, would have disappeared with privatization (Pei 1998: 150–151). It may be true that collective landownership constituted a barrier to development in the Mao era. That conclusion has made many researchers, including myself in the past, assume that collective landownership could play no positive role in development; it perhaps explains why collective landownership's role in China's transition has not been well studied, and has even been regarded as irrelevant. Indeed, both communist and capitalist ideological biases hinder scientific research into the question of collective land and its relationship to rural industrialization. In economic history, collective landownership creates a distinctive pattern of surplus labor moving to industry that does not fit the Lewis model. As an empirical matter, in China it has driven the transfer of about 140 million surplus laborers to industry since 1970. Here lies the best-kept secret of China's rapid development over the past quarter century.

Notes

1 I follow China's practice in defining the category of TVE to include not just township and village enterprises (*xiangcun qiye*) but also individual household enterprises (*huban qiye*) and partnerships (*lianhu qiye*), because all these enterprises, as will be seen, rely on the resource allocation of collective land ownership. When focusing on township and village enterprises, I use the term "collective TVEs." Unless otherwise noted, all data are from various annual issues of the *China Agricultural Statistical Yearbook*, *China Statistical Yearbook*, and *China Township Enterprise Statistical Yearbook*.

2 When the HRS was instituted in rural China between 1983 and 1984, the contract period was set at 15 years. In 1998, it was extended to another 30 years.
3 As early as the pre-reform era, rural collective industry (commune and brigade enterprises) had the rights to sell or purchase industrial equipment, though their rights regarding land were quite different.
4 One referee argues that the land shares of village residents are a meaningless kind of ownership. If one moves out of the village, he or she cannot cash in the ownership right. Indeed, the shareholders of collective land differ from the shareholders in a market economy when they have no right to sell land. However, it is hard to regard the use and income rights as meaningless ownership if the rights guarantee the shareholders' survival. In fact, this is just the reason why the purchase and sale of collective land are not allowed when most of China's population depends on land to survive.

References

Alchian, A.A. and Demsetz, H. (1973) "The Property Rights Paradigm." *Journal of Economic History*, 33(1): 16–27.

Bao Yongjiang (2000) *Chengjiaoxing xiangzheng qije de erci chuangye* (The secondary launch of the suburban-type township enterprises), Tianjin: Tianjin Renmin Chubanshe.

Byrd, William A. (1990) "Entrepreneurship, Capital, and Ownership." in W. Byrd and Q. Lin (eds) *China's Rural Industry: Structure, Development, and Reform*, Oxford: Oxford University Press, pp. 189–217,

Byrd, William A. and Lin, Q. (eds) (1990) *China's Rural Industry: Structure, Development, and Reform*, Oxford: Oxford University Press.

Che, J. and Qian, Y. (1998) "Insecure Property Rights and Government Ownership of Firms." *Quarterly Journal of Economics*, 113: 467–496.

China Agricultural Statistical Yearbook (1980–1998, annual) Beijing: China Agricultural Press.

China Statistical Yearbook (1981–1997, annual) Beijing: China Statistical Press.

China Township Enterprise Statistical Yearbook (1987–1998, annual) Beijing: China Agricultural Press.

Dang-zhibu [party branch of CCP] of Houji Village, Liangshan Township, Liangshan County, Shandong province (1985) "Tadan gaige, guangkai menglu, zonghe fazheng, gaohuo jingji" (Boldly reform, open all avenues to prosperity, synthetically develop and make economy brisk), in Chen Wenkui (ed.), *Zhonghua dadi shang de xuanli chunhua: xiangzheng qije wenji* (The gorgeous spring flowers on the broad land of China: a collection of TVE studies), Shandong: Shandong Renmin Chubanshe, pp. 283–290.

Du, Haiyan (1990) "Causes of rapid rural industrial development," in W. Byrd and Q. Lin (eds) *China's Rural Industry*, Oxford: Oxford University Press, pp. 47–62.

Du Ying (1997) "Xiangzeng qiye de zhengce huanjing, xingtai tezeng yu zhidu chuangxin" (The policy environment, features, and institutional innovation of TVEs), in Lin Qingsong and Du Ying (eds) *Zhongguo gongye gaige yu xiaolu* (China's industrial reform and efficiency), Yunnan: Yunnan Renmin Chubanshe, pp. 305–340.

Huang, Philip C.C. (1990) *The Peasant Family and Rural Development in the Yangzi Delta, 1350–1988*, Stanford:, CA Stanford Univ. Press.

Lewis, W. Arthur (1954) "Economic Development with Unlimited Supplies of Labour," *Manchester School*, 22(2): 139–191.

Lin, Nan (1995) "Local Market Socialism: Local Corporatism in Action in Rural China," *Theory and Society*, 24: 301–354.

Lin, Qingsong (1990) "Private Enterprises: Their Emergence, Rapid Growth, and Problems," in W. Byrd and Q. Lin (eds) *China's Rural Industry*, Oxford: Oxford University Press, pp. 172–188.

Naughton, Barry (1994) "Chinese Institutional Innovation and Privatization from Below," *American Economic Rev*, 84(2): 266–270.

Nee, Victor (1992) "Organizational Dynamics of Market Transition: Hybrid Forms, Property Rights, and Mixed Economy in China," *Administrative Science Quarterly*, 37: 1–27.

Oi, Jean C. (1992) "Fiscal Reform and the Economic Foundations of Local State Corporatism in China," *World Politics*, 45 (October): 99–126.

Pei, Xiaolin (1994) "Rural Population, Institutions, and China's Economic Transformation," *European Journal of Development Research*, 6(1): 175–196.

Pei, Xiaolin (1996) "Township-village Enterprises, Local Governments, and Rural Communities: the Chinese Village as a Firm During Economic Transition." *Economics of Transition*, 4(1): 43–66.

Pei, Xiaolin (1998) *The Institutional Root of China's Rural Industry and Gradual Reform*, Lund, Sweden: Lund University Press.

Pei, Xiaolin and Gunnarsson, Christer (1996) "Agrarian Structures, Property Rights, and Transition to Market Economy in China and the Former Soviet Union." in J. Hersh and J.D. Schmidt (eds) *The Aftermath of "Real Existing Socialism" in Eastern Europe*. Vol. 1, *Between Western Europe and East Asia*, London: Macmillan, pp. 247–268.

Ranis, Gustav and Fei, John C.H. (1961) "A Theory of Economic Development." *American Economic Rev*, 51: 533–565.

Selden, Mark and Lu, Aiguo (1993) "The Reform of Landownership and the Political Economy of Contemporary China." in Mark Selden, *The Political Economy of Chinese Development*. Armonk, NY: M.E. Sharpe, pp. 187–205.

Solow, Robert M. (1956) "A Contribution to the Theory of Economic Growth.", *Quarterly Journal of Economics*, 70: 65–94.

Umbeck, John R. (1981) *A Theory of Property Rights: With Application to the California Gold Rush*, Ames: Iowa State University Press.

Walder, Andrew G. (1995) "Local Governments as Industrial Firms: An Organizational Analysis of China's Transitional Economy." *American Journal of Sociology*, 101: 263–301.

Wang, Xiaolu (1990) "Capital Formation and Utilization." in W. Byrd and Q. Lin 9eds) *China's Rural Industry*, Oxford: Oxford University Press, pp. 222–242.

Weitzman, M. and Xu, C. (1994) "Chinese Township-village Enterprises as Vaguely Defined Cooperatives." *Journal of Comparative Economics*, 18: 121–145.

Zhou Qiren (1994) *Nongcun biange yu Zhongguo fazhan* (Rural reform and China's development), Hong Kong: Oxford University Press.

Part III

Rethinking property rights

Natural resources and gender

9 Property rights reform in pastoral areas

Dilemmas on the road to the household ranch*

Tony Banks

The introduction of the Household Responsibility System (HRS) in Chinese agriculture in the early 1980s re-established the household farm as the basic unit of production. Farm management decisions were largely devolved to the household level and households were entitled to residual income after their meeting of certain quota and tax obligations. The rapid growth of agricultural output and income in the immediate reform period has been widely attributed to improved production incentives under the HRS versus the commune system that it replaced (see e.g. Lin *et al.* 1996; Putterman 1993). Cropland tenure arrangements under the HRS have been characterized by the assignment of land use rights to individual households, but the ongoing collective ownership of land (with associated restrictions on transferability and alienability), and the periodic reallocation of land use rights in response to demographic changes and in accordance with the equal entitlement rule. The practice of periodic reallocations has continued despite it being incongruous with national policy (see the Introduction to this book).

Two general types of analyses of Chinese rural property rights can be distinguished. On the one hand, there is the conventional microeconomics approach that highlights some characteristics of contemporary Chinese cropland tenure, especially periodic reallocations, that may give rise to land tenure insecurity and related inefficiencies (Hu 1997; Li *et al.* 1998; Wen 1995). This approach is closely related to the private property paradigm that is critically discussed by Bromley in Chapter 1, and Ho in the Introduction, although its focus is on usufruct rather than ownership rights *per se.* The implication of this approach is that the further privatization of usufruct, if not land itself, is desirable. On the other hand, there are those who take a more institutional or new institutional economics approach (Dong 1996; Kung 2000; Liu *et al.* 1998). This approach questions whether the degree of land tenure insecurity is actually that high and, more fundamentally, places efficiency in the context of the broader social and economic environment, characterized by incomplete and imperfect markets and positive transaction costs. The implications of the institutional and new institutional perspectives are that the benefits of further privatization may be overstated and the opportunity costs, including the provision of social insurance via equal entitlement, overlooked. Those adhering to this approach emphasize the regional diversity and complexity of land tenure arrangements and partially explain this in terms of a process of decentralized institutional innovation that has enabled local interests and conditions to shape such arrangements.

This chapter attempts to extend the above land tenure debate to China's extensive rangelands, which account for some 40 per cent of its total territory. The conventional analysis of the Chinese rangeland tenure situation is that, prior to the implementation of rangeland policy, there was complete open access to rangelands and, consequently, a classic "tragedy of the commons" was in progress. The supposed Tragedy of the Commons has frequently been blamed for rangeland degradation problems in China (e.g. Ho 2001; Li and Duo 1995; Longworth 1990, 1993; NRC 1992; Tuoman 1993; Wang 1995; Yu *et al.*, 1996), which are widely perceived to be worsening.[1] On the basis of this prognosis, contemporary rangeland policy prescribes the partial privatization of pastures, with exclusive and long-term use rights to pasture being allocated to the household level. It is believed that this will give rangeland users the incentive to both stock rangeland within carrying capacity and invest in improvements.

The conventional view of Chinese rangeland tenure is contested both empirically and theoretically in this chapter. The empirical focus of this chapter is Xinjiang-Uygur Autonomous Region (hereafter Xinjiang) in western China. Xinjiang constitutes one-sixth of China's total area and has rangelands almost as large in size as those of Inner Mongolia and Tibet (Miller 2000; NRC 1992). Its pastoral population of 1.2 million is predominantly comprised of Muslim ethnic minority groups. Evidence is introduced that rangeland tenure in Xinjiang is neither completely open access, as implied by the descriptor "tragedy of the commons", nor, at the other end of the property rights continuum, the exclusive household tenure system that is enshrined in rangeland policy. This suggests that the extent of open access and the associated inefficiencies that it gives rise to may be less than what is commonly supposed. More fundamentally, given the resource, social and economic context, it is argued from a new institutional economics perspective that seemingly inefficient aspects of rangeland tenure may actually facilitate the realization of certain benefits, benefits that are missed in the conventional analysis and could represent "opportunity costs" of further rangeland privatization.

The remainder of this chapter is organized as follows. In the second section, a new institutional economics framework for understanding rural institutions is introduced and features of the economic, resource and social context that have a bearing on the relative "efficiency" of different tenure arrangements are identified. Key characteristics of pastoral tenure in Xinjiang Uygur Autonomous Region, identified from rapid tenure appraisals conducted by the author in 11 pastoral counties[2] in the region in 1998 and 2001, are then presented in the third section. These characteristics include group tenure and fuzzy boundaries, which are associated with inefficiencies in the conventional analysis. However, the case is put in the fourth section that group tenure and fuzzy boundaries facilitate certain benefits, namely, external exclusion; economies of size with respect to herd supervision; provision of social insurance; and the abatement of environmental risk. In the fifth section, the implications for future institutional change are discussed. Finally, a conclusion is drawn.

Land tenure institutions, efficiency and context

According to mainstream microeconomics, private property represents the most efficient type of land tenure institution because it embodies the efficiency-enhancing characteristics of completeness, exclusivity, transferability and enforceability[3] (Posner 1977; Randall 1975). However, underpinning this proposition are the assumptions of perfect information and zero transaction costs. Transaction costs are invariably associated with the acquisition of information about exchange and include search and information costs, bargaining and decision costs, and policing and enforcement costs (Eggertsson 1990). In the presence of imperfect information and positive transaction costs, the property rights associated with Pareto-optimality cannot be used as a benchmark for efficiency and it becomes more meaningful to gauge the "efficiency" of an institutional arrangement through comparing it with other, real alternatives to achieve the same objective (Demsetz 1969; Furubotn and Richter 1997).

Transaction cost considerations are at the core of the New Institutional Economics approach to land tenure. The transaction costs associated with a given land tenure system, and thus its relative costliness, are in part determined by the degree of completeness and perfection in land and complementary markets. Incomplete or imperfect markets, arising from the presence of positive transaction costs or state intervention, are common in developing rural areas, including those of China (Ellis 1993; Lin 1995; Nyberg and Rozelle 1999; Oi 1999). The land market in China is considerably incomplete and imperfect because of the prohibition on the private ownership of land, restrictions on the transferability of land use rights and high transaction costs. Complementary markets, including those for rural credit, labor and grain, are likewise characterized by considerable incompleteness and imperfections, owing to transaction costs and state intervention. Even in the absence of state intervention, these markets would remain to some degree incomplete and imperfect because of transaction costs.

Incomplete and imperfect markets have two implications for land tenure analysis. First, the hypothetical benefits of private property rights in land, including improved access to credit and efficiency-enhancing land transfers, are at best only partly realizable (Dong 1996). Second, given incomplete and imperfect markets, some institutional arrangements can be explained in terms of being substitutes for markets or acting as non-price controls (Ellis 1993; Hoff *et al.*, 1993). Thus, what appears to be a seemingly inefficient institutional arrangement can actually be a device to organize exchange in a transaction costs-saving manner (Furubotn and Richter 1997). This approach does not necessarily overlook the efficiency losses that are generated by existing institutional arrangements but takes the position that, given the broader economic environment, there may be net benefits associated with the status quo. The recent literature on rural property rights in China has emphasized the role that the land tenure system plays in the provision of social insurance, given the absence of either well-developed insurance markets or a comprehensive state welfare system (Dong 1996; Kung 2000; Liu *et al.* 1998). Collective ownership, coupled with the periodic reallocation of land in accordance with demographic changes, enables village collectives to ensure relatively equitable household access to land resources. Periodic reallocations have been found to be most frequent and comprehensive in those regions where off-farm work opportunities are limited and land relatively scarce, thus confirming their role in social insurance provision (Kung 2000; Liu *et al.* 1998).

The relative costliness of different institutional arrangements also depends on the characteristics of the natural resource. The resource characteristics of rangelands and cropland differ considerably. Rangelands are larger and more spatially dispersed than the case of cropland, and this can make it more costly to establish private exclusion. They also have lower productivity per unit of area and thus the potential benefits of private exclusion are less. Finally, rangelands in arid and semi-arid regions, including western China, are characterized by considerable variability in climate and thus the spatial and temporal distribution of forage (Behnke *et al.* 1993; Miller 2000; Scoones 1995). A common implication of the extensiveness, low productivity and variability of rangelands is that group tenure may be superior to exclusive individual household tenure. Group tenure is associated with a lower cost of exclusion than household tenure, because it reduces the total length of the boundaries to be monitored and enforced (Field 1989). Opportunistic grazing strategies, necessitated by the temporal and spatial variability in forage, are also better facilitated by group tenure arrangements and, in addition, fuzzy boundaries (Behnke *et al.* 1993; Scoones 1995). The potential environmental risk-abating function of land tenure will be particularly important in situations where other environmental-risk management mechanisms, such as fodder markets and access to credit, are lacking or poorly developed, as in the case of Tibet (Miller 2000). An additional and widely recognized benefit of group tenure in rangelands is that it facilitates the capturing of economies of size with respect to herd supervision (Baland and Platteau 1998) and at lower cost than that possible under an individualized tenure regime, in the absence of well-developed markets for grazing rights and herding labor.

When comparing the relative benefits and costs of different land tenure arrangements, the cost of internal governance in a group tenure situation also need to be considered (Baland and Platteau 1998; Field 1989). These are the costs associated with the negotiation, monitoring and enforcement of rules for the joint use of a resource. Collective action theory, reinforced by empirical studies of common property regimes, indicates that the difficulty and thus costs associated with the overcoming of the problem of collective action are related to group size and homogeneity (Baland and Platteau 1996; Field 1989; Ostrom 1990). The smaller the size of the group and the more homogeneous the group, in terms of mutual dependence on and shared interests in the resource, the lower the costs of internal governance. Social structure also has a bearing on the cost of collective action. Social structures that are characterized by a degree of closure of social networks and repeated and multiplex social relations are associated with a high rate of voluntary rule compliance and the presence of reputation mechanisms with bite (Coleman 1994). This in turn lowers the cost of collective action. Another typical characteristic of such communities is that they have low-cost mechanisms for the monitoring of rules and arbitration of disputes, including disputes over land rights (Baland and Platteau 1996; Ostrom 1990). Thus, the cost of internal governance is dependent on the size, homogeneity and social structure of the group and in some social contexts the cost of internal governance may be minimal.

Although the cost of internal governance has been emphasized in the conventional property rights literature, internal governance may have an advantage over the alternative of external regulation. Namely, endogenously evolved rules are more likely to be appropriate to the local resource, social and economic context than externally imposed ones, and this can enhance economic efficiency (Baland and Platteau 1996; Ostrom 1990). The external governance of rangeland use encounters two, often insurmountable, problems. First, the cost to a central agency of acquiring detailed resource knowledge and devising appropriate rules is high because of the diversity and complexity of rangeland ecologies. Second, the cost of externally monitoring and enforcing resource use rules is also high, given the disparate nature of rangeland resources. High costs coupled with the common phenomenon of under-resourced enforcement agencies, that are also prone to corrupt practices, can render effective centralized regulation impossible (Baland and Platteau 1996). Through the devolution of some authority regarding the derivation and monitoring and enforcement of rules to resource users, the cost of governance can be reduced and its efficacy improved (Swift 1995).

Finally, when comparing land tenure arrangements, it needs to be emphasized that there are governance costs associated with individual tenure, not just group tenure (Runge 1986). These transaction costs include social overhead investment in structures for the recording and administering of individual property rights, and the adjudication of disputes. Thus, not only are there various potential benefits arising from group tenure and fuzzy boundaries, but the cost of internal governance may be less than that of external regulation.

Institutional reform in pastoral Xinjiang

The decollectivization of the Xinjiang pastoral sector was initiated in 1983, with the contracting out of commune livestock, and completed by 1985, when the communes were formally de-established and livestock distributed in ownership to households, on the basis of household population and labor force. The marketing system for most livestock products was simultaneously liberalized and only wool marketing still remains under state monopoly control. Initially, when the communes were abolished, use rights to rangelands were informally allocated to small groups of households, which formed on a voluntary basis, and use rights to hayfields and cropland were allocated to individual households. Over 90 of the rangelands of Xinjiang are utilized on a seasonal basis (Zhang 1992) and when rangelands were distributed to groups in 1985, groups received a parcel in each of the major seasonal pastures. Summer pasture is located at high elevation in the Tian Shan and Altay Shan mountains, winter pasture in the desert basins and spring–autumn pasture in the hill country in between. The relatively high productivity of mountain pastures compels migration there during summer, while extreme climate forces a retreat to the desert basins over winter. The area of pasture allocated to the groups was roughly based on the total number of commune livestock that had been allocated to their constituent members, thus ensuring a degree of equitable land allocation. Boundaries were defined by natural landmarks or line-of-sight between natural landmarks, rock piles and posts.

A major step towards the introduction of a more formal framework for rangeland tenure in Xinjiang was the introduction of the Xinjiang Rangeland Law in 1989 and this has since been augmented by a number of regulations issued by the regional government.[4] Contemporary rangeland policy in Xinjiang provides for the continuation of collective or state ownership of grasslands[5] but the contracting out of use rights, with emphasis on the household as the basic unit of contract.[6] According to the Xinjiang Animal Husbandry Bureau (AHB), the contracting of rangeland to individual households is nearly completed, with some 94 percent of useable rangelands having been contracted to individual households by 1999. Yet the findings from the rapid appraisals that were conducted in the Tian Shan and Altay regions of Xinjiang reveal a considerable disjuncture between *de jure* and *de facto* tenure. Grassland use contracts have been issued to individual households and the contracts specify the area of different seasonal pastures that have been assigned to the households. However, the area specified is based on the number of commune livestock that were distributed to households in 1985 and often does not refer to an actual defined household pasture.[7] In practice, the issuance of grassland contracts has not usually resulted in the delineation of household boundaries in rangelands and the group tenure arrangements that were formed in 1985 have largely persisted.[8] Individual tenure has only been firmly established in hayfields and croplands.

Rangeland policy's emphasis on establishing exclusive individual use rights is also contradicted by the persistence of fuzzy boundaries. There has been virtually no fencing of group or household rangeland boundaries in Xinjiang and there is significant seasonal variation in the degree to which internal boundaries are monitored and enforced by pastoralists. In spring–autumn pasture, internal boundaries in pasture, whether group or household, are often not enforced at all and a form of internal open access prevails. In summer pasture, in contrast, there is some adherence to internal boundaries, particularly with respect to the herding of small livestock, and in winter pasture for small livestock internal boundaries are strictly enforced. External (village) boundaries are less fuzzy than internal ones, with communities generally enforcing both external exclusion and seasonal exclusion from their village pastures. Community leaders and pastoralists in the field enforce external (village) boundaries in pasture during their proper season of use, and station one or several households in major village pastures all year round to protect them from out-of-season encroachment. Movement times between different seasonal pastures are established by the local AHBs, to ensure inter-community coordination, and enforced by community leaders who are represented in the field.

Another point of disjuncture between *de jure* and *de facto* tenure relates to resource use regulation. Rangeland policy provides for the derivation of household stocking rates, their inclusion in grassland use contracts, and their monitoring and enforcement by local AHBs. However, stocking rates for household pastures either have not been derived or, where they have been, neither the local Animal Husbandry Bureau nor pastoral communities or groups make any effort to monitor and enforce them.[9] A final characteristic of regional rangeland policy is its emphasis on maintaining land tenure stability.[10] On this account, there has been essential congruency between policy and practice. Rangeland allocation at the village, pasture group and household levels has essentially remained the same since 1985 and rangelands have not been subject to the kind of periodic reallocations experienced in croplands.[11] More detailed descriptions of the pastoral and pastoral tenure situation in Xinjiang in general, and Altay prefecture in particular, are given in Banks (2001, 2003).

The tragedy of the commons reconsidered

The prevalence of group tenure and fuzzy boundaries, and the lack of enforced stocking rate controls, indicate the presence of a significant degree of open access in pastoral Xinjiang. Nevertheless, the *de facto* pastoral tenure situation lies somewhere between the complete open access situation that is commonly assumed to have existed before rangeland policy was implemented, and the individualized tenure system enshrined in policy. External and seasonal exclusion from village pastures is enforced and complete internal open access only prevails in spring–autumn pasture. However, at least a partial tragedy of the commons appears to be in progress, given the evidence that long-term rangeland degradation is occurring, particularly in spring–autumn pasture where tenure arrangements are least exclusive. Yet the relationship between exclusivity and rangeland degradation does not hold in the case of winter and summer pasture: tenure arrangements are more exclusive in winter pasture but degradation problems are also worse there. Knowledge gaps regarding rangeland ecology dynamics and the relative contribution of grazing versus other factors to rangeland degradation compound the problem of establishing a definitive link between tenure arrangements and rangeland degradation.[12]

Aside from rangeland degradation, the observed lack of investment in rangeland improvements could also be interpreted as an indicator of a tragedy of the commons. Pastoralists do not make any investment in the improvement of rangelands, where group tenure arrangements and fuzzy boundaries prevail, but they do invest in the improvement of hayfields and cropland, where individual household tenure prevails. However, as with the case of rangeland degradation, the lack of investment in improvement of rangelands may be less attributable to tenure than what is commonly implied. Arguing in the tradition of Schultz (1964), the lack of private investment may first and foremost reflect a lack of appropriate and financially viable investment opportunities. Although fencing is promoted and partially subsidized by the state, it is not sufficient to establish strict exclusion, given the problems of out-of-season encroachment, and nor does it necessarily save on herding labor, as both fencing materials and livestock are vulnerable to theft and thus still need to be actively monitored. The viability of fencing is further undermined by its considerable direct costs. Aerial sowing and pest eradication more definitely contribute to rangeland improvement but are inherently subject to problems of scale economies, externalities and coordination, and for this reason remain solely undertaken and funded by the state.

It is commonly implied that individual tenure induces households to invest in the conversion of natural pasture to artificial pasture.[13] Although the correlation between individual tenure and artificial pasture is irrefutable, the role of individual tenure in precipitating household investment in artificial pasture is more questionable. In northern Xinjiang, state investment in irrigation schemes usually precedes the implementation of household tenure and the establishment of artificial pasture. It should furthermore be noted that a large proportion of natural pasture is not suitable for conversion to artificial pasture, either because it cannot feasibly be irrigated or it is simply too remote from households' winter bases. Thus, the presence of rangeland degradation and the lack of household investment in rangeland improvement or conversion do not necessarily constitute evidence of an ongoing tragedy of the commons, even though they are often cited as such.

Contemporary institutional arrangements and economic advantage

A major deficiency of the conventional analysis is its lack of treatment of transaction cost considerations. This omission has three major repercussions. First, the cost of establishing individualized property is overlooked. Second, the benefits arising from the existing arrangements, or the opportunity costs of further exclusion, are ignored. Third, the lack of transaction cost considerations gives rise to undue pessimism regarding the possibility of successful collective action.

External exclusion

The costs of establishing individual household tenure in pastoral Xinjiang include social overhead and direct private costs. Social overhead costs include the costs associated with administering a detailed cadastral survey, establishing and maintaining a comprehensive land registration system, and the resolution of disputes through form adjudication channels. Characteristics of rangeland resources, including their extensiveness and spatial dispersion, not only exacerbate the cost of implementing a formal cadastral survey and land registration system but also pose problems for the private monitoring and enforcement of household boundaries. It will be recalled from the previous section that fencing is not sufficient to ensure exclusion. During the season in which a rangeland is in use, households could conceivably monitor and enforce their individual boundaries through direct observation in the field. However, the total length of the internal boundaries to be monitored and enforced is greater under an individual versus group tenure situation and, furthermore, there are economies of size to be captured in boundary monitoring and enforcement activities. These economies are realizable at least cost through group herding arrangements which, as it will be argued shortly, are facilitated by group tenure arrangements. There are also considerable economies of scale to be realized with respect to the protection of household pastures and hayfields from out-of-season encroachment. These economies are currently realized through community-based mechanisms, including the stationing of grassland protector households in pastures all-year round and community monitoring and enforcement of seasonal movement rules. Thus, exclusion can be less costly established in the case of group versus individual tenure, and even individual tenure will require community-based mechanisms to aid its enforcement.

Economies of size in herd supervision

Economies of size with respect to herd supervision exist because one herder household can typically supervise the livestock of three or four households. Economizing on the use of herding labor is imperative to households because their resource utilization patterns place considerable spatial demands on their labor.[14] Households realize economies of size with respect to herd supervision through forming group herding arrangements. A typical arrangement involves a small group of close kin pooling their small livestock into a single herd and young families or men in the group taking care of their supervision, whilst others in the group tend to the large livestock, cultivation and haymaking. Alternatively, some households are now contracting commercial herders to supervise their livestock. Because they are remunerated on a per livestock basis, commercial herders also have the incentive to reap economies of size through herding several households' livestock together.

It is postulated that, given the broader institutional environment, group tenure represents a low-cost mechanism for facilitating group herding arrangements and thus the reaping of economies of size with respect to herd supervision. Group herding arrangements imply joint use of pasture. In principle, joint use of pasture could be obtained under an individualized land tenure system, with households that have adjoining pastures combining them into one large, contiguous pasture. However, there are no obvious benefits from doing this, given that the intended outcome, *de facto* group tenure, exists anyway. Alternatively, group herding arrangements could conceivably operate without the formation of a contiguous pasture, as group livestock could be rotated through individual member's pastures even if they were not adjoining. In practice, however, such an arrangement would entail frequent transition across non-members' pasture and present the additional challenge of monitoring and enforcing the boundaries of parcels within the same seasonal pasture that were not being used at any given moment in time. A change in the institutional environment in favor of making use rights freely transferable between rangeland users could help to mitigate the difficulties of an individual tenure – joint operation system. However, aside from being outside the realm of current political possibility, a market for rangeland use rights would invariably have high transaction costs. The observation that group herding arrangements are almost always exclusive to members of the same pasture group provides evidence of the essential complementarities between group tenure and herding arrangements.

Social insurance

The pastoral tenure system, as with the cropland tenure system, plays a role in the provision of social insurance. Pastoral regions share in common with arable regions deficiencies in markets and an absence of state social welfare. Furthermore, given that pastoral regions are characterized by a relatively low incidence of off-farm work opportunities, it can be expected from the Chinese cropland tenure literature that equal access to land constitutes an important form of social insurance in these regions (Kung 2000; Liu *et al.* 1998). The pastoral land tenure system has been found to facilitate equal access to resources in several different ways. First, group tenure is coupled with rules that grant new households the right to use their parent's pasture and migrant households the right to reuse their former group's pasture should they return.

This raises the puzzle as to why group tenure provides social insurance in the pastoral context but another land tenure mechanism, the periodic reallocation of household use rights, provides social insurance in the arable context. Because of the differences in rangeland and cropland resource characteristics, the periodic reallocations of rangelands would be a much more complex process than that of croplands. Periodic reallocations in croplands are aided by the existing fragmentation of household holdings into numerous plots, each with clearly defined physical boundaries, and the lack of any obvious need for those plots to be contiguous (with the exception, possibly, of reaping economies of size with respect to mechanical technologies). In the case of rangelands, however, it is imperative for a household's holdings in any single seasonal pasture to be kept contiguous, or else problems regarding the realization of economies of size with respect to herding labor, monitoring and enforcement of boundaries and transit rights would be exacerbated. Furthermore, in contrast to croplands, the periodic reallocations of rangelands would necessitate the periodic delineation of new line-of-sight boundaries, which could be a contentious and exhaustive task. Finally, given that the boundaries in rangelands are only fuzzily observed in the first place, the making of continuous changes to them at the margins could become a rather meaningless exercise. Group tenure, in short, constitutes a more feasible way to ensure access to pasture, and thus the provision of social insurance, than the periodic reallocation of individual holdings.

Fuzzy boundaries also facilitate the realization of the political and social objective of ensuring equal access. Internal boundaries are at their fuzziest in spring–autumn pasture, where *de facto* internal open access prevails. The distribution of pastoral resources in spring–autumn pasture is particularly patchy and this renders the task of ensuring an equitable distribution of rangeland to groups, let alone individual households, very difficult. Another unique resource characteristic of spring–autumn pasture is the spatial concentration of water resources in just a few streams and/or spring ponds. This contrasts with the case of other pastures, where water resources are much more evenly dispersed: in summer pasture, by the numerous mountain streams and in winter pasture, by snowfall. Stock routes could conceivably be delineated but they would have to be numerous in order to connect with all the groups' pastures and the process of delineation would be complex. Internal open access represents the lowest-cost and less contentious method for ensuring equitable access to water, as well as patchy forage, in spring–autumn pasture.

Fuzzy boundaries also serve another purpose that is related to guaranteed household access to pasture and thus the provision of social insurance. An informal rule allows pastoralists to herd their livestock over the pasture of another group or community for transit purposes and this in turn enables them to access their dispersed seasonal pastures. Gaining access to pasture would not otherwise be an insurmountable problem, as stock routes between seasonal pastures could, and to some extent already have, been delineated. Yet having to keep to formal stock routes would significantly prolong movements for some households. Given the location of spring–autumn pasture in the transition zone between summer and winter pasture, the need for mobility across spring–autumn pasture is particularly important and this constitutes another reason for the high degree of open access observed in this pasture.

While pastoral tenure facilitates equal access to land, equal access does not necessarily translate into equal appropriation. Household appropriation is a function of household herd size and, given the considerable disparities in household herd size that have developed since 1985,[15] some households are appropriating significantly more forage than others from jointly used pasture. Thus, although equal access potentially provides social insurance by guaranteeing households minimal access to forage, households' capacity to claim such insurance is also contingent on them having significant livestock to support a basic livelihood.

Environmental risk abatement

As has been generally proposed by others (Behnke *et al.* 1993; Miller 2000; Scoones 1995), flexibility in land tenure arrangements has been found to help mitigate environmental risk in Xinjiang. During severe winters, characterized by blizzards and heavy snowfall, households that normally graze small livestock on the southern flanks of hill pastures sometimes temporarily reallocate to winter pasture in the desert basin, with pasture boundaries in winter pasture being temporarily redefined in order to accommodate the new arrivals. Within spring–autumn pasture, where pastoral resources are relatively patchy and temporally variable, the practice of internal open access helps to ensure that environmental risk is distributed across the whole community. More evidence of land tenure flexibility enabling the management of environmental risk is provided in the form of local governments and community leaders slightly varying movement times between seasonal pastures in accordance with climatic conditions.

Nevertheless, the potential for land tenure flexibility to help abate environmental risk is limited because of the high covariance of such risks over feasible migratory zones.[16] This leads to the observed tendency for communities and groups to become, if anything, even more protective of rangeland boundaries when adverse climatic events induce forage scarcity. Finally, households have at their disposal mechanisms other than land tenure flexibility to help them cope with environmental risk, including the pre-emptive sale of livestock and the purchase of feed, which is supplied by local government on a partially subsidized and credit basis.

The costs of governance

The group tenure arrangements found in Xinjiang are largely based on pre-socialist social formations and have certain characteristics that are conducive to low-cost and thus successful collective action. Pasture groups are relatively small in size, typically comprising of several to one dozen households, and are homogeneous in terms of ethnicity. Furthermore, given the general lack of alternative livelihood opportunities in pastoral areas and pastoralists' lack of participation in non-pastoral uses of rangeland resources, the groups are homogeneous in terms of their mutual dependence on and interest in pastoral resources. Being based on pre-existing kinship structures, the groups have natural authority structures, and group members also have repeated and multiplex relations (Hudson 1938; Tsui 1996). All of these characteristics are conducive to the accumulation of social capital and the overcoming of first- and second-order collective action dilemmas. Group characteristics, furthermore, can be somewhat generalized to the community level. Evidence of successful collective action at this level exists in the form of relatively effective mechanisms for external and seasonal exclusion and the arbitration of disputes. Communities can quite conceivably undertake these tasks at lower cost than the alternative of external regulation, because of the disparate nature and seasonal use of rangeland resources.

Given the presence of characteristics conducive to successful collective action, and evidence of successful collective action in some spheres, the collective inaction of communities and pasture groups with respect to the regulation of stocking rates represents a puzzle. This puzzle cannot be explained through recourse to new range ecology, as the natural check on livestock numbers that environmental adversities and the winter feed constraint may play are moderated in the Xinjiang context by the availability of external feed inputs. In addition, the scientific evidence that is available indicates that long-term rangeland degradation is occurring in spring–autumn pasture and that overstocking is a contributory factor.[17] This signifies the need for some form of regulation of stocking rates, particularly in spring–autumn pasture. It could be argued that the presence of fuzzy boundaries potentially complicates the problem of collective action by transforming it into a multi-tier problem. Not only households, but groups and communities as well, need assurance that if they follow stocking rate constraints, others will follow suit. Yet, as is exemplified by the government's derivation of seasonal movement rules and communities' monitoring and enforcement of these rules, a co-management approach can facilitate the resolution of multi-tier collective action problems.

The lack of community action with respect to stocking rate regulation is instead due to the lack of space for such action allowed for by the state. The limitations of the current centralized state approach to the derivation and monitoring and enforcement of stocking rates are evident. Pastoralists widely perceive the government's fixed stocking rate approach to be inappropriate, given the high degree of inter-annual variability in rangeland productivity. Furthermore, because of the disparate nature and seasonal utilization of rangelands, the task of externally monitoring and enforcing household stocking rates is costly and certainly beyond the limited resources that the designated agency has at its disposal.[18] Given that the transaction costs associated with external regulation are prohibitive, a co-management approach to the derivation and monitoring and enforcement of resource use rules constitutes a more feasible alternative.

Implications for institutional evolution

The conventional and new institutional analyses above respectively highlight some of the potential efficiency costs and benefits associated with contemporary *de facto* pastoral tenure in Xinjiang. On the one hand, there is a partial tragedy of the commons occurring because of the presence of fuzzy boundaries and group tenure arrangements without internal regulation mechanisms. On the other, the NIE analysis has highlighted some of the potential benefits associated with group tenure and fuzzy boundaries, given the broader economic, resource and social context. These findings may be generalized to Tibet Autonomous Region, where rangelands have also been allocated to groups, boundaries in rangelands are fuzzy and the state does not attempt to monitor and enforce household stocking rates, even if they have been derived (Goldstein and Beall 1991; Miller 2000). There is also evidence of over-stocking causing rangeland degradation in parts of Tibet (Miller 2000).

From a conventional property rights perspective, it can be expected that the pastoral tenure cost–benefit nexus in Xinjiang and Tibet will change in favor of greater exclusivity over time. Efficiency losses in the form of rangeland degradation will continue, if not worsen, under the existing pastoral tenure regime. The use of fencing to establish strict exclusion will become more feasible over time, as social acceptance of it increases and its cost declines relative to the rising opportunity cost of herding labor. Fencing cannot completely substitute for herding labor, but to the extent that scale economies in herd supervision are still present, the development of markets for grazing rights and herding labor could enable their capturing under an individualized tenure system. Thus, the need to capture economies of scale in herd supervision will not indefinitely constitute a rationale for group tenure. The social insurance role that group tenure plays is likewise likely to decline in importance in the future, as population growth stabilizes, off-farm employment opportunities increase and, possibly, a more comprehensive state welfare system evolves. The land tenure system currently only plays a secondary role in the mitigation of environmental risk and, with increased household fodder production as well as improvement in markets for grazing rights, credit and feed, this role will further diminish in importance in the future. Finally, applying collective action theory, it can be expected that further market integration will erode the conditions necessary for collective action and increase the cost of internal governance, thus reinforcing the shift in the cost–benefit nexus in favor of individualized tenure.

The major implication of the conventional analysis, and the goal of national rangeland policy, are the creation in due course of the household ranch. Recent developments in select parts of western China outside of Tibet and Xinjiang represent the materialization of the type of land tenure transitions envisaged in national rangeland policy.[19] Winter pastures and winter–spring household pastures have been extensively fenced in some areas and there is a high expectation among local officials and pastoralists that summer household pastures are about to be fenced too. Stocking rates for household pastures have been included in grassland use certificates and pastoralists have been warned that they will need to adhere to them within a set time frame, after which township officials and village committee members are planning to jointly enforce them. If coupled with the careful monitoring of rangeland conditions, such areas can serve as a test bed for contemporary rangeland policy.

Although the above transitions are closely based on national rangeland policy, alternative pathways have been followed in some areas (Banks *et al.* 2003; Banks and Sheehy 2000). In Maqu County of Gansu Province, for example, household boundaries in winter pasture have been delineated but groups of households have pooled their pastures together and fenced their outer boundary. The benefits of fencing group versus individual household boundaries, as construed by the pastoralists themselves, lend further support to some of the propositions made earlier in this chapter. The perceived benefits include lower fencing costs and the realization of economies of size with respect to herd supervision, as households take turns at supplying labor for supervision of the joint herd. The group tenure arrangement also facilitates the provision of social insurance. Reflecting the ongoing emphasis of policy on equitable distribution, the area of rangeland allocated to households remains based on their 1985 livestock number. However, as household herd sizes are now considerably differentiated, there is a mismatch between the size of household herds and the rangelands allocated to them. Under the Maqu County pilot program, the total number of stock units that can be grazed on the joint pasture and each household's share of this are calculated. Households that graze fewer livestock than the hypothetical carrying capacities of their portions of the joint pasture are compensated by those households that graze more. Poor households are thus guaranteed access to forage equivalent to that produced by their pasture if they need it, and can earn supplementary income in the form of grazing fees to the extent that they do not.

A new institutional economics approach would explain variations in the pace and direction of pastoral tenure change in western China in terms of variations in underlying environmental, economic and social conditions. The slow pace of pastoral tenure change in Xinjiang and Tibet, for example, could be explainable in terms of a combination of their relatively higher environmental variation, greater dependence on pastoralism, poor market integration and more intact traditional social structures tipping the cost–benefit nexus in favor of a continuation of group tenure and fuzzy boundaries. Yet the political dimension is also important, given that institutional change in the Chinese countryside has been directed as well as induced (Liu *et al.* 1998). In Xinjiang and Tibet, not only does the strict implementation of rangeland policy not rank high in terms of regional government priorities, but it is also perceived to be potentially conflicting with more pressing policy priorities, namely ethnic/social stability and economic development. The strict implementation of rangeland policy could undermine ethnic and social stability, through alienating pastoral groups and exacerbating land right disputes. Furthermore, it is widely perceived by government officials that the implementation and strict enforcement of stocking rate controls would have an adverse impact on pastoral incomes and would counter poverty alleviation efforts, at least in the short to medium term. Thus, the regional governments of Tibet and Xinjiang have created political space for rangeland policy to be heavily mediated at the local level. In contrast, in other regions where the ethnic issue in particular is not so sensitive, governments have been less reticent to pursue the strict implementation of national rangeland policy.

The case of pastoral tenure change in Maqu County embodies elements of both directed and induced institutional change. The change was precipitated and facilitated by external agents but, through the piloting and participatory nature of the process, resource users have been able to ensure that the new arrangements are suited to local conditions. A co-management approach has also been taken with respect to the ongoing monitoring and enforcement of the new rules, and the measurement of their biophysical impacts. The result is a new regime that improves on the old by enabling stricter exclusion and appropriate internal regulation. At the same time the potential benefits of group tenure, including the facilitation of economies of size with respect to herd supervision and the provision of social insurance, are still realizable. Thus, the Maqu pastoral tenure model represents an alternative to the continuation of the status quo or the strict implementation of the yet unproven household ranch system, and cannot necessarily be assumed to be a stopover on a linear path between the two. Similarly, the co-management process underpinning the model represents an important alternative to either sole reliance on local level collective action or state action. Reliance solely on local collective action may not result in improved institutions, even if the state created space for it, given the limitations of local knowledge and the presence of the second-order collective action dilemma, or the problem of institutional supply. Likewise, unilateral state action will also not necessarily lead to improved institutional arrangements, given the informational problems associated with the centralized derivation of appropriate arrangements, coupled with the problems associated with their external monitoring and enforcement.

Conclusion

The aim of this chapter has been to extend the debate on rural property rights in China to its extensive pastoral sector. Land tenure institutions in rangelands and croplands have been found to share in common collective ownership but little else. The distinguishing features of rangeland tenure include group arrangements, fuzzy boundaries, and relatively stable land allocation. While the collective ownership of rangelands and croplands, and associated restrictions on transferability and alienability, give rise to common efficiency concerns, the land tenure differences between them give rise to divergent efficiency concerns as well. The joint use of land and fuzzy boundaries are the major potential sources of inefficiencies in the case of rangeland tenure, whereas the periodic reallocations of land have constituted the focus of the efficiency debate with respect to croplands. In the same way that the cropland tenure debate has proceeded, it has been argued in this chapter that the efficiency losses attributed to rangeland tenure are overstated and the direct and opportunity costs associated with further privatization are understated. Differences between rangeland and cropland tenure are ultimately attributable to differences in resource characteristics, with rangelands being more extensive, less productive and more variable than cropland. Evidence of the paramount role of resource characteristics is provided by the observation that pastoral households that both graze livestock on extensive rangelands and cultivate fodder crops do so under two different tenure regimes.

It has been argued in this chapter that the unique resource characteristics of rangelands give rise to unique transaction cost considerations that in turn largely account for the type of pastoral tenure institutions observed. Group tenure and fuzzy boundaries facilitate, at relatively low cost, external exclusion, the realization of economies of size with respect to herd supervision, the abatement of environmental risk, and the provision of social insurance via equal access. The latter is also a benefit associated with the cropland tenure system. However, equal access is provided through different tenure mechanisms in the different resource contexts: in grasslands via group tenure and fuzzy boundaries, and in croplands via periodic reallocations. This reaffirms the crucial role that nature resource endowments have in explaining the diversity of property rights in rural China.

Kung's (2000) statement that a "uniform system of land tenure in rural China is unlikely to be successful given its immense diversity" becomes an understatement when rangelands are explicitly considered. Although future changes in underlying social and economic conditions may tilt the cost–benefit nexus in the direction of greater exclusion, the resource characteristics of rangelands are essentially immutable and thus it cannot be assumed that a convergence of rangeland tenure with cropland tenure will eventually be induced. Nor can it be assumed that the cropland tenure system necessarily constitutes a template for improved rangeland management. The major implication for the role of the state is that an innovative and decentralized approach to pastoral tenure change, focused on system improvement versus system transformation, is likely to be less risky and more effective than directed institutional innovation based upon contemporary rangeland policy.

This conclusion reaffirms the three principles distilled by Bromley, albeit at a more micro level, in his analysis of international transition experience: do no serious harm; incentives matter; and focus on transitional strategies versus tactics. The likelihood of doing serious social or environmental harm through a process of incremental and participatory pastoral tenure improvement is low relative to the alternative of imposing (or attempting to impose) private pastoral tenure. Evidence of the social and environmental harm that the latter can do is provided by the case of Inner Mongolia (Williams 2002), where directed innovation based on rangeland policy has been pursued with more vigor than in the case of Xinjiang and the Tibetan plateau region. With respect to incentives mattering, contemporary problems related to rangeland management are less to do with the ownership structure of rangeland *per se*, and more to do with the "working rules" that govern their use. In parts of contemporary China, the collective *ownership* of rangelands, and even the collective *use* of rangelands, is proving viable in terms of efficiency, equity and environmental outcomes (Banks *et al.* 2003). The final principle of Bromley, the need to focus on transitional strategies versus tactics, is also reflected in the argument of this chapter. A long-term view of institutional change, one that gives due cognizance to the role of path dependency and culture, is necessary, rather than the simple imposition of pre-ordained designs from alien contexts. Related to this, the process of institutional improvement needs to involve learning-by-doing at the local level. Although Bromley's principles are presented as "lessons for China" in the context of institutional change in parts of rangeland China they could be deservedly described as "lessons from China" as well.

Notes

* Adapted from *World Development*, Vol. 31, Banks, Property Rights Reform in Rangeland China: Dilemmas on the Road to the Household Ranch, pp. 2129–2142, Copyright (2003), with permission from Elsevier.

1 According to official sources, some 90 percent of China's rangelands are degraded to some degree, including 42 percent moderately to seriously (SDPC 1996; SEPA 1998).

2 The pastoral counties where rapid tenure appraisals were conducted were: Altay and Buerqin (Altay Prefecture); Bole and Wenquan (Bertala Prefecture); Ermin and Wusu (Tacheng Prefecture); and Huocheng, Zhaosu, Cabucaer, Tekeshi and Gongliu (Yili Prefecture). All of these are located in northern Xinjiang, where its extensive rangelands and mobile pastoralists (principally Kazaks and Mongolians) are also concentrated.

3 Exclusivity ensures that users have the incentive to invest in land improvements and adoptable sustainable land management practices. Transferability provides owners with access to credit, since land constitutes an important form of collateral in developing rural areas, and also facilitates the gravitation of resources to the most dynamic agents and their highest-value use. Completeness and enforceability imply that property rights are well specified and enforced.

4 The two significant Xinjiang Government regulations issued since 1989 are the "Regulation on the Collection and Use of Grassland Management Fees in Xinjiang Uygur Autonomous Region" (Regulation No. 247, 1992) and "Regulation on the Grassland Contract in Xinjiang Uygur Autonomous Region" (Regulation No. 88, June 1996). These are based on national regulations issued by the Grassland Division of the Ministry of Agriculture.

5 Xinjiang Rangeland Law, Article 8.

6 Xinjiang Rangeland Law; Xinjiang Regulation No. 88 (June 1996), Article 5; Xinjiang AHB Document No. 9 (March 1994).

7 The underlying purpose for the specification of the area of different seasonal household pastures appears to be tax related. As grassland use fees vary according to different types of seasonal pastures and apply on a per *mu* basis, the area of each seasonal pasture needs to be known before the total grassland use fees payable by the household can be calculated.

8 In two pastoral villages in Buerqin County, for example, some 6 percent and 36 percent of the original groups formed in 1985 had subdivided by 1998. However, the average size of the groups in both villages increased over the same period, due to population growth (see Banks 2001).

9 In Yili Prefecture stocking rates have yet to be derived; in Altay Prefecture they have yet to be enforced.

10 Policy first prescribed that the term of use rights was "a long time" (Xinjiang Rangeland Law, Articles 9 and 35), before a 30-year term was introduced in 1993 and this was subsequently amended to 50 years in 1996 (Xinjiang Regulation No. 88, Article 4). Furthermore, use rights are inheritable.

11 Circumstances under which boundaries have been modified include when land reclamation projects have diminished the size of pastoral villages' rangeland endowments, and some pasture groups have elected to subdivide their pastures, though usually not down to the individual household level.

12 Other causes of rangeland degradation including rodents, pests and the use of pasture (in the past) for cropping (Tuoman 1993).

13 'Artificial pasture' is Chinese terminology for perennial grass species, such as alfalfa.

14 In Altay Prefecture pastoral households' large and small livestock are grazed in distant pastures for between three to seven and a half months a year. In addition, during summer when all livestock are being grazed together in alpine pasture, households must make provision for the cultivation of crops over spring and summer, or the cutting of hay in summer, at their winter bases over 100 kilometres away.

15 In Altay Prefecture household herd sizes averaged about 141 livestock (June 1997 AHB data) but 28% of households had less than 50 livestock and 10% over 300, and some households had over 800 livestock (June 1998 AHB data).

16 Altay Prefecture's winter of 2000–01, its worst in 50 years, adversely affected rangelands throughout the prefecture. The prefectures of Bertala, Tacheng and Yili experienced low snowfall during the same winter and a dry spring in 2001, and this likewise adversely impacted on the rangelands throughout these prefectures.

17 That the effects of growing livestock populations has first materialized in spring–autumn pasture is in part due to the double-use of this pasture in the seasonal migratory cycle (Tuoman, 1993).

18 The Grassland Supervision section of the Xinjiang AHB, tasked with the monitoring and enforcement of stocking rates has a total of 2050 employees based in 470 locations at the regional, prefecture, county and township levels. The thinness of spread this represents on the ground is illustrated by the case of Buerqin County, in Altay Prefecture, which has some 3,100 pastoral households and 500,000 livestock, utilizing a total of about 670,000 hectares of grassland. The total number of county AHB staff amounts to 36, most of whom are assigned to grassland research and extension duties, and the agency only has three jeeps at its disposal.

19 Based on rapid tenure appraisal conducted in Sunan County, Gansu Province, by the author in May 2001, and Miller (2000).

References

Baland, J.-M. and Platteau, J.-P. (1996) *Halting Degradation of Natural Resources: Is There a Role for Rural Communities?* Oxford: FAO and Clarendon Press.

Baland, J.-M. and Platteau, J.-P. (1998) "Division of the Commons: A Partial Assessment of the New Institutional Economics of Land Rights," *American Journal of Agricultural Economics*, 80: 644–650.

Banks, T.J. (2001) "Property Rights and the Environment in Pastoral Xinjiang: Evidence from the Field," *Development and Change*, 32: 703–726.

Banks, T.J. (2003) "Pastoral Commons in Western China: A New Institutional Economics Perspective," PhD dissertation, Brighton: University of Sussex

Banks, T.J. and Sheehy, D. (2000) "Grassland Study," unpublished report for the World Bank Gansu and Xinjiang Pastoral Development Project.

Banks, T.J., Richard, C., Li, P. and Yan, Z. (2003) "Community-based Grassland

Management in Western China: Rationale, Pilot Project Experience, and Policy Implications," *Mountain Research and Development*, 23(2): 132–140.

Behnke, R.H., Scoones, I. and Kerven, C. (1993) *Rangeland Ecology at Disequilibrium: New Models of Natural Variability and Pastoral Adaptation in African Savannas*, London: Overseas Development Institute.

Coleman, J.S. (1994) "A Rational Choice Perspective on Economic Sociology," in: N.J. Smelser and R. Swedberg (eds) *The Handbook of Economic Sociology*, (Princeton, NJ: Princeton University Press, pp. 166–180.

Demsetz, H. (1969) "Information and Efficiency: Another Viewpoint," *Journal of Law and Economics*, 12: 1–22.

Dong, X.-Y. (1996) "Two-tier Land Tenure System and sUstained Economic Growth in Post-1978 China," *World Development*, 24(5): 915–928.

Eggertsson, T. (1990) *Economic Behaviour and Institutions*, Cambridge: Cambridge University Press.

Ellis, F. (1993) *Peasant Economics: Farm Households and Agrarian Development* 2nd edn, Cambridge, NY: Cambridge University Press.

Field, B.C. (1989) "The Evolution of Property Rights," *KYKLOS*, 42(3): 319–345.

Furubotn, E. and Richter, R. (1997) *Institutions and Economic Theory: The Contribution of New Institutional Economics.*, Ann Arbor, MI: University of Michigan Press.

Goldstein, M.C. and Beall, C.M. (1991) "Change and Continuity in Nomadic Pastoralism on the Western Tibetan Plateau," *Nomadic Peoples*, 28: 105–122.

Ho, P. (2001) "Rangeland Degradation in China Revisited?" *Journal of Development Studies*, 37(3): 99–132.

Hoff, K., Braverman, A. and Stiglitz, J.E. (eds) (1993) *The Economics of Rural Organisation: Theory, Policy and Practice*, New York: Oxford University Press.

Hu, W. (1997) "Household Land Tenure Reform in China: its Impact on Farming Land Use and Agro-environment," *Land Use Policy*, 14(3): 175–186.

Hudson, A.E. (1938) *Kazakh Social Structure*, New Haven, CT: Yale University Press.

Kung, J.K. (2000). "Common Property Rights and Land Reallocations in Rural China: Evidence from a Village Survey," *World Development*, 28(4): 701–719.

Li, G. and Duo, L.K. (1995) "Qiantan caoyuan youchang chengbao shiyong (Preliminary survey of the grassland payment contract)," *Xinjiang Xumuye* (Xinjiang Animal Husbandry Journal), 2: 36–37.

Li, G., Rozelle, S. and Brandt, L. (1998) "Tenure, land rights, and Farmer Investment Incentives in China," *Agricultural Economics*, 19: 63–71.

Lin, J., Cai, F. and Li, Z. (1996) *The China Miracle: Development Strategy and Economic Reform*, Hong Kong: Chinese University Press.

Lin, J.Y. (1995) 'Endowments, Technology, and fActor Markets: A Natural Experiment of Induced Institutional Innovation from China's Rural Reform," *American Journal of Agricultural Economics*, 77: 231–242.

Liu, S., Carter, M. R. and Yao, Y. (1998) "Dimensions and Diversity of Property Rights in Rural China: Dilemmas on the Road to Further Reform," *World Development*, 26(10): 1789–1806.

Longworth, J.W. (ed.) (1990) *The Wool Industry in China: Some Chinese Perspectives*, Mount Waverley: Inkata Press.

Longworth, J.W. (1993) *China's Pastoral Region: Sheep and Wool, Minority Nationalities, Rangeland Degradation and Sustainable Development*, Wallingford: CAB International.

Miller, D. (2000) "Tough Times for Tibetan Nomads in Western China: Snowstorms,

Settling Down, Fences and the Demise of Traditional Nomadic Pastoralism," *Nomadic Peoples*, NS4(1): 83–109.

National Research Council (NRC) (ed.) (1992) *Grasslands and Grassland Sciences in Northern China*, Washington, DC: National Academy Press.

Nyberg, A. and Rozelle, S. (1999) *Accelerating China's Rural Transformation*, Washington DC: World Bank.

Oi, J.C. (1999) "Two Decades of Rural Reform in China: An Overview and Assessment," *The China Quarterly*, 159: 617–628.

Ostrom, E. (1990) *Governing the Commons: The Evolution of Institutions for Collective Action*, Cambridge: Cambridge University Press.

Posner, R.A. (1977) *Economic Analysis of Law*, Boston: Little Brown.

Putterman, P. (1993) *Continuity and Change in China's Rural Development: Collective and Reform Eras in Perspective*, New York: Oxford University Press.

Randall, A. (1975) *Resource economics*, New York: Wiley.

Runge, C.F. (1986) "Common Property and Collective Action in Economic Development," *World Development*, 14(5): 623–635.

Scoones, I. (ed.) (1995) *Living with Uncertainty: New Directions in Pastoral Development in Africa*, London: Intermediate Technology Publications.

Schultz, T.P. (1964) *Transforming Traditional Agriculture*, New Haven, CT: Yale University Press.

State Development Planning Commission (SDPC) (1996) *Report on the Population, Resources and Environment of China*, Beijing: China Environmental Sciences Press.

State Environmental Protection Agency (SEPA) (1998) *China Ecological and Environmental Situation Report 1998*, Beijing.

Swift, J. (1995) "Dynamic Ecological Systems and the Administration of Pastoral Development," in: I. Scoones (ed.) *Living with Uncertainty: New Directions in Pastoral Development in Africa*, London: Intermediate Technology Publications, pp. 153–173.

Tsui, Y. (1996) "The Development of Social Organisations in the Pastoral Areas of Northern Xinjiang and Their Relationship with the Environment," in: C. Humphrey and D. Sneath (eds) *Culture and Environment in Asia: 2*, (Cambridge: White Horse Press, pp. 205–230.

Tuo, M. (1993) "Xinjiang caodi xianzhuang, tuihua yuanyin ji qi fangzhi duice (The current state of the grasslands, causes of degradation and countermeasures in Xinjiang)," *Xinjiang Xumuye* (Xinjiang Animal Husbandry Journal), 2: 28–33.

Wang, R. (1995) "Shixing caodi youchang cheng bao shi yong zhi jiagiang caodi ziyuan guanli yu jianshe (The practice of grassland tenureship to strengthen management and construction of grassland resources)" *Zhongguo Caodi* (Grasslands of China), 1: 59–63.

Wen, G.J. (1995) "The Land Tenure System and its Saving and Investment Mechanism: The Case of Modern China," *Asian Economic Journal*, 9(31): 233–259.

Williams, D.M. (2002) *Beyond Great Walls: Environment, Identity and Development of the Chinese Grasslands of Inner Mongolia*, Stanford, CA: Stanford University Press.

Yu, Z., Sun, L., Yu, Z., Chang, F. and Ba, T. (1996) "Zhong guo caodi chanquan zhidu chubu yanjiu (A preliminary study on the grassland property right system of China)," *Zhongguo Caodi* (Grasslands of China), 4: 47–51.

Zhang, X. (1992) "Xinjiang," in National Research Council (ed.) *Grasslands and Grassland Sciences in Northern China*, Washington, DC: National Academy Press, pp. 109–120.

10 Collective forests and forestland

Physical asset rights versus economic rights

Yaoqi Zhang and Shashi Kant

The critical role of land in human existence has been widely recognized for time immemorial, and that is why in some cultures, specifically Aboriginal culture, land is known as the mother of human existence. Historically, probably due to such importance of land, land reforms have been integral parts of all the world-wide revolutions, including the cultural revolution and the recent reforms in China. In this book, all the previous chapters have focused on land reforms in the agriculture sector of China. However, in the modern era, forest resources have become as important, if not more, as agriculture, and analyses of land reforms of any country without including forestland reforms will be incomplete.

During the 1990s, many global issues associated with forests such as the decline of biological diversity, deforestation and forest degradation, the fate of forest people, climate change, and desertification have dominated the public and political debates at international as well as national levels. China has played a major role in these debates, as well as in the development of new policies and programs to address these issues. China is uniquely placed on many dimensions of the forestry sector and, hence, experiences from the Chinese forestry sector might have important international implications.

China's forestry sector features four critical dimensions. First, in terms of the share of the total global forest area, China belongs to the top five countries (with Russia, Brazil, Canada, and the United States) (FAO 1997). However, in terms of proportional forest cover (percentage of the total land area) China is among the countries which have lowest cover, and the North and Northwest China have the lowest forest cover within China. Second, China is the second largest roundwood producer (only after the United States) and the second largest fuelwood and charcoal producer (only after India) (FAO 1998). Third, China accounts for one of the world's largest reserves in biodiversity, and the variety of wild plants and animals is greater than that of North America and Europe, equaling one-eighth of all species on the earth (Raun 1995; Harkness 1998). Fourth, China has faced remarkable damages due to forest destruction and deforestation which have led to soil erosion and floods (Lang 2002).

For example, in 1998 the Yangzi drainage area suffered from the largest flood since 1954, which caused an economic loss of 166 billion yuan (20 billion US dollars) (Yin and Li 2001). The increase in sand and dust storms in Northern China, as a result of deforestation and desertification, received world-wide attention after sand was blown over to Japan and even the United States.

In response to these critical problems, China has taken many initiatives in the past 20 years. For example, in 1999 China launched the Natural Forest Conservation Program (NFCP), which bans logging in the upper areas of major rivers. Second, China is a signatory of the United Nations Convention on Biological Diversity (CBD). In 2002 China signed the Cancun Declaration of like-minded high-biodiversity countries, and reaffirmed its commitment to the objectives of the CBD. One of the most important experiments in institutional reform in the Chinese forestry sector started with the proclamation of the "Decisions on the Issues of Forest Conservation and Forestry Development" by the State Council in 1981. This document, popularly known as the "Three Fixes" or *San-Ding,* was intended to stabilize ownership of forest and forestland, to specify private use rights on collective forestland and to establish a system of management responsibility. In this sense, it effected the de-collectivization of collectively-owned forests or forestlands. As the land reforms of state-owned forests are governed by a different set of rules and deserve a separate discussion, this chapter is primarily concerned with the reforms in the collective forest sector.

Over the past two decades, many scholars have investigated China's reforms of collective forestland, yet, compared with the agricultural sector, studies in forestry are still limited. Generally, these studies have tried to establish a relationship between de-collectivization (allocation of forest management rights to households) of forestlands and economic efficiency of forest production from these lands (Rozelle *et al.* 2002; Yin and Newman 1997; Zhang *et al.* 2000a, 2000b). No doubt the allocation of management rights is an important ingredient to economic efficiency, but it is not the sole determinant. Economic efficiency is measured in terms of the net economic returns to the forest management right holder, which not only depends on his physical assets and/or management rights but also on other factors such as the prices received for the forest products, and the costs paid for the protection of management rights and physical forest products. In western market economies, prices and costs may not be such an issue as they are determined in a competitive market system, but in China, these are still critical determinants for the economic outcome of forest-sector reforms because the state still controls prices and costs either directly or indirectly.[1] Hence, the studies of forest-sector reforms which have focused on de-collectivization only may give some indication of the production efficiency of collective forest sector but cannot provide a comprehensive view of the economic efficiency.

Most of the land reforms studies, including studies on collective forestland, seem to promote, either deliberately or non-deliberately, the Washington Consensus – private property rights are essential for the future of developing countries including China. Such conclusions are based either on an incomplete understanding or a partial use of property rights framework which leads to conclusions that only "ownership of assets" and "prices matter" for economic efficiency. However, as Bromley, in Chapter 1, has argued, it is not only the ownership structure of assets and/or prices that matter but also the whole structure of working rules for economic incentives. In this chapter, we will analyze the structure of property rights for economic incentives in collective forest sector.

In Chapter 1, Bromley emphasized institutions (working rules) for economic incentives. However, as Ho said in the Introduction, the words "institutions" and "property rights" are frequently used side by side – even to the point that the distinction between them becomes blurred. A property right is an institution, yet an institution is not necessarily a property right. Hence, our analysis is limited to a particular set of institutions – property rights – and even in property rights, it is limited to the property rights arising from statutory and customary legal sphere and not from the social and cultural sphere.

The property rights framework is useful in understanding the differences between ownership and property rights, and provides an insightful classification of property regimes – state, private, common and open access (Bromley 1989, Randall 1975). As per this framework, property is not a physical object, but it is a benefit stream (Bromley 1991). Property rights bring together legal concepts of rights and duties with settings and circumstances (including objects) capable of producing income (ibid.). Hence, in this framework, all property rights are clubbed together as "bundle of rights" as mentioned by Ho in the Introduction. The weakness of clubbing all property rights together as "bundle of rights" is that analysts have focused only on the rights related to the ownership and management of physical assets, and have overlooked other rights related to economic incentives. In Chapter 2, Wang distinguishes between "personal rights" and "real rights," but this distinction is based on legal position of the rights. Surprisingly, an objective classification of property rights is missing from the literature. The only exception may be the classification by Barzel (2002) who groups property rights into "legal rights" and "economic rights." He defines legal rights as the claims over assets delineated by the state as the property of particular individual or group, where the assets are all inclusive – physical assets, intellectual creations, and brand names, etc. and economic rights as an individual's ability, in expected terms, to directly consume the services of an asset, or consume it indirectly through exchange. It should be understood that having legal rights does not necessarily implys having economic rights. A legal right is only a means while an economic right is an end. This classification is very useful at least in shedding some light on distinction between the rights associated with physical assets and economic returns. However, the terminology is confusing and may not be appropriate for the discussion of the property rights arising from statutory and customary legal sphere. For example, economic rights may also be legal rights, and all the rights arising from statutory sphere are legal rights. Hence, we propose and use in this chapter a slightly different classification of property rights: (1) physical asset rights; and (2) economic rights.

Physical asset rights are "the claims over physical assets, such as forest land, and forest products, delineated by the government, local, provincial, or federal, as the property of particular individual, household, or group." Hence, in the context of collective forest sector, physical asset rights will include management and production rights over collective forest-land and ownership rights over forest products. However, ownership does not necessarily mean economic rights. For example, in some situations, a household may own trees on a collective-forest land allocated to them, but cannot harvest trees or sale trees without government permission, and thus cannot enjoy economic returns.

Economic rights are "the claims over economic returns from physical assets, delineated by the government." Even after allocation of physical assets to households, either ownership or management, the government can constrain economic returns to households by controlling prices and costs and imposing taxes. Hence, similar to Barzel's argument, having physical asset rights does not necessarily imply having economic rights. A physical asset right is only a means while an economic right is an end. Physical asset rights will contribute to physical production mainly while economic rights will contribute to economic efficiency.

In our case, both types of rights, physical asset rights and economic rights are legal rights, and the rulers of the state (a specialized protector-ruler or the government) are supposed to safeguard all the legal rights. Normally, the state is efficient in safeguarding legal rights merely due to scale of economies in its operations, but on the other hand, the state may also display rent-seeking and self-interested behavior. For this reason, it is imperative to establish mechanisms to control the protectors (the state) from becoming rent-seeking agents. Otherwise the economic rights of civilians and farmers may be at risk when the protectors become the proprietor (Barzel 2002). Therefore, to effectively evaluate the economic performance of collective forestland reforms, we need a property rights framework that distinguishes between physical asset rights and economic rights.

It is not our aim to assess the economic performance of property rights reforms in terms of physical asset rights and economic rights. We wish to highlight the various critical aspects of physical asset rights and economic rights on collective-owned forestland, and their current status. In addition, we examine the changing role of the government from forest owner to a specialized protector of rights. The next section provides some facts and figures about China's forests and forestland. The section is followed by a short historical overview of forest property rights. In the third section, physical asset rights arising from the changes in forest property rights are analyzed, while in the fourth part, economic rights are examined.

Forests and forestland in China

China's forest area is 158.9 million ha with a stock volume of 11.3 billion m^3, accounting for 7 percent of the total land of the globe and 16.6 percent of the total land of China (see Figure 10.1). In 1999, 52 million m^3 of timber and 539 million stems of bamboo were produced, while the total output value of forestry was 31.88 billion yuan in current prices (NFAB 2001). In addition, China's forest are also an important source of forest by-products, particularly in northern China, where agro-forestry systems cover 45 million ha (Huang *et al.* 1997). The forest sector provides

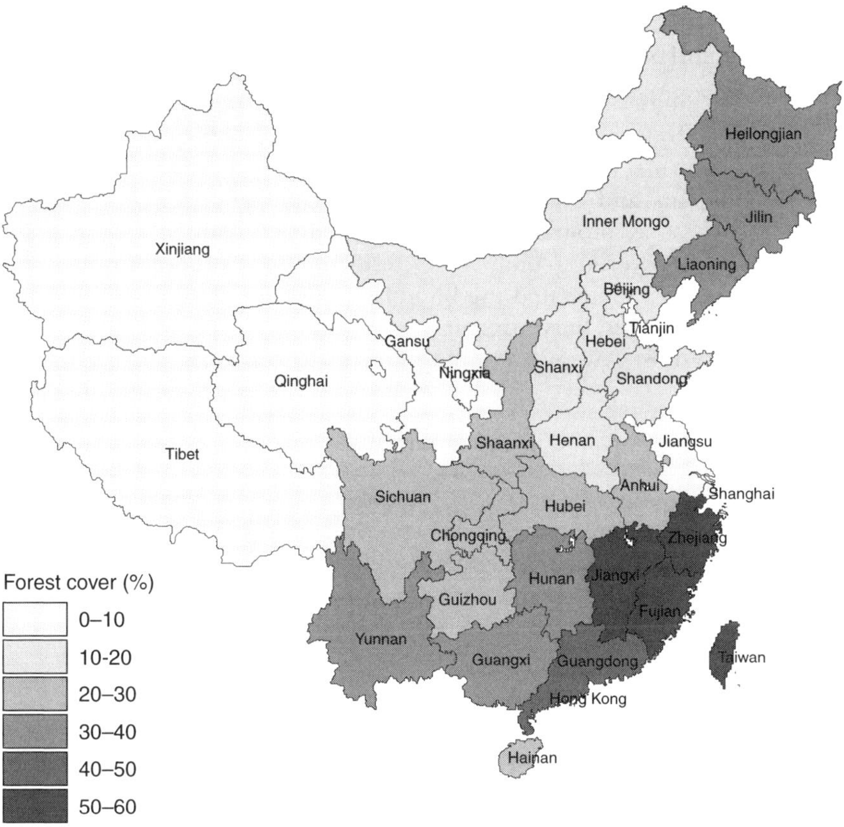

Figure 10.1 Forest cover in China.

over 3 million job opportunities and many more jobs are related to the forest sector, such as the tourism industry. Currently, China is one of the few developing countries where the trend in deforestation has shifted to forest expansion – mainly due to large-scale plantations (with nearly 50 million ha) (NFAB 2001).

China's forests are unevenly distributed across provinces (see Table 10.1 and Table 10.2). The structure of forest ownership also varies across regions. The northeast and southwest are dominated by state ownership, primarily managed by about 130 state-owned forestry enterprises and 4,000 state forest farms (that manage 30 million ha of forests across the whole country). The central, south and southeast are dominated by collective-owned forests. The distribution of forest types according to ownership is listed in Table 10.3. It should be noted that the collective forests account for a substantially larger share in planted timber forests, economic forests and bamboo forests. Currently, the timber from collective-owned forest accounts for 70 percent of industrial timber, approximately 500 million m^3 per annum.

Historical shifts in ownership and control over forest

Historically, the rights in forests and forestlands in China were recognized and enforced by local communities, not by a central agency, and were governed by informal institutions, such as customary norms, conventions, beliefs, religions and ethics (Zhang 2001). Quasi-governmental organizations, such as a "mountain council" (or "village council") were quite common as a governing body for forest land in southern China. The mountain council delineated the boundaries of land, designated and regulated hunting rights, harvesting and even output-sharing (Wu 1962).

The first Forest Law and Hunting Law in China were enacted by the

Table 10.1 China's forest resources, 1973–1998

Years of inventory	*Forestry land**		*Forest*		*Forest cover*
	Area (million ha)	*Stock bill (m^3)*	*Area (million ha)*	*Stock bill (m^3)*	*(%)*
1973–1976	257.6	10.3	121.9	9.4	12.7
1977–1981	267.1	10.3	115.3	9.0	12.0
1984–1988	267.4	10.6	124.7	9.1	12.3
1989–1993	262.9	11.8	133.7	10.1	13.9
1994–1998	263.3	12.5	158.9	11.3	16.6

Sources: China's National Forest Resources Inventories (1973–1998).

Note

* The concept of *forestry land*, frequently used in China, refers to the land with a present or potential future forest cover, or the land that is allocated for forestry purposes. So not all forestry land is forested, but may be with some trees.

Table 10.2 Forest ownership and other characteristics of four forest regions of China

Region	*Characteristics*	*Ownership*
North-east	Rich forest resources and low population density, important timber supplier, providing nearly half of the industrial wood	Dominated by state ownership
North/north-central/ north-west	(i) The north/north-central China is a major timber consumption region and has the highest population density. Land use is dominated by agricultural land, and forestry land is dominated by plantation forests and agroforestry. (ii) North-west China has dry climate and a very low forest cover and population	Largely owned by collective ownership
South/south-east	Important timber supply and consumption region, which is dominated by mountains and forests, and natural and plantation forests co-exist	Dominated by collective ownership
South-west	Rich natural forest resources, but mostly inaccessible	Dominated by state ownership

Source: Research by the authors.

Republic of China in 1915 (Chen 1982: 71–95). The law stipulated that "All mountains and forests within the country, unless they are owned by private persons and in charge by the local governments, belong to the state and are administrated by the ministry and the local government" (Article 1). A series of comprehensive institutions concerning property rights of trees and land, zoning, timber harvesting, and trade were also established shortly after the proclamation of the law. Unfortunately these laws were not effectively implemented, partly due to armed conflicts among contending warlords, the ensuing civil wars and the war with Japan.

Forests and forestland tenure have undergone significant changes in past half-century (see Table 10.4). The Land Reform Law of China was issued in the following year after the establishment of the People's Republic of China in 1949.[2] Land was allocated to farmers in recognition of their support for the revolution. During land reform all land owned by private landlords was confiscated and mostly redistributed to local farmers, while the remainder in particular remote and large plots, were placed under state ownership.

However, the period of private holding in the collective forest area was to be very brief. In the name of the revolution, the government expropriated the land shortly afterwards. The subsequent Socialist Transformation

Table 10.3 Distribution of forest types according to ownership

	Total forest		*Timber forest*		*Plantation timber forest*		*Economic forest area (share)*	*Bamboo forest area (share)*
	Volume (share)	*Area (share)*	*Volume (share)*	*Area (share)*	*Volume (share)*	*Area (share)*		
State	7,641 (68%)	64 (42%)	7,124 (71%)	62 (48%)	378 (37%)	62 (26%)	1.6 (8%)	0.3 (7%)
Collective	3,665 (32%)	90 (58%)	2,961 (29%)	67 (52%)	1,013 (63%)	29 (74%)	18.6 (92%)	3.9 (93%)

Sources: NSFB (2000).

Note
Units: Volume in million m^3, area in million ha.

Table 10.4 Forest tenure changes in China

Period	*Institutional changes*	*Tenure system*
Before 1949		Warlords, landlords, bureaucrats, merchants, self-sufficiency farmers, common and open access (legally by the state)
1950–1952	Land reform and economic recovery	Government confiscated all forestlands owned by landlords and bureaucrats and evenly distributed to the farmer within the community for the community forests. The rest, mostly in remote and less populated area, such as the North-east and South-west, were claimed belong to the state
1953–1955	Primary collectivization	Private trees, forest and forestland were allowed, but encouraged to bring the resources and join in the mutual aid teams and elementary agricultural producers' cooperatives
1956–1958	Advanced collectivization, and towards socialism	Upgraded to higher agricultural producers' cooperatives and transition to collectively owned and People's Commune
1958–1981	People's commune system	Collectively owned (often shared by commune and village levels for forests, but agricultural land was often owned by the production team, the lowest level of the three-levels of the commune system), state-owned by central, provincial and local (county) governments
1981–1984	Stabilization and consolidation of ownership	Private held timberland (allocated to individuals), contracted timberland (i.e, the use rights were contracted out to the individual farmers); collective timberland (shareholding system), state-owned
1985–1992	Privatization and decentralization	Private timberland (the use rights were divided into individual farmers); contracted timberland; collective timberland (including shareholding system), state-owned
1993–1998	Towards market economy	Longer-term contract for forest and forestland, auction of non-forestland for long-term (up to 100 years) holding, state-owned

Source: Research by the authors.

vested the ownership of private forestland into the collectives (villages) during the first phase of collectivization from 1952 to 1955. During this period, individual farmers were still allowed to hold some forestland. In the second phase since 1956, however, private forests and forestland, except for a small number of dispersed trees, were gradually forced under collective ownership – initially, in the Agricultural Producers' Cooperatives, later in the People's Communes (usually several villages within one commune).

Since then, private forestland has completely disappeared. In its place came a large number of collective forest farms, which amounted to 8,000 in 1960 (MoF 1987). For the majority of collective forests and forest land, both the ownership and use or management rights are controlled by three levels of collectives: People's Communes, a group of villages, and villages. In many cases one village had been broken down to several groups. It was often that forestland was kept more centralized than the agricultural lands. This structure had been unchanged throughout the 1960s and the 1970s even though some specific structure might slightly differ from time to time and region to region.

Comparatively, the nature and management of state-owned forests and forestland were not changed. The reform of property rights is characterized by the decentralization of authority from the central government to provincial governments and the enterprises, which involves increasing commercialization of forest operations (Zhang 2000, 2002). In addition, profound changes in property rights have occurred in the collective-owned forests. These changes will be examined in the following two sections, respectively, from the perspectives of physical asset rights and economic rights.

Physical asset rights

After de-collectivization ownership was retained by the collective (usually at village or township levels), but management rights were transferred to households or individuals. Hence, households obtained physical asset rights in terms of use and management rights over the forests and forest products and ownership rights over forest produce. The two key aspects of physical asset rights are, first, the right of ownership versus the right of use, and, second, the right of transfer of forests and forestlands. However, having use rights does not imply having full rights of use for which reason we must examine the limitations on these two aspects – use rights and transfer rights.

Ownership versus use right over forests and forestland

As discussed above, prior to 1980, the ownership and use rights of forest and forestland were not separated, either in the private forest between

1949 and 1953, or later in collective forests. But the land reform of China since 1978 separate of the management right of land from the ownership of land, and categorized forests into "state owned, collectively managed" and "collectively owned, privately managed." The 1982 Constitution and the Land Administration Law both determined that the administrative villages[3] that succeeded the ownership of the land were allowed to allocate the land to smaller units or households for management. In the forest sector, the "Three Fixes" document (1981) declared that: (1) for all the forest stands and forestland with clear ownership, the government, at or above the county level, should issue a property certificate to the owner to recognize the property right and guarantee its stability; (2) in accordance with the needs of the local forest farmers, plots of forestland, including waste hills, river sites or beaches, should be allocated to the farmers for the purpose of long-term planting of trees and grass; and (3) the trees, planted by the farmers around their houses, on allocated land and on the land designated by the village committee, shall be everlasting property of the farmers and can be inherited. Note, the main purpose of this policy was not only to allow private holding forest management rights, but to further clarify the ownership of the collective forestland to whom (e.g., which villages or communities).

The "Three Fixes" schedule was implemented during the following four years after 1981. With the exception of Shanghai and Tibet, 1,781 counties or 77.5 percent of all the counties that participated in the implementation of the "Three Fixes," had completed their duties. Private management certificates were issued, covering about 100 million ha of forestland for confirmation of their rights, while approximately 1.3 million disputes on forest and forestland were settled (90 percent of all disputes). The main reason for the dispute was less clearly defined property resulted from historical changes. The disputes often led to trees being cut or even fighting between villages or communities. A total area of 31 million ha of collective land was re-allocated to about 56 million households under the household responsibility system with an average of 0.56 ha per household (MoF 1987). It is relatively difficult to know the exact figures of the various household holdings that are generally classified as (1) responsibility land; (2) contract land; and (3) allocated lands (*ziliudi*). According to the former Ministry of Forestry (MoF 1987), these three types of land accounted for about two-thirds of the total collective forest land in the mid-1980s. But these figures vary from province to province, for example, Jiangxi and Guangdong Provinces had the highest share (about 90 percent), while Fujian was at the lowest (less than one-third because it had also adopted a share-holding system, a more moderate restructuring of forest tenure (see Zhang *et al.* 1999)).

During the implementation of the "Three Fixes," the government had intended to expand private use and management rights of forestland, via lease or allocation to the local farmers. For instance, in 1983 it stipulated that: (1) the plots of land allocated to the farmers should be enlarged; (2) the acreage of wasteland under a contract should not be limited and the term of contract could amount to 30 or 50 years; and (3) the contracts could be transferred to other persons. At the time, the consequences of, and even the political debates on such "privatization" were not clear at all. There was no one in the central government who could provide clear direction on the forestland reforms. The actual implementation was very much dependent on the local understanding and perception of officials, which resulted into huge regional variations in the system. Simultaneously, the de-collectivization of forestland was frequently accompanied by forest destruction because of farmers' uncertainty over future policies. However, this situation occurred only in the initial few years of forest tenure reforms (Zhang *et al.* 2000b). However, throughout the reform process, the government never officially claimed to change the nature of the ownership of forestland.

At the beginning of the economic reforms, the separation of ownership and use rights was in all likelihood a political and ideological compromise to avoid a full-fledge privatization. As Ho (2001) pointed out, "to avoid an escalation of land disputes between the various levels of collective ownership, the law maintains a deliberately vague definition of collective ownership." However, over time, it appears that the privatization of land property rights has become more acceptable. In this sense, the revised Forestry Law, effective since 1998, reflects the rising legal status of private property rights compared to the Forest Law of 1985. The 1998 Forest Law clearly recognizes the rights of the owners and users of the forests, trees and forestland, and includes provisions for the protection against and control of infringements on these rights (Article 3, Forestry Law of China, 1998).

Forest and forestland transfer rights

An important step in the tenure reforms, after the implementation of the "Three Fixes", was to allow *forest ownership (note that it is the ownership of trees only and not of the forest land)* and *forestland use right* to be legally transferable by contracting for a fixed period of time. By 1988, forest transfer (lease) had become widely practiced, particularly in the provinces of Guizhou, Fujian, Guangdong, Hunan, and Sichuan. The young and middle-aged forests are traded in the market, while the mature forests are open to enterprises, such as paper mills. Some of the wood-based panel factories have also bought forests to establish their own raw material bases. The transferred land included forested and non-forested, stated-owned as well as collective-owned land in Sichuan Province (Zhang, L., Wu and Zhu 2000). The prices of the land use rights ranged from 7.5–7,500 yuan/ha, depending on the land quality and the length of contract. Usually the governments only charge some re-registration fees, varying from 1–10 percent of the transferred value. The negotiated lease price should not be less than 50 percent of the appraisal value determined by the local authorities. The lease terms range from 30 to 100 years with an average of 50–70 years. In general, the impacts are positive, reflected in increased forestation and forest protection on transferred land, and a change to higher value use. For instance, in Ya'an County of Sichuan Province, a company for eco-tourism purchased 50 years use right on 400 ha of state-owned forestland with a commitment of additional investments of 140 million yuan to be paid off within three years (ibid.).

The introduction of forestland transaction by auction has been another important development. The auctions seem to have been developing. Almost a decade ago, more than 10 provinces made use of auctions, and over 730,000 ha have come under a new management authority in the first few years of the auctions (Ai 1995). In Shaanxi Province, the use rights for over 267,000 ha of wasteland were transferred by auction between 1992 and 1995 (Wang and Jian 1996). In Lüliang Prefecture in Shanxi Province, about 200,000 ha of wasteland were auctioned during the same period (Yao 1996; Hanstad and Ping 1997). To date, no national survey has been conducted on such auctions. A study by the Ministry of Water Resources (1997) is probably the most comprehensive report (see Table 10.5).

Usually the auction is limited to the households within the community (called a closed auction), but in some cases, it is also open to households from other villages (called an open auction). Forestland transaction by

Table 10.5 "Four Wastelands" auction until 1996

Province	*Area (1,000 ha)*	*Price (US $)*	*Number of households purchasing*	*Area planted in (1,000 ha)*
Shanxi	990	–	315,000	327
Shaanxi	498	6,867,470	180,000	134
Yunnan	482	14,615,663	426,061	198
Inner Mongolia	396	1,781,253	234,500	104
Hebei	347	6,144,578	208	–
Heilongjian	333	–	–	–
Henan	200	4,819,277	39,360	–
Liaoning	145	7,313,976	105,000	100
Shandong	133	–	–	64
Gansu	140	–	–	–
Guizhou	92	2,336,627	12,550	–
Niningxia	1	47,880	24,092	–
Sichuan	7	301,205	4,000	–
Jiangxi	10	–	–	–
Hilin	5		7,700	–

Source: Ministry of Water Resource (1997).

auction has become more popular in recent years (Xu and Huang 1999; Ho 2000). The auction and transactions have been further formalized by the 1998 Forestry Law (Article 15):

> The use rights of the following types of forests, trees and forestland can be legally transferred to other owners, as well as valued as inputs for share or as initial input conditions to start joint venture, co-operative plantation and forest management. But the forestland cannot change to other purpose of use: ... The felling quota permits are legally transferable after being legally transacted, or shared, or meeting the conditions of joint venture, co-operative plantation and forest management. However, the two sides of transaction must still follow the regulations of forest, tree harvesting and reforestation stipulated in this law.

Limitations on use rights and transfer rights

The rights of ownership and management, and forest and forestland transfer rights are subject to many limitations, unlike property rights over agricultural land and other properties. Most of these constraints are due to increasing environmental and ecological concerns, although at times these concerns may be used as an excuse for controlling the private property rights of individuals or households. The first constraint is that forestland cannot be used for any other purpose, such as for agriculture or development, while some types of forest and forestland (for example, protection forest) cannot even be altered into any other types of forests (Forestry Law, Article 15). Second, in many cases, even the tree species to be planted are determined by the government. Third, rights holders do not have free harvesting rights, and they can only harvest a limited quantity of timber after receiving a logging license from the local forest authorities. An annual logging quota, which sets the maximum forest harvest during a given year in a given region, is calculated and approved by relevant authorities. Logging licenses are issued to different farmers in the region so that the total annual logging does not exceed the logging quota, and reforestation must be enforced following logging. Fourth, timber can be transported only after receiving a transportation license from the local authorities.

Similarly, the introduction of sustainable forest management criteria and indicators, and forest management certification imposes new constraints on forest property rights. The Natural Forest Conservation Program (NFCP) bans logging in the natural forests and restricts silvicultural practices in these areas. Although the natural forests are mostly located in state-owned territory, some are situated in collective-owned land. In those areas, the NFCP imposes major constraints on the physical asset rights of forest owners or forest use right holders. These constraints mean a reduction on the physical assets rights, and consequently, a reduction on economic rights of a household.

Economic rights

Economic rights of the land, as mentioned earlier, are essentially the rights to economic benefits from the land. The difference between the physical asset rights and economic rights can be illustrated by a simple example. Suppose a farmer is given all the management rights on a forest in addition to all the rights to the final product except that the final product must be sold to a government agency at a price fixed by the state. In such a case, the farmer has physical asset rights over forestland and his final product, but his economic rights are curtailed. Being an economic rights holder mean that he is able to claim benefits of the product. But, the proportion of the residual value available to the right holder will mainly depend on three factors: (1) the cost of exercising physical asset rights or the costs for the protection of physical asset rights; (2) the availability of competitive market prices for the products; and (3) the share from the residual value that is extracted by government agencies. These three aspects of economic rights will be discussed in the following section.

The costs of exercising physical asset rights

Forest that is not under (or lacks) active management is often interpreted by economists to be lacking well-defined property rights (a situation of open access). This is true for many cases. However, a common situation in China is that households are given the rights of ownership or management, but they fail to exercise the economic rights when it is too costly to implement their management rights, which leads to open access. Unlike the great successes in the agricultural reforms, forestry reforms have met with more problems and the positive effects are more limited (Yin and Newman 1997; Zhang 2000; Zhang *et al.* 2000a). This is due to the nature of the forests, which is significantly different from agricultural crops. For example, the location of agricultural crops is closer to human habitation while forestland is generally situated far away from human settlement. This implies that the threat from timber theft is higher, while also the costs for protection and supervision are higher. In addition, the threat of theft of agricultural crops is only during a very short period when it has ripened, whereas trees face a threat all year.

In addition, trees are in general considered to be a product from nature, and not resulting from human labor and intensive inputs, in contrast to agriculture. Hence, the crime for timber theft is considered less serious compared to the theft of agricultural crops. Organized illegal logging by one community in another village community's forest is not uncommon. An example of this is provided in the account of village communities in Yunnan by Yeh (2000). Even though the "Three Fixes" scheme provided the *de facto* rights with *de jure* documentations, it could not reduce the costs for protecting the right holders. In fact, due to the economic reforms and large-scale decentralization of management rights, the governmental supply for policing forces has grown weaker.

It is generally believed that the early economic reforms in forestry were the third greatest cause for the destruction of forests, apart from the Great Leap Forward in 1958 and the Great Proletarian Cultural Revolution (1966–1976). Scholars have attributed political uncertainty about management rights as one of the factors leading to large-scale deforestation, yet, exposure to theft (illegal access) and the high costs of protection are other important factors in deforestation. The costs for the protection of management rights are substantial. According to MoF (1992) and Wang (2000), one million people were engaged in the prevention of illegal logging and resource monitoring.[4] The cost hovers around 1 to 3 billion yuan. These are huge costs in comparison to the silvicultural investments of 10 billion yuan per annum. Moreover, these costs are mainly borne by the forestland users, rather than by the local government budget (Chen, G. 2001), which results in reduced economic rights to physical asset right holders.

Several studies (e.g. Kant and Chiu 2000; Ruiz-Peres *et al.* 1999) have reported a positive impact of the economic reforms on forestry, but these primarily concern the economic forests (such as for fruits and nuts) and the bamboo forests in southern China. According to the MoF (1994), economic forests account for 36 percent of the total area of plantation forests. In fact, the physical asset rights of these non-timber forests are not much different from the timber forests. However, the enforcement of these rights is easier (economic forests, like bamboo and fruit trees, are more similar to agriculture than timber forest), while the residual value per unit land area available to the management right holder of these forests is greater than in the case of other forest types. As Bruce and other authors have noted, farmers' rational response to the erosion, of economic rights to the other categories of forests is not to invest (see Bruce *et al.* 1995; Rozelle *et al.* 2002; Yin and Newman 1997; Zhang, L. *et al.* 2000).

Competitive market prices and government price control

A second critical factor for economic rights is the availability of a free market and market prices. In 1950, the timber trade for collective forest enterprises was monopolized by the central government that controlled timber production, prices, and distribution. This means that although the collectives were the owners and management right holders over collective forestland, they did not enjoy significant economic rights, whereas the state did not hold management rights, yet did enjoy major economic rights. During this period, the central government kept timber prices low, and the price differences between the variations in species, quality, location, and size were small. The economic reforms since 1978 did increase the procurement price significantly. In 1985 the central government issued the "Ten Policy Issues for Promoting Rural Economy Development," which abolished the state monopoly for timber trade in southern China. Unfortunately, the overnight liberalization of the market caused much economic disruption and led to the biggest episodes of deforestation since 1949. In reaction, the government reactivated in 1987 the traditional government timber procurement agencies and re-imposed its monopoly on the market in major timber-producing counties. As market mechanisms and the socio-economic environment improved, all price controls were finally lifted and free competition has been practiced since 1993.

The trends in timber prices, as well as the difference between the controlled price and the free market price are shown in Figure 10.2. For this comparison, four provinces were selected. Two provinces – Anhui and Henan – were selected because, although they were less important for the timber supply, the relatively small timber production in these provinces was not subject to government-controlled prices. Hence, there are market timber prices available from these two provinces. The other two provinces, Fujian and Jiangxi, were chosen because the timber prices were controlled by the government in these provinces until 1993. From the figure, we can see that there were substantial differences between government-controlled prices and market prices, while these differences persisted during the entire period 1978–1993. However, after 1993 the difference in timber prices among the four provinces started to decrease. We can conclude

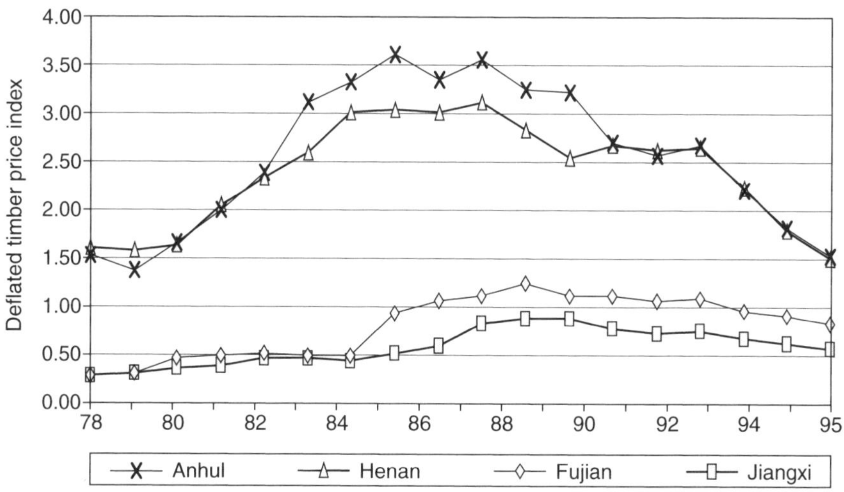

Figure 10.2 Trends in timber prices in four provinces.

that even though forestry land reforms granted physical asset rights (management rights) over collective-owned forestlands to the households, the government-controlled timber prices still restricted the economic rights of these households.

Forest taxation and fees

Another important constraint over economic rights of forests is the system of government taxes and fees. Economically non-neutral taxes not only affect farmers' (the physical asset right holders) share in the residual value of forest products, but they also introduce economic inefficiencies in resource allocation. Even before the liberalization of the timber market, farmers suffered from arbitrary and high taxes and fees, which withdrew a large amount of the economic rights from the farmers. Many investigations have been undertaken on the forest-related taxes and charges, which vary over place and time. A summary of these studies is given in Table 10.6. Although the data are at times not fully accurate, we can safely assume that the reported figures are underestimated because the data for some fees was not available at all. As indicated, the physical asset right holders usually only receive around 10–30 percent of the sale price.

The government has taken major steps to transfer and allocate the physical asset rights over collective-owned forest lands, and to reform the timber market. However, due to the high costs for the protection of the interests of physical asset right holders, and high forest taxes and fees, physical asset rights holders enjoy only a fraction of their economic rights. As the economic reforms progress, the price issue that used to be a traditional barrier (see Li *et al.* 1988), and even the problem of protection costs, are becoming less prominent. On the other hand, however, the lack of progress in the reform of the taxation and fees system is becoming a serious bottleneck for forestry development. One important reason for

Table 10.6 Forest-related taxes and charges on timber sales

Location (county/province)	*Tax and charge (% of retail price)*	*Farmer held asset (% of retail price)*	*Data sources*
Kahua/Anhui	50	–	Wang (1996), Chen (2000)
Jiangzhou/Hunan	62	38*	FEDRC (1999)
Shanming/Fujian	76	6.8	Zhang, Z. (2000)
Fujian	70	30	Zhang *et al.* (1999)
Haihua/Hunan	45–55	–	Wang *et al.* (2000)
Jingpin/Guizhou	–	7.5	Hou (1993)
Shaowu/Fujian	70	30*	Zhou (2000)

Note
*Including logging cost.

the disproportionately high taxes and fees is the inefficiency in the collection system: there are too many different taxes and fees – in many cases, there are more than 20 types of taxes and fees imposed on a single product (see Zhang *et al.* 1999); different authorities collect different taxes and fees; and, finally, significant efforts are wasted in the actual tax collection. It was estimated that over 50 percent of the manpower and resources are assigned to collection and management (Chen 1995). In more extreme but not too uncommon cases, the collected revenues are insufficient to cover the costs.

The amounts of taxes are often not predictable and less transparent since they are changeable across time, and measuring how much timber is harvested on the mountains and transported across the checkpoint is very much dependent upon how much you are willing to bribe the officers or your connection with the authority. Such a system in forestry provides more opportunities for local governments and officials to practice rent-seeking behavior and to exercise arbitrary taxes, fees and corruption. It was suggested adopting a more simplified taxation system, e.g., the more neutral land productivity tax that had been used in Finland for several decades and also used in China agricultural system.[5]

The worst thing is the misuse of the revenue generated from the taxes and fees. Officially it is usually claimed the revenue be finally used for forestry development. In reality, the majority of the revenue has been channeled to higher level forestry administration bodies, to non-forestry sectors as general expenditure, such as governmental running, infrastructure development, education, health, and so forth.

Conclusion

In the previous sections, we have discussed the current status of physical asset rights and economic rights associated with the collective forestland, and we are inclined to conclude that there has been a sufficient progress on the front of physical asset rights. However, the progress on economic rights front is very slow and is falling behind the progress on physical asset rights, and such non-synchronized collective forestland reforms will continue to contribute to economic inefficiencies in the forest sector of China.

In countries like China, which are on the path of transformation from planned economies to market economies, the fundamental question associated with collective forestland reforms, and probably with other land reforms also, is the transformation of the government's role in economic activities associated with land-based production. In the pre-reform era, the government not only was an owner of land, but it was in control of all land-based production activities. In the post-reform era, the government, whether local, provincial, or central, can play the role of an owner of land or a specialized protector of the interest of households responsible for land-based production. The economic behavior of the government, with respect to land-based production activities, will depend upon the role identified by itself. The government as owner means all final residual rents created from land belong to the government, while the government as a specialized protector means government is hired by the land managers to protect their property rights, not necessarily ownership rights, and from this aspect, there is no difference between the government and other third-party enforcement agents (Barzel 2002). The government may continue to be the owner of land, but it can play the role of a specialized protector of the property rights, use and management rights in the present case, of households. On the other hand, government may not be the owner of land, but it still can play the role of an owner of land. Hence, in the land reforms in China, ownership of land is not a major issue, as Bromley, in Chapter 1, pointed out, that private ownership of land is both necessary and sufficient for wise and sustainable use of natural resources is a particularly widespread fiction. The current household responsibility system, in which ownership remains with the local government and only management and use rights are transferred to households, may be as good as transfer of ownership to households, and this type of land tenure satisfies the condition of "do no serious harm" proposed by Bromley in Chapter 1. However, the critical issue, associated with forestland reforms, is the role of government in land-based production activities.

The analysis of forestland reforms in terms of physical asset rights and economic rights is useful in understanding the role of government in forest production activities on collective forestlands. The gradual reforms and current form of physical asset rights indicate that the government is trying to change its role from the owner of land to a specialized protector of the interests of households. For example, prior to reforms, the local government, together with its higher level of government, was the owner as well as manager of collective forestland. But, in the de-collectivized system, even though land ownership is with the local government, all management rights are with the households.[6] However, the analysis of economic rights provides no evidence of the seriousness of the government about transformation in its role from an owner to a specialized protector. In the new property right arrangements, management right holders pay taxes to the government that should provide protection services. However, it is universally acknowledged (by farmers, forestry administration officers, and academia) that the taxes and charges are excessive and misused, and are the most serious barrier to improving investment and forest management.[7] The tax payers have no voice in the determination of tax types and tax levels, and in the use of tax revenue. Even after such high taxes, the government is unable to provide adequate protection services to forest produce from collective forestlands. As a result, households get too little a share and the government gets the major share of land residual. It seems that efforts made by various level governments are not primarily to provide services, but to intervene in the forest management and claim the major share of land residual. Apparently, an observation by Barzel (2002) – "the specialized protectors will gradually retreat back into proprietors again if no rules are established to prevent the specialized protectors becoming owners in the first place" seems to a be true reflection of the collective forestland reforms in China.

The central government is aware of this situation and has attempted to reduce farmers' tax burdens. The 1998 Forestry Law (Article 7) states:

> To protect the legal rights of the forestry-based farmers and ease the economic burden, it is prohibited to illegally charge any fine on the farmers. It is also prohibited to arbitrary raise and collect fund from the farmers.
>
> The legal rights of the collectives and individuals who contracted and plant trees are protected by the state. Any institutions and individuals cannot infringe the rights on the trees and other legal property owned by the collectives and individuals who contract and plant trees.

However, due to various sources of inefficiencies in government, it is very difficult to reduce the cost of enforcement and taxes and fees, specifically when the local governments have not given up the ownership of these lands, and when they face lack of financial resources due to inefficiencies in other sectors. For instance, for a short period of time in 2001, the government attempted to change various arbitrary fees system to a single taxation system, but gave up finally because that made the local governments face lack of financial sources for basic services, including rural education. More importantly, since the farmers have no voice in determining the use of tax revenue, there is no incentive or pressure on local governments to improve their governing and administration system.

The results of an inefficient governing system, specifically of local governments, and total freedom of local governments in terms of provision of protection services and tax imposition and collection are the conversion of "*de jure* private property rights," allocated under collective forestland reforms, into "*de facto* open access" system. Normally, open access terminology is used in the context of individuals and households. In this case, it is an open access to governing and/or political agencies. As pointed out earlier, not only various levels of governments, but also various administration agencies at the same level jump into claiming the residuals with different names of taxes and fees. That is why often more than two dozen taxes and fees can be observed on a single product. In addition, the high cost of enforcement and the low share in the residual reduce the incentives to the right holders to exercise their management rights, and this reinforces conversion of *de jure* "private rights" into an open access situation, this time by individuals and households. Hence, the net effect of inefficient governing system is double-sided pressure on the *de jure* "private management and use rights" allocated to households on collective forestlands.

In conclusion, land reforms, in countries like China, should be followed by political and governance reforms and the focus of these reforms should be on (1) synchronization of economic rights with physical asset rights; (2) identification and enforcement of the government's role as a specialized protector of the interest of households responsible for land-based production; and (3) jurisdictional demarcation of powers, duties and responsibilities of governments at various levels.

Notes

1 Prices and costs, associated with forest production, are also controlled in Western market economies but the degree of control and the methods of control are different than in China. For example, prices of standing timber on government forestlands in Canada are fixed by respective provincial governments and not through the market. Similarly, import taxes used by the USA for Canadian lumber affect timber prices in the USA.

2 In fact, "The Principles of Land Law" had already been developed and enforced in the regions controlled by the Communists since 1947.

3 There are some differences between administrative villages and natural villages. Usually, the ownership is devolved to the natural villages based on the ownership prior to collectivization. However, due to vague ownership problems, conflicts and fights have erupted over land, see also the Introduction.

4 This figure depends on the definition. According to the National Forestry Bureau, it was estimated that about 0.2 million people were engaged in the forest law enforcement (NFAB 2001).

5 See, for more details Chen (1995), Zhang and Liu (1999).

6 In addition to household responsibility system, three other forms of physical asset rights are present (i) township or village forest farms; (ii) joint-forest farms; and (iii) the share-holding system. Under these forms, the land use rights belong to the collective; collective, households, and some other institutions; and a group of households, respectively. Hence, except township or village forms, in other two forms, management rights are being shared by households and other groups.

7 For a recent study, see Li (2003).

References

Ai, Y. (1995) "Auction the Use Right to Speed up the Development of 'Four Kinds of Wasteland' Resources," *Forestry Economics*, 3: 1–6, (in Chinese).

Barzel, Y. (1997) *Economic Analysis of Property Rights*, 2nd edn, Cambridge University Press. New York.

Barzel, Y. (2002) *The Theory of the State: Economic Rights, Legal Rights and the Scope of the State*, Cambridge: Cambridge University Press.

Bromley, D.W. (1989) *Economic Interests and Institutions*, New York: Basil Blackwell.

Bromley, D.W. (1991) *Environment and Economy*, New York: Basil Blackwell.

Bruce, J.W. and Zhongmin, L. (1995) "Experimenting with Approaches to Common Property Forestry in China," *Unasylva*, 46: 22–48.

Chen, Genchang (2001) A Study on Adjusting Forestry Institutional Arrangement," *Forestry Economics*, (Jan.): 11–15 (in Chinese).

Chen, R. (1982) *Historical Materials of China's Forests*, Beijing: China's Forestry Publishing House, (in Chinese).

Chen, W. (2000) "Recommendations to Develop China's Forestry Sector," *Forestry Work Research*, 2: 28–36, (in Chinese).

Chen, Y. (1995) "Levy Taxes on Forest Area Instead of on Timber," *Forestry Economics*, 6: 44–47, (in Chinese).

FAO (1997) *State of the World's Forest*, Rome: FAO.

FAO (1998) *Yearbook of Forest Products 1996*, Rome: FAO.

FEDRC (Forestry Economic Development Research Centre) (1999) "A Survey of Forest-related Taxes and Fees," *Forestry Economics*, 6: 26–35.

Hanstad, T. and Ping, L. (1997) "Land Reform in the People's Republic of China: Auction Rights to Wasteland," *Loyola of Los Angeles: International and Comparative Law Journal*, 19(3): 545–583.

Harkness, J. (1998) "Recent Trends in Forestry and Conservation of Biodiversity in China," *The China Quarterly*, 156: 191–934.

Ho, P. (2000) "The Four Wastelands Auction Policy: Removing the Rural-Urban Divide or Another Commandist Mass Campaign?" *China Information*, 14(1): 1–37.

Ho, P. (2001) "Who Owns China's Land? Policies, Property Rights, and Deliberate Institutional Ambiguity," *The China Quarterly*, 166, June: 394–421.

Hou, Z. (1993) "A Survey and Analysis of Forestry-related Taxes and Charges," *Forestry Economics*, January: 37–44, (in Chinese).

Huang, W., Kanninen, M, Xu, Q. and Huang, B. (1997) "Agroforestry in China: Present State and Future Potential," *AMBIO*, 26(6): 393–397.

Kant, S. and Chiu, M. (2000) "Forestry Reforms and the Local Economy of Linan County, Zhejiang, China," *Forest Policy and Economics*, 1: 283–299.

Lang, G. (2002) "Forests, Floods, and the Environmental State in China," *Organizations and Environment*, 15(2): 109–130.

Li, J., Kong, F., He, N. and Ross, L. (1988) "Price and Policy: the Keys to Revamping China's Forestry Resources," in Repetto and M. *Public Policies and the Misuse of Forest Resources*, Cambridge: Cambridge University Press.

Li, Xiande 93003) "Rethinking the Peasant Burden – Evidence from a Chinese Village," *The Journal of Peasant Studies*, 30(3–4): 45–74.

Ministry of Water Resource. (1997) "Proceedings of Workshop on Wasteland Auction and Erosion Control," unpublished paper, Beijing, (in Chinese).

MoF (Ministry of Forestry) (1987) *Forestry Yearbook*, Beijing: China's Forestry Publishing House, (in Chinese).

MoF (Ministry of Forestry) (1992) *Forest Resources Administration and Monitoring*, Beijing: China's Forestry Publishing House, (in Chinese).

MoF (Ministry of Forestry) (1994) *Forestry Yearbook*, Beijing: China's Forestry Publishing House, (in Chinese).

National Forestry Administration Bureau (NFAB) (2000) *National Forest Resources Statistics: 1994–1998*, Beijing: China's Forestry Publishing House, (in Chinese).

National Forestry Administration Bureau (NFAB) (2001) *China's Forestry Development Report 2000*, Beijing: China's Forestry Publishing House, (in Chinese).

Randall, A. (1975) "Property Rights and Social Microeconomics," *Natural Resources Journal*, 15: 729–747.

Raun, P. (1995) "Biodiversity and the Future of China." *Pacific Science Association Information Bulletin*, 47(1–2): 1–8.

Rozelle, S., Huang, J. and Benziger, V. (2003) "Forest Exploitation and Protection in Reform China: Assessing the Impact of Policy, and Economic Growth," in W. Hyde (ed.) *China's Forests: Global Lessons from Market Reforms*, Washington DC: Resources for the Future.

Ruiz-Peres, M., Zhong, M., Belcher, B., Xie, C., Fu, M. and Xie, J. (1999) "The Role of Bamboo Plantations in Rural Development: The Case of Anji County, Zhejiang, China.," *World Development*, 27(1): 101–114.

State Council of P.R. China (1981) *The Decisions on the Issues of Forest Conservation and Forestry Development*, Beijing, (in Chinese).

Wang, G., Liu, J. and Xiang, D. (2000) "A Survey of Huaihua Forest-related Taxes and Charges," *Forest Research Work*, 9: 35–46, (in Chinese).

Wang, S. (1996) "Things I Saw and Heard and my Thoughts," *Forest Work Research*, 11: 5–9, (in Chinese).

Wang, X. and Jian, L. (1996) "Auction Using Right of "Four Kinds of Wasteland" and Countermeasures," *Forestry Economics*, 1: 37–42, (in Chinese).

Wang, Z. (2000) "Study on Strengthening the Enforcement of the Law on Forest Policy," *Forestry Economics*, (June): 63–69, (in Chinese).

Wu, X. (1962) *A Compendium of Chinese Popular Customs*, Taipei: Wenxing Publishing House, (in Chinese).

Xu, J. and Huang, H. (1999) "Investigation on the Collective Forest Property Rights in Nanping," *Problems of Forest Economics*, 1: 46–49, (in Chinese).

Yao, X. (1996) "Practice and Thought on the Auction of "Four Kinds of Wasteland," *Forestry Economics*, 1: 30–36, (in Chinese).

Yeh, E.T. (2000) "Forest Claims, Conflicts and Commodification: The Political Ecology of Tibetan Mushroom-Harvesting Villages in Yunnan Province," *The China Quarterly*, 161 (March): 264–278

Yin, H., and Li. C. (2001) "Human Impact on Floods and Flood Disasters on the Yangtze River," *Geomorphology*, 41: 105–109.

Yin, R and Newman, D. (1997) "Impacts of Rural Reforms: The Case of the Chinese Forest Sector," *Environment and Development Economics*, 2: 289 – 303.

Zhang, L., Wu, Z. and Zhu, F. (2000) "Push Forward Forestland Marketing and Improve Forest Sustainable Management," *Forestry Economics*, (August): 15–22, (in Chinese).

Zhang, Y. (2000) "Deforestation and Forest Transition: Theory and Evidences," in M. Palo and H. Vanhanen (eds) *World Forests from Deforestation to Forest Transition?*, Dordrecht: Kluwer Academic Publishers.

Zhang, Y. (2001) "Institutions in Forest Management: Special Reference to China," in M. Palo, J. Uusivuori and G. Mery (eds) *World Forests, Market and Policy*, Dordrecht: Kluwer Academic Publishers.

Zhang, Y. (2002) "The Impacts of Economic Reforms on the Efficiency of Silviculture: A Non-Parametric Approach," *Environment and Development Economics*, 7(1): 107–122.

Zhang, Y. and Liu, D. (1999) "Site Productivity Tax and China's Forest Taxation Reform," *World Forestry Research*, 12(1). 68–73, (in Chinese).

Zhang, Y., Dai, G., Huang, H., Kong, F., Tian, Z., Wang, X. and Zhang, L. (1999) "The Forest Sector in China: Towards a Market Economy," in M. Palo and J.

Uusivuori (eds) *World Forests, Society and Environment*, Dordrecht; Kluwer Academic Press, pp. 371–394.

Zhang, Y., Uusivuori, J. and Kuluuvainen, J. (2000a) "The Impacts of Economic Reforms on Rural Forestry in China," *Forest Policy and Economics*, 1: 27–40.

Zhang, Y., Uusivuori, J. and Kuuluvainen, J. (2000b) "Econometric Analysis of the Causes of Forest Land Use Change in Hainan, China," *Canadian Journal of Forest Research*, 30: 1913–1921

Zhang, Z. (2000) "Distribution of Forestry Income Needs to be Adjusted," *Forest Work Research*, 8: 42–45, (in Chinese).

Zhou, X. (2000) "Private Forest Research," *Forestry Development*, 6: 6–14, (in Chinese).

11 Gender, landlessness and equity in rural China

Zongmin Li and John Bruce

The return to family farming and the rapid development of off-farm opportunities in China since the late 1970s have had a major effect on rural households and their members in China. Men and women have played increasingly differentiated economic roles in their families and communities since these changes. At the same time that gender roles have changed, China has extended strong property rights to farm households. Has this strengthening of property rights affected men and women in the same ways? And how have changes in property rights and in economic roles interacted to affect women's access to and control over land resources? Has the Chinese government addressed gender equality issues in these reforms, and if so, how effective have these measures been? What is the reality faced by women in accessing and controlling farmland and how is this affecting their welfare and that of their families?

These critical questions require answers, particularly so as in the late 1990s, researchers and women's groups in China began voicing concerns about growing landlessness by women. Landlessness in this context means that a woman, if she heads a household, has no land of her own, or if she is part of a household headed by a man, has had no share of land allocated to the household for her by the village. They argued that recent legal reforms in the rural land tenure system, while gender-neutral on their face, had the effect of discriminating against women. This appeared to be taking place in spite of the sweeping guarantees of gender equity in Chinese law, not only in the Constitution but in more specific legislation such as the Law on Protecting Women's Rights and Interests, which mandates equal rights to property for women (including equal rights to farmland) and protection for women's land rights in cases of marriage or divorce.[1] As articles 28 to 29 of the Law state:

> Article 28. The state protects the property rights which women enjoy equally with men. Women's legal rights to common property of marriage and family brook no infringement.
> Article 29. Women enjoy equal rights with men to farm responsibility fields and fields for growing grain rations in rural areas and to obtain

land for housing construction. These legal rights of women brook no infringement.

This chapter argues that landlessness on the part of women is growing as the result of interaction between legal reforms intended to increase tenure security for households, on the one hand, and traditional patterns of patrilocal residence and patrilineal inheritance of land, on the other. This interaction has effectively deprived women of *land rights of their own* during marriage, in both the parental village and their husband's village. It has also deprived them of *access to land* as a productive asset upon divorce or widowing. While the central government has recognized and sought to deal with these problems in the 2002 Rural Land Contracting Law, the principal remedial provisions face serious implementation problems, and there is a need for further action.

This chapter explores these issues by examining the relationship between land rights, development, and women's welfare. After reviewing how households received initially fragile property rights in farmland in the 1980s it notes that reforms in the 1990s provided them with greater security of tenure. The chapter examines the evidence of growing landlessness among women, and the causes of this landlessness, and reviews policy reform proposals for solving these problems.

Gender and land rights

There is a substantial body of international literature on the relationship between rural women's livelihood and their land rights, one that is increasingly couched in terms of the phenomenon of the "feminization of agriculture," Throughout the world, in recent decades there have been pronounced tendencies toward the feminization of agriculture. FAO statistics now indicate that worldwide 40 percent of the economically active population in agriculture consists of women (FAO 2003: 2), while in countries in East and South Asia the percentage is substantially higher. For instance, in India, 78 percent of economically active women are involved in agriculture (ibid.).

The proportion of the work in agriculture done by women is increasing as men shift into other sectors. When employment opportunities develop outside agriculture, they are often seized by men. Although many young women have obtained industrial and service employment, often far from home, married rural women tend to remain at home, caring for children and playing an active role in farming. Moreover, women are increasingly heads of rural households, either *de facto* where husbands have migrated to find employment, or legally, as widows and divorcees. FAO statistics indicate that women now head a quarter of rural households, and in some countries the number is more than half (ibid.).

The economic reforms in China have opened up alternative employment opportunities for women outside the agricultural sector.[2] However, although figures are fragmentary and difficult to obtain, the overall trend shows that the female share in the agricultural labor force (agriculture, animal husbandry, forestry, and fisheries) is steadily on the rise.[3] This increased responsibility of women for agricultural production is partly due to out-migration of men to better paid jobs in townships, towns and cities. In a joint study by the FAO and the UNDP it was found that of the total population of the eight villages investigated, 41.65 percent of the residents had migrated. Of the total number of migrants, 64.3 percent were male (Huang 1997). According to the State Commission for Reform and Development (*Guojia Fazhan Gaige Weiyuanhui*), the proportion of female workers in agriculture has risen from 52.4 percent in 1990 to 61.6 percent in 2000 (China Labor Bureau 2004: 1). Currently, Chinese women contribute more to agricultural production than ever before, and now account for between 60–70 percent of all farm labor (Duncan and Li 2001: 3).[4] In some parts of commodity grain production areas this percentage is as high as 90 percent (IFAD 1995).

Recognition of the increasing number of women heading rural households and making key production decisions has focused the attention of donor agencies on how women access land, credit and extension services. Women are generally disadvantaged in all these areas, but especially with regard to land. Property rights in land around the globe are unequally distributed. In 1998 the German Gesellschaft für Technische Zusammenarbeit (GTZ 1998:145), and Seager (Seager *et al.* 1997: 76) concluded that globally women owned only about 1 percent of all land. For China, there are no national data available for the land titled in the name of women. However, the situation is not likely to be much better than elsewhere. Based on a study in Hainan, Duncan and Li found that none of the women interviewed had their name on the land use contract. As they noted:

> We did not find any instances where a woman's name appeared on a contract. Some interviewees told us that women signed the contract when they were the heads of household (for example, a woman without an adult son, whose husband had died), but we did not see any such contracts first-hand. Each of the contracts we observed listed, and was signed by, the male head of household only.
>
> (2001: 34)

Turning to post-socialist and post-collective societies in Eastern Europe and Central Asia, one finds the emergence of a common pattern.[8] Following the dismantling of the collective enterprise, where household landholdings are divided among former members of the collective, the holdings tend to be constituted based on the labor force or size of household. Each member counts. But in the end, the titling of the land is most often in the name of the husband, as head of household, leaving the spouse effectively without land rights (Saxena 1993; Quisimbing *et al.* 1995). Examples of this trend can be found in transitional economies ranging from Russia (Bridger 1992; Holt 1995) to Albania (Lastarria-Cornhiel and Wheeler 1998). A recent comparative study by Tinker and Summerfield (1999) noted similar problems in China, Vietnam and Laos.

How are we to assess the significance of this lack of connection between greater decision-making in agriculture by women and the parallel failure to accord them clear land ownership rights? Agarwal (1994: 572) classifies the arguments on impacts into three broad categories:

1 *The productivity argument:* Women who have the incentives associated with secure access ensured by property rights will make better decisions about investment and good husbandry of the resource, and will have better access to credit and services.
2 *The welfare argument:* Women, especially women whose households have disintegrated due to divorce or widowing, fall into poverty without access to land. Land produces for markets, but also has a social security function.
3 *The empowerment argument:* Women who have equal rights to land will be empowered economically, socially and politically, both within their households and their communities.

All three arguments are plausible with respect to China, but reliable empirical data on these critical issues are still lacking. Comparatively, however, considerable progress has been made in empirical work on how the relative assets of spouses affect household decision-making and welfare outcomes. For instance, studies from several countries using unitary and collective models of the household recently reviewed by Quisimbing and Maluccio (2003), confirm that women's entitlements to land assets during marriage increase their bargaining power within the rural household, and that women's assets at marriage are positively correlated with household outcomes such as children's clothing, educational expenditures and health expenditures.

Such data dealing with assets within the household does not exist for China,[6] but much of the broader reasoning about changes in household landholdings and their potential impacts on decision-making and welfare outcomes seems relevant to the Chinese case. The role of women in agriculture has been increasing. During the collective period, women were active in agriculture, especially in south China, indeed, this was promoted by government to break down traditional gender roles. Then as China returned to household farming in 1980s, a larger proportion of women came to work in agriculture. This was in part due to new farming tasks being undertaken by the household, necessitating reallocation of tasks within the household, but at the same time male labor was beginning to shift into rural industries, resulting in the "feminization of agriculture."[7]

Similar to other countries-in-transition, at the same time that the role of women in farm operations was increasing over the 1990s, women's direct rights and access to land were weakened. Researchers and policy-makers became concerned that a new class-based poverty was emerging in the form of a class of asset-poor women (Zhu Ling 2000: 11). The pages that follow examine the evidence for growing landlessness of women and attempt to understand its causes and implications in the Chinese context. To do so, it is necessary to go back briefly to the beginning of the return to family farming in the late 1970s and understand how a new land tenure system for family land developed.

Households, women and land during reform

During the period of collective farming, gender issues relating to land received little attention for the obvious reason that not even men had rights in farmland. This began to change in 1978, when the Household Responsibility System (HRS) reforms initiated the return of China's farmland to households, gradually increased their freedom to make production decisions, and strengthened their use rights. Zhang Linxiu found in a 1995 village survey (2001: 3–7) that 71.6 percent of the areas had the unencumbered right to transfer land to whoever wanted to rent it. In her 2000 survey (ibid.: 3), more than 95 percent of farmers said they could rent land out to whoever they wanted and did not require any village approval.[8] Other studies confirm that farmers came to enjoy greatly enhanced rights to determine the use of their land (Li, Z. 1993, 1997; RDI 2002: 29).

The question is how women were treated with regard to land rights in the early years of the HRS. Although there is wide regional variation, the system had from the outset a strong egalitarian ethos, with shares of land allocated based on number of persons, male and female, in the household. Because households change with marriage, birth and death, it was deemed that regular readjustments of landholdings were needed to keep holdings equal. In many villages there were frequent (every three to five years) reallocations of land among the households to account for changes in household size, including those caused by the movement into the village of new wives of male residents. In a nation-wide survey at the end of the 1990s, the Communist Party Central Policy Research Office found that 80 percent of the observed villages had readjusted the leased plots since the introduction of the household responsibility system (of which 66 percent had adjusted twice or more).[9] Distribution was generally not sensitive to gender. The new household was allocated land that included a portion based on the presence of the new wife. If a man already had an allocation, the household allocation would be increased when he married. New wives felt they had land of their own in the household pool and that this made them partners in the household (Duncan and Li 2001; Li, Z. 1993, 1999; Summerfield, forthcoming).

Although more empirical research is necessary, the HRS may have negatively affected women in various ways. First, the HRS transferred authority over women's labor from the production team back to the head of the household. Whereas the shift to the new system may have strengthened the authority of rural women and men over their labor, it might simultaneously have shifted the balance of power *within* the household, thereby reducing women's authority relative to that held by their husbands, fathers, and fathers-in-law. Moreover, women's domestic duties have generally increased as collective social services terminated. For instance, a study in Sichuan and Jiangsu carried out by the All-China Women's Federation demonstrated that over the period 1978–1986 the proportion of women engaged in housework went up by 6.4 percent (All-China Women's Federation, 1993: 3). Finally, the HRS provided an incentive to households to maximize production on the leased land, which resulted in increased responsibility by the household unit in working on the land. In some cases this meant an increase in women's workload in the field, especially if their husbands and/or adult children worked in factories. We have seen some of this evidence earlier in this chapter.

A second stage of the HRS reforms began in the early 1990s, one that altered the land rights position of women. Government sought gradually to increase the term of household land use rights, to enhance household incentives to produce and invest by providing them with greater tenure security. Initially the government allowed a five-year use right, then in 1984 a 15-year right, and in 1993, the addition of 30 years to the original contract period (Bruce and Harrell 1989: 8; Ho 2001: 394). Such longer terms implied a reduction in the frequency of periodic redistributions of land among village households. Still, these terms were stated as maximum allowable terms rather than required terms. In many villages annual adjustment of use rights continued to be the rule, and frequent redistributions continued. It was only with the introduction of the 30-year term in 1993 that government began to exert serious pressure to reduce reallocations.

The second phase of the HRS reform was consolidated legally in 1998. In that year the Standing Committee of the National People's Congress adopted a new Land Administration Law (LAL) that confirmed the right of all farmers to a 30-year use right, over and in addition to their existing contract term. The LAL also strongly discouraged readjustments of landholdings during the contract term. Article 14 of the Law limits adjustments to "isolated cases," makes all readjustments subject to agreement by two-thirds of the villagers' conference or two-thirds of the villagers' representatives, and requires approval by the township government and the county administrative agency responsible for agriculture (RDI 2002: 29). In the period from 1994 to 1999 there was a burst of readjustments, called the "second round of contracting," as the existing land use contracts in many communities expired, but after 1999 the Land Administration Law has slowed readjustments significantly, though it has not eliminated them entirely. What were the implications of this second phase of reform for women? When there are major changes in systems of landholding and land rights, there are winners and losers. In this case, women may have been both (Summerfield forthcoming: 1). Women have benefited from these reforms as members of households with new rights to land, and yet there is growing evidence that in their own individual entitlements to land, women have been disadvantaged by the changes (Zhang 2001: 3; Zhu and Jiang 2000: 5). How did these reforms contribute to growing female landlessness?

Female landlessness emerges

Women's rights to land and gender issues generally were long thought of by policy-makers in China as a "western-interest issue", one that does not fit China's reality. Many Chinese scholars and researchers have stressed that China has had very tight family ties and that land was the property of the family as a whole. There were, they urged, no land right issues between men and women within a family.[10]

But toward the end of the 1990s, the issues of gendered land rights and women's loss of land rights began to attract the attention of the All-China Women's Federation and other institutions. Initially, very little data on the magnitude of the problem were available. Government survey data, including the agricultural census data, are household-based. They indicate male and female labor involved in agriculture, but so far as farm management or land holdings are concerned, they are not gender disaggregated, even to distinguish between male and female-headed farm households. Because leases are made with the family, government statistics on leases are similarly unhelpful. Evidence was largely anecdotal, but this did not prevent the *China Women's Daily* from carrying a vigorous debate on women's land rights in 14 issues published in January–April, 1999. This was the first major public airing of these problems.

How serious was the problem? Information was scarce, but there were some preliminary indications that women in practice were being discriminated against in land allocation on a significant scale. Land is allocated to households, but for each individual in the household, and the evidence suggested that households were receiving less land for women than for men. The All-China Women's Federation has said flatly that in rural arable land allocation, women had not enjoyed the same rights with men (All-China Women's Federation 1999). From the complaint letters that the Federation received a disturbing picture arose. After divorce, death of the partner, or when marrying into a new household, women in certain regions were only entitled to 50 to 70 percent of the amount of land men were getting. Moreover, in the aforementioned cases 40 percent of female laborers had never been allocated agricultural land or residential land even though they worked the land every day (All-China Women's Federation 2000: 318). The same report indicated that the All-China Women's Federation had received 2,076 letters complaining about loss of land rights from rural women in 22 provinces during just the first half of 1999. These complaints about property disputes accounted for more than 40 percent of the total letters of complaint receiving during that period. These disputes concerned primarily failure to allocate land to women upon marriage into a new village and their deprivation of any land upon divorce or widowing.[11] Researchers were also beginning to produce some quantitative indications on landlessness:[12]

- A national survey conducted by Lin Zhibin (2001) in 22 villages in 17 provinces found that 5 percent of women were landless versus 2 percent of men. A total of 163 married women were interviewed to find the causes of landlessness. It was found that 32 percent had not been allocated land on marriage into their husband's village. Significantly, 80 percent of those who did not receive land had been married after 1995. Among married women, the more recently married were more likely to have no land because readjustments of land distributions were by 1995 strongly discouraged by government.
- A study in 10 villages in 10 different counties in Shanxi by Zhu and Jiang (2000: 7) found that while there had been no significant discrimination against women in early land distributions under the household responsibility system, by the time of her study every village had women with no access to land, and in some villages, the rate of landless women was as high as 34.4 percent. Again, women married more recently were less likely to have received land in their husband's village.
- A survey conducted in 100 counties in 10 provinces and cities (Beijing, Shanxi, Liaoning, Zhejiang, Anhui, Hubei, Guangxi, Sichuan, Shanxxi, and Gansu) on implementation of Law on Protecting Women's Rights and Interests (All-China Women's Federation 2002: 13–14), found that about 12 percent of women did not have land shares and 13 percent of women had partial shares. About 23 percent of women with no land shares had never had one; 30 percent had lost their land after they got married and moved to their husbands' villages; about 1 percent of women had lost their land when they divorced; and about 46 percent of women had lost their land shares through government redistribution, widowing or other reasons. Women's land rights were often not reflected in the land certificates issued to households. While 86 percent of land use certificates were in the name of the husband or father, including father-in-law, only 7 percent of certificates were in the name of the woman, while 5 percent of the certificates were issued to a man and woman jointly.

- Yang (2003: 59–63) in a household survey of 416 households in Hunan and Shanxi (with an additional 163 in-depth interviews with women to assess their land rights) found that women, particularly married women, faced increasingly insecure rights to land. Almost 10 percent of women had not received a land share when they moved to their husbands' village. Among these landless women, 90 percent were under 30 years of age and married after 1995. One-quarter of the landless women had lost their land share in their parental village and did not get land in their husband's village. The study concluded that since the second round of land distribution, the number of landless women had increased and would increase in the future.
- Zhang Linxiu reported, based on her survey of 1,200 households and 60 villages in six provinces (Hebei, Shaanxi, Sichuan, Liaoning, Zhejiang, and Hunan) (Zhang 2001), that only 6 percent of women could get land rights after they married; that 10 percent of women's access to land depended upon whether there was extra land in the village into which the women married; that 60 percent of women had to wait to get land until a land reallocation took place in the village, and that 24 percent of the women were unable to get any land. If a newly married woman is fortunate enough to get land, it is usually a smaller plot of poorer quality.

Why was women's landlessness increasing in the wake of the second phase of the HRS reforms? We will delve into this question in the following sections.

New laws, old norms

Several studies have examined the causes of the growing landlessness of women in China. For example, this author examined these issues in villages in Hebei Province (Li, Z. 1993, 1999), as did Duncan and Li in Hainan Province (2001). More general treatments have appeared by Lin (2001) and Zhang Linxiu (2001), while several chapters in Tinker and Summerfield (1999) deal with women's land rights in China in the context of access to housing.

Generally these authors conclude that the cause of the emerging landlessness of many women lies in the decrease of readjustments under the new Land Administration Law of 1998, followed by a reassertion of traditional social norms. In this transitional period, villages had considerable latitude in determining new rules. Cultural values and social norms involving male dominance, neutralized with regard to land distribution during the collective period, resurfaced or, where they had been present all along, developed new consequences. What were these norms?

With regard to women and land, the first traditional norm is the tradition that when boys grow up and marry, they bring their wife home; when girls grow up and marry, they marry away to their husband's village. As the saying goes, "Marry a chicken, follow a chicken; marry a dog, follow a dog" (*jia ji sui ji, jia gou sui gou*). Or there is another saying, "Women who grow up to move away are like water we throw out" (*jia chuqu de nü'er, po chuqu de shui*). Today, women who marry generally move to the villages of their husbands, and their presence there creates a need for additional land for the new household (Chen 2002: 3; Summerfield forthcoming; Zhu and Jiang 2000: 4–5). Prior to the 1998 Land Administration Law, readjustments were frequent and provided an opportunity for landholdings to be adjusted to reflect changing family demographics including the arrival of a wife and, in some instances, the birth of children (Li, Z. 2003: 9, Summerfield forthcoming; Zhu and Jiang 2000: 14). Since that time, however, redistribution has been rare, with dire consequences particularly for women who marry in as brides.

The second norm is that of patrilineal inheritance. Chinese inheritance of land has historically been patrilineal, with ownership passing from father to sons. During the 20 years of the collective period, residences, which were privately owned, continued to pass in the male line (Li Weisha 1999: 236). Now, with long terms to farmland contracts that allow the contract to be inherited by heirs, this pattern is reasserting itself with regard to farmland (Cohen 1992: 368; Gao 1994: 85; Zhang 2001). While the pattern runs counter to national law, which guarantees daughters' inheritance rights to land as well as other property, the trend is clear. Heather Zhang Xiaoquan found in her survey of attitudes on inheritance of property by married daughters a strong expectation of patrilineal inheritance (2001: 262).

The situation developing today based on these two norms is reminiscent of that which existed in pre-revolutionary China. It is the son who inherits land, and daughters, as do daughters under patrilineal and patrilocal systems around the world, come to live with their husbands and their land. The assertion of these norms by villagers, however, is not only a matter of survival of older values, but also a response to growing population pressure on land. Chen Benjian in a personal communication (April 8, 2002) made this connection:

> The problem of increasing population and decreasing land size has become more and more severe. A simple method to deal with it is to limit beneficiaries. But who should be excluded and who should be beneficiaries is decided in light of rural social and culture norms. The "normal" way, of course, is to limit women's rights to land because they are the people who are moving between villages due to changes in their marital status.

Even though women may in theory and law be able to inherit land from their parents, when they move away, they most commonly marry into another village, and in practice they lose their share of land rights in their parental village. In the early days of the HRS this was sometimes mitigated by adjustments in landholdings which recognized the presence of new wives. But as readjustments in landholdings have slowed in the late 1990s, marriage and inheritance norms detrimental to women frequently deprived women of their legal rights to land.

Several studies confirm this. Brides typically move to the villages of their husbands, and their presence there creates a need for additional land for the new household (Summerfield forthcoming; Zhang Lingxiu 2001: 9; Zhu and Jiang 2000: 4–5). With the growing official discouragement and legal limitation of readjustments, women increasingly have difficulty obtaining land in their husbands' villages (Duncan and Li 2001: 17–18). With growing pressure on land, daughters who move away find their share in the parental land used by other family members, and find it impossible in practice to derive any benefit from that land share (Lin 2001:8, All China Women's Federation 1999:1–3). In the absence of readjustments, then, the position of women is fundamentally different from that of men (Chen, 2002[13]; Duncan and Li 2001: 31–33).[14]

How does this play out in the lives of women, in concrete terms? Families are dynamic and over 30 years, old people die, babies are born, and children mature and marry. Women are widowed and divorced. The disposition of women's land rights at these critical points in their lives are governed by norms of marriage and inheritance. To get a sense of what is happening, it is best to examine women's land rights in terms of the impact of major life events such as marriage, widowing, and divorce.

Life events and landlessness

Girls and women in their parental villages

In the "second round of land adjustments" in 1995 and in subsequent readjustments (which sometimes still take place contrary to the clear policy against them), there is evidence of an unwillingness on the part of villages to count girls in calculating the amount of land a family should receive, on the assumption that girls will move away upon marriage. In some areas, under the 30-year contract, young men get more land than young women on assumption that they will bring women, while communities use the 30-year rule as a reason for not giving unmarried young women land: they will be leaving and so to give them land will create problems later. In some areas the villages have developed rules that are based upon predictions of the ages of marriage. Girls who do not marry by the customary age face growing discrimination in land allocations in many villages, being allocated a smaller share of land than boys or no share at all (Chen 2002: 6, Fang 2002).[15] For example:

- Nanchong Village in Lingdi Township of Leqing County in Zhejiang Province made a rule that married men could get 1.5 units of land, while young men who were not married could get 2 units of land; girls who were between 14 and 23 years old could only get 0.5 of a unit of land, while unmarried women who were over 24 years old could get no land (All-China Women's Federation, 2000: 2). In short, the village gave women one-third of the land rights of men, including women who might marry into the village (hence 1.5 units to married men and 2 units to unmarried men), while depriving unmarried women of land rights at age 24.
- In Anhui Province, the land redistribution in 1995 was based on sex and age. From ages one to seven, boys and girls were treated equally, but then after seven a boy got more points on the assumption that in 15 years he would get married and have children and so need more land. But girls after age seven got fewer points as they got older because it was assumed that a girl would be married by age 22 and would move to her husband's village, so there was no point in giving girls more land. By age 22, young men got three land shares but young women got none (Research Center for Rural Economy of the Ministry of Agriculture, 2001: 267).

Where village rules allow, a woman who continues to reside unmarried in her home village might continue to have a share of land within the share of the parental household, but she will not receive separate land. If the parents die, she could conceivably inherit a share of that land as an heir, especially if there are no male heirs, but the author has found no examples of this. Zhang Xiaoquan (2003: 264) notes that in the village she studied, even when there are only female children in a household, and a daughter married a man who, contrary to the norm, comes to live in her village, it is very difficult for her to inherit land.

The All-China Women's Federation (1999: 2) sounds a slightly more positive note, observing that when a husband moves to his wife's village, he may be given land, adding, however, that if there are several daughters in a family whose husbands move to the village, only one daughter will be able to get land for her husband. But their report goes on to say:

> "In areas where land is under intense pressure because of expanding non-agricultural uses, the villagers will often vote to determine whether women applicants can have land. These include both new wives moving to their husbands' village and women who marry but do not move to the husband's village. For example, in Huoqiu County in Anhui, there were 45 married women who stayed in their villages of origin; their farmland and residential land was taken away by force by the village committee. They sued the village, and the court ruled in their favor. But the village leader said: "You may have won the suit,

but we are still not going to give you anything. You can bring Jiang Zemin here, and we still won't give you anything." The 45 women remain landless. Cases like this can be found around the country.[16]

Married women who move away and land shares in their parental village

A daughter who marries and moves away to her husband's village has little chance of retaining land in her parental village. In theory, if under village rules she had had a share interest in the family land, a woman moving away could ask for a partition and sale of her share, perhaps to her brothers. But this virtually never happens. In the discussions of the Focus Group on Gender and Land in May 2002 and January 2003, the women discussants struggled to imagine this and could not. They felt it ran contrary to deep values in the Chinese family. It would be shameful for a daughter to fight over land with her family.[17] No shame, however, accrues to brothers who deprive a sister of her land rights. Land is thought of a family property, and it is the sons who remain in the family village and will control the family assets. This inability of a woman to "cash in" her land share when she leaves the village, notes Li Ping (2001), deprives her of the opportunity to use those funds to acquire land on the market in her new village or to invest in some non-agricultural opportunity.

There is also a legal dimension to this problem, having to do with uncertainty as to the nature of the joint family ownership of land at Chinese law, but the fact is that while married daughters are rarely allowed to partition and transfer their share of the household land use rights, a married son typically partitions his land share from the holding of the entire household when he establishes his own family.[18]

The married woman and land in her husband's village

Before the Land Administration Law and the second land distribution, a husband's village would usually allocate more land to the new household for the new wife. Now, she still effectively gives up her land in her home village, leaving it with her parents and siblings, but will likely not get land in her new village until there is a new adjustment of landholding. This may not happen for a generation in many villages under the newly revised Land Administration Law.

This is the area for which we have the most satisfactory empirical data. All the surveys noted in the section of this chapter on the emergence of female landlessness not only establish the existence of that landlessness, but that it is a recent phenomenon, arising largely among women who have married and moved to their husbands' villages in the years since 1995 (Lin 2001; Yang 2003; Zhang, L. 2001; Zhu and Jiang 2000). The timing and the qualitative studies by these and other authors make clear the link between growing female landlessness and the end of readjustments.

Some women have special problems. Married women whose husbands have non-agricultural residential status are usually allowed by their home village to retain their *hukou* (residential registration) in their home village after they marry someone with an urban or other non-agricultural (teachers, health workers) registration, but they cannot keep their farmland. If they move to their husbands' parents' villages, they cannot get land. There are also some women who have married men who have non-agricultural residential registrations in other villages. Their husbands' residency status is often described as "empty residence" (*konggua hukou*), implying that they receive no benefits. These husbands and by extension their wives cannot get land in those villages (All-China Women's Federation 2000: 2).[22]

The divorced or widowed woman

Li Ping points out (2001) that the importance of rights within the household, which are ambiguous in Chinese law, become clear when the family structure changes through divorce or death of a spouse. What rights do women have to land from the household's holding in these circumstances?

China has surpassed other countries-in-transition in creating a gender-sensitive legal framework for land rights. The Marriage Law of 2001 provides that a wife's interest in land use rights should be protected by law and that the court's decision should not only favor wife and children in a property settlement, but also that the wife's household's land use rights should be protected under the law in the event of divorce. The Inheritance Law of 1985 states that when a person dies without a will, his or her separate property goes first, in equal amounts, to spouse, children and parents. Under Article 13, if a woman who is an heir has lived with the deceased or provided major support to the deceased, the court can award her a larger share. Article 26 provides that the widow is entitled to one-half of the jointly owned property that both spouses earned during the marriage, unless otherwise agreed, and Article 29 allows indivisible property to be distributed through sales with appropriate compensation or be held as jointly owned property among heirs on the same tier.

However, despite the legislation cited above, many widowed or divorced women face difficulty in retaining land in their husbands' village or, if they return to their parental village, being allocated land there (All-China Women's Federation, 1999: 1–3; Chen, 2002; Zhu and Jiang, 2000: 4–6).

In the case of women who are widowed, in some areas "only the children will keep the father's residential status and land; the widow must move back to her home village" (All-China Women's Federation, 2000: 2). Such a move would, of course, leave a woman bereft of land rights. Duncan and Li (2001: 42), however, note variations. Their fieldwork in

Hainan Province indicated that in some places, the widow steps into the shoes of the deceased husband as the head of household with control over household property including land use rights. In other villages, the husband's land rights will be assumed by the husband's parents or brothers. In still other villages, the widow will hold such land rights until her son (if any) becomes an adult.

Divorced women seem to be in a more unfavorable position. Zhu Ling, in her 2000 study, concluded that divorce rendered women's land rights profoundly insecure. The All-China Women's Federation (1999: 2) reported that

> If women divorce, some husbands' villages force them to move out and take back their responsibility land. Their parental village will not usually give them land. Even in husbands' villages where divorcing women are allowed to stay in the village and continue to use land initially, once the husband remarries, the former wife's land is allocated to the new wife.

Duncan and Li (2001: 41) explain that because a woman does not bring land use rights into the family, it would be difficult for her to claim land use rights as part of the property settlement in case of divorce. Zhu Ling and Jiang Zhongyi report (2000: 9) that divorced and widowed women frequently protect themselves by quick remarriage in their former or late husband's village. Remarriage continues their access to land and, they explain, may be the lowest cost strategy for this group of women.

If a divorced woman chooses to return to her parental village upon divorce, she may find that the land use rights initially allocated to her have been in effect assigned to her parents or brothers through an informal intra-household transaction. Although the land use rights initially allocated to her remain, in principle, her own, it is likely that concerns over potential conflicts among family members with respect to such land use rights will compel her to accept that she will not be able to partition them (Duncan and Li 2001: 38–39).[20]

It is clear that these outcomes for women have less to do with national law than with family and village norms. This reflects the fact that local communities have in recent decades had the ability, within certain parameters such as collective ownership of land, to make important rules concerning the allocation and administration of land among their members. In the absence of detailed instructions ensuring women's rights, local communities routinely deprive women of access and rights to land. And in the absence of strong pressures from the center, villages can persist in local policies (*cun gui min yue,* or customary law) in violation of national law (Chen 2002: 2). The 1999 *China Women's Daily* series on female landlessness is full of complaints about abuse by local authorities and the failure of higher authorities to remedy them.

To sum up, women facing critical life events are disadvantaged: (1) by a lack of clarity as to the rights of the wives and daughters within the family right to an allocation; (2) by their inability to get land in their name in their husband's village because of the restrictions on adjustments under the 1998 Land Administration Law; (3) by the resurgence of traditional norms that violate the requirements and the intention of national laws on gender equity; (4) by growing pressure on land which is leading communities to deny land to the vulnerable, in particular women; and (5) by a significant shift of power and control over land to local authorities.

The impact of women's landlessness

The emergence of landlessness on the part of women is a recent phenomenon in China, and there has been little research to examine its impacts. There is, however, information in general work including some that use categories followed in the international discussion of these impacts: productivity, welfare, and empowerment.

What impact might we expect from a lack of land rights for women to have on productivity? Here we need to extrapolate the conclusions from studies, such as that of Guo Li and Scott Rozelle (1998)[21] which found that secure tenure rights had a significant and positive effect on farmers' investment incentives and yields. They conclude that land tenure and associated land rights in rural China have affected the production behavior of farmers and in particular have encouraged land-saving investments. If male-headed households respond positively to these incentives, female-headed households deprived of such incentives should be less productive as a result. There is also some evidence that lack of land contracts may have other negative impacts on productivity. Zhu and Jiang (2000: 10) found that women's lack of land rights (even though they farmed the land) affected their access to credit and extension services. Zongmin Li (1997: 29) found that women's lack of property rights adversely affected their bargaining power within the home and within the community. Improved land rights for women could give them access to the facilities they need to boost productivity and family incomes. Unfortunately, China lacks any survey data which examines land rights in relation to productivity by gender of household head.

Landlessness for women can translate easily into poverty. This pattern has been noted in a number of discussions of female landlessness. Zhu and Jiang in their Shanxi study (2000) make this connection between landlessness and poverty, and argue that recent policies have made rural women a permanent landless class, vulnerable to poverty. Duncan and Li (2001: 40) note "widely reported cases where divorced women in rural areas have great difficulty supporting their life because they are deprived of land use rights upon divorce." In the *Women's Daily*'s debate of women's land rights in 1999, there were numerous cases cited that showed that women who lost land contracting rights in the villages also lost other benefits from the village, for example, compensation generated by sale or taking by government of village land. Compensation was only given to people who had land shares. (*China Women's Daily*, March 4, 1999).

But the first statistical evidence only recently became available. Yang Li (2003: 17–25) found in Hunan and Shanxi that landlessness on the part of women (landlessness in the sense that they had been allocated no land in their own right in their husbands' village) affects family food supply negatively in three ways. First, those households had arable land of 4.28 *mu*, and their production per family was 2,836 *jin* of grain compared with other families that held 5.61 *mu* and produced 3,624 *jin* of grain. They found that the first category of households had to purchase grain to feed their families, increasing their poverty. The same families, by the end of 2001, had only roughly half as much grain per person in storage as the other families, enough to feed themselves for three months, as opposed to seven months for the other families. Looking at grain sale information, by 2001 the families in the first category had income from grain sales of ¥21 per person, while the others had income of ¥91 per person. Families in which women did not have land were significantly worse off in welfare and food security terms. They find that especially in cases where families have no off-farm employment opportunities, their income is substantially less than other families.

In terms of empowerment, Yang's study (2003: 21) found that women who lacked land had lower participation rates in farming (almost 20 percent lower than women who had land) and fewer opportunities to make production decisions. In addition, they were less able to influence other families' decision-making. This impact of landlessness on participation in decision-making extended to political participation. Women who did not have land shares were not even regarded as citizens of the villages, and were not seen as entitled to vote or otherwise have a say in village decisions. Yang (ibid.: 22) found that in Shanxi, landless women were often called by their husbands or other villagers "illegal persons" (*heiren*). Husbands expressed unhappiness when guests came from their wives' families because their wives had not brought land to the family, and so, the husbands felt, the wives should not bring guests to eat the family food.

The land issue is of great importance for China's rural women in that it involves both their material conditions and the way in which they see themselves and others see them. If women have ceased to count in land allocation, becoming the nation's largest landless group, what does this mean for the image of women? There is already a strong preference for male children, and there is evidence (the high rate of female suicide[22]) that women feel undervalued. Pan Jintang urged in 1999 that women's freedom of marriage and divorce will not be fully realized if they do not have equal rights to land. He warned that inequality in land rights will encourage families to seek to have sons, because daughters offer no economic security. The problems of gender inequity, he suggests, will be more severe in rural areas. Gender inequality with regard to land may thuse be one factor contributing to the present demographic crisis, in which the much higher percentage of young males is condemning many of them to perpetual bachelorhood.

Today, the Chinese government has accepted the validity of these concerns. It has recognized that women's landlessness is a problem, and grappled with these issues in connection with the development of a new law on contracting of rural land to farmers by their villages. It addresses them directly. It is worth considering carefully, however, how effectively the new law addresses the problem.

Mitigation: the Rural Land Contracting Law, 2003

The Rural Land Contracting Law (RLCL) (Law No. 73/2002) was enacted on August 29, 2002, and came into effect on March 1, 2003. The Agricultural Group in the People's Congress managed the drafting of this law, and as the work proceeded, consulted the All-China Women's Federation, various Chinese research institutions, and foreign advisors on gender issues. The law is a further important step towards security of tenure for China's farmers, and attempts to address the gender issue in landholding.

The RLCL provides in Article 6 that men and women have equal rights in contracting rural land, which would seem to prohibit discrimination such as girls counting for less than boys in the allocation of land to households, and Article 57 makes officials who deny women their land rights liable for their actions, and subject to civil and criminal penalties. But the main thrust of the new law is to affirm the primacy of contracted rights and protect them from readjustment. The only circumstances in which Article 27 allows readjustments are "where a natural disaster has seriously damaged contracted land and other special circumstances." Women marrying into a village would obviously constitute no such special circumstance. The RLCL also allows, however, for specified land to be used for "readjustment of contracted land or contracted to newly added population within the village" (Article 28). This specified land is "flexible land" that has been reserved by the village collective in accordance with law, and lands reclaimed or voluntarily returned by contracting parties. However, under Article 27 even such limited readjustment requires a two-thirds' vote in village institutions and subsequent local government approvals.[23]

The key issue regarding women's land rights, however, is where, in light of the end to readjustments, women can look for a right to land of their own. The general approach of the new law to this issue was presaged in a 1999 interview in the *China Women's Daily* with Du Runsheng, a pioneer of property rights reform in China and the former director of the late Research Center for Rural Development of the State Council (Lu and Chen 1999: 9):

> Equality is important, and so the law gives women equal shares with men. But from an efficiency standpoint, it is important that we do not adjust the landholdings too often. That's why when a village distributes land they should not make assumptions about whether women will eventually stay or leave their home village; it should be done strictly according to the present population. That's consistent with the Government's guaranteeing thirty-year land rights, giving people the security they need in land. I have learned that there are three situations in which women's land rights are in danger: (1) married women, when they move in; (2) when women marry non-rural residents but stay in the rural areas, and (3) when women are divorced. How to solve this problem? Women, once they marry and move away, should retain their plot in their village of origin. Women who marry urban residents, if they still live in the countryside, should have a right to land. Divorced women should keep their existing residential registration and land use rights. These women must have the right to transfer their use rights to others, but they should not be forced to do so. After land has been distributed, and before any new adjustment, women in these situations should not receive new land. The only way land should be shifted from one person to another is by voluntary transactions.

The RLCL follows this pattern, stipulating in Article 30:

> When a woman marries during the contract term, the contract-issuing party cannot take back her original contracted land unless she receives land where she moves. When a woman is divorced or widowed, the contract-issuing party cannot take her land back if she still lives at her current place of residence or moves to a new place of residence where she cannot get land."

Article 30 does little to help young women to obtain land rights in their new husbands' villages, but it does seek to protect the land rights of young women in their parental village when they marry and move away, at least until such time that they receive land in the new village. It may be effective in protecting these rights against village officials, but can it protect them against appropriation by the young woman's parents and siblings? The benefits women actually derive from this provision will depend upon the extent to which their families recognize that their daughter retains an interest in the household land, and allow her to derive benefits from it. Lin (personal communication, 2003) worried that "women's claim to their land rights runs against the interest of their family, including father, brother and mother, and means a rebellion against the patriarchal system, a cut-off of the kinship ties . . . women who are ready to do so are unlikely to succeed in practice, because it is unlikely that they will get any legal support."[24]

On the other hand, Article 30 is potentially very helpful to widows and divorcees. There is a need for appropriate enforcing regulations that address more specifically how land distribution should be handled following a divorce. One ambiguity needs clarification: does "her land" include land acquired by the husband prior to the marriage?[25]

Finally, the new law does not address the problems of women who have already lost their land rights through discriminatory acts in the last decade, and especially in the second cycle of reallocations in the late 1990s. Will they have no remedy, at least until a possible next round of readjustments after the end of the current 30-year term? (This may or may not happen.) This is a major failing of the new law. The studies cited earlier in this chapter suggest that there are substantial numbers of women in this position.

The Rural Land Contracting Law is still an important *legal* step forward for women. Women will benefit as members of households from the greater security of tenure it creates for those households. They should also benefit from the clarification that the principle of equal treatment for women applies to land contracting. The challenge will be to enforce the provisions of the law, to monitor the effectiveness of the new law, and to work to address unresolved issues, including that of women who became landless prior to the enactment of this law.

Next steps?

What more needs to be done for women has been debated among the scholars, policy-makers, practitioners, and international agencies. In the discussions in China among those with gender concerns during the period leading up to enactment of the 2003 RLCL, different legal reform strategies were put forward. Some proponents, including the All-China Women's Association, tended to focus on preserving the right of villages to carry out readjustments to give women access to land. But it is clear now that government is strengthening long-term land rights, and so ways need to be found to promote women's access to and rights in land that work within that context.

Are further legal reforms needed? This is, after all, as Lin Zhibin and Liu Donghua pointed out to the author,[26] a constitutional issue. Women must receive the treatment to which they are morally and constitutionally entitled. Most commentators, such as Duncan and Li (2001: 47–48)[27] focus on realizing the promise of Article 30 in the new Rural Land Contract Law by making partition and sale of the woman's share in the parental holding easier and ensuring that women receive the money so that they can rent land in their husbands' village. Jennifer Brown of RDI (2003), proposing implementing regulations under the new law, identifies a number of opportunities. She suggests promulgation of both national and provincial regulations that require that every land use contract must specify, consistent with the new law, that:

- The contract must be signed by both husband and wife.
- The land use right cannot be sold by either the husband or wife alone, without the consent of the other.
- The land use right must be partitioned if a household member requests partition.
- After partition, a right-holder may sell his or her share, possibly with a right of first refusal for the other household members.

In addition, steps need to be taken to rectify the landlessness of women that has resulted from the discriminations of past years; this could be accomplished by legislation that clarified that a household allocation received by the husband before marriage is nonetheless jointly owned with a wife he subsequently marries. Such legislation should similarly give the husband joint ownership of a wife's land, if any.

These reforms would align the position in China with that in many legal jurisdictions in Europe and the United States. There are significant differences in approaches as among countries, but protection of women's land rights are achieved through some combination of (1) broad recognition of land acquired or held by the household during marriage as marital property, co-owned with the wife; (2) the guarantee of a substantial share in the inheritance of that property by the wife as principal heir, in the event of the death of the husband, and (3) on divorce, equal division between the husband and wife of the land classified as marital property (Cunningham *et al.* 1993: 187–199; Glendon 1989: 120).

This author, writing elsewhere (Li 2003a: 15), concludes that as important as these legal reforms are, there are equally urgent needs on other fronts:

1 A major effort is needed to realize the promise of the new Rural Land Contracting Law through implementing regulations. Already, local and provincial regulations may be establishing best practices in this area.[28]

2 Those who support women's land rights need to develop programs that provide financial, technical and social assistance to women seeking to enforce their rights.

3 While landlessness among women is already of concern, there is danger that it will continue to increase. Government and research institutions must invest seriously in the monitoring and evaluation of progress (or lack of progress) under the RLCL.

4 Government should re-declare at the highest level its commitment to the principle of gender equality with regard to land. It should follow

through on this by undertaking well-publicized gender-and-land-equity audits, punishing local officials where there are failures to enforce existing law.

5 Government must rethink its primary reliance on women retaining rights in their parental villages, and adopt proactive policies requiring instead that they receive land in their village of marriage. This can be accomplished without unduly disturbing existing landholders through the creation of a substantial reserve in each village for this purpose.

As many advocates realize, however, the major need is to change perceptions and behavior. The critical activities will be building the consciousness and will of women on these issues, creating networks to support them, and sensitizing officials to the justice of their demands. This will need to be done locality by locality, because as suggested earlier, the power to determine many of the outcomes lies in the hands of local governments.

Conclusion

This chapter has found that in spite of good intentions and specific attention to gender equity in land legislation, women's landlessness has grown since government has sought to end readjustments in landholdings. Patrilocal marital and residential patterns and patrilineal inheritance practices, coupled with increased competition for land, account for the slighting of women's land rights. Particularly with the virtual elimination of land redistribution since 1997, an increasing number of women do not receive land shares in their husband's village when they move there, nor are they able to preserve their land share in their parental village, if they ever received one. The result is a pattern of deep gender inequality in land ownership in direct violation of the law of the land. This chapter has examined the process of the creation of landlessness in terms of key events in women's lives, and has distinguished between women's lack of land rights of their own, during marriage, and their loss of access to land upon widowing or divorce. It has stressed that the latter is to a large extent a consequence of the former.

The impact of this growing landlessness has yet to be adequately assessed empirically, in spite of some very recent provincial studies. Students of the phenomenon of female landlessness believe that it is affecting productivity, both through an impact on incentives and the lack of access by women to services such as credit and extension given their landlessness. There is concrete evidence that this landlessness is affecting the welfare of women and their families, reducing food security and incomes and making these families prone to falling into poverty. Equally important, lack of land undermines women's position in the household and society, reducing their role in decision-making and their sense of self-worth.

Government recognized the seriousness of these problems in the 2003 Rural Land Contracting Law. It took steps to guarantee land rights for married women, divorcees and widows, and it has affirmed the right of women who marry out to retain land rights in their parental village, if they have them, at least until they obtain land in the husband's village. But it seems this may not end the problem. Women will continue to have difficulty obtaining land in their husbands' villages. Their families will resist any attempt to partition their land share from the holding of the parental household. And women who have already become landless since the mid-1990s lack a remedy under the new law.

There are proposed remedies to these remaining problems, and they are not limited to legal reforms. Education and advocacy will play critical roles. In the end, it is the issue of enforcement of national norms of gender equity that may prove most difficult. Local authorities have gained much greater control over land in recent years, and are often able to ignore national law. District and provincial officials and the courts are not yet ready to take seriously gender equity with regard to land, and for the most part reject women's complaints out of hand.

In conclusion, those concerned with reform in this area need to think clearly about the relative roles of be played by legal and administrative controls to enforce gender equity, on one hand, and on the other, the use by women of opportunities posed by expanding private rights in land and the liberalization of land markets. There may be a tendency to rely too much on the first strategy, given China's history of planning to achieve social objectives. It is equally or more important, given the shape of the emerging system of private land rights in China, that women and those who support them learn how women can work within and use that system to attain their welfare objectives.

Acknowledgments

An initial version of this chapter was prepared on the basis of discussions in 2002 with a Ford Foundation-supported group of gender and land researchers in Beijing, drawn from economics, development studies, women's studies, law and social studies. It has gone through several iterations. The authors would like to thank Peter Ho for his encouragement in developing what was originally a synthesis paper based on group discussions into publishable form. For their insights and advice at various stages of writing, the authors wish to express gratitude to Zhang Linxiu, Lin Zhibin, Chen Benjian, Liu Donghua, Du Jie, Fang Yuzhu, Li Ping and other Chinese colleagues, as well as Sarah Cook, Hein Mallee, and Ma Jifang at the Ford Foundation.

Notes

1 The Inheritance Law of 1986 and the Marriage Law of 2001 also provide substantial and specific protection. For a thorough and thoughtful review of Chinese law affecting women's land rights, see Duncan and Li (2001).

2 For example, a study of 9,729 households in two townships in Jiangsu and Sichuan (respectively Hengtang and Jiahong), showed that the proportion of women in the agricultural sector declined from 83 percent in 1978 to 58.7 percent in 1986. Over the same period, the proportion of women in non-agricultural work increased by 17.9 percent (All-China Women's Federation 1993: 3).

3 Note that the official statistics from the National Bureau of Statistics show that the proportion of female workers in agriculture has been steady over the period from 1993 until 2001, hovering between 37 and 38 percent (see National Bureau of Statistics at www.stats.gov.cn). This is most likely due to the difference between "formally employed female workers" as registered by the National Bureau of Statistics, and the actual proportion of female farmers active in agriculture. The figures for the latter are fragmentary and difficult to obtain as they are not officially recorded.

4 IFAD (1995) states slightly different figures, with women only constituting 46.2 percent of the agricultural labour force in 1982, rising to 50 percent in 1987, and reaching 60 percent in 1994.

5 For other case studies on countries in East and Central Europe and Central Asia, see UNICEF (1995) and Giovarelli and Duncan (1999).

6 The author's dissertation (Li 1997), however, compares the impact of employment in agriculture and rural industry on women's bargaining power and welfare outcomes in households in three villages in Yutian County, Hebei Province.

7 In 1999, UNDP estimated that women now perform more than 80 percent of the routine farm labor, though there is considerable variation from place to place (Song and Jiggins 2002: 7). Differences in estimates might be seasonal, due to the fact that many men return to their home village to assist with farming during the busy season. Zhang Linxiu indicates that women are contributing as much as, if not more, labor days to agriculture as men these days in China (Zhang 2001: 2).

8 Zhang found in the same survey that the percentage of regions in which farmers had complete rights to decide what to plant, increased from 73.4 percent in 1995 to 97 percent in 2000. She found that greatest improvement in rights came in the rights of farmers to convert their land to other uses: from 53.6 percent in 1995 to around 85 percent in 2000.

9 The survey included 271 observation villages. See Wang (1998: 56–57).

10 Chen Benjian, Editor of the *Women's Daily*, noted that it was only from 1999, as complaints about women's land rights grew rapidly, that there was any public awareness that this was a common problem. When the women's media tried to find experts who knew about land tenure and gender issues, she remembers, it proved very difficult. "If you talked to policy-makers, women's land rights were out of the picture. If you talked to people who did women's studies, they didn't know land tenure issues, but if you talked to economists who knew land issues, they didn't believe there was a women's issue in land tenure, and if you talked to sociologists they were also puzzled by the issues." Chen Benjian, personal communication, April 12, 2002.

11 Fang Yuzhu, Deputy Director, Deputy of Inspection of the Department of Women and Children's Rights and Interests of the All-China Federation. Personal communication, April 8, 2002.

12 As stated earlier, but deserving reiteration here, is that "landless" in this context means that a woman heading a household has no land or, if she is part of a household headed by a man, no share of land has been allocated to the household for her by the village.

13 Chen Beijan, personal communication, June 2002.

14 It is worth noting that the rigidities introduced by restrictions on readjustments has impacts in other contexts as well, for instance when children are born into the household or a household member dies.

15 Fang Yuzhu, Deputy Director, Deputy of Inspection of All-China Women's Federation. Personal communication, April, 8, 2002.

16 There is evidence that these patterns exist with regard to peri-urban as well as rural land. Fang Yuzhu, Coordinator, the Division of Inspection of the Department of Women and Children's Rights and Interests, All-China Women's Federation, in a personal communication on April 15, 2002, relates that in built-up peri-urban areas near Beijing, where land is no longer available for farming and houses are allocated to villagers instead, a man receives two houses while a woman receives one apartment.

17 The first author's experience in Central Asia suggests that attitudes there are very similar. In Africa, in the experience of the second author, women may also hesitate to quarrel over land with their parents while married because they want to be able, if they are divorced by their husbands, to return to their family.

18 Arable land use rights allocated to individuals in households are treated as property jointly owned by all household members, and an individual does not have a right to a particular piece of land (Li P, 2001). Duncan and Li (2001) explain that at law, in a formal sense, a daughter's right to a partition of land may depend on whether the family ownership of the land right is "share joint ownership" or "mutual joint ownership". Article 78 of the General Principles of Civil Law (1986) provides that a share joint owner may transfer his or her share of the interest in the property, with the other joint owners having a first right of refusal, but it is silent on transferability under mutual joint ownership. Chinese law does not state which type of joint ownership applies to the property jointly owned by husband and wife, or to the property jointly owned by all household members.

19 The All-China Women's Federation in 2000 (2–3) found that in the rural areas around Nanning, Guangxi, some villages said that women who married non-agriculturists could not receive the same treatment as women whose husbands engaged in agriculture. In Yuxi City, Yunnan, where the tobacco industry has taken most arable land, the local customary rule says that families in the village can get residential land in proportion to the number of sons they have; but families with only girls get only one share of residential land regardless of the number of daughters. In Shandong, some villages near the cities have residential land use planning, and there women who marry in their home village are penalized and must pay a price two to four times the usual price to get a residential plot half the size of normal family plots.

In four counties in Sichuan, the same study found that in cases in which a husband is residing in an urban area but his wife must stay with his parents in the rural areas, and his parents are still agricultural residents, neither the wife's village of origin nor the in-laws' village will give her land. Often she will not be registered as a villager in the in-laws' village. Sometimes, a woman in this position can purchase a residential registration in the village, but this does not guarantee land rights. In the four counties, there are 11 townships that allow this. Some 55 percent of the women in this situation who had purchased registration still did not have land. But in some areas the wife can pay a contribution to the agricultural development fund to get both registration and a small piece of land. In this case there is payment required for children as well as the wife, children being counted as half-residents and getting less land until 14 years of age.

20 Duncan and Li (2001: 40) illustrate this with a case from Hainan Province, in which

> the sister-in-law of a divorced woman told us that the woman had returned to the village with her four-year old child after divorce. Although her land rights were retained with the maiden family when she married, she could not farm on the land she had a right to because her land rights had been assigned to her brother when she was married. She had to lease in land in another village and work there while leaving her child in the maiden village with her parents. When asked why she could not farm on her own land in the maiden village, the sister-in-law said that she had no right to land because she "eats with us".

21 The study surveyed 664 households from 31 villages in six counties in Hebei and Liaoning Provinces in 1995.

22 Please read the series Protecting Women's Legal Rights in Land Contracting, China *Women's Daily*, January 14–April 8, 1999. See Kleinman and Lee on rural female suicide in Perry and Selden (eds), *Chinese Society*.

23 A readjustment must, under Article 27, be agreed upon by two-thirds of a villagers' meeting of the collective economic organization or two-thirds of the villagers' representatives, and must be reported to and approved by the appropriate agricultural or administrative department of the township and county governments. A similar provision in the Land Administration Law made it very difficult to get approval for readjustments for the benefit of women, or even for creation of reserves for their benefit, and this provision will likely have the same effect.

24 Mark Selden makes an important point (personal communication, June 1, 2004): the desire of women to continue to have access to parental family land may encourage a trend already underway in more prosperous areas and villages toward intra-village marriage. Selden notes that "This does not challenge the patriarchal family system so directly, but it has a powerful impact on it, favorable to young people and young women in particular."

25 An earlier draft of the Rural Land Contracting Law had addressed this problem by categorically including rural land rights as jointly owned property of husband and wife regardless of the time such land use rights are acquired. In the final draft, however, this is not made clear. Jiang Zhongyi, Senior Researcher, Research Center for Rural Economy, Ministry of Agriculture, a participant in development of the law, in a discussion with the Gender and Land Focus Group in Ford Foundation's Beijing Office on January 13, 2003.

26 Personal communications, July 3, 2002.

27 This is the strategy reflected in the pre-law interview with Du Runsheng, "Efficiency and Gender Equality," by Lu Xiaofeng and Chen Benjian, in one of a series of reports on protection of women's rights to land, *Chinese Women's Daily*, April 15, 1999.

28 The All-China Women's Federation endorsed regulations in Heilongjiang and Fujian Provinces and in the city governments of Changsha City (Hunan Province) and Tangshan City (Hebei Province). The Federation concluded that in 2000 there were five provinces, thirty-one cities and more than one hundred counties providing effective guidance. They especially commended Meishan County in Sichuan, which in 1990 issued rules improving the land responsibility contracts, with detailed guidance on protecting women's land rights (All-China Women's Federation, 2000: 9).

References

All-China Women's Federation (ed.) (1993) *The Impact of Economic Development on Rural Women in China*, Tokyo: United Nations University.

All-China Women's Federation (1999) *Report on Violation of Women's Land Rights under the Second Land Adjustment: A Working Paper*, Beijing: Department of Women's Rights and Interests.

All-China Women's Federation, Department of Women's Rights and Interests (2000) *Situation and Suggestions on Problems of Rural Married Women's Land Contracts*, September, Beijing: All-China Women's Federation.

All-China Women's Federation, Department of Women and Children's Rights and Interests (December, 2002) "Survey Report on Implementation of Law on Protecting Women's Rights and Interest, People's Republic of China", Beijing: All-China Women's Federation.

All-China Women's Federation, Deputy of Inspection, Women's Rights and Interests (1999) *Protection of Women's Rights and Interests in Rural Land Contract*, at 318, Papers from the Workshop for the Fifth Anniversary of the Fourth World Women's Conference, Beijing: All-China Women's Federation.

Agarwal, Bina (1994) *A Field of One's Own: Gender and Land Rights in South Asia*, South Asian Studies 58, Cambridge: Cambridge University Press.

Bridger, Susan (1992) *Women in the Soviet Countryside; Women's Role in Rural Development in the Soviet Union*, Cambridge: Cambridge University Press.

Brown, Jennifer (May 2003) "Protecting Women's Land Rights through RLCL Implementing Regulations," Draft for Comment, Seattle: Rural Development Institute.

Bruce, John and Harrell, Paula (1989) "Land Reform in the People's Republic of China 1978–1988," Land Tenure Center Research Paper No. 100, Madison: Land Tenure Center, University of Wisconsin-Madison.

Buvinic, Mayra (1997) "Women in Poverty: A New Global Underclass," 108 *Foreign Policy* 38.

Chen, Benjian (2002) "Find the Lost Land Rights", a special report of the *China Women's Daily*, Beijing: *China Women's Daily*.

China Labor Bureau (ed.) (2004) *Rural Working Women in China: A Short Summary of Concerns*, Hong Kong: China Labor Bulletin.

Cohen, Myron (1992), "Family Management and Family Division in Contemporary China," *The China Quarterly*, 13: 357–377.

Cunningham, Roger, Stoebuck, William and Whitman, Dale (1993) *The Law of Property*, 2nd edn, St Paul, MN: West Publishing Co.

Du, Ying (2001) *Improving Land Tenure System for Rural China*, Beijing: Research Center for Rural Development, Ministry of Agriculture.

Duncan, Jennifer and Li Ping (2001) *Women and Land Tenure in China: A Study of Women's Land Rights in Dongfang County, Hainan Province*, RDI Reports on Foreign Aid and Development #110, Seattle: Rural Development Institute.

FAO (2003) "A Gender Perspective on Land Rights – Equal Footing, Gender and Development Service," *Sustainable Development*, Rome: FAO.

Gao, Xiaoxian (1994) "China's Modernization and Changes in the Social Status of Rural Women," in C. Gilmartin *et al.* (eds) *Engendering China: Women, Culture, and the State*, Cambridge, MA: Harvard University Press, pp. 80–97.

Giovarelli, Renee and Duncan, Jennifer (1999) "Women and Land in Eastern

Europe and Central Asia," paper prepared for a workshop on Women Farmers: Enhancing Rights and Productivity", Bonn, Germany, August 26–27, 1999, Seattle: Rural Development Institute.

Glendon, Mary Ann (1989) *The Transformation of Family Law: State, Law, and Family in the United States and Western Europe*, Chicago, University of Chicago Press.

GTZ (1998) *Land Tenure in Development Cooperation: Guiding Principles*, Schriftenreihe der GTZ, No. 264, Wiesbaden: Universum Verlagsanstalt.

Ho, Peter (2001) "Who Owns China's Land? Policies, Property Rights and Deliberate Institutional Ambiguity," *The China Quarterly*, 166, June: 394–421.

Holt, Sharon (1995) *Gender and Property Rights: Women and Agrarian Reform in Russian and Moldova*, Washington, DC: The World Bank.

Huang, Ping (1997) *Rural Migration in Rural Development in the Evolving Market Economy: Micro-and Macro-Studies*, Rome: UNDP/FAO.

IFAD (1995) *The Status of Rural Women in China*, Rome: International Fund for Agricultural Development.

Kumar, Kabir (September 2002) *Land Use Rights and Gender Equality in Vietnam*, Washington, DC: The World Bank.

Lastarria-Cornhiel, Susana and Wheeler, Rachael (1998) *Gender, Ethnicity, and Landed Property in Albania*, LTC Working Paper 18, Madison: Land Tenure Center, University of Wisconsin-Madison.

Lee, S. and Kleinman, A. (2000) "Suicide as Resistance in Chinese Society," in J. Elizabeth, E. Perry and Mark Selden (eds) *Chinese Society: Change, Conflict and Resistance*, London and New York: Routledge.

Li, Guo, Rozelle, S. and Brandt L. (1998) "Tenure, Land Rights and Farmer Investment Incentives in China" *Agricultural Economics*, 19: 63–71.

Li, Ping (2001) "Women's Land Rights in China," paper presented at a workshop on women's land tenure rights, May 22–24, 2001, Beijing: Rural Development Institute.

Li, Weisha (1999) "Changing in Housing Patterns for Rural Chinese Women," Irene Tinker and Gale Summerfield (eds) *Women's Rights to House and Land: China, Laos, Vietnam*, Boulder, Co: Lynne Rienner Publishers, pp. 231–240.

Li, Zongmin (1993) *Changes in the Role of Rural Women under the Household Responsibility System: A Case Study of the Impact of Agrarian Reform and Rural Industrialization in Dongyao Village, Hebei Province, North China*, Land Tenure Research Paper 113, Madison, WI: Land Tenure Center, University of Wisconsin-Madison.

Li, Zongmin (1997) *The Impact of Rural Industrialization on Intra-Household Labor Division and Individual Members' Welfare*, PhD dissertation (Development Economics), Land Tenure Center, University of Wisconsin-Madison.

Li, Zongmin (1999) "Changing Land and Housing Use by Rural Women in North China," in Irene Tinker and Gale Summerfield (eds) *Women's Rights to House and Land: China, Laos, Vietnam*, Boulder, CO: Lynne Rienner Publishers, pp. 241–264.

Li, Zongmin (2003a) *Women's Land Tenure Rights in Rural China: A Synthesis*, Beijing: Ford Foundation.

Li, Zongmin (2003b) "Preserving Women's Rights in Land Titling in Laos," in Module 9, Investments in Land Administration, Policy and Markets, *Agricultural Sourcebook*, Washington, DC: Agricultural and Rural Development Department, World Bank.

Lin, Zhibin (2001) "Gender Equality in China's Land Tenure System", *Journal of Agricultural Observation*, October.

Lu, Xiaofei, and Chen Benjian (1999) "Efficiency, Equality, and Gender Equality – an Interview with Mr. Du Rensheng," *Chinese Women's Daily*, April 15, 1999.

National Peoples Congress, Legislative Committee (2001) *Report on the Amended Marriage Law of 2001*, Issue 9, April 24, 2001, Beijing: National Peoples Congress.

Pan, Jintang (1999) "Land Contract Rights: Women's Survival Rights," *Chinese Women's Daily*, March 18, 1999.

People's Republic of China (2002) Rural Land Contracting Law, August 29, 2002.

Popular Coalition (2002) *A Common Platform on Access to Land*, Rome: The Popular Coalition, IFAD.

Quisimbing, Agnes and Maluccio, John (2000) *Intrahousehold Allocation and Gender Relations: New Empirical Evidence from Four Developing Countries*, Washington, DC: International Food Policy Research Institute.

Quisimbing, Agnes, Brown, Lynn, Feldstein, Hilary Sims, Haddad, Lawrence and Pena Christine (1995) *Women: The Key to Food Security*, Food Policy Report, Washington, DC: International Food Policy Research Institute.

RDI (Rural Development Institute) (2002) *Report on the Results and Recommendations for Chinese Land Tenure*, Seattle: Rural Development Institute.

Saxena, N.C. (1993) "Women and Wasteland Development in India,", in Andrea Singh and Neera Burra (eds) *Women and Wasteland Development in India*, New York: Sage Publications and the International Labor Organization, pp. 124-170.

Seager, Joni, *et al.* (1997) *The State of Women in the WorldAtas*, 2nd edn,. London and New York: Penguin.

Song, Yiching and Jiggins, Janice (2000) "Feminization of Agriculture and Related Issues: two case studies in marginal rural area in China," paper presented at the European Conference on Agricultural and Rural Development in China (ECARDC VI), Leiden, 5–7 January 2000.

Summerfield, Gale (forthcoming) "Gender Equity and Land Reform in China: The Household Responsibility System 1980–2000," in Jane Jaquette and Gale Summerfield (eds) (forthcoming) *Institutions, Resources and Mobilization: Women and Gender Equity in Development Theory and Practice.*

Tinker, Irene, and Gale Summerfield (eds) (1999) *Women's Rights to House and Land: China, Laos, Vietnam*, Boulder, CO: Lynne Rienner Publishers.

UNICEF (1995) "Progress Achieved in the Implementation of the Convention on the Elimination of All Forms of Discrimination against Women. Report by the Committee on the Elimination of Discrimination against Women," paper at Fourth World Conference on Women, Beijing, China, September 4–15, 1995, A/CONF.177/7, New York: UNICEF.

Wang, Huimin (1998) "Dangqian Nongcun Tudi Chengbao Jingying Guanli de Xianzhuang ji Wenti" (The Present Situation and Problems Facing the Management and Administration of Rural Land Leases), *Zhongguo Nongcun Guancha*, 5: 56–57.

Yang, Li (2003) *Research Issues on Women's Land Rights in Rural Land Contracting*, Research Center for Rural Economy (RCRE), OXFAM Project (CHN-1411-01A/02A), Beijing: RCRE.

Zhang, Heather Xiaoquan (2003) "Gender Difference in Inheritance Rights: Observations from a Chinese Village", *The Journal of Peasant Studies*, 30: 25–277.

Zhang, Linxiu (2001) "The Situation of Rural Land Contracts; a Gender Perspective," presentation at a workshop on women's land rights, Beijing, May 24–25.

Zhu, Ling and Zhongyi Jiang (2000) "Gender Inequality in Land Tenure System of Rural China," in *Impact of Labor Migration on Agricultural Women in Poor Areas*, Beijing: Ford Foundation.

Index

Page references in italics refer to figures and tables